Pleased to meet you!
My name is Tsutsui. I want to thank you,
from the bottom of my heart, for picking
up the first volume of *We Never Learn*. I'll
be deeply delighted if you enjoy this slightly
strange romantic comedy about teenagers
who struggle in school. I'll be struggling
to succeed right along with them!

I hope you'll also enjoy finding this little
character, the Galiole doll, which is
hidden in each story. Secret: there's
no prize for finding it.

• **Taishi Tsutsui** •

We Never **Learn**

We Never Learn

Volume 1 • SHONEN JUMP Manga Edition

STORY AND ART **Taishi Tsutsui**

TRANSLATION Camellia Nieh
SHONEN JUMP SERIES LETTERING Snir Aharon, Steve Dutro
GRAPHIC NOVEL TOUCH-UP ART & LETTERING Erika Terriquez
DESIGN Shawn Carrico
SHONEN JUMP SERIES EDITOR John Bae
GRAPHIC NOVEL EDITOR David Brothers

Printed in the U.S.A.

Published by VIZ Media, LLC
P.O. Box 77010
San Francisco, CA 94107

10 9 8 7 6 5 4 3 2 1
First printing, December 2018

VIZ MEDIA
viz.com

SHONEN JUMP
shonenjump.com

ratings.viz.com
RATED T+ OLDER TEEN

PARENTAL ADVISORY
WE NEVER LEARN is rated T+ for Older Teen and is recommended for ages 16 and up. This volume contains mild language and sexual themes.

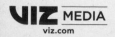

SHONEN JUMP MANGA

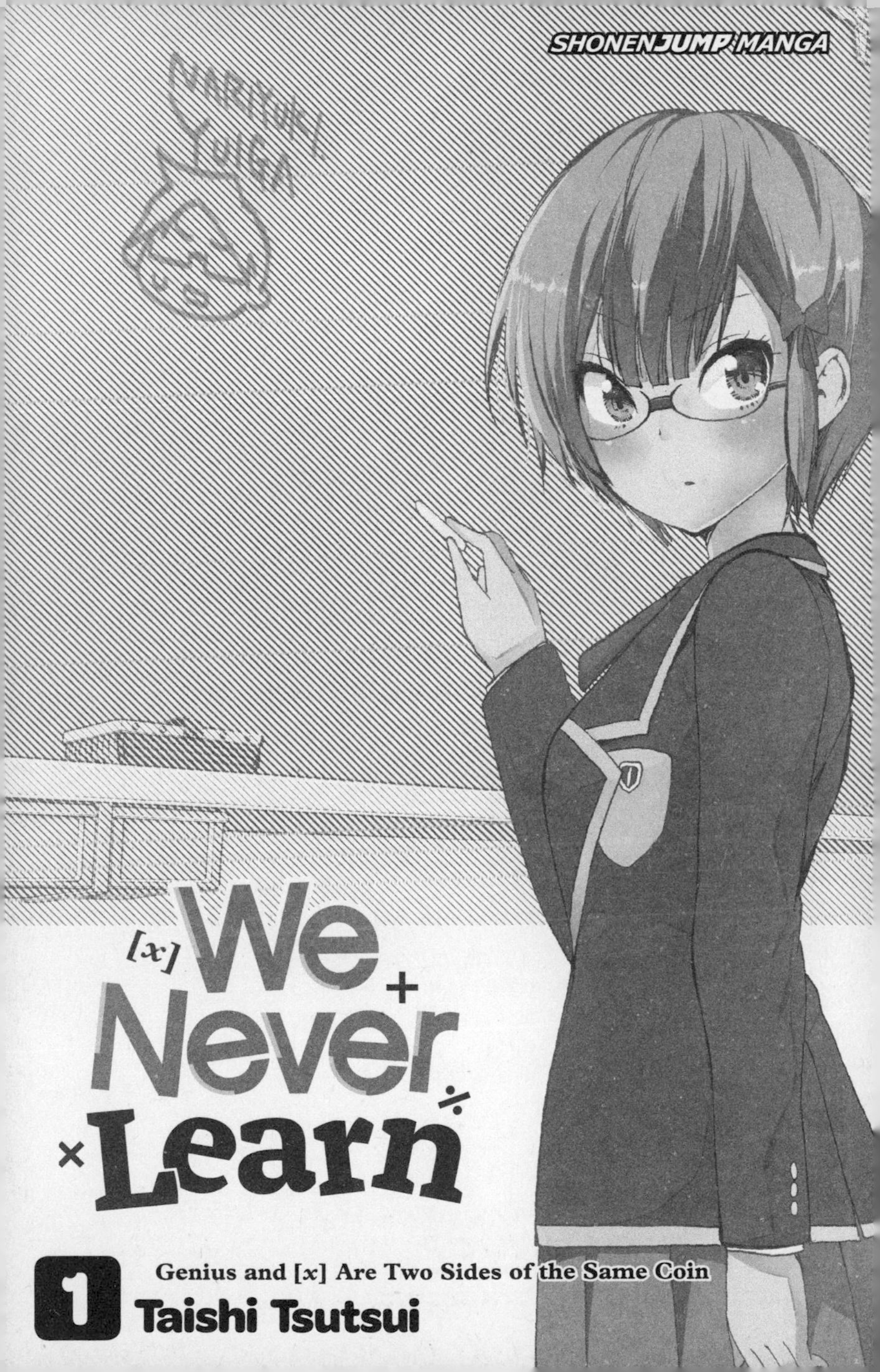
NARIYUKI YUIGA

[x] We + Never ÷ × Learn

1

Genius and [x] Are Two Sides of the Same Coin

Taishi Tsutsui

TITLE

We Never Learn

CONTENTS

VOLUME **1** Genius and [X] Are Two Sides of the Same Coin

NAME **Taishi Tsutsui**

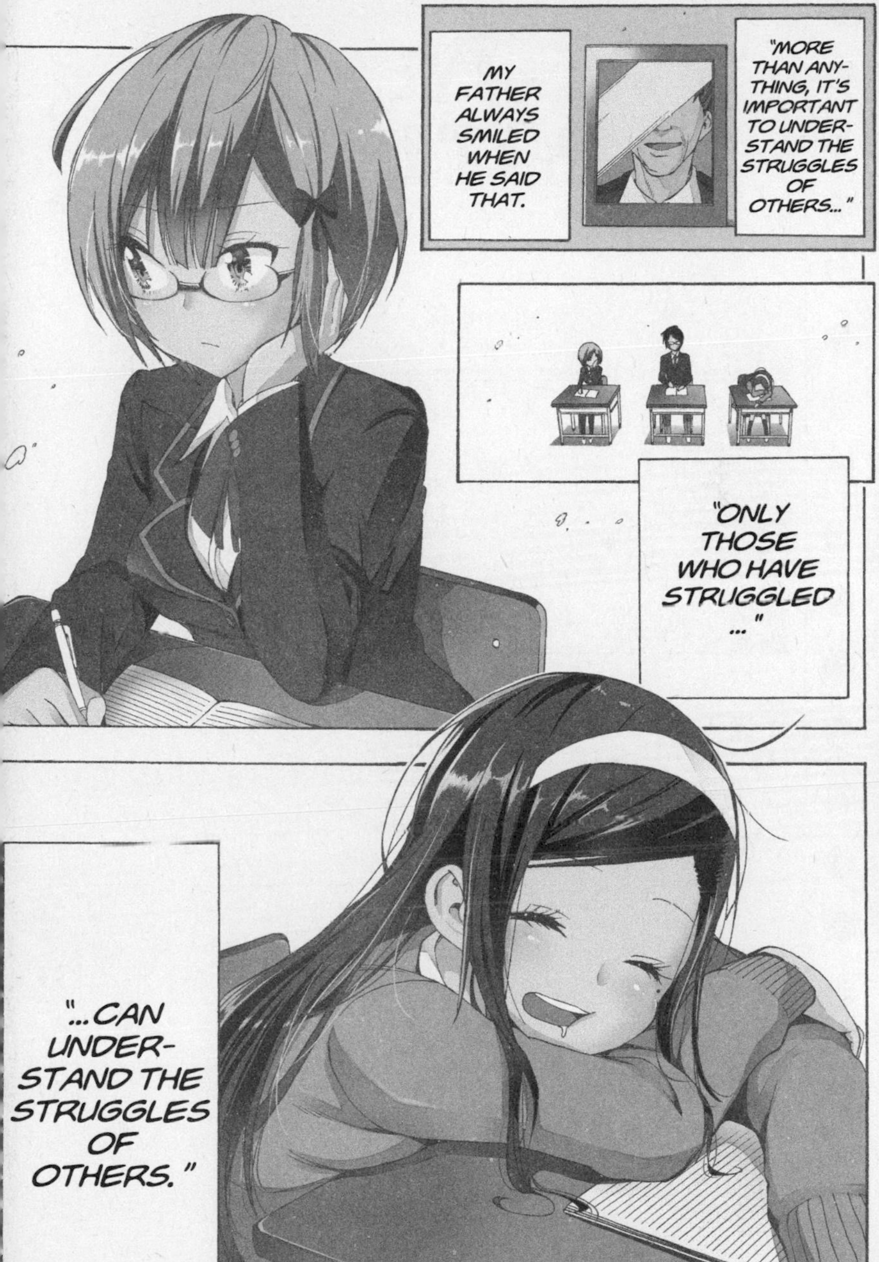
"MORE THAN ANYTHING, IT'S IMPORTANT TO UNDERSTAND THE STRUGGLES OF OTHERS..."
MY FATHER ALWAYS SMILED WHEN HE SAID THAT.
"ONLY THOSE WHO HAVE STRUGGLED..."
"...CAN UNDERSTAND THE STRUGGLES OF OTHERS."

Question 1: Genius and [*X*] Are Two Sides of the Same Coin

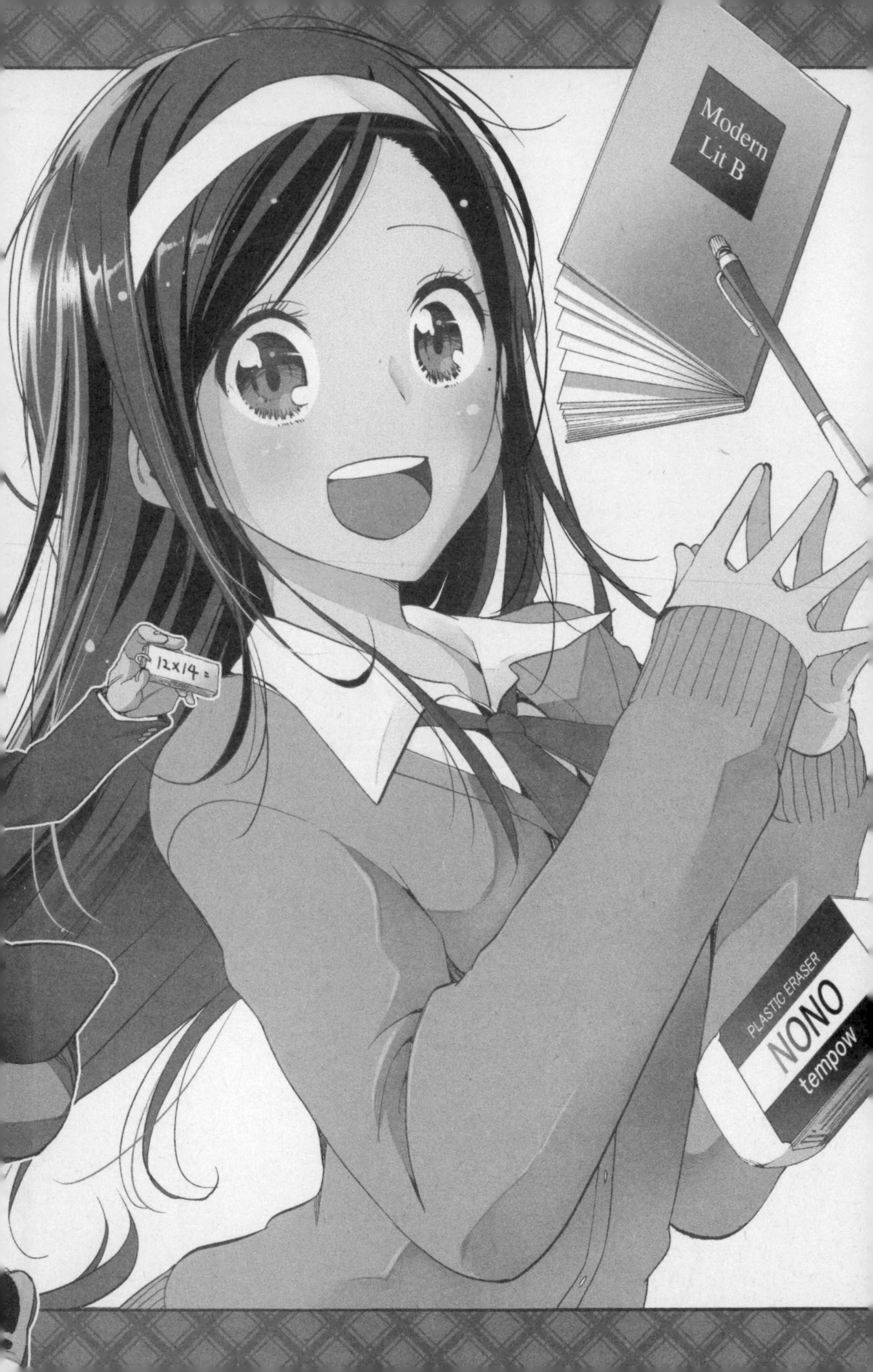
Modern
Lit B
12x14=
PLASTIC ERASER
NONO
tempow

Question 1: Genius and [X] Are Two Sides of the Same Coin

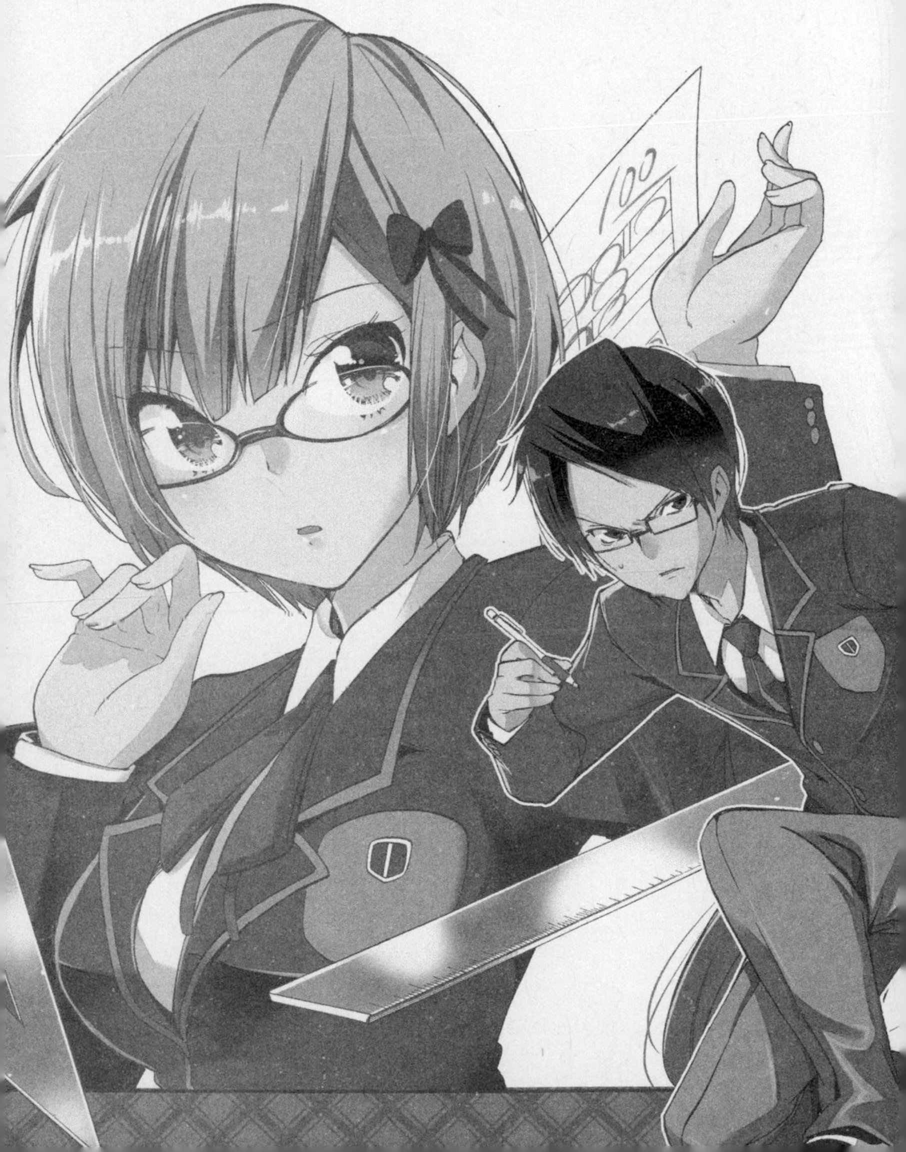

[x] We
Never
Learn

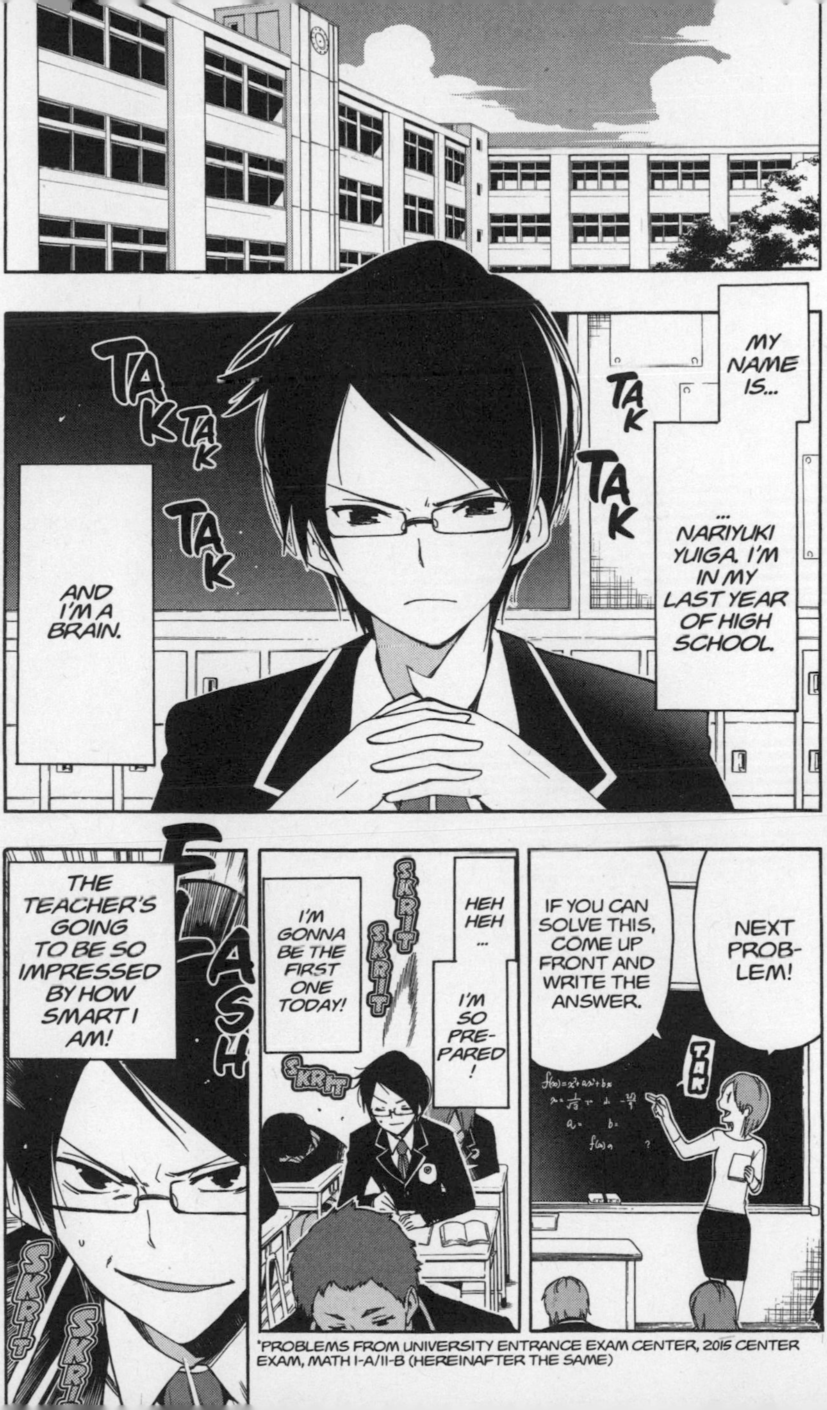
MY NAME IS...
TAK
TAK
... NARIYUKI YUIGA. I'M IN MY LAST YEAR OF HIGH SCHOOL.
TAK TAK
TAK
AND I'M A BRAIN.
NEXT PROB-LEM!
IF YOU CAN SOLVE THIS, COME UP FRONT AND WRITE THE ANSWER.
TAK
HEH HEH ...
I'M SO PRE-PARED!
SKRIT
SKRIT
I'M GONNA BE THE FIRST ONE TODAY!
SKRIT
FLASH
THE TEACHER'S GOING TO BE SO IMPRESSED BY HOW SMART I AM!
SKRIT
SKRI

*PROBLEMS FROM UNIVERSITY ENTRANCE EXAM CENTER, 2015 CENTER EXAM, MATH I-A/II-B (HEREINAFTER THE SAME)

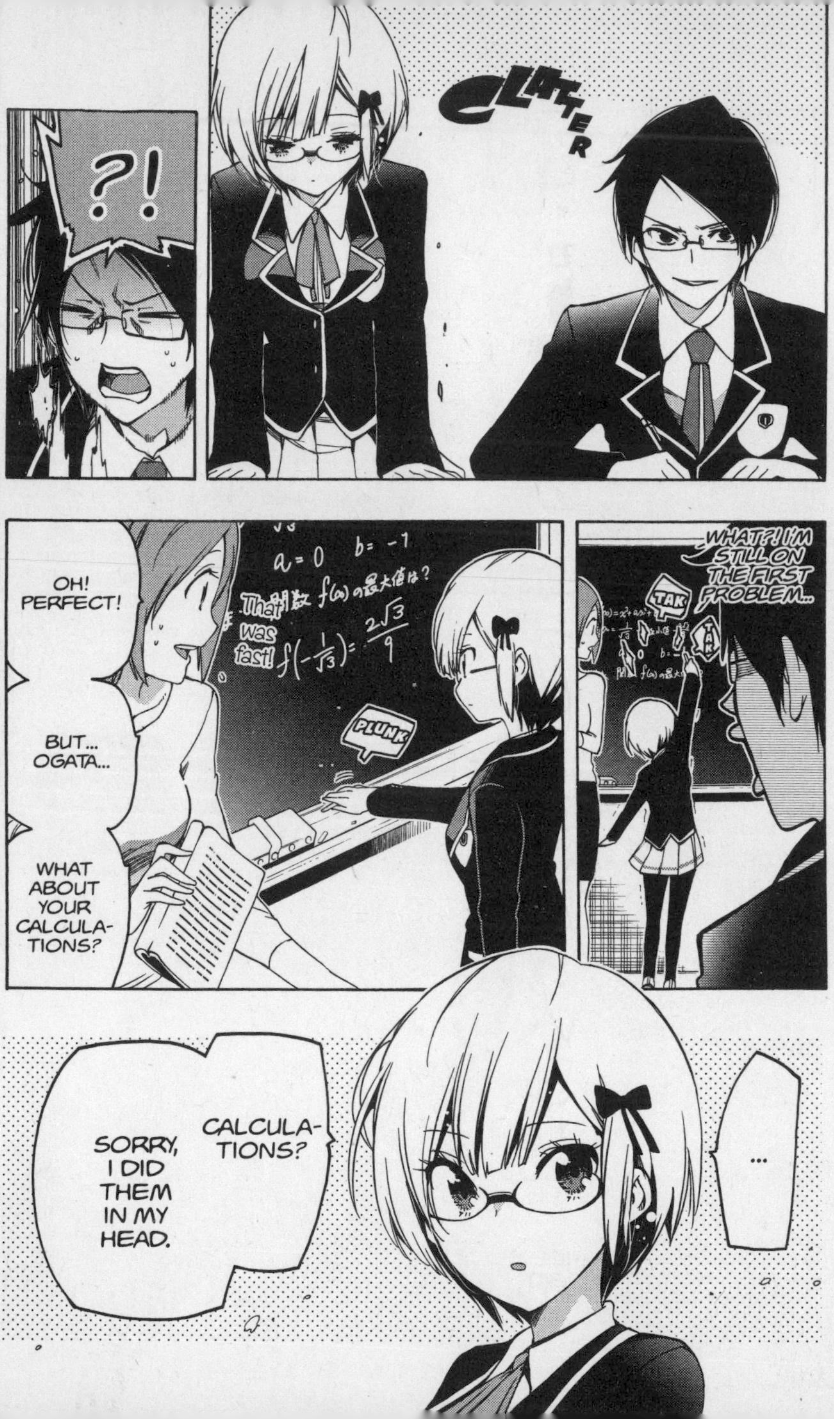
CLATTER
?!
WHAT?! I'M STILL ON THE FIRST PROBLEM...
TAK
TAK
That was fast!
PLUNK
OH! PERFECT!
BUT... OGATA...
WHAT ABOUT YOUR CALCULATIONS?
...
CALCULATIONS?
SORRY, I DID THEM IN MY HEAD.

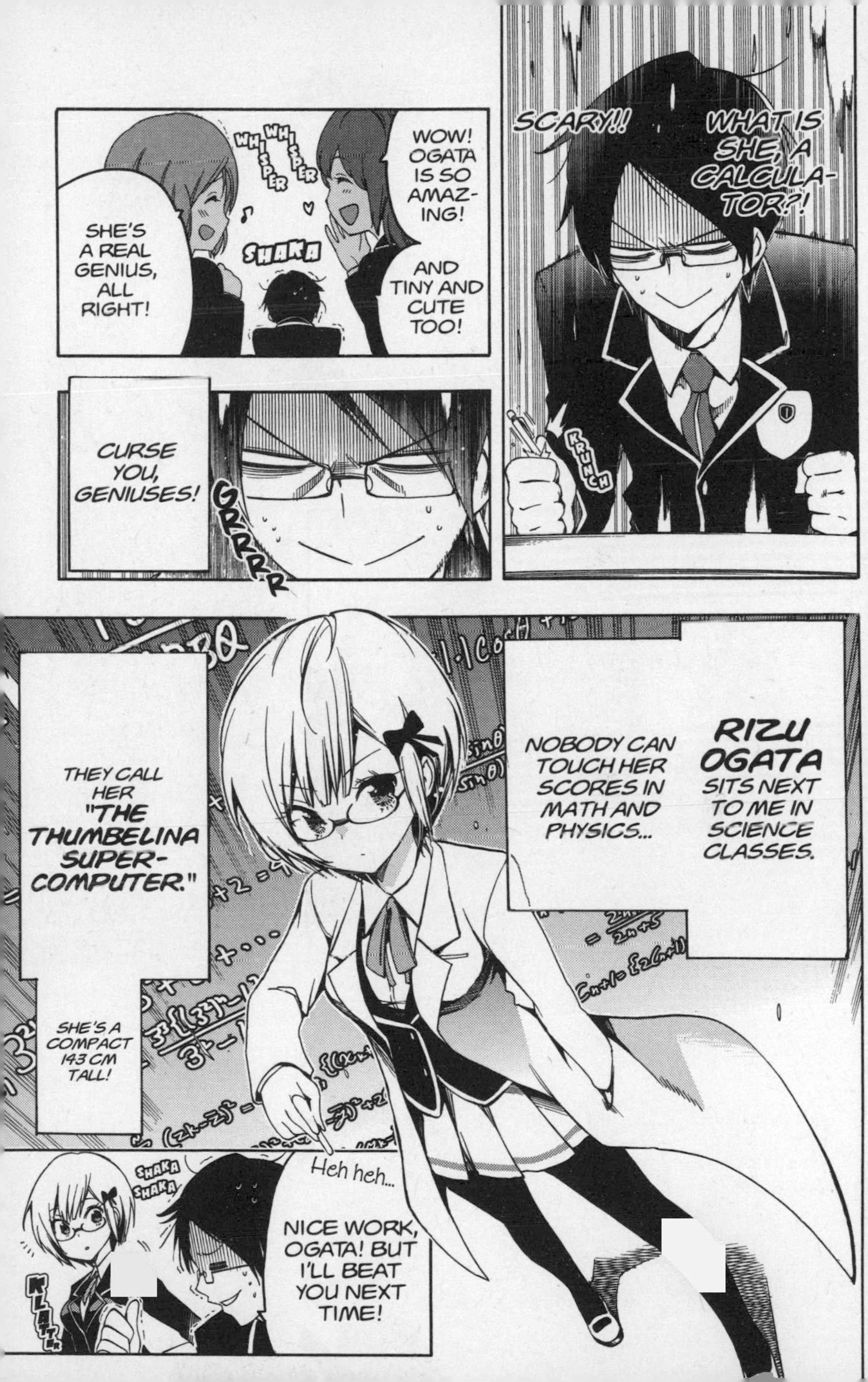
WHAT IS SHE, A CALCULATOR?!
SCARY!!
KRUNCH
WOW! OGATA IS SO AMAZING!
AND TINY AND CUTE TOO!
WHISPER WHISPER
SHAKA
SHE'S A REAL GENIUS, ALL RIGHT!
GRRRRR
CURSE YOU, GENIUSES!
RIZU OGATA SITS NEXT TO ME IN SCIENCE CLASSES.
NOBODY CAN TOUCH HER SCORES IN MATH AND PHYSICS...
THEY CALL HER "THE THUMBELINA SUPER-COMPUTER."
SHE'S A COMPACT 143 CM TALL!
Heh heh...
NICE WORK, OGATA! BUT I'LL BEAT YOU NEXT TIME!
SHAKA SHAKA
KLATTER

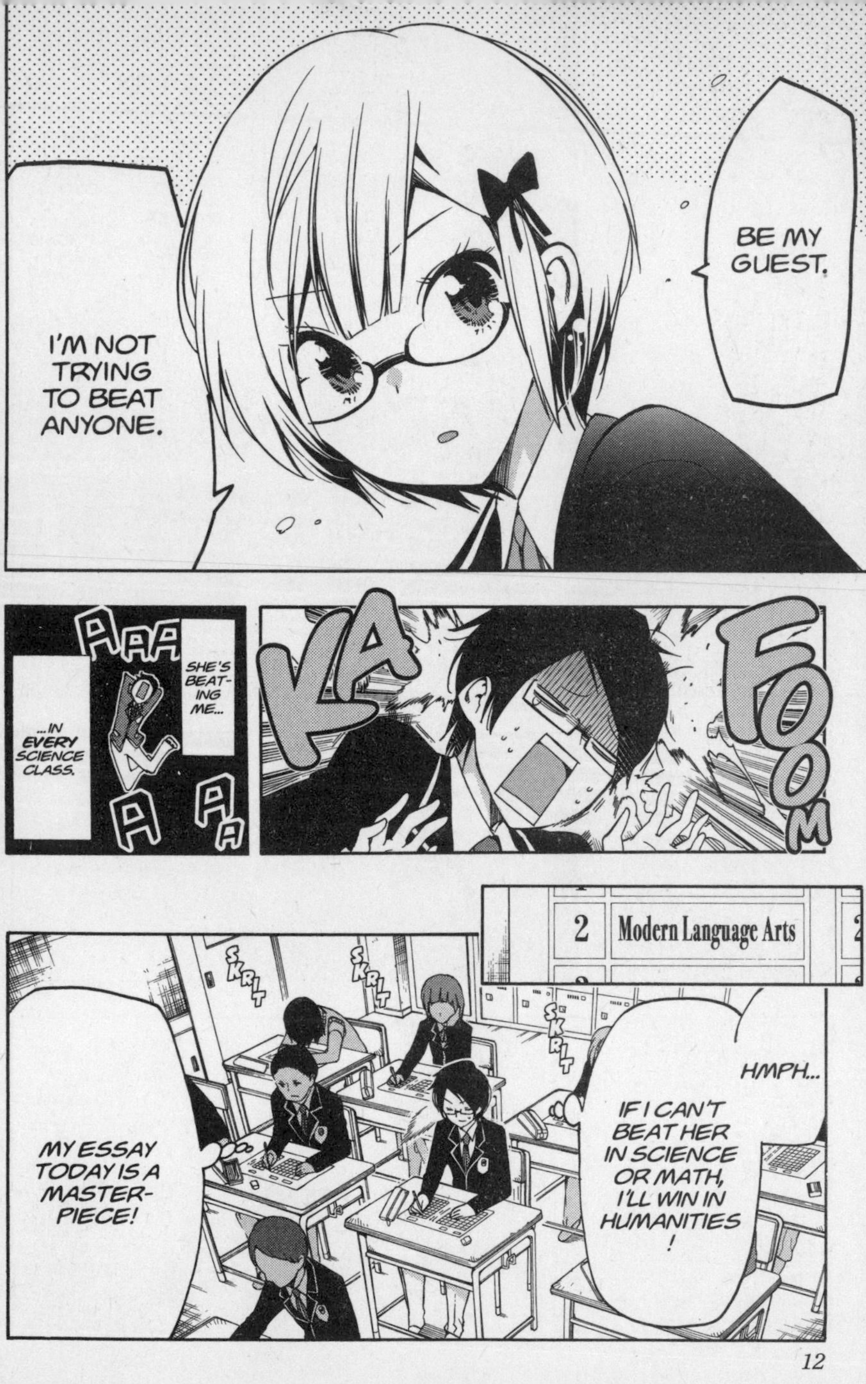
BE MY GUEST.
I'M NOT TRYING TO BEAT ANYONE.
KA
FOOM
SHE'S BEAT-ING ME...
...IN EVERY SCIENCE CLASS.
AAAAAA
2 Modern Language Arts
SKRIT
SKRIT
SKRIT
HMPH...
IF I CAN'T BEAT HER IN SCIENCE OR MATH, I'LL WIN IN HUMANITIES!
MY ESSAY TODAY IS A MASTER-PIECE!

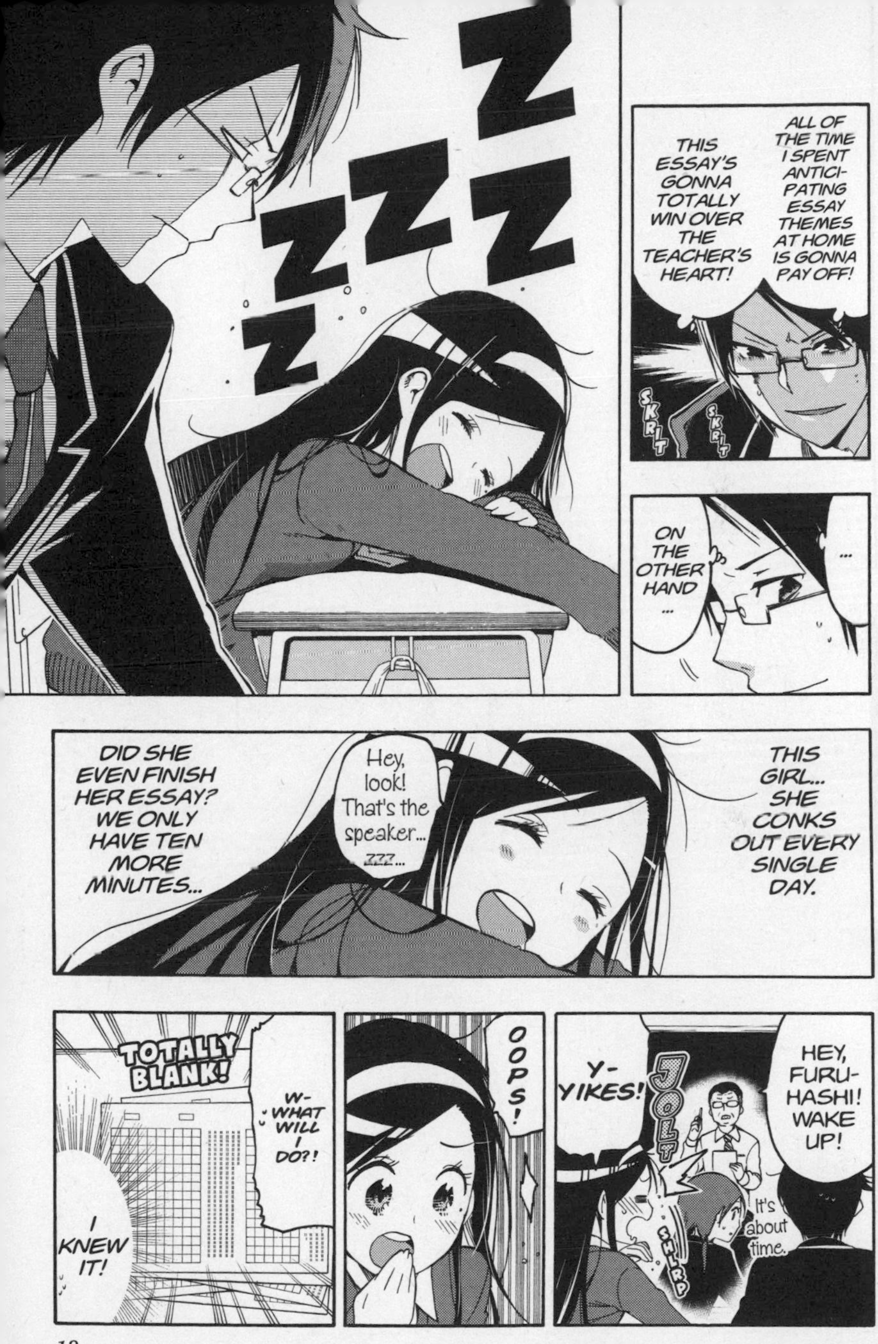
ALL OF THE TIME I SPENT ANTICIPATING ESSAY THEMES AT HOME IS GONNA PAY OFF!
THIS ESSAY'S GONNA TOTALLY WIN OVER THE TEACHER'S HEART!
SKRIT
SKRIT
...
ON THE OTHER HAND...
ZZZZZZ
THIS GIRL... SHE CONKS OUT EVERY SINGLE DAY.
Hey, look! That's the speaker... zzz...
DID SHE EVEN FINISH HER ESSAY? WE ONLY HAVE TEN MORE MINUTES...
HEY, FURUHASHI! WAKE UP!
JOLT
Y-YIKES!
It's about time.
SHLRP
OOPS!
W-WHAT WILL I DO?!
TOTALLY BLANK!
I KNEW IT!

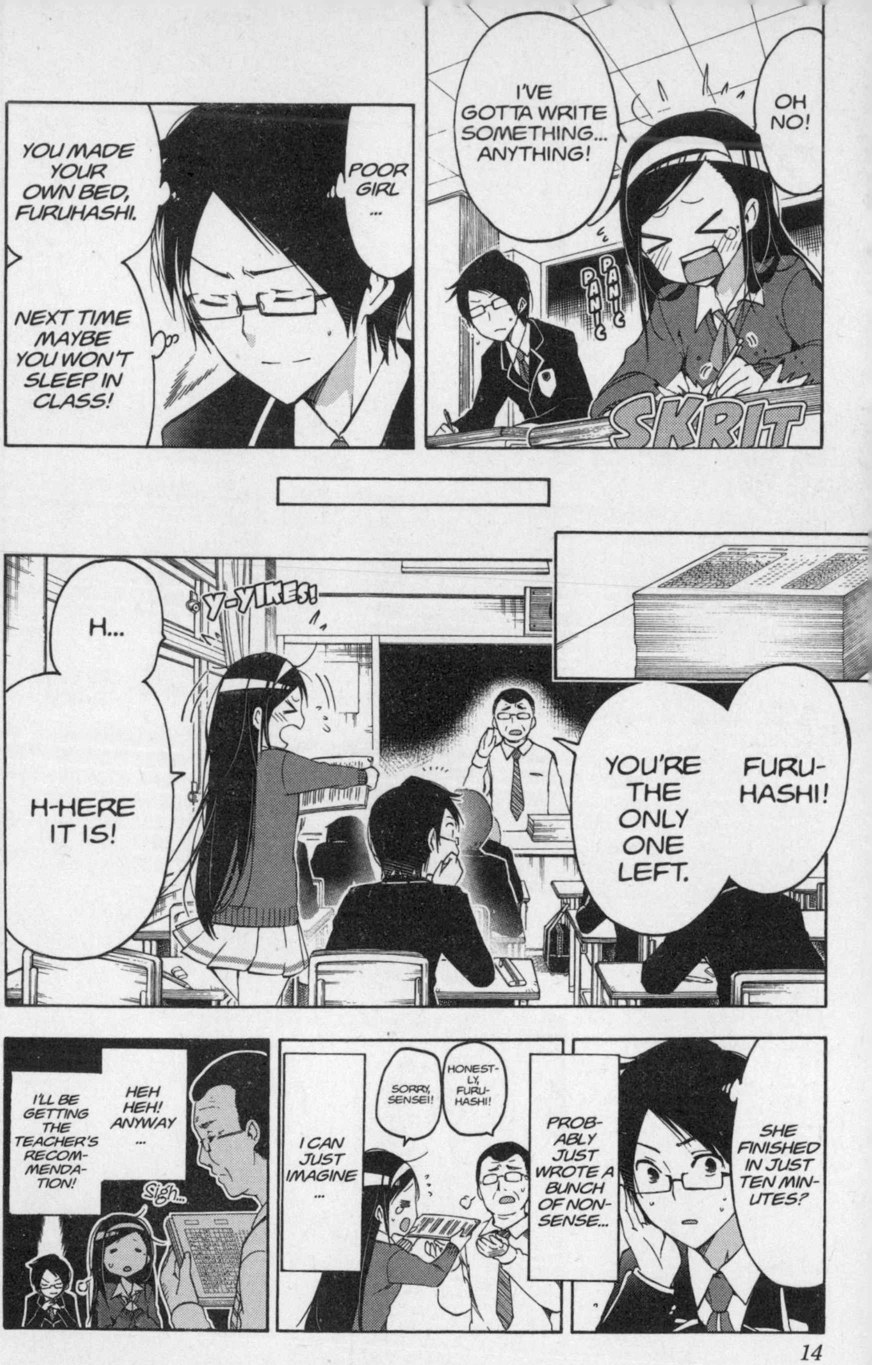
OH NO!
I'VE GOTTA WRITE SOMETHING... ANYTHING!
PANIC PANIC
SKRIT
POOR GIRL ...
YOU MADE YOUR OWN BED, FURUHASHI.
NEXT TIME MAYBE YOU WON'T SLEEP IN CLASS!
FURUHASHI!
YOU'RE THE ONLY ONE LEFT.
Y-YIKES!
H...
H-HERE IT IS!
SHE FINISHED IN JUST TEN MINUTES?
PROBABLY JUST WROTE A BUNCH OF NONSENSE...
HONESTLY, FURUHASHI!
SORRY, SENSEI!
I CAN JUST IMAGINE ...
HEH HEH! ANYWAY ...
I'LL BE GETTING THE TEACHER'S RECOMMENDATION!
Sigh...

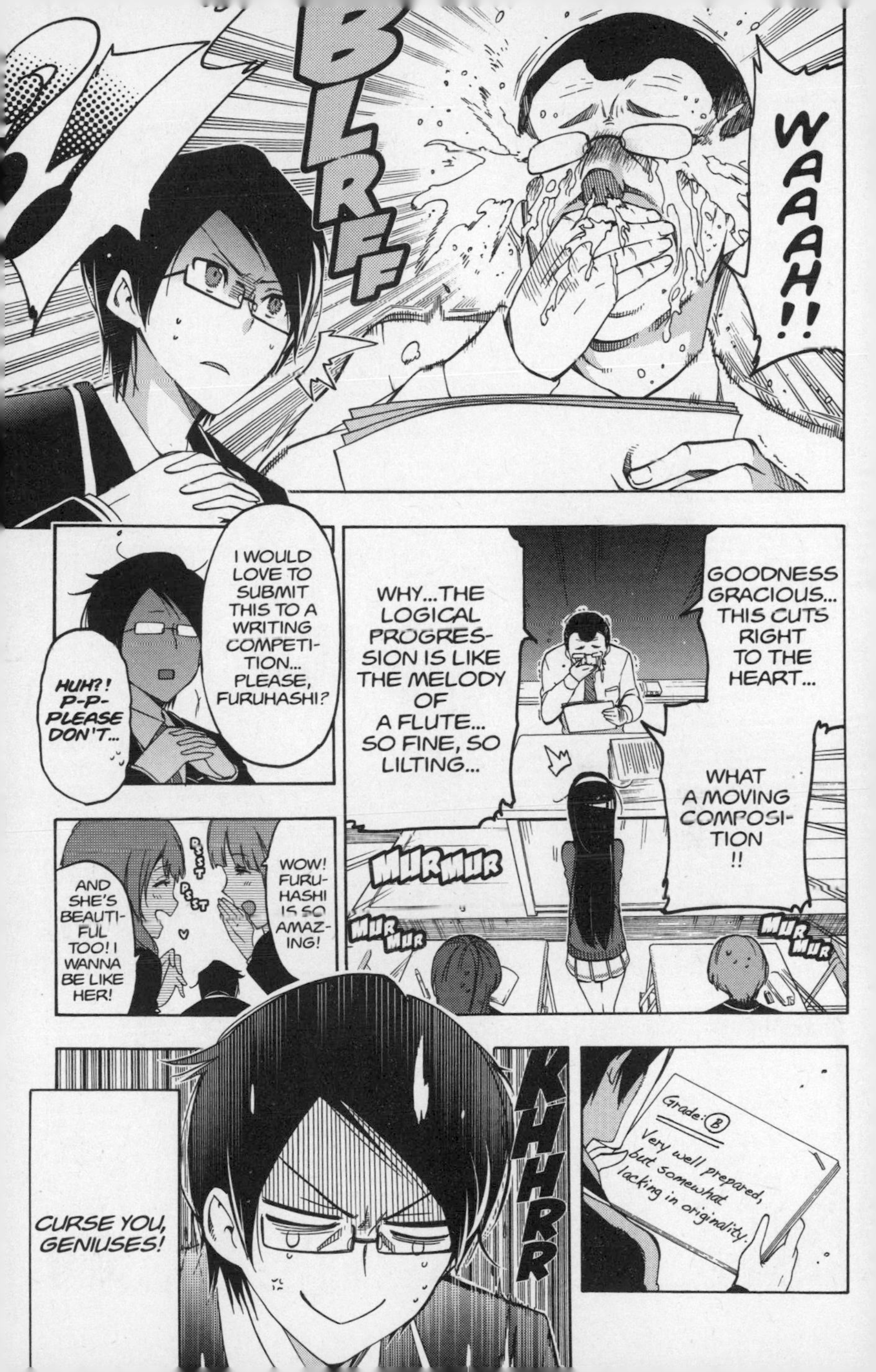
WAAAAH!!
BLRFF
GOODNESS GRACIOUS... THIS CUTS RIGHT TO THE HEART...
WHY... THE LOGICAL PROGRESSION IS LIKE THE MELODY OF A FLUTE... SO FINE, SO LILTING...
WHAT A MOVING COMPOSITION !!
MURMUR
MUR MUR
MUR MUR
I WOULD LOVE TO SUBMIT THIS TO A WRITING COMPETITION... PLEASE, FURUHASHI?
HUH?! P-P-PLEASE DON'T...
WOW! FURUHASHI IS SO AMAZING!
PSST PSST
AND SHE'S BEAUTIFUL TOO! I WANNA BE LIKE HER!
Grade: B
Very well prepared, but somewhat lacking in originality.
KHHRR
CURSE YOU, GENIUSES!

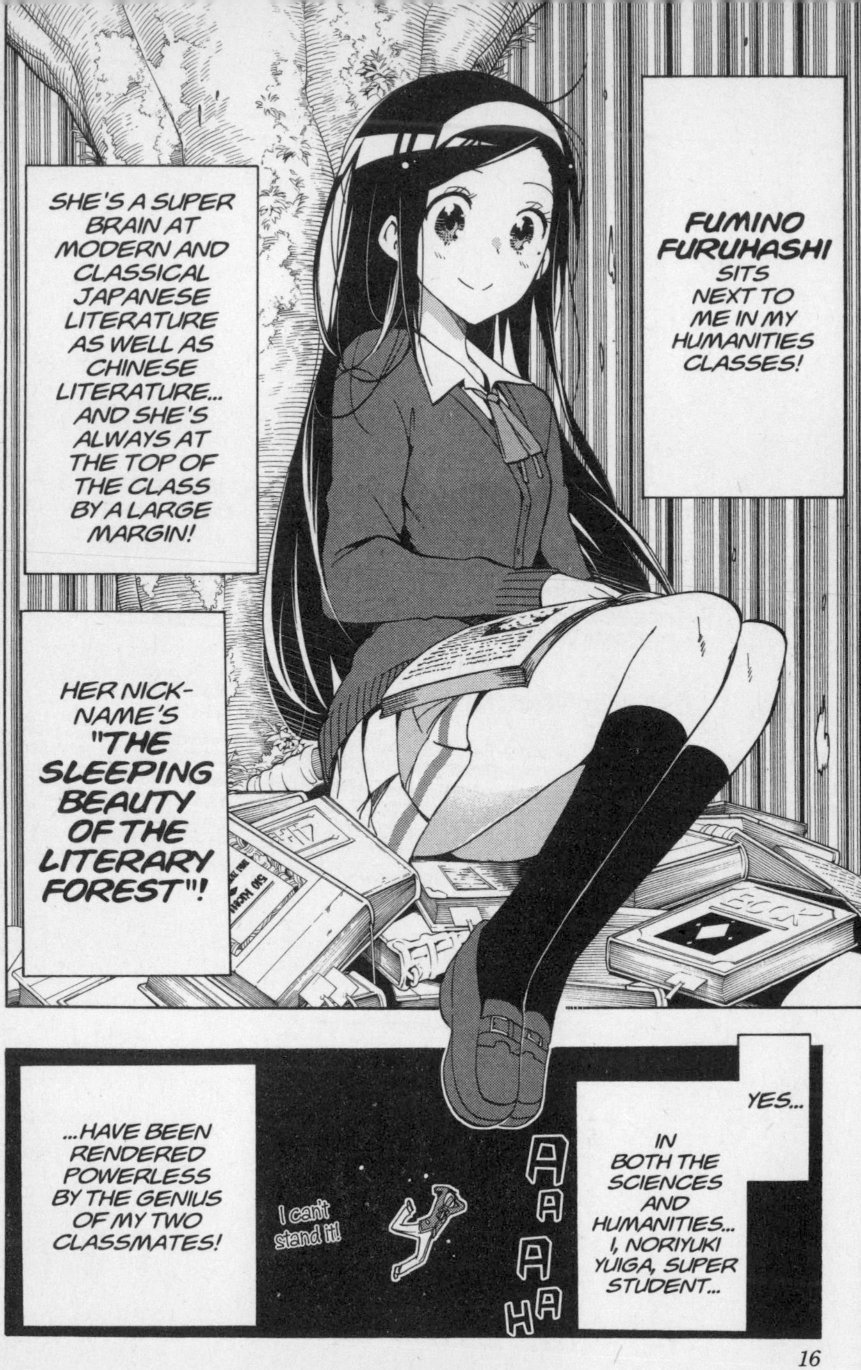
FUMINO FURUHASHI SITS NEXT TO ME IN MY HUMANITIES CLASSES!
SHE'S A SUPER BRAIN AT MODERN AND CLASSICAL JAPANESE LITERATURE AS WELL AS CHINESE LITERATURE... AND SHE'S ALWAYS AT THE TOP OF THE CLASS BY A LARGE MARGIN!
HER NICK-NAME'S "THE SLEEPING BEAUTY OF THE LITERARY FOREST"!
YES...
IN BOTH THE SCIENCES AND HUMANITIES... I, NORIYUKI YUIGA, SUPER STUDENT...
AAAAHA
I can't stand it!
...HAVE BEEN RENDERED POWERLESS BY THE GENIUS OF MY TWO CLASSMATES!

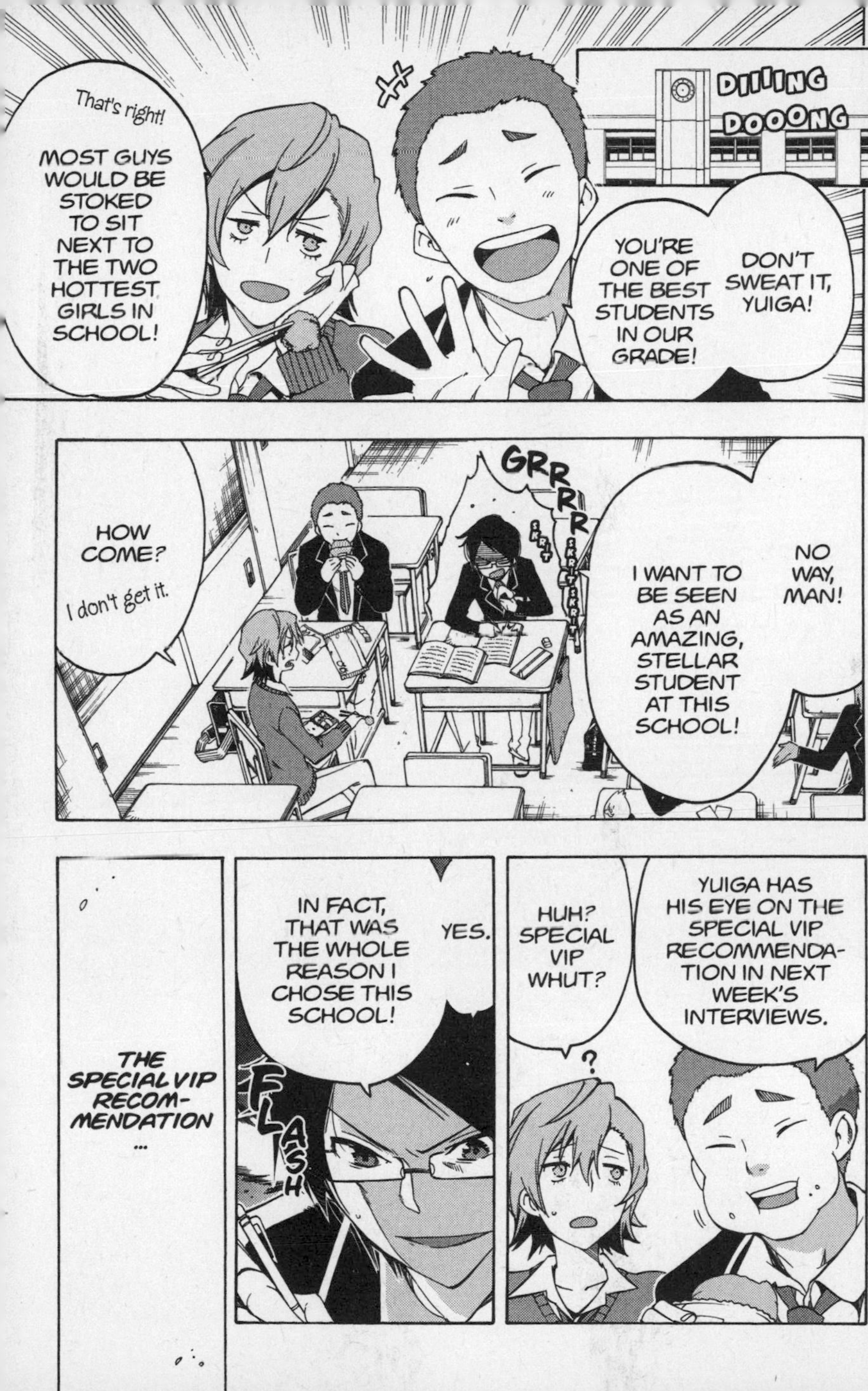
DIIIING DOOONG
DON'T SWEAT IT, YUIGA!
YOU'RE ONE OF THE BEST STUDENTS IN OUR GRADE!
That's right!
MOST GUYS WOULD BE STOKED TO SIT NEXT TO THE TWO HOTTEST GIRLS IN SCHOOL!
NO WAY, MAN!
I WANT TO BE SEEN AS AN AMAZING, STELLAR STUDENT AT THIS SCHOOL!
GRRRRR
SKRIT SKRIT SKRIT
HOW COME?
I don't get it.
YUIGA HAS HIS EYE ON THE SPECIAL VIP RECOMMENDATION IN NEXT WEEK'S INTERVIEWS.
HUH? SPECIAL VIP WHUT?
YES.
IN FACT, THAT WAS THE WHOLE REASON I CHOSE THIS SCHOOL!
FLASH
THE SPECIAL VIP RECOMMENDATION ...

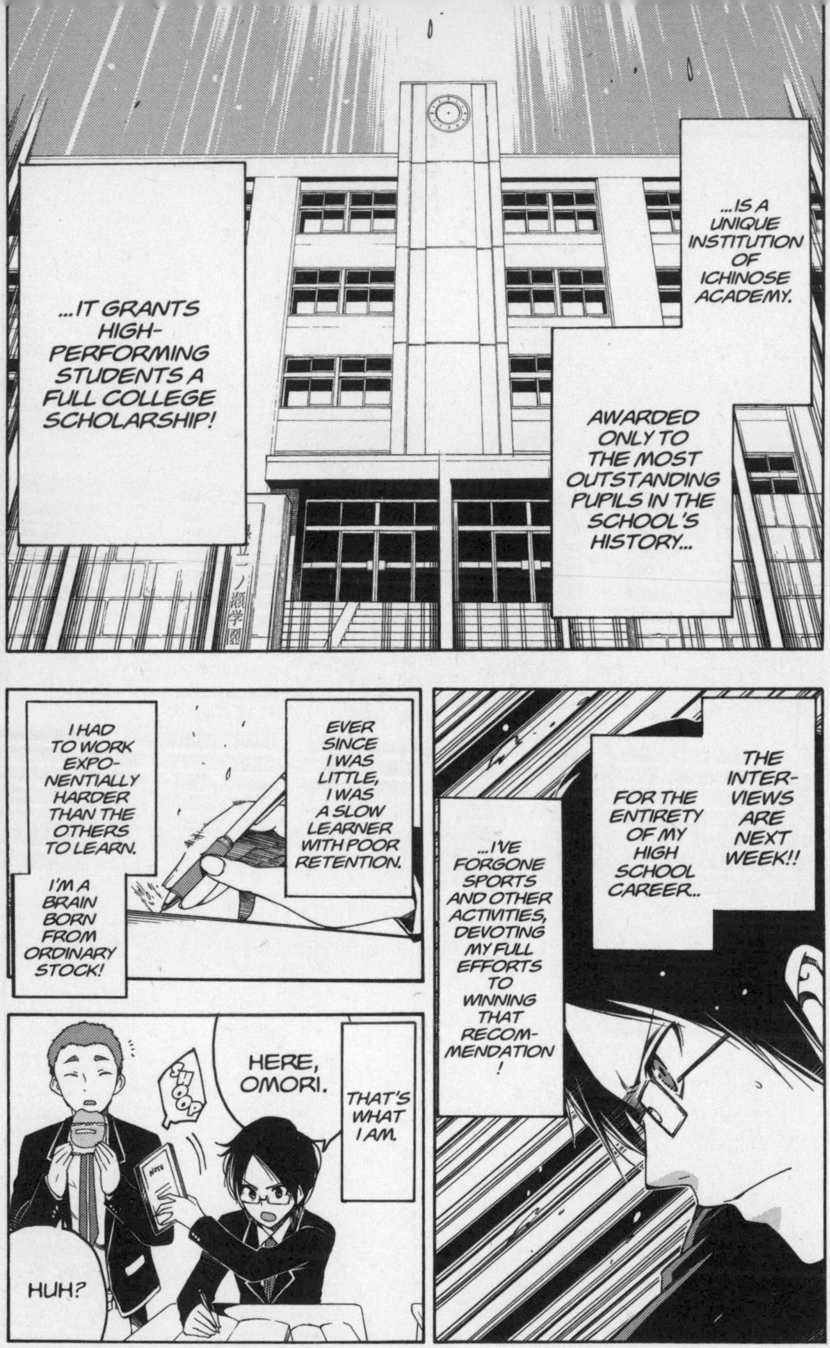
...IS A UNIQUE INSTITUTION OF ICHINOSE ACADEMY.
AWARDED ONLY TO THE MOST OUTSTANDING PUPILS IN THE SCHOOL'S HISTORY...
...IT GRANTS HIGH-PERFORMING STUDENTS A FULL COLLEGE SCHOLARSHIP!
THE INTERVIEWS ARE NEXT WEEK!!
FOR THE ENTIRETY OF MY HIGH SCHOOL CAREER...
...I'VE FORGONE SPORTS AND OTHER ACTIVITIES, DEVOTING MY FULL EFFORTS TO WINNING THAT RECOMMENDATION!
EVER SINCE I WAS LITTLE, I WAS A SLOW LEARNER WITH POOR RETENTION.
I HAD TO WORK EXPONENTIALLY HARDER THAN THE OTHERS TO LEARN.
I'M A BRAIN BORN FROM ORDINARY STOCK!
THAT'S WHAT I AM.
HERE, OMORI.
SHOOP
NOTE
HUH?

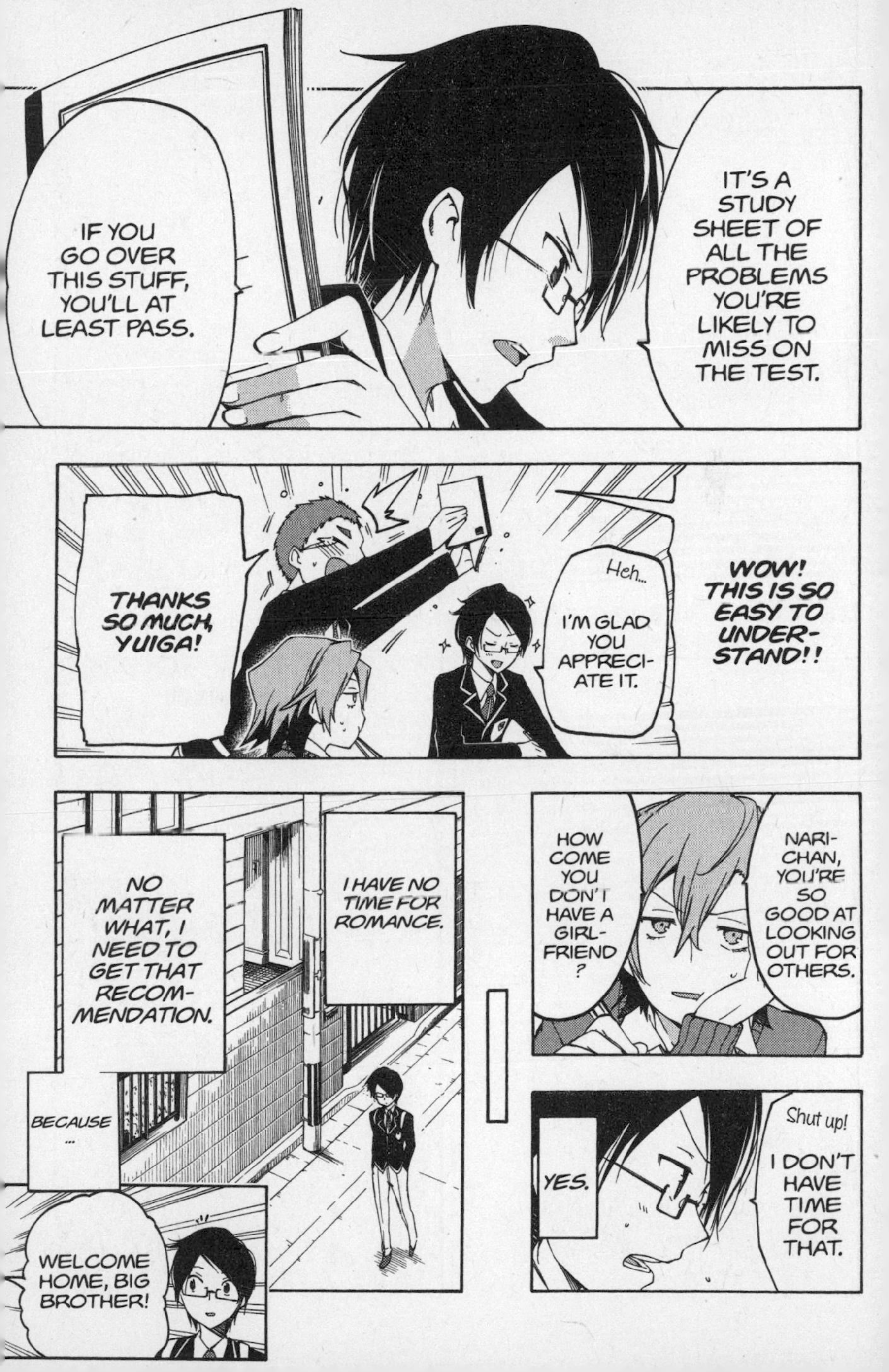
IT'S A STUDY SHEET OF ALL THE PROBLEMS YOU'RE LIKELY TO MISS ON THE TEST.
IF YOU GO OVER THIS STUFF, YOU'LL AT LEAST PASS.
WOW! THIS IS SO EASY TO UNDERSTAND!!
Heh...
I'M GLAD YOU APPRECIATE IT.
THANKS SO MUCH, YUIGA!
NARI-CHAN, YOU'RE SO GOOD AT LOOKING OUT FOR OTHERS.
HOW COME YOU DON'T HAVE A GIRLFRIEND?
Shut up!
I DON'T HAVE TIME FOR THAT.
YES.
I HAVE NO TIME FOR ROMANCE.
NO MATTER WHAT, I NEED TO GET THAT RECOMMENDATION.
BECAUSE...
WELCOME HOME, BIG BROTHER!

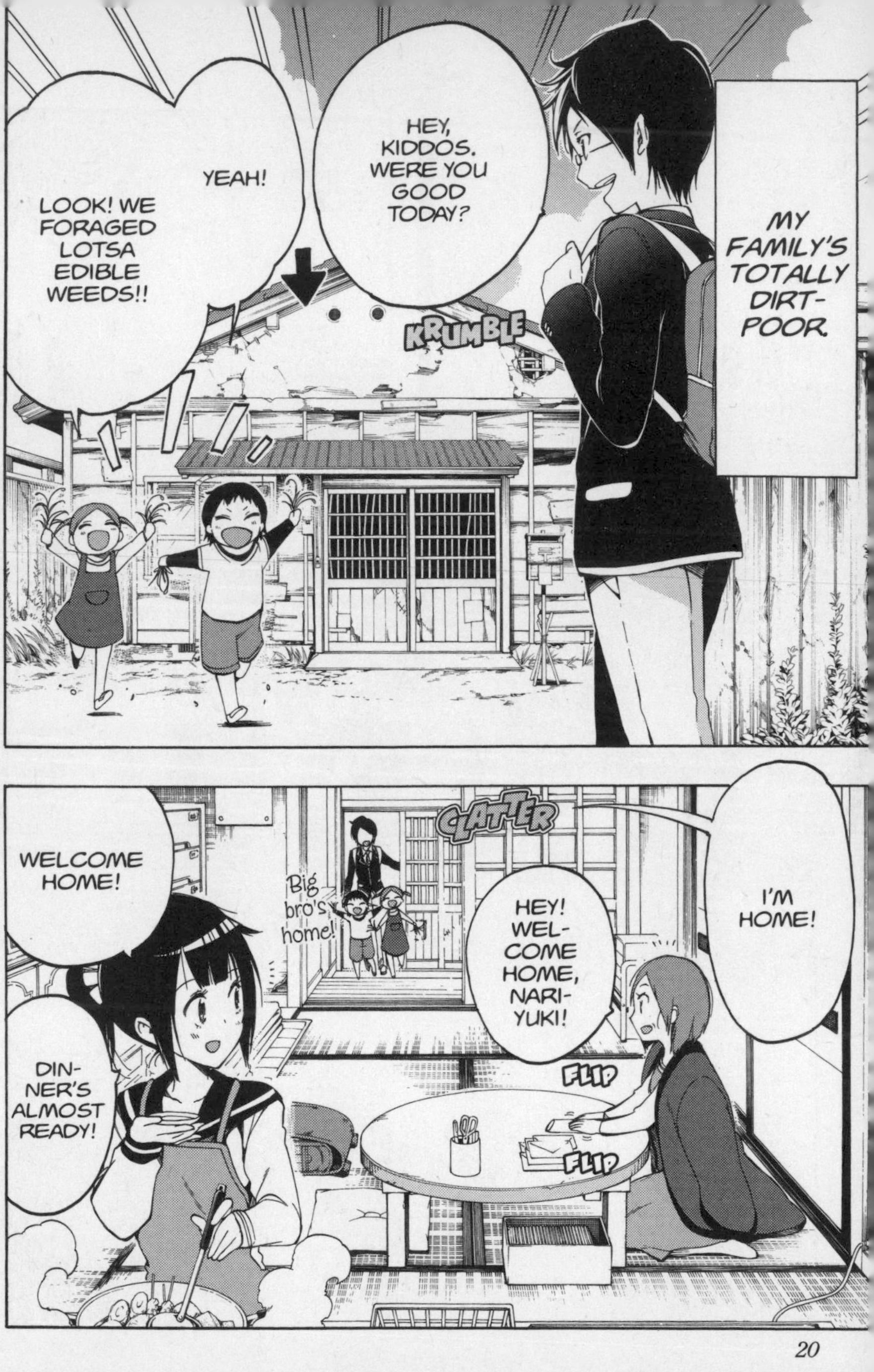
MY FAMILY'S TOTALLY DIRT-POOR.
HEY, KIDDOS. WERE YOU GOOD TODAY?
KRUMBLE
YEAH!
LOOK! WE FORAGED LOTSA EDIBLE WEEDS!!
I'M HOME!
CLATTER
HEY! WEL-COME HOME, NARI-YUKI!
Big bro's home!
FLIP
FLIP
WELCOME HOME!
DIN-NER'S ALMOST READY!

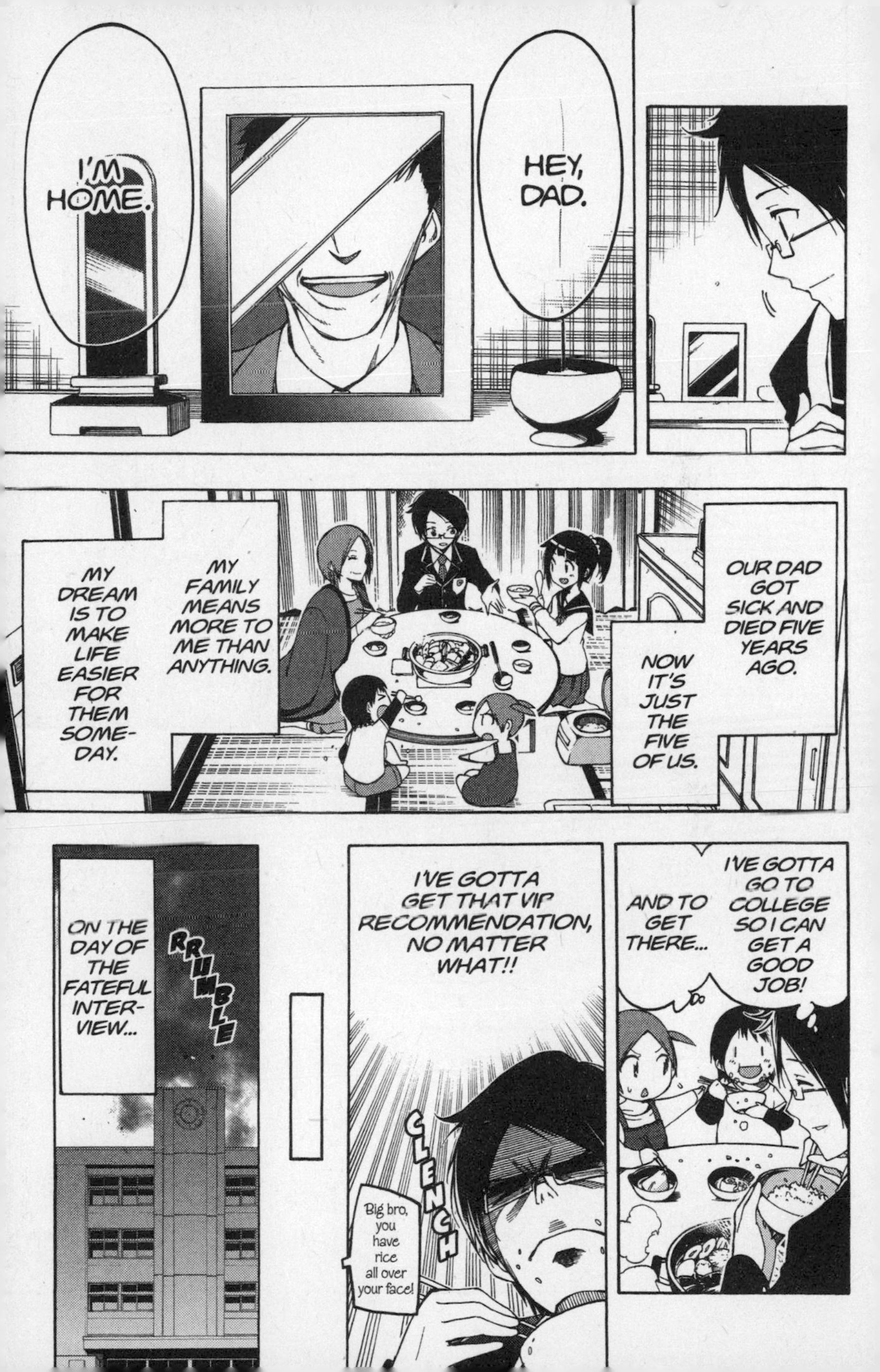
HEY, DAD.
I'M HOME.
OUR DAD GOT SICK AND DIED FIVE YEARS AGO.
NOW IT'S JUST THE FIVE OF US.
MY FAMILY MEANS MORE TO ME THAN ANYTHING.
MY DREAM IS TO MAKE LIFE EASIER FOR THEM SOME-DAY.
I'VE GOTTA GO TO COLLEGE SO I CAN GET A GOOD JOB!
AND TO GET THERE...
I'VE GOTTA GET THAT VIP RECOMMENDATION, NO MATTER WHAT!!
CLENCH
Big bro, you have rice all over your face!
RRUMBLE
ON THE DAY OF THE FATEFUL INTER-VIEW...

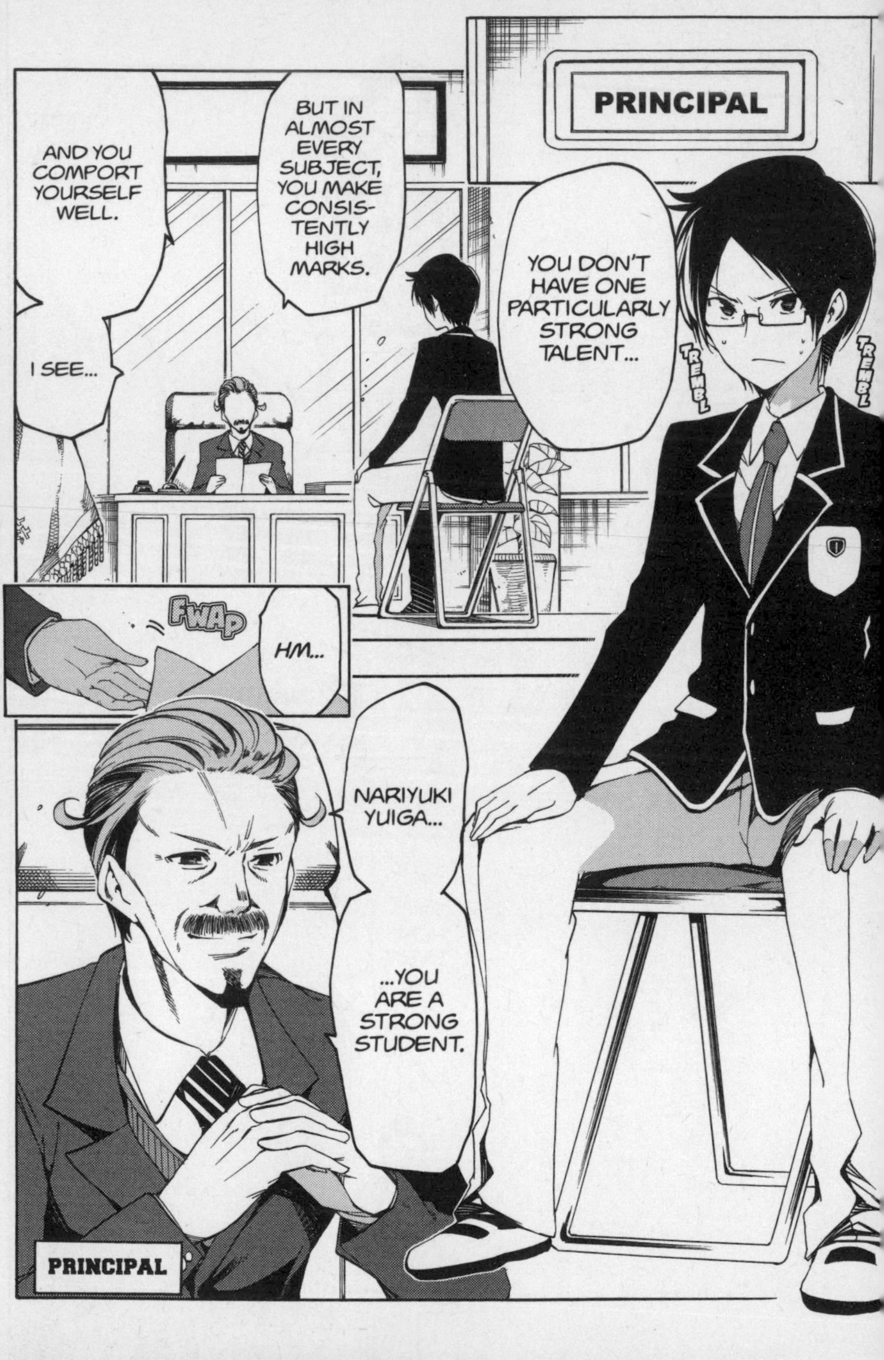
PRINCIPAL
YOU DON'T HAVE ONE PARTICULARLY STRONG TALENT...
TREMBL
TREMBL
BUT IN ALMOST EVERY SUBJECT, YOU MAKE CONSIS-TENTLY HIGH MARKS.
AND YOU COMPORT YOURSELF WELL.
I SEE...
HM...
FWAP
NARIYUKI YUIGA...
...YOU ARE A STRONG STUDENT.
PRINCIPAL

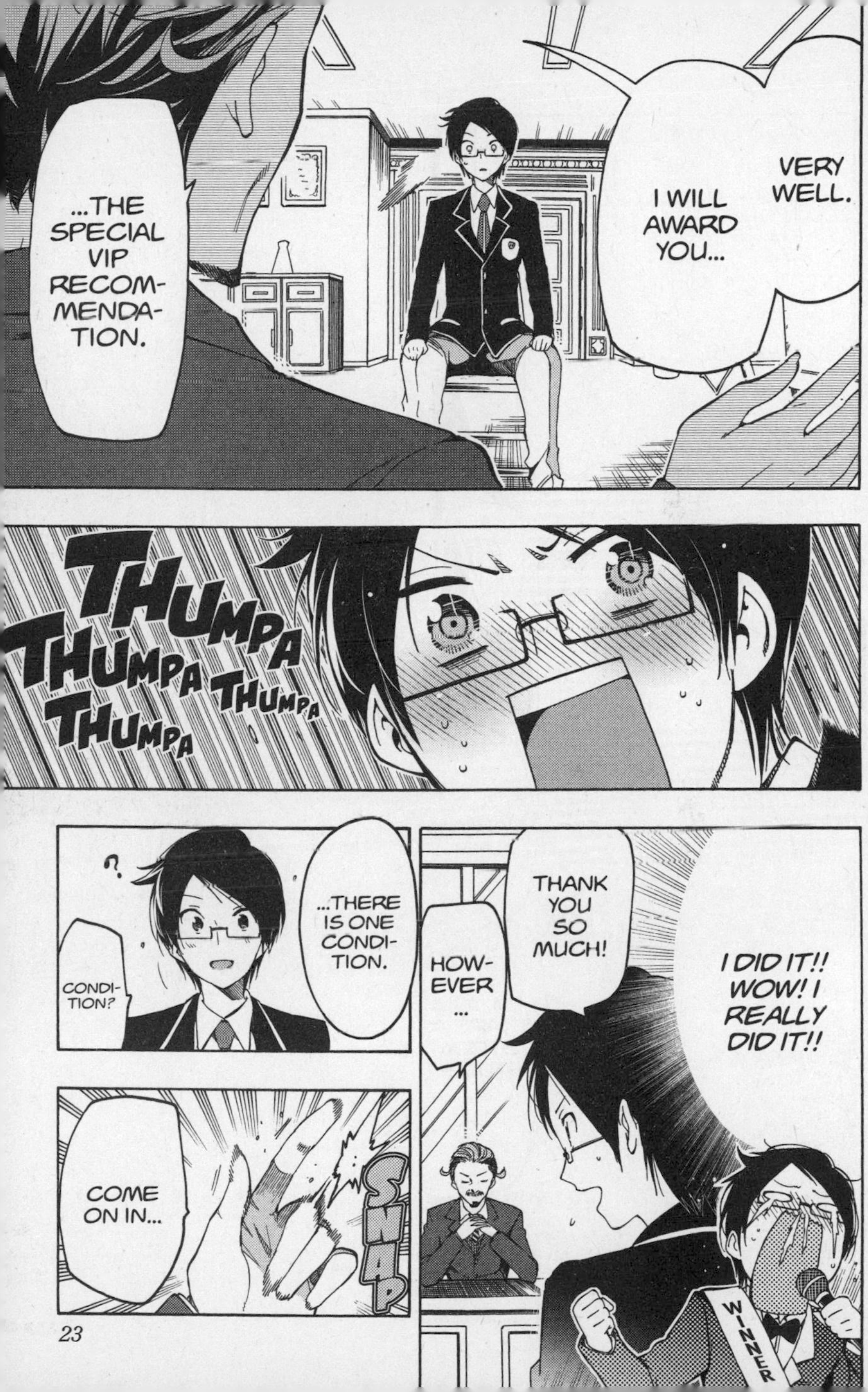
VERY WELL.
I WILL AWARD YOU...
...THE SPECIAL VIP RECOMMENDATION.
THUMPA THUMPA THUMPA THUMPA
I DID IT!! WOW! I REALLY DID IT!!
THANK YOU SO MUCH!
HOWEVER...
...THERE IS ONE CONDITION.
CONDITION?
SNAP
COME ON IN...
WINNER

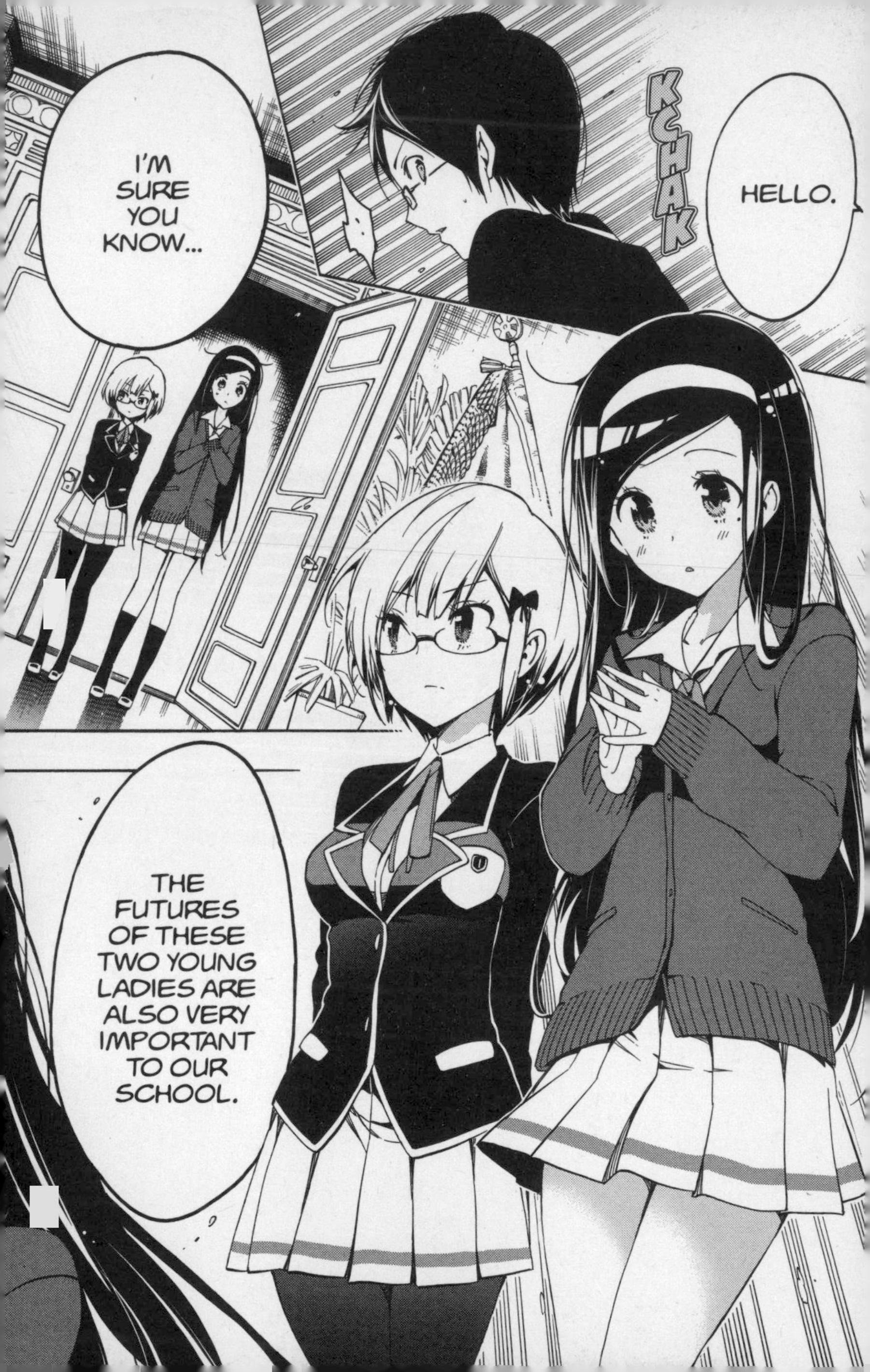
HELLO.
KCHAK
I'M SURE YOU KNOW...
THE FUTURES OF THESE TWO YOUNG LADIES ARE ALSO VERY IMPORTANT TO OUR SCHOOL.

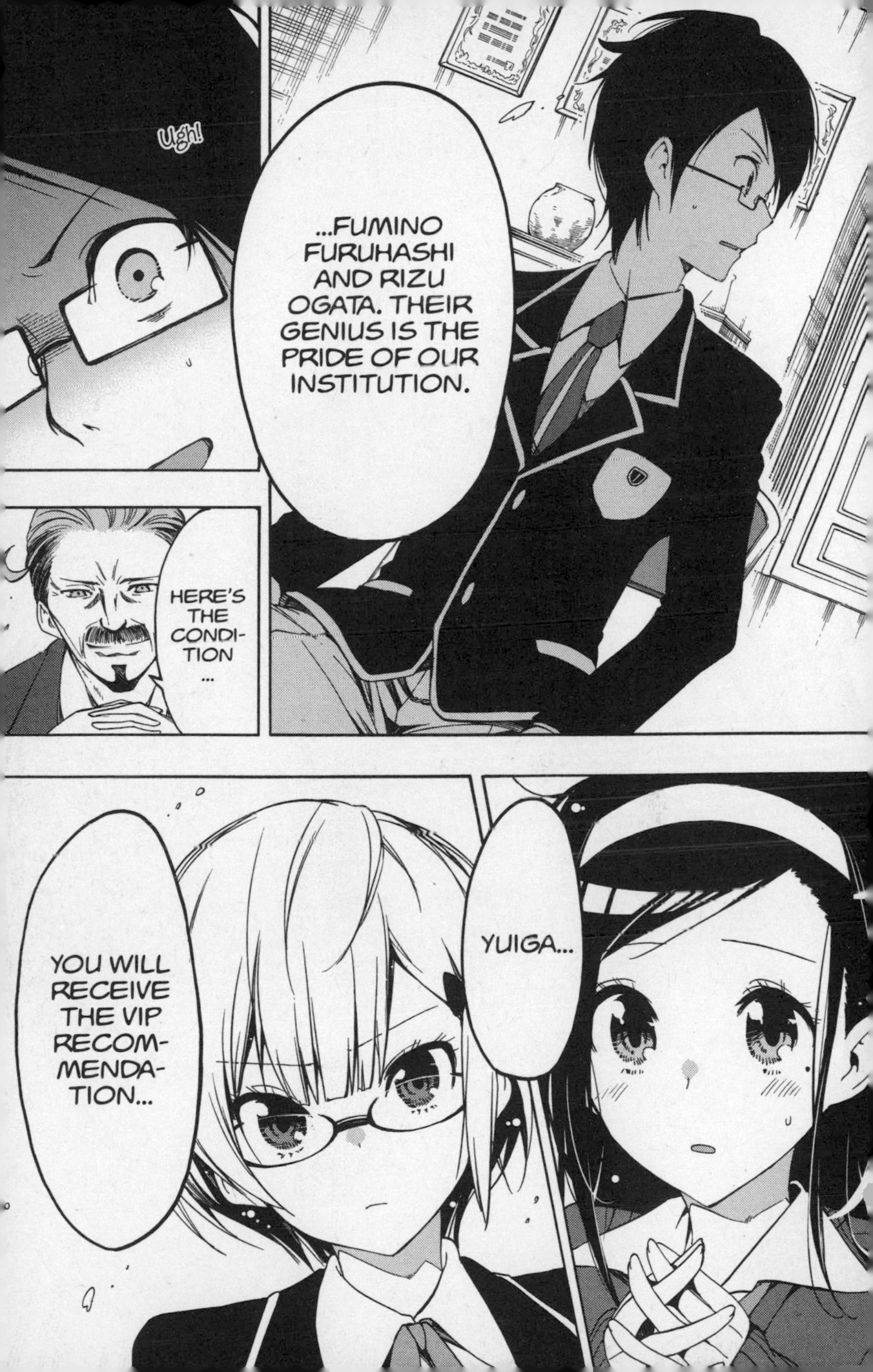
...FUMINO FURUHASHI AND RIZU OGATA. THEIR GENIUS IS THE PRIDE OF OUR INSTITUTION.
Ugh!
HERE'S THE CONDITION...
YUIGA...
YOU WILL RECEIVE THE VIP RECOMMENDATION...

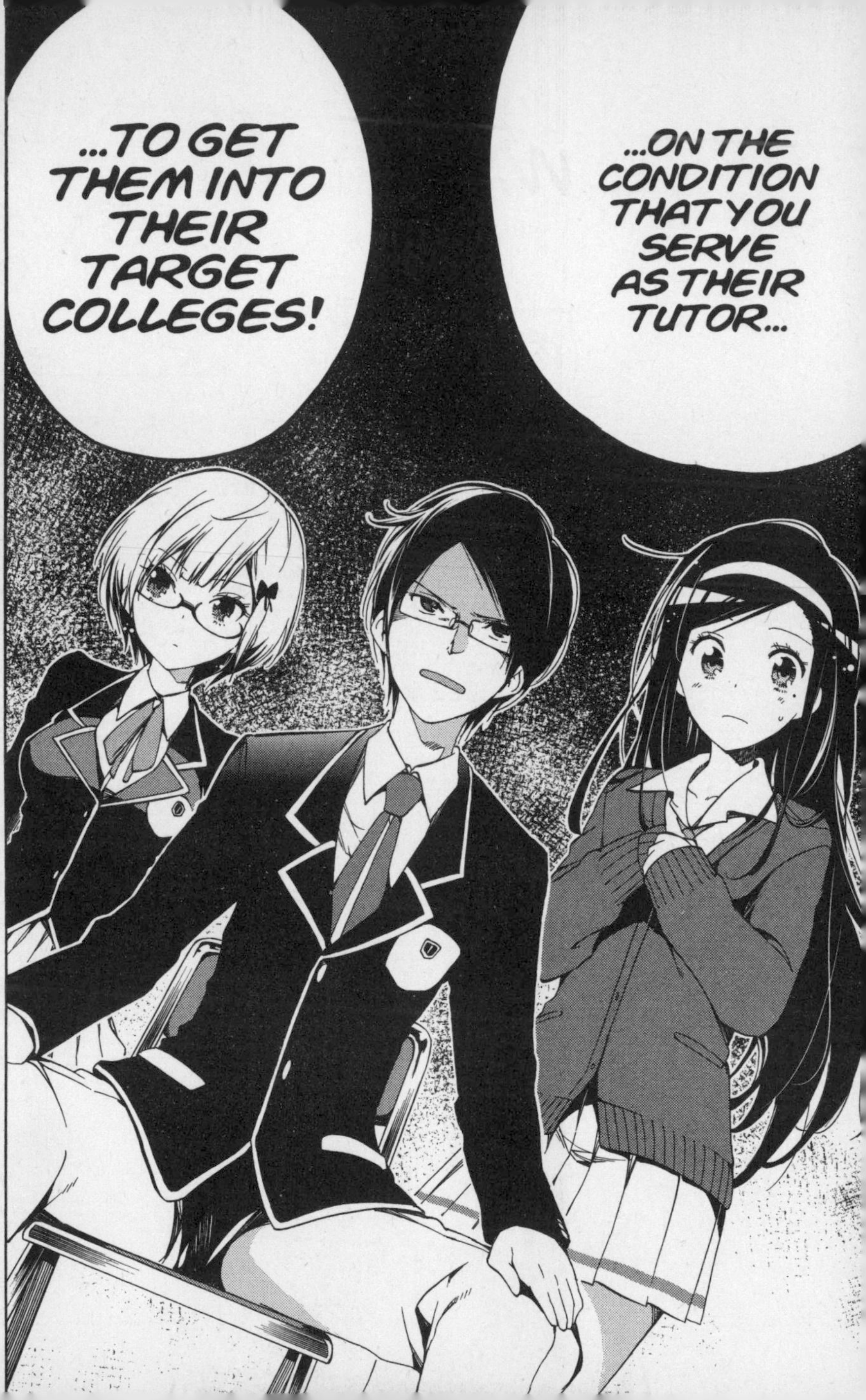
...ON THE CONDITION THAT YOU SERVE AS THEIR TUTOR...
...TO GET THEM INTO THEIR TARGET COLLEGES!

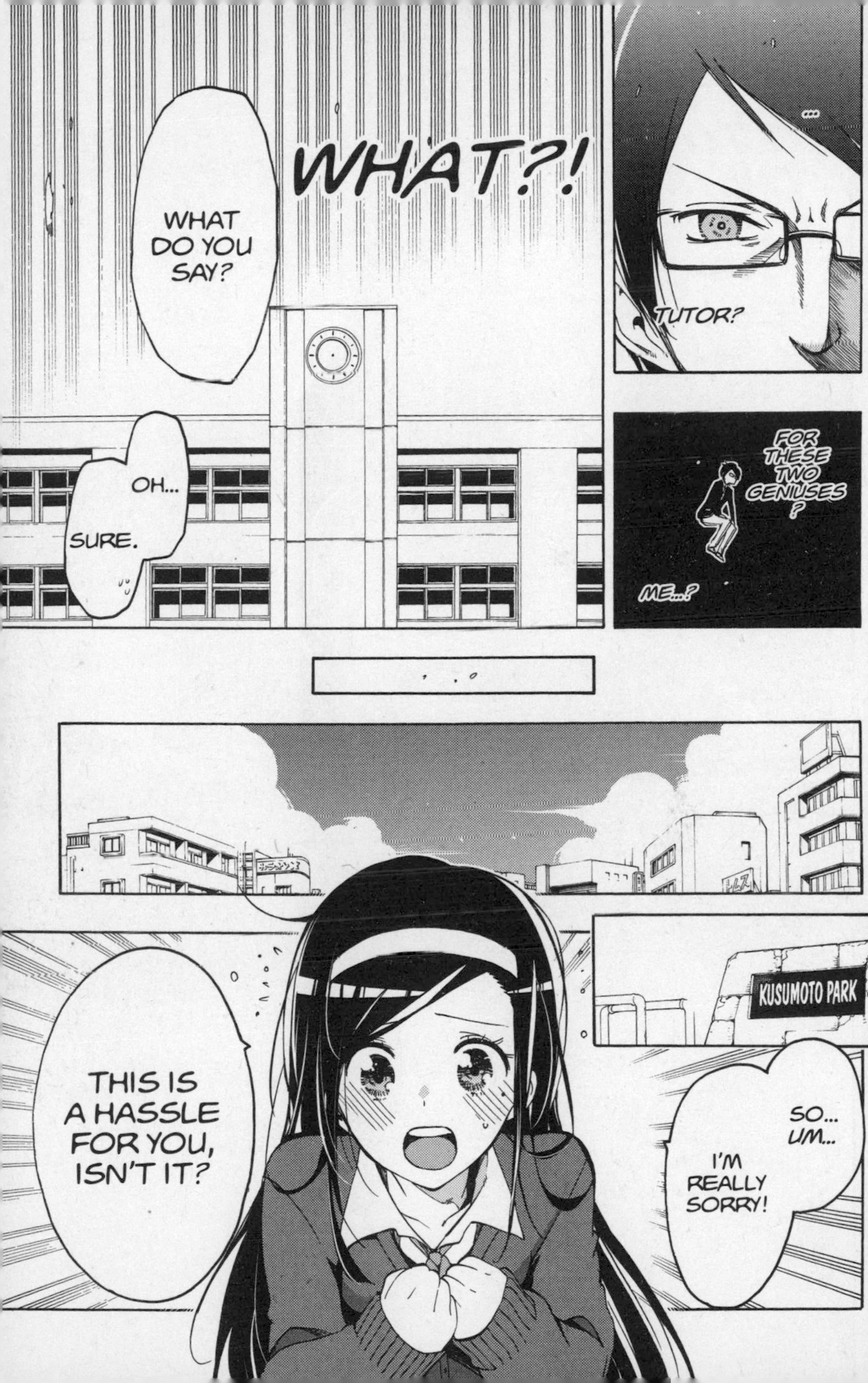
...
TUTOR?
FOR THESE TWO GENIUSES?
ME...?
WHAT?!
WHAT DO YOU SAY?
OH... SURE.
KUSUMOTO PARK
SO... UM... I'M REALLY SORRY!
THIS IS A HASSLE FOR YOU, ISN'T IT?

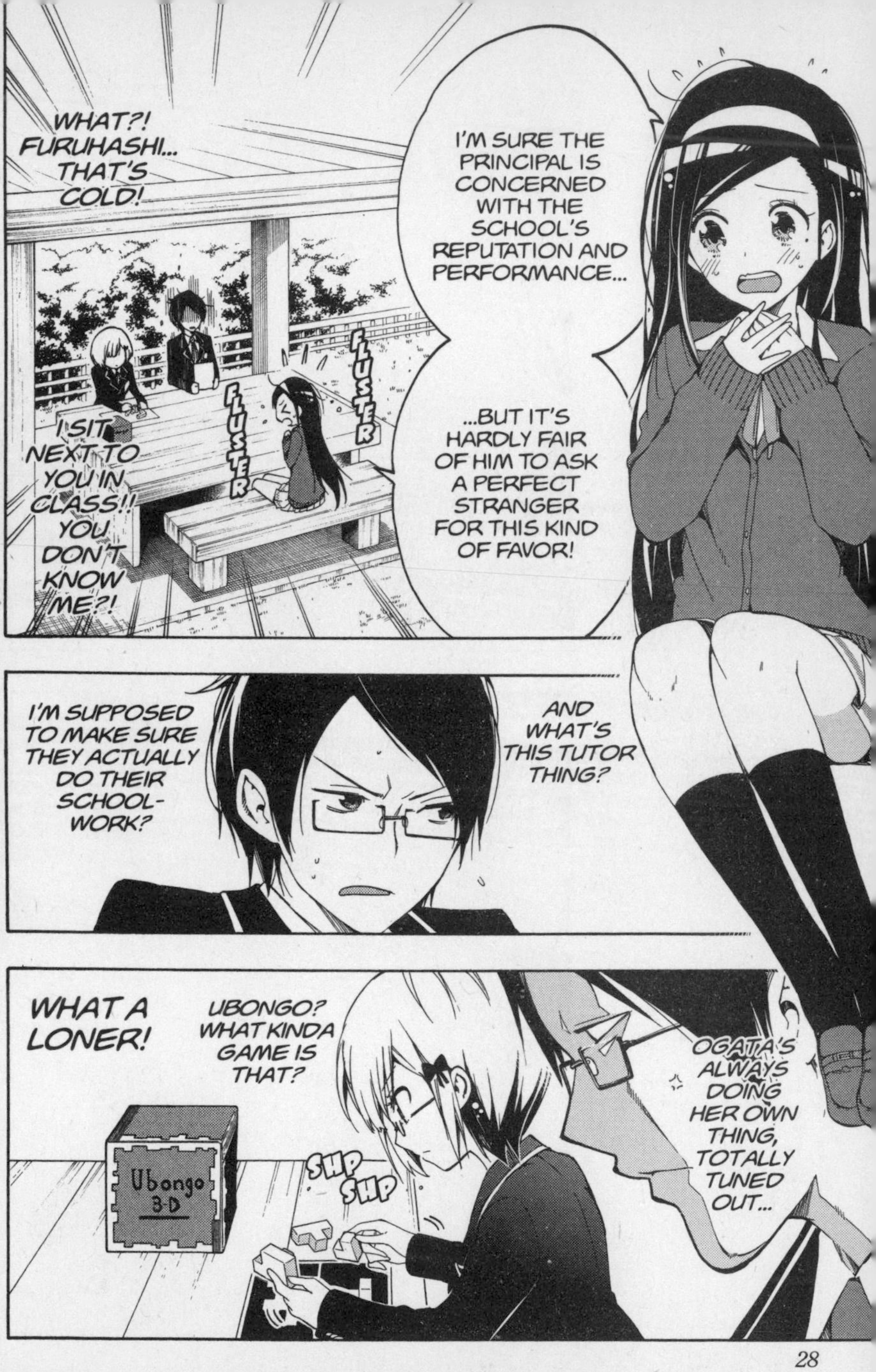
I'M SURE THE PRINCIPAL IS CONCERNED WITH THE SCHOOL'S REPUTATION AND PERFORMANCE...
...BUT IT'S HARDLY FAIR OF HIM TO ASK A PERFECT STRANGER FOR THIS KIND OF FAVOR!
WHAT?! FURUHASHI... THAT'S COLD!
FLUSTER
FLUSTER
I SIT NEXT TO YOU IN CLASS!! YOU DON'T KNOW ME?!
AND WHAT'S THIS TUTOR THING?
I'M SUPPOSED TO MAKE SURE THEY ACTUALLY DO THEIR SCHOOL-WORK?
OGATA'S ALWAYS DOING HER OWN THING, TOTALLY TUNED OUT...
SHP SHP
UBONGO? WHAT KINDA GAME IS THAT?
WHAT A LONER!
Ubongo 3-D

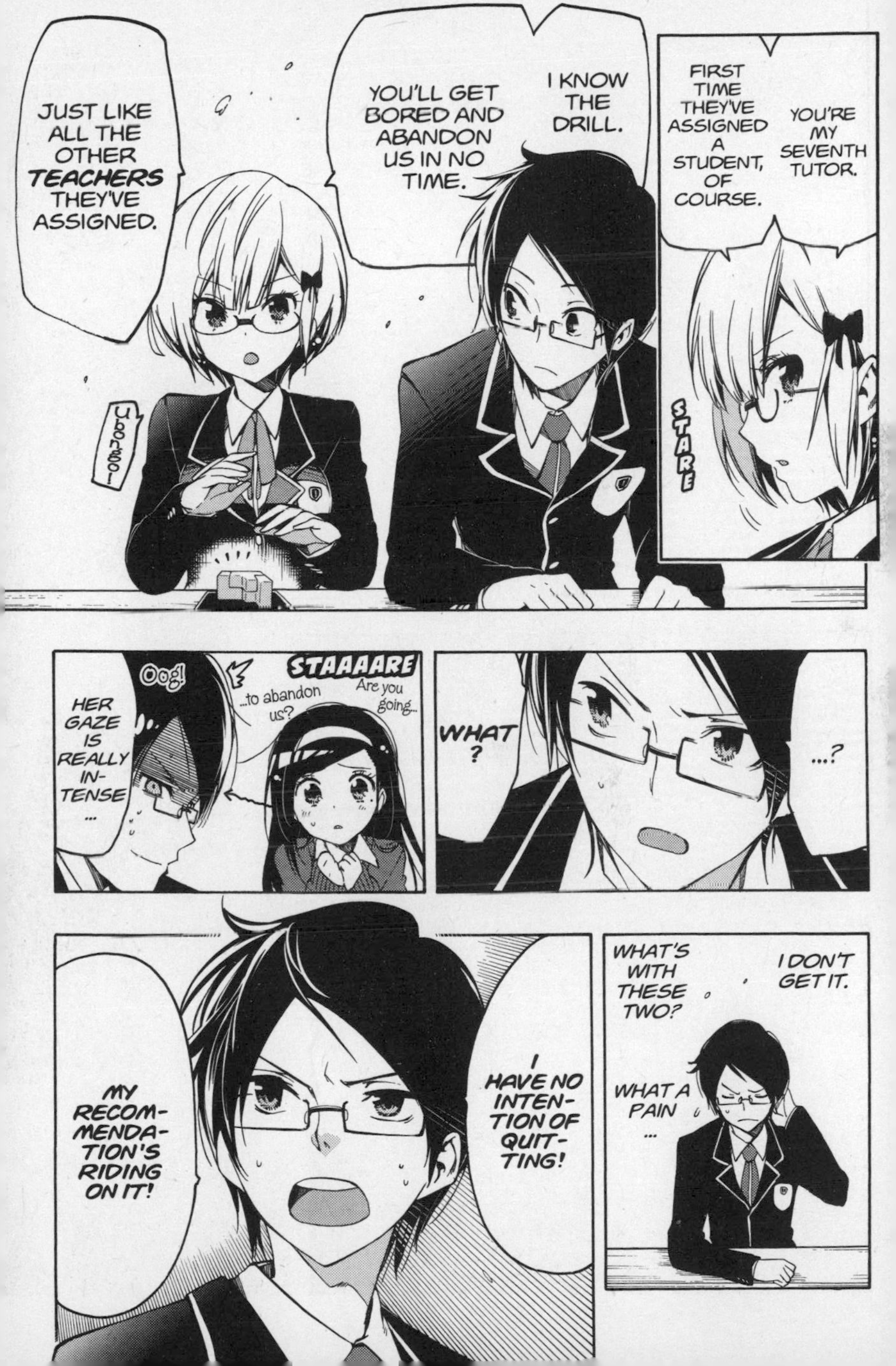
YOU'RE MY SEVENTH TUTOR.
FIRST TIME THEY'VE ASSIGNED A STUDENT, OF COURSE.
STARE
I KNOW THE DRILL.
YOU'LL GET BORED AND ABANDON US IN NO TIME.
JUST LIKE ALL THE OTHER TEACHERS THEY'VE ASSIGNED.
Ubonsoo!
...?
WHAT?
STAAAARE
Are you going...
...to abandon us?
Oog!
HER GAZE IS REALLY IN-TENSE...
I DON'T GET IT.
WHAT'S WITH THESE TWO?
WHAT A PAIN...
I HAVE NO INTEN-TION OF QUIT-TING!
MY RECOM-MENDA-TION'S RIDING ON IT!

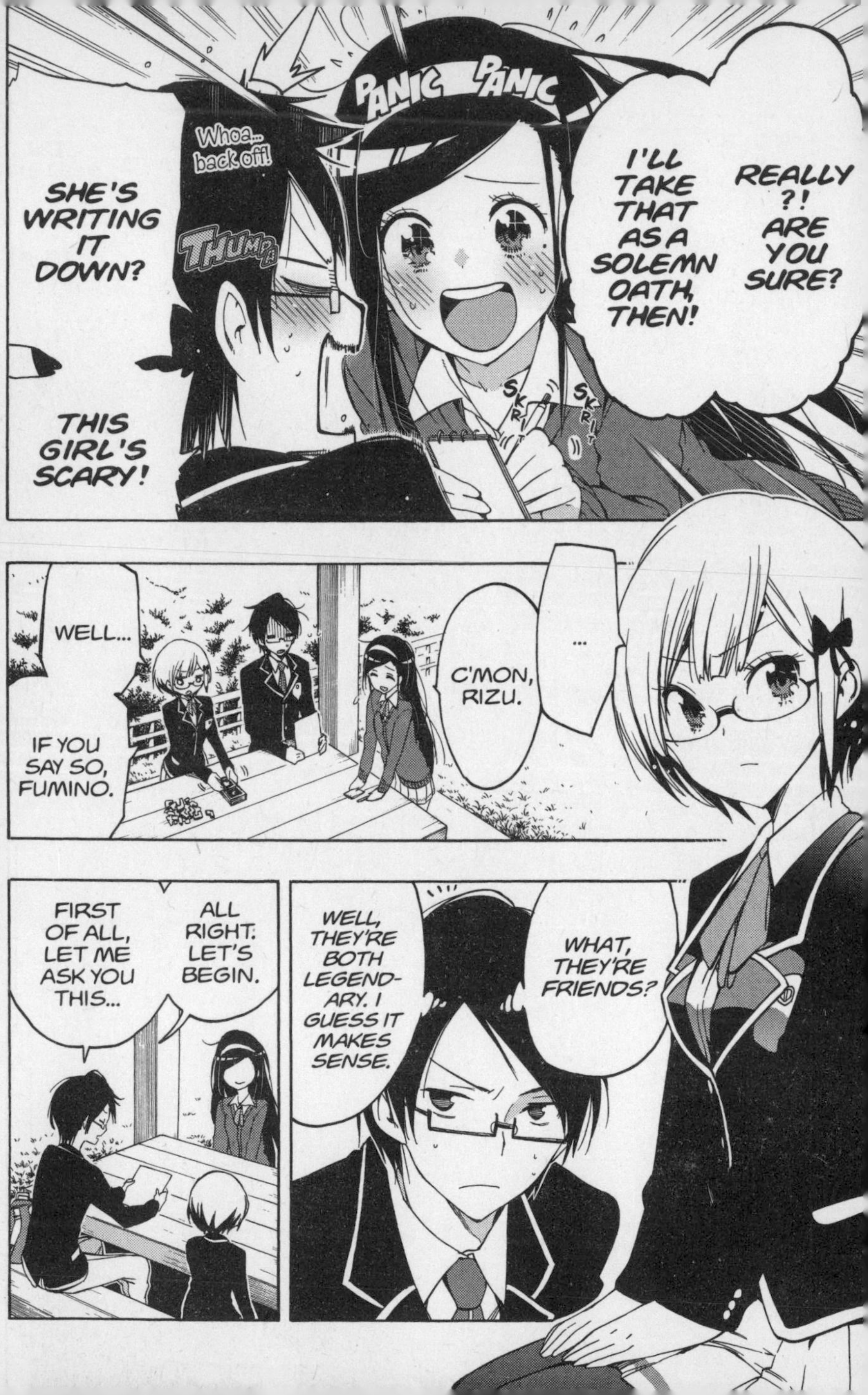
PANIC PANIC
REALLY?! ARE YOU SURE?
I'LL TAKE THAT AS A SOLEMN OATH, THEN!
SKRIT SKRIT
Whoa... back off!
THUMP
SHE'S WRITING IT DOWN?
THIS GIRL'S SCARY!
...
C'MON, RIZU.
WELL...
IF YOU SAY SO, FUMINO.
WHAT, THEY'RE FRIENDS?
WELL, THEY'RE BOTH LEGENDARY. I GUESS IT MAKES SENSE.
ALL RIGHT: LET'S BEGIN.
FIRST OF ALL, LET ME ASK YOU THIS...

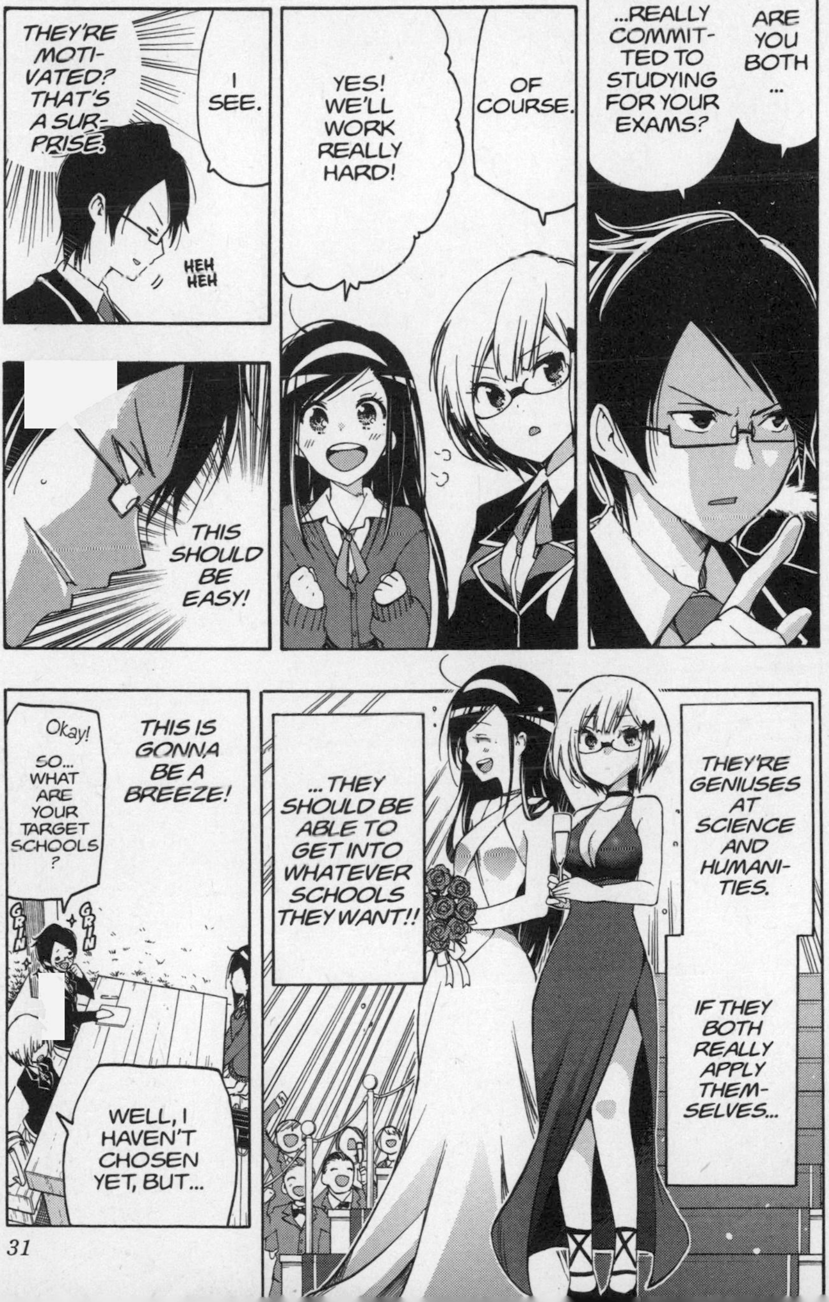
ARE YOU BOTH ...
...REALLY COMMITTED TO STUDYING FOR YOUR EXAMS?
OF COURSE.
YES! WE'LL WORK REALLY HARD!
I SEE.
THEY'RE MOTIVATED? THAT'S A SURPRISE.
HEH HEH
THIS SHOULD BE EASY!
THEY'RE GENIUSES AT SCIENCE AND HUMANITIES.
IF THEY BOTH REALLY APPLY THEMSELVES...
...THEY SHOULD BE ABLE TO GET INTO WHATEVER SCHOOLS THEY WANT!!
THIS IS GONNA BE A BREEZE!
Okay!
SO... WHAT ARE YOUR TARGET SCHOOLS?
GRIN GRIN
WELL, I HAVEN'T CHOSEN YET, BUT...

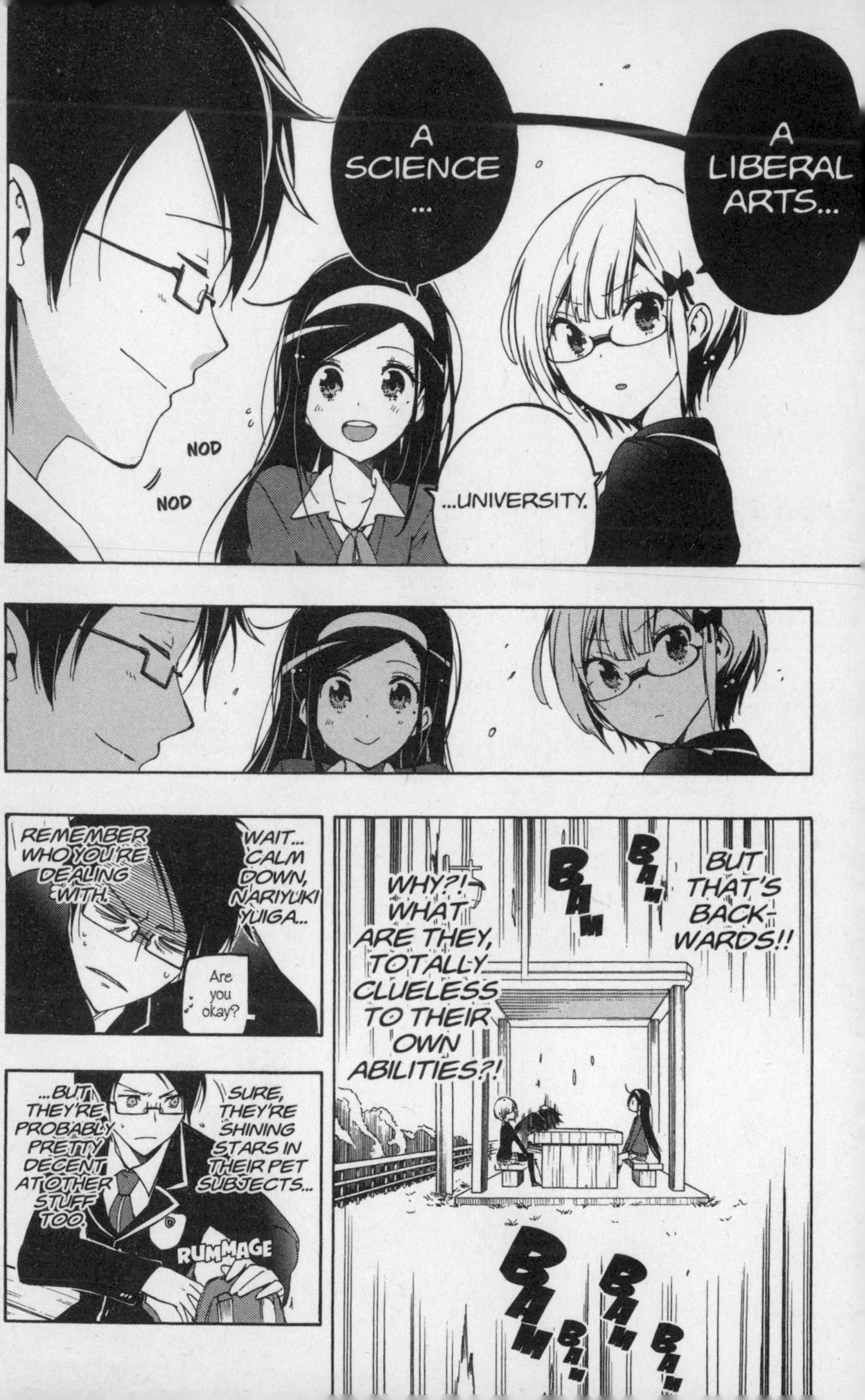
A LIBERAL ARTS...
A SCIENCE ...
...UNIVERSITY.
NOD
NOD
BAM
BAM
BUT THAT'S BACK-WARDS!!
WHY?! WHAT ARE THEY, TOTALLY CLUELESS TO THEIR OWN ABILITIES?!
BAM BAM BAM BAM BAM
WAIT... CALM DOWN, NARIYUKI YUIGA...
REMEMBER WHO YOU'RE DEALING WITH.
Are you okay?
SURE, THEY'RE SHINING STARS IN THEIR PET SUBJECTS...
...BUT THEY'RE PROBABLY PRETTY DECENT AT OTHER STUFF TOO.
RUMMAGE

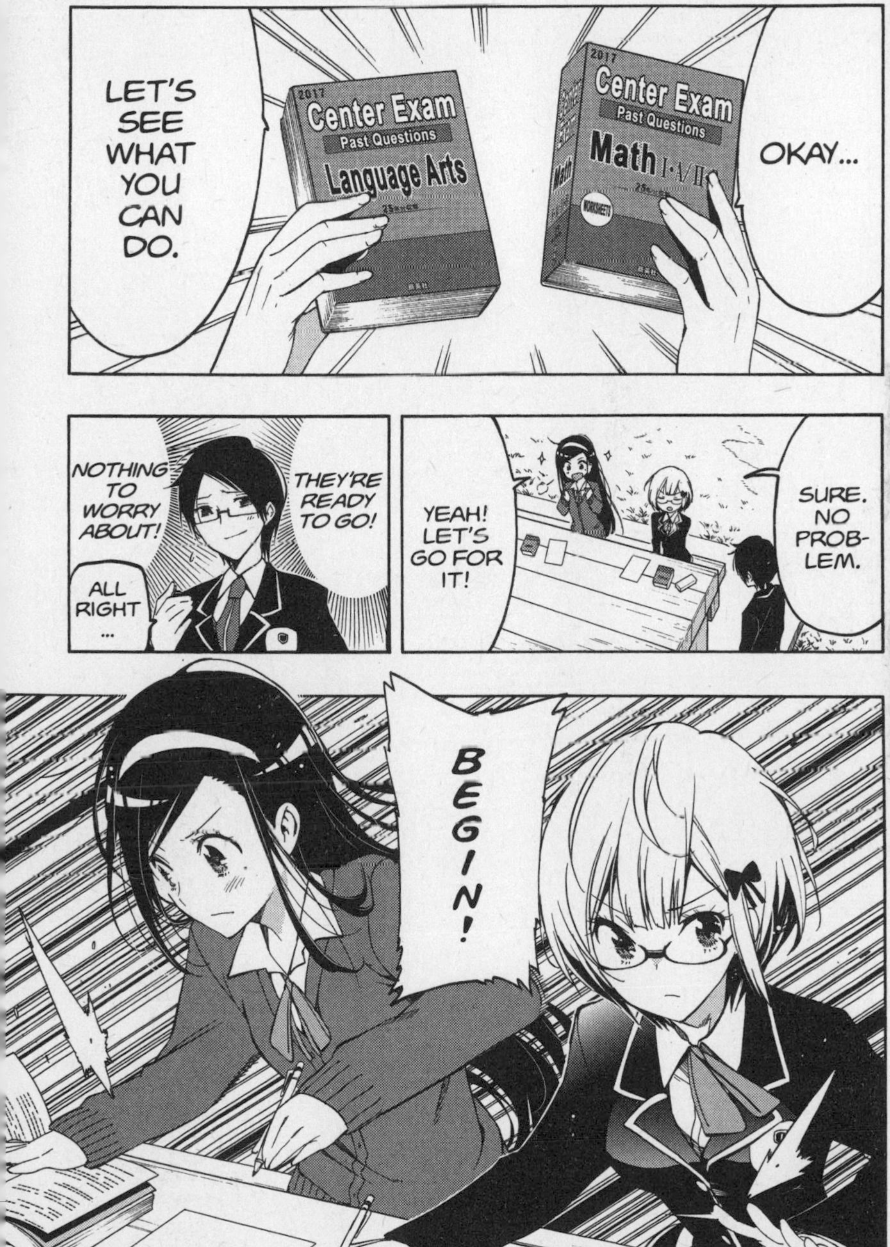
2017
Center Exam
Past Questions
Math I·A/II·B
WORKSHEETS
OKAY...
2017
Center Exam
Past Questions
Language Arts
LET'S SEE WHAT YOU CAN DO.
SURE. NO PROB-LEM.
YEAH! LET'S GO FOR IT!
THEY'RE READY TO GO!
NOTHING TO WORRY ABOUT!
ALL RIGHT ...
BEGIN!

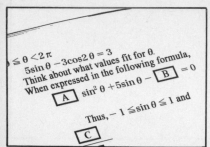

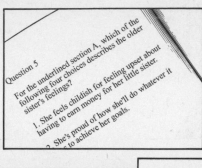

Question 5
For the underlined section A, which of the following four choices describes the older sister's feelings?
1. She feels childish for feeling upset about having to earn money for her little sister.
2. She's proud of how she'll do whatever it takes to achieve her goals.
$\leqq \theta < 2\pi$
$5\sin\theta - 3\cos 2\theta = 3$
Think about what values fit for θ.
When expressed in the following formula,
A $\sin^2\theta + 5\sin\theta -$ B $= 0$
Thus, $-1 \leqq \sin\theta \leqq 1$ and
C
TUNK
HUH?
...
WE HAVE NO CLUE!

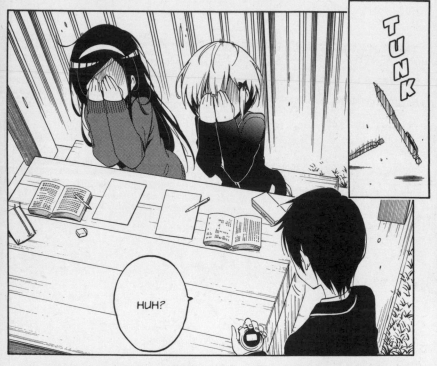

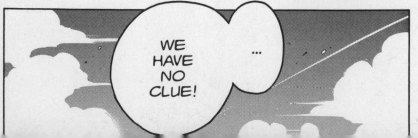

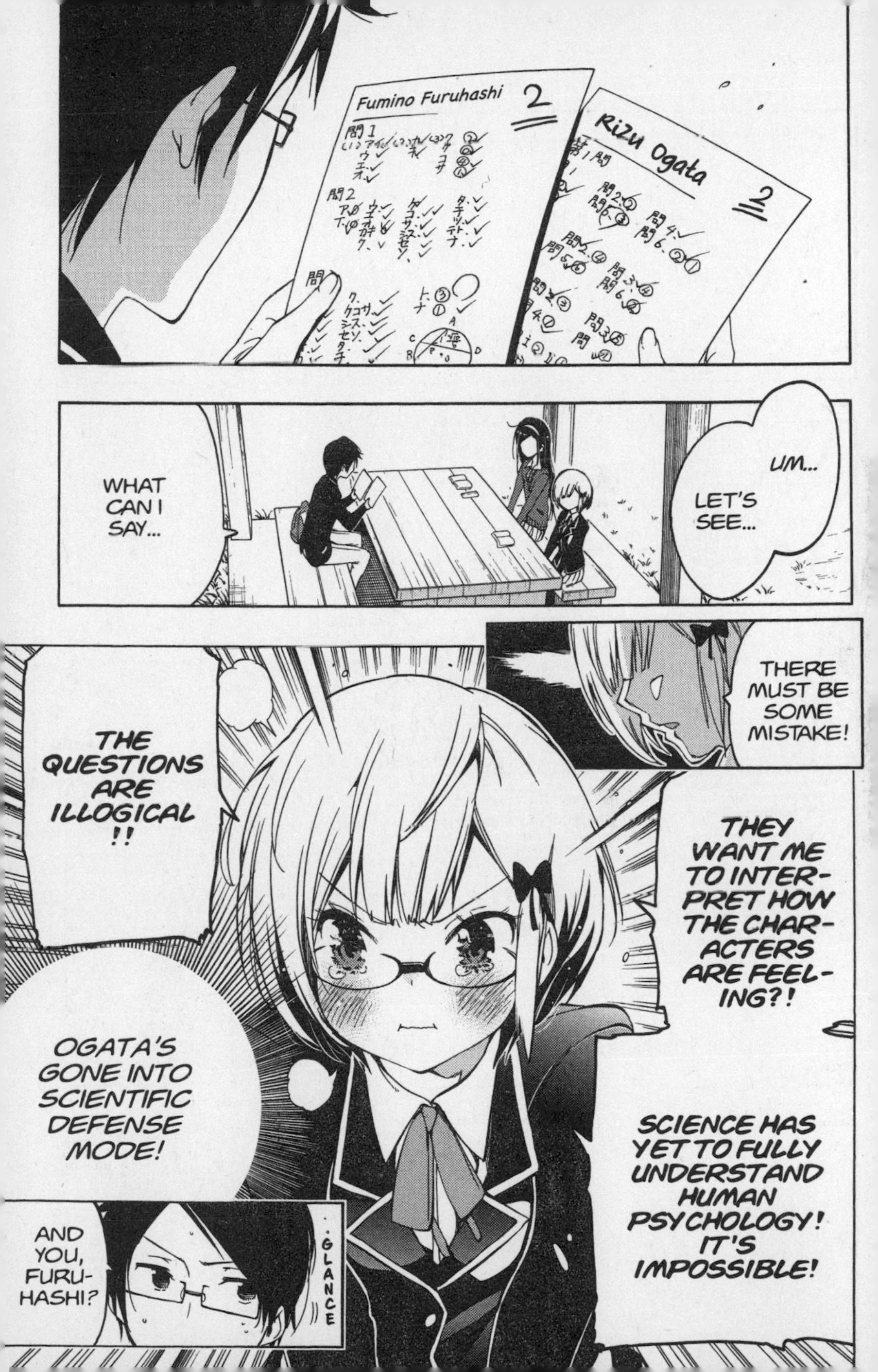
Fumino Furuhashi
2
Rizu Ogata
2
UM... LET'S SEE...
WHAT CAN I SAY...
THERE MUST BE SOME MISTAKE!
THE QUESTIONS ARE ILLOGICAL!!
THEY WANT ME TO INTERPRET HOW THE CHARACTERS ARE FEELING?!
SCIENCE HAS YET TO FULLY UNDERSTAND HUMAN PSYCHOLOGY! IT'S IMPOSSIBLE!
OGATA'S GONE INTO SCIENTIFIC DEFENSE MODE!
...GLANCE
AND YOU, FURUHASHI?

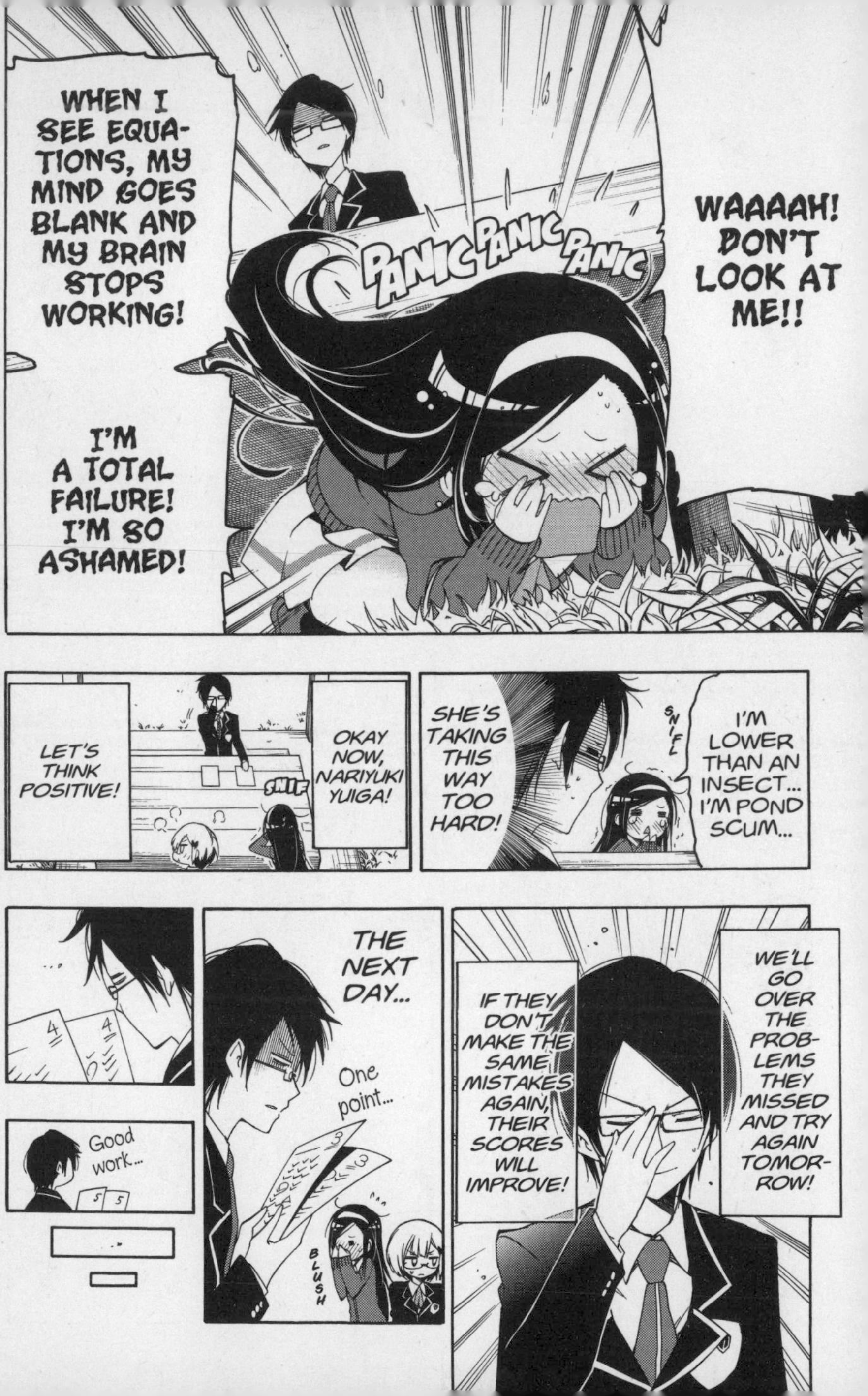
WAAAAH! DON'T LOOK AT ME!!
PANIC PANIC PANIC
WHEN I SEE EQUATIONS, MY MIND GOES BLANK AND MY BRAIN STOPS WORKING!
I'M A TOTAL FAILURE! I'M SO ASHAMED!
I'M LOWER THAN AN INSECT... I'M POND SCUM...
SNIFL
SHE'S TAKING THIS WAY TOO HARD!
OKAY NOW, NARIYUKI YUIGA!
SNIF
LET'S THINK POSITIVE!
WE'LL GO OVER THE PROBLEMS THEY MISSED AND TRY AGAIN TOMORROW!
IF THEY DON'T MAKE THE SAME MISTAKES AGAIN, THEIR SCORES WILL IMPROVE!
THE NEXT DAY...
One point...
BLUSH
Good work...

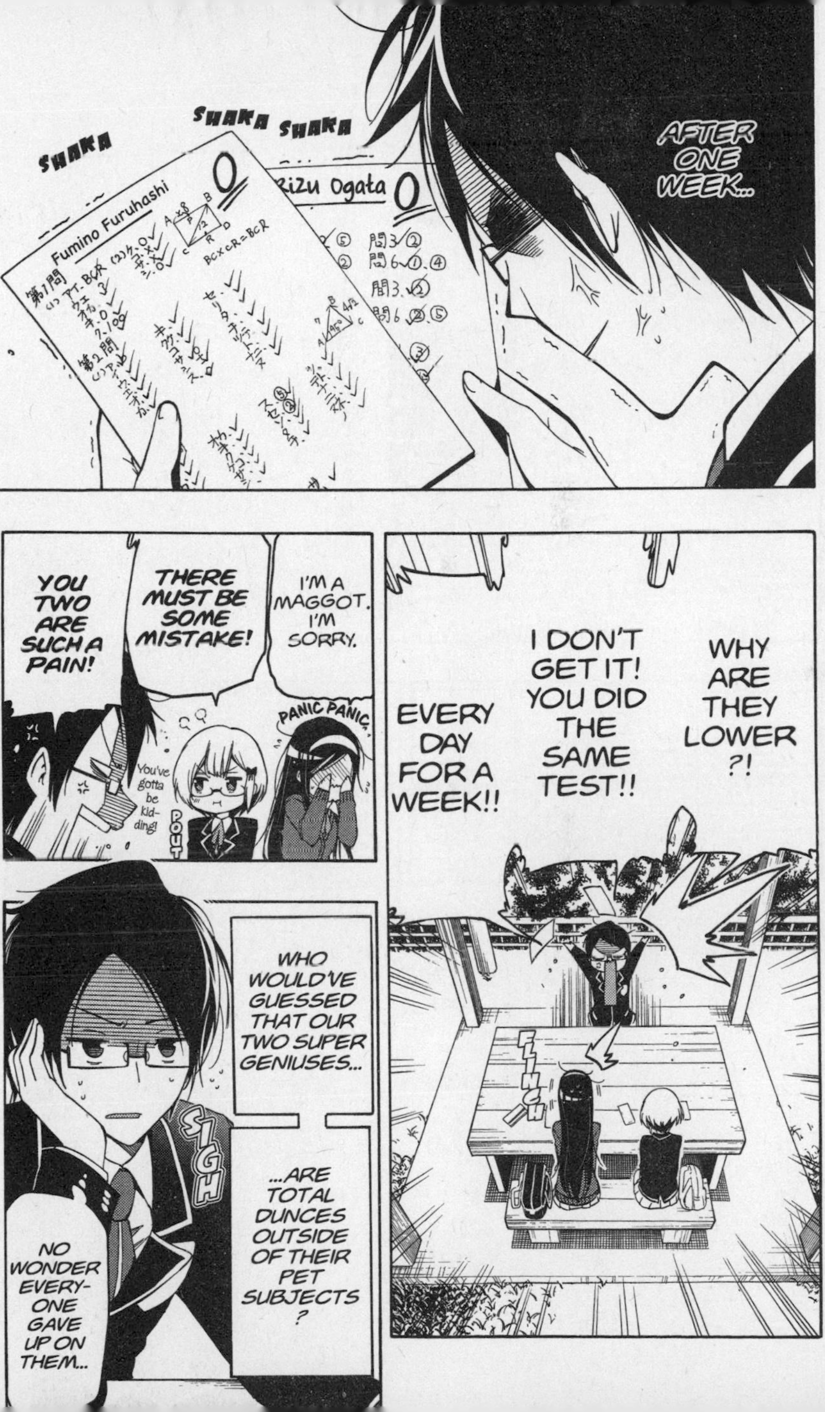
AFTER ONE WEEK...
SHAKA SHAKA
SHAKA
Rizu Ogata
Fumino Furuhashi
WHY ARE THEY LOWER?!
I DON'T GET IT! YOU DID THE SAME TEST!!
EVERY DAY FOR A WEEK!!
FLINCH
I'M A MAGGOT. I'M SORRY.
THERE MUST BE SOME MISTAKE!
YOU TWO ARE SUCH A PAIN!
PANIC PANIC
You've gotta be kid-ding!
POUT
WHO WOULD'VE GUESSED THAT OUR TWO SUPER GENIUSES...
...ARE TOTAL DUNCES OUTSIDE OF THEIR PET SUBJECTS?
SIGH
NO WONDER EVERY-ONE GAVE UP ON THEM...

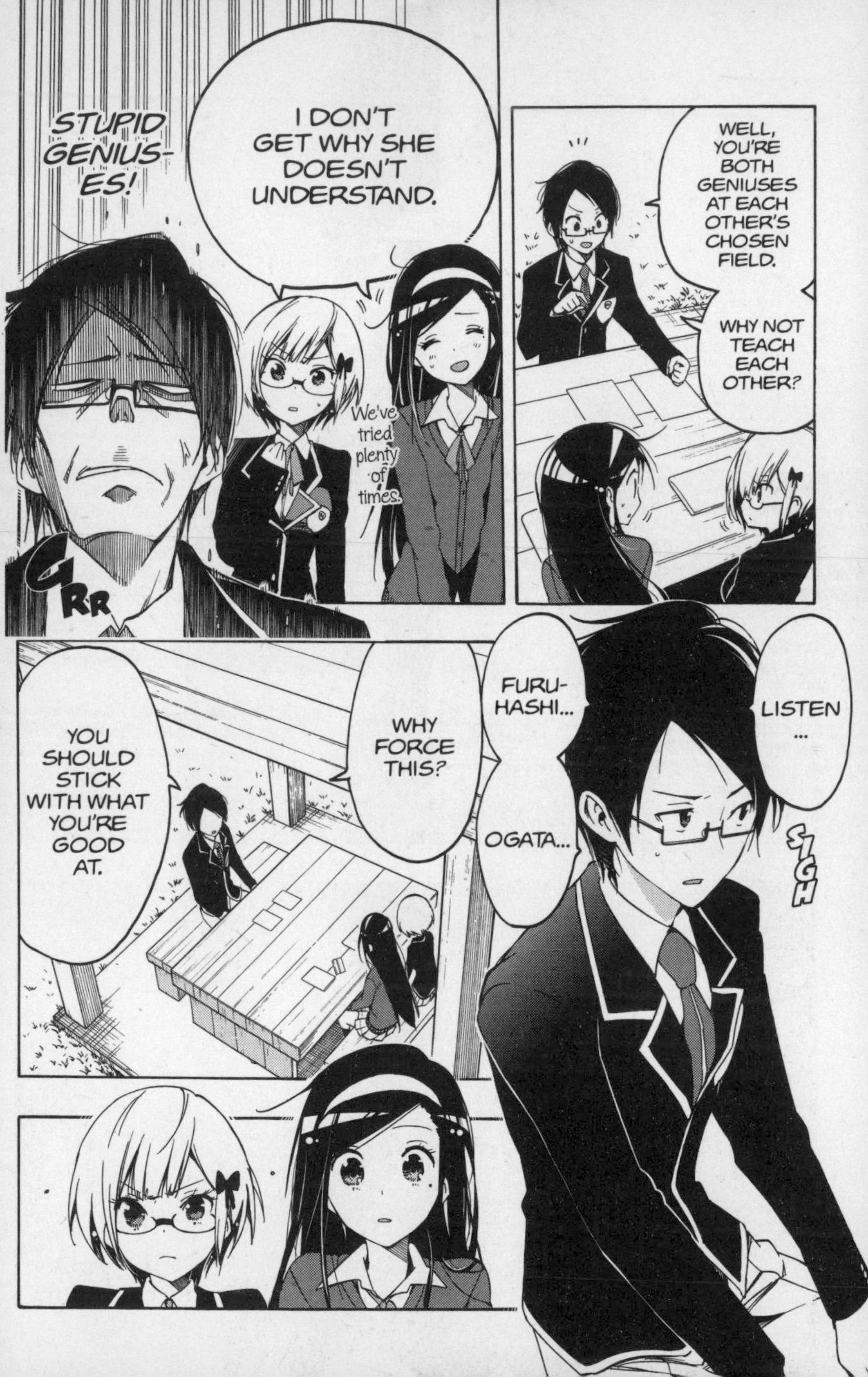
WELL, YOU'RE BOTH GENIUSES AT EACH OTHER'S CHOSEN FIELD.
WHY NOT TEACH EACH OTHER?
I DON'T GET WHY SHE DOESN'T UNDERSTAND.
STUPID GENIUS-ES!
We've tried plenty of times.
GRR
LISTEN...
SIGH
FURU-HASHI...
OGATA...
WHY FORCE THIS?
YOU SHOULD STICK WITH WHAT YOU'RE GOOD AT.

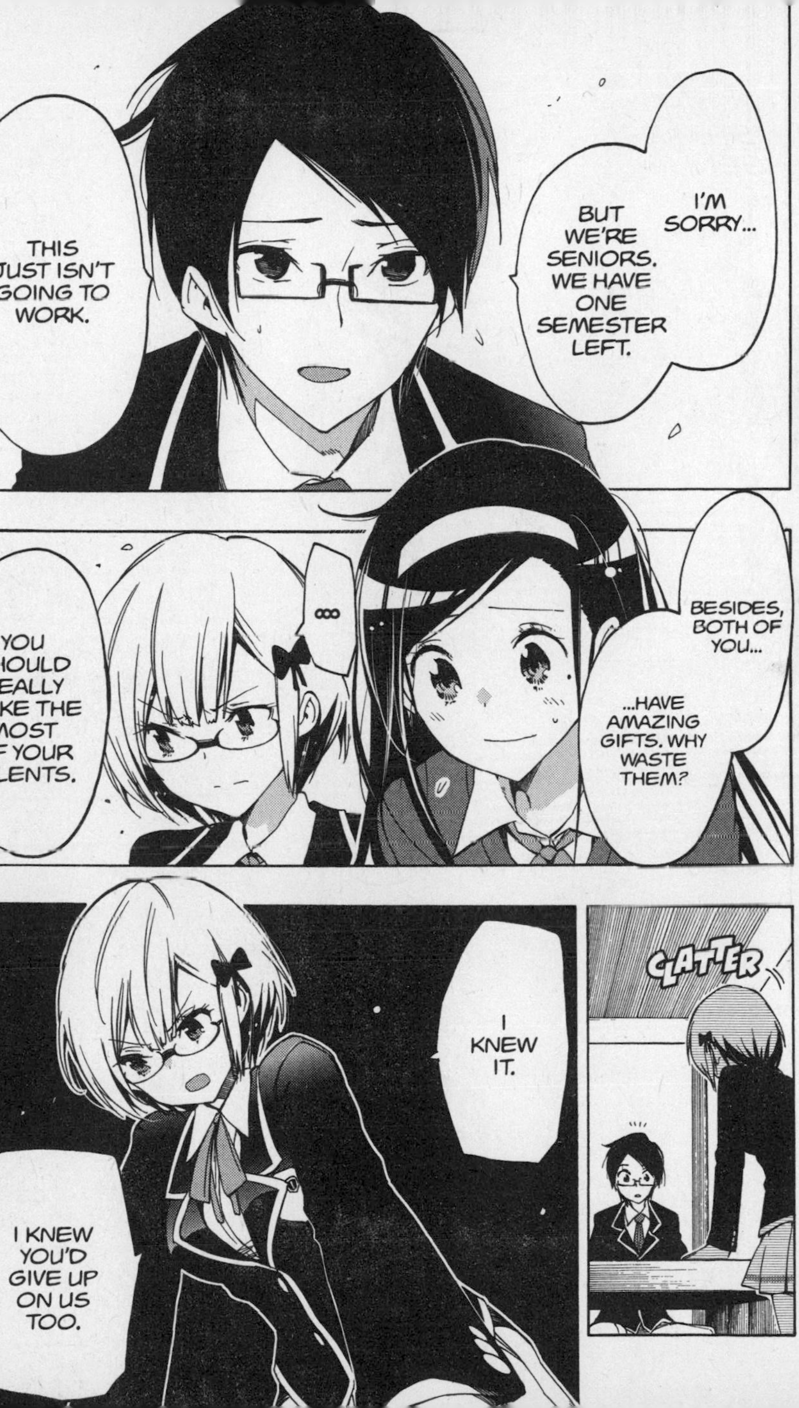
I'M SORRY...
BUT WE'RE SENIORS. WE HAVE ONE SEMESTER LEFT.
THIS JUST ISN'T GOING TO WORK.
BESIDES, BOTH OF YOU...
...HAVE AMAZING GIFTS. WHY WASTE THEM?
...
YOU SHOULD REALLY MAKE THE MOST OF YOUR TALENTS.
CLATTER
I KNEW IT.
I KNEW YOU'D GIVE UP ON US TOO.

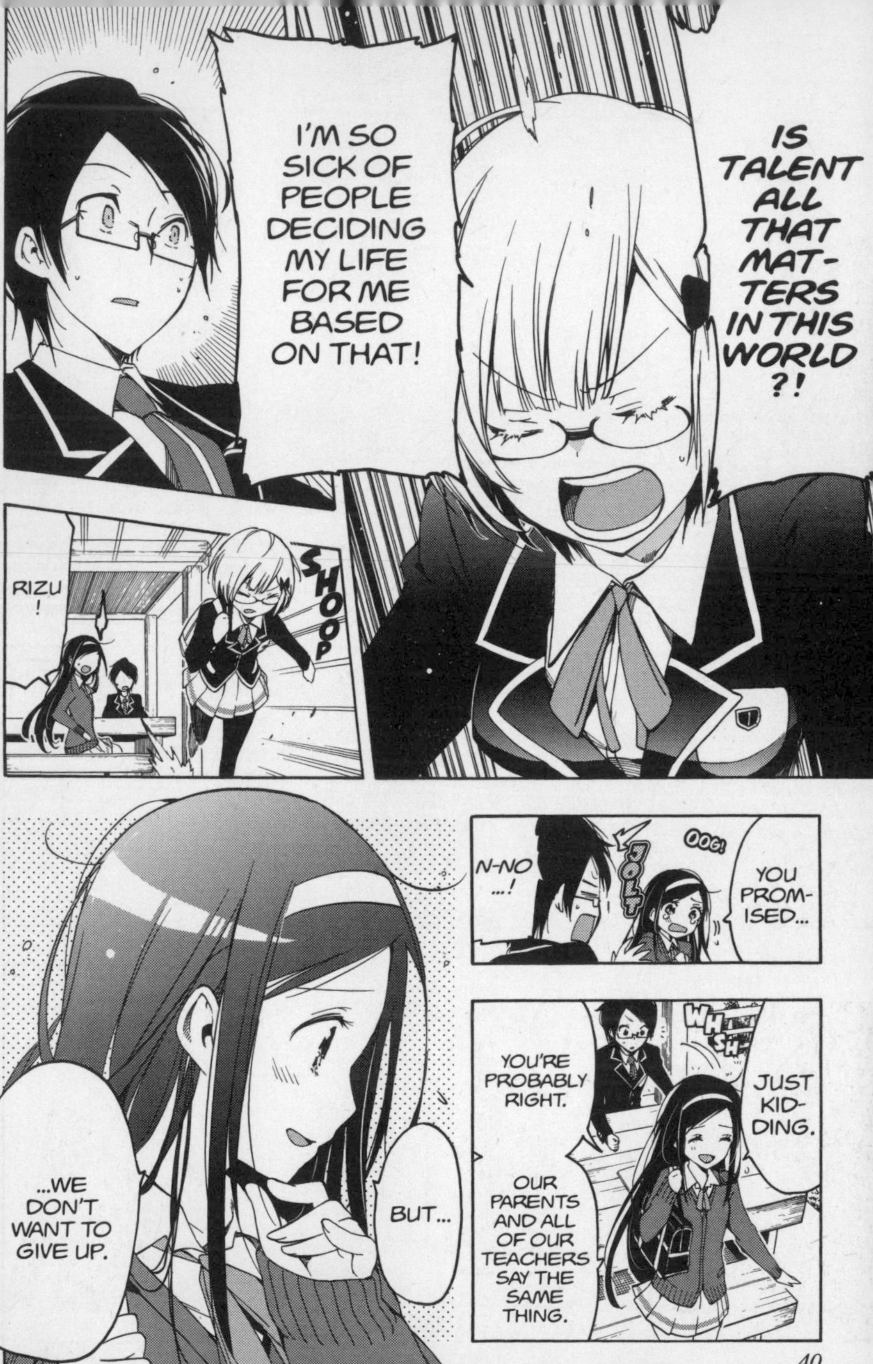
IS TALENT ALL THAT MAT-TERS IN THIS WORLD?!
I'M SO SICK OF PEOPLE DECIDING MY LIFE FOR ME BASED ON THAT!
SHOOOP
RIZU!
OOG!
YOU PROM-ISED...
JOLT
N-NO...!
WHSH
JUST KID-DING.
YOU'RE PROBABLY RIGHT.
OUR PARENTS AND ALL OF OUR TEACHERS SAY THE SAME THING.
BUT...
...WE DON'T WANT TO GIVE UP.

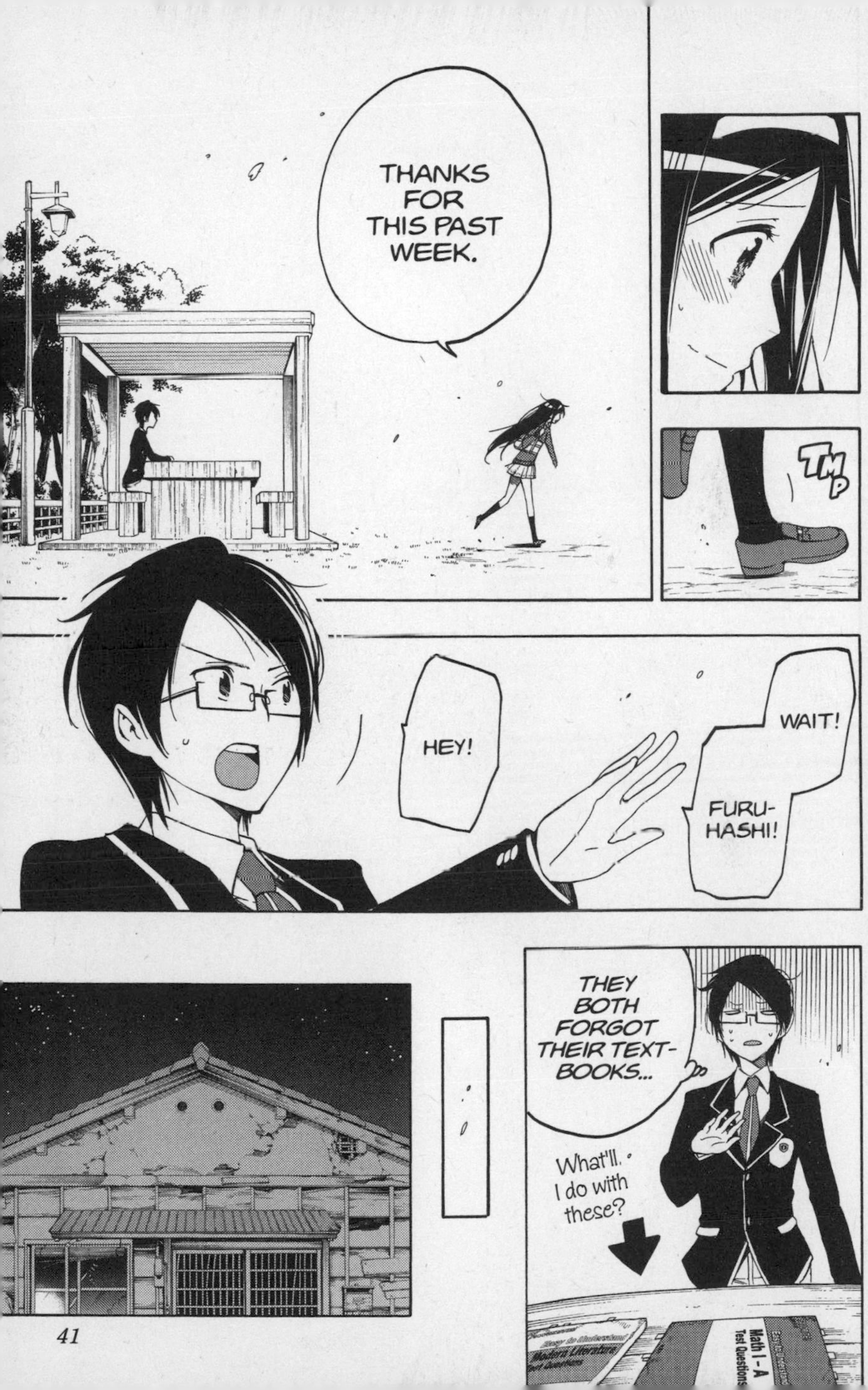
TMP
THANKS FOR THIS PAST WEEK.
WAIT!
FURU-HASHI!
HEY!
THEY BOTH FORGOT THEIR TEXT-BOOKS...
What'll I do with these?
Math I-A
Test Questions
Modern Literature

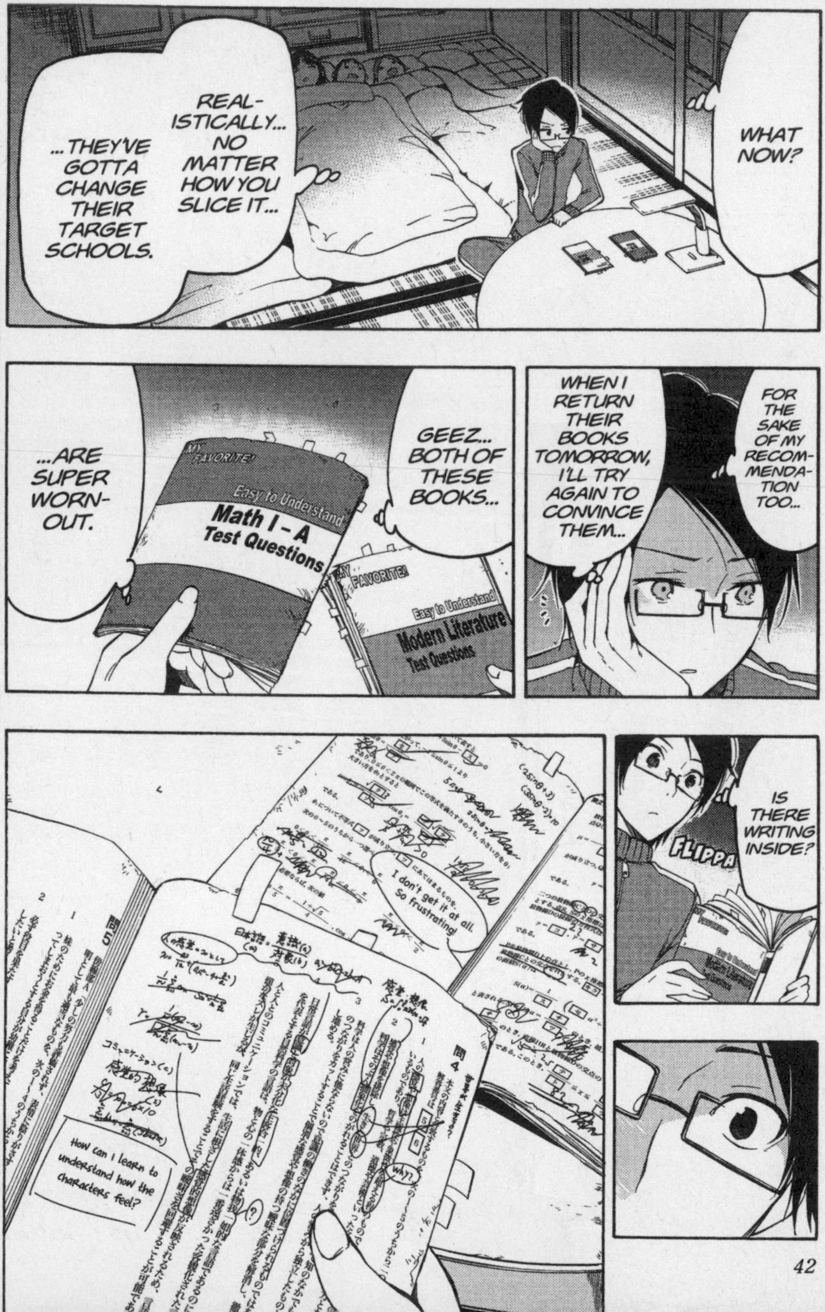
WHAT NOW?
REAL-ISTICALLY... NO MATTER HOW YOU SLICE IT...
...THEY'VE GOTTA CHANGE THEIR TARGET SCHOOLS.
FOR THE SAKE OF MY RECOMMENDATION TOO...
WHEN I RETURN THEIR BOOKS TOMORROW, I'LL TRY AGAIN TO CONVINCE THEM...
GEEZ... BOTH OF THESE BOOKS...
MY FAVORITE! Easy to Understand Modern Literature Test Questions
MY FAVORITE! Easy to Understand Math I - A Test Questions
...ARE SUPER WORN-OUT.
IS THERE WRITING INSIDE?
FLIPPA
I don't get it at all. So frustrating!
why?
How can I learn to understand how the characters feel?

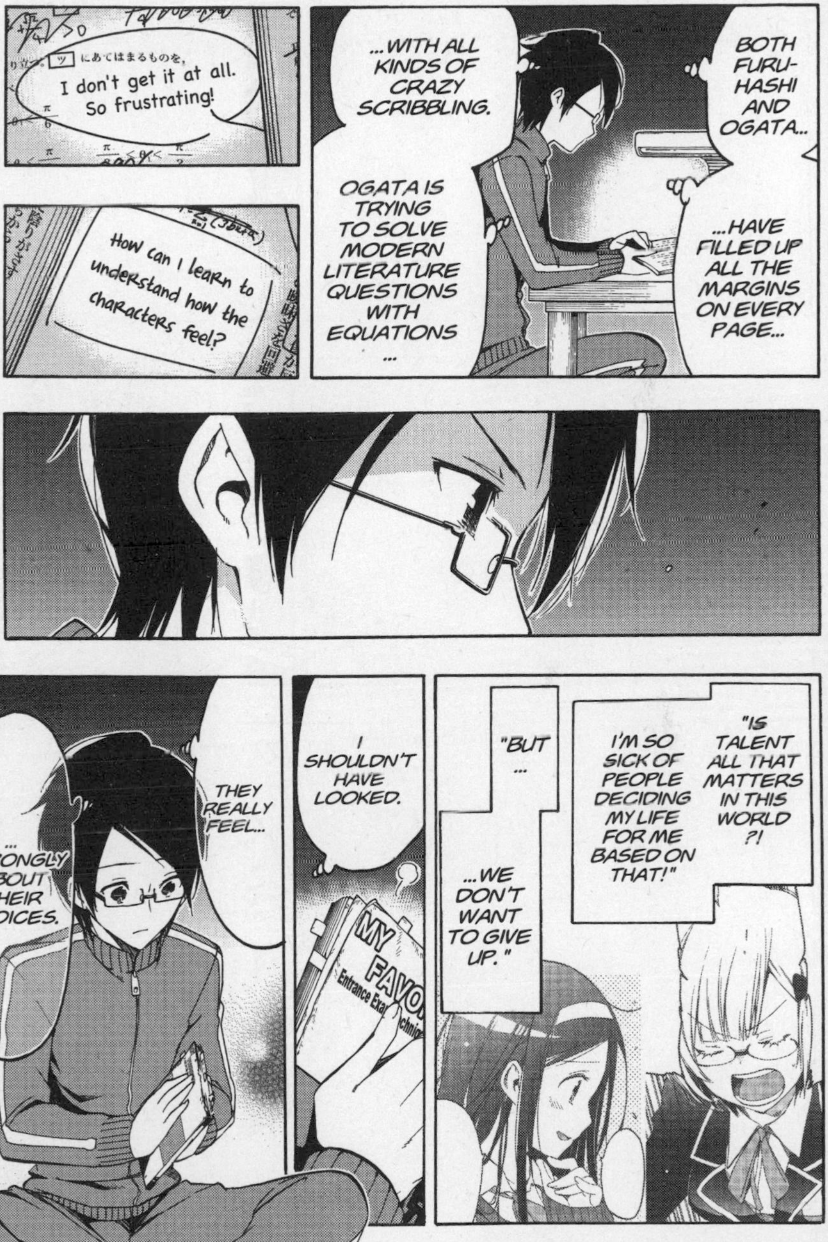
BOTH FURU-HASHI AND OGATA...
...HAVE FILLED UP ALL THE MARGINS ON EVERY PAGE...
...WITH ALL KINDS OF CRAZY SCRIBBLING.
OGATA IS TRYING TO SOLVE MODERN LITERATURE QUESTIONS WITH EQUATIONS ...
にあてはまるものを、
I don't get it at all. So frustrating!
How can I learn to understand how the characters feel?
"IS TALENT ALL THAT MATTERS IN THIS WORLD ?!
I'M SO SICK OF PEOPLE DECIDING MY LIFE FOR ME BASED ON THAT!"
"BUT ...
...WE DON'T WANT TO GIVE UP."
I SHOULDN'T HAVE LOOKED.
THEY REALLY FEEL...
... STRONGLY ABOUT THEIR CHOICES.

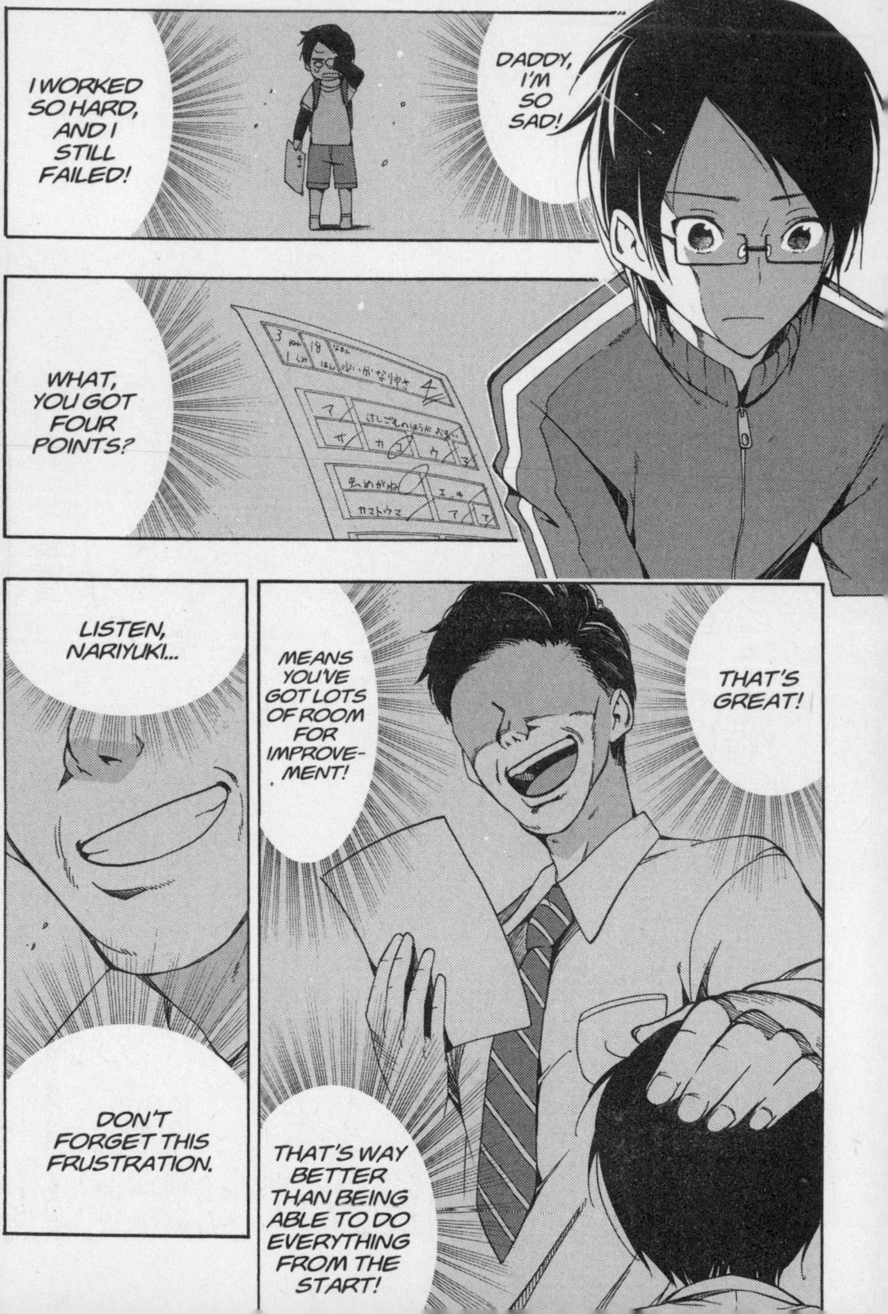
DADDY, I'M SO SAD!
I WORKED SO HARD, AND I STILL FAILED!
WHAT, YOU GOT FOUR POINTS?
THAT'S GREAT!
MEANS YOU'VE GOT LOTS OF ROOM FOR IMPROVE-MENT!
THAT'S WAY BETTER THAN BEING ABLE TO DO EVERYTHING FROM THE START!
LISTEN, NARIYUKI...
DON'T FORGET THIS FRUSTRATION.

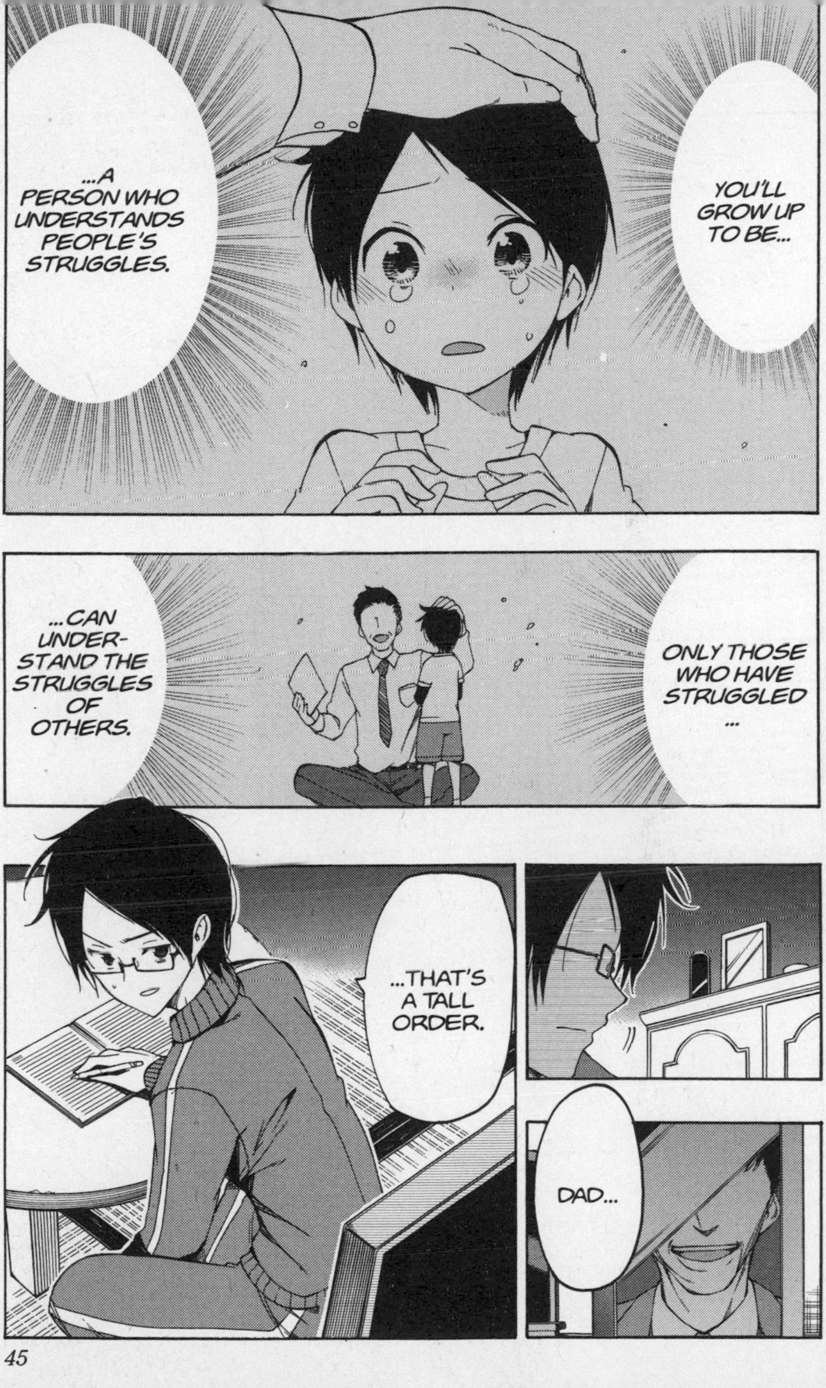
YOU'LL GROW UP TO BE...
...A PERSON WHO UNDERSTANDS PEOPLE'S STRUGGLES.
ONLY THOSE WHO HAVE STRUGGLED ...
...CAN UNDERSTAND THE STRUGGLES OF OTHERS.
DAD...
...THAT'S A TALL ORDER.

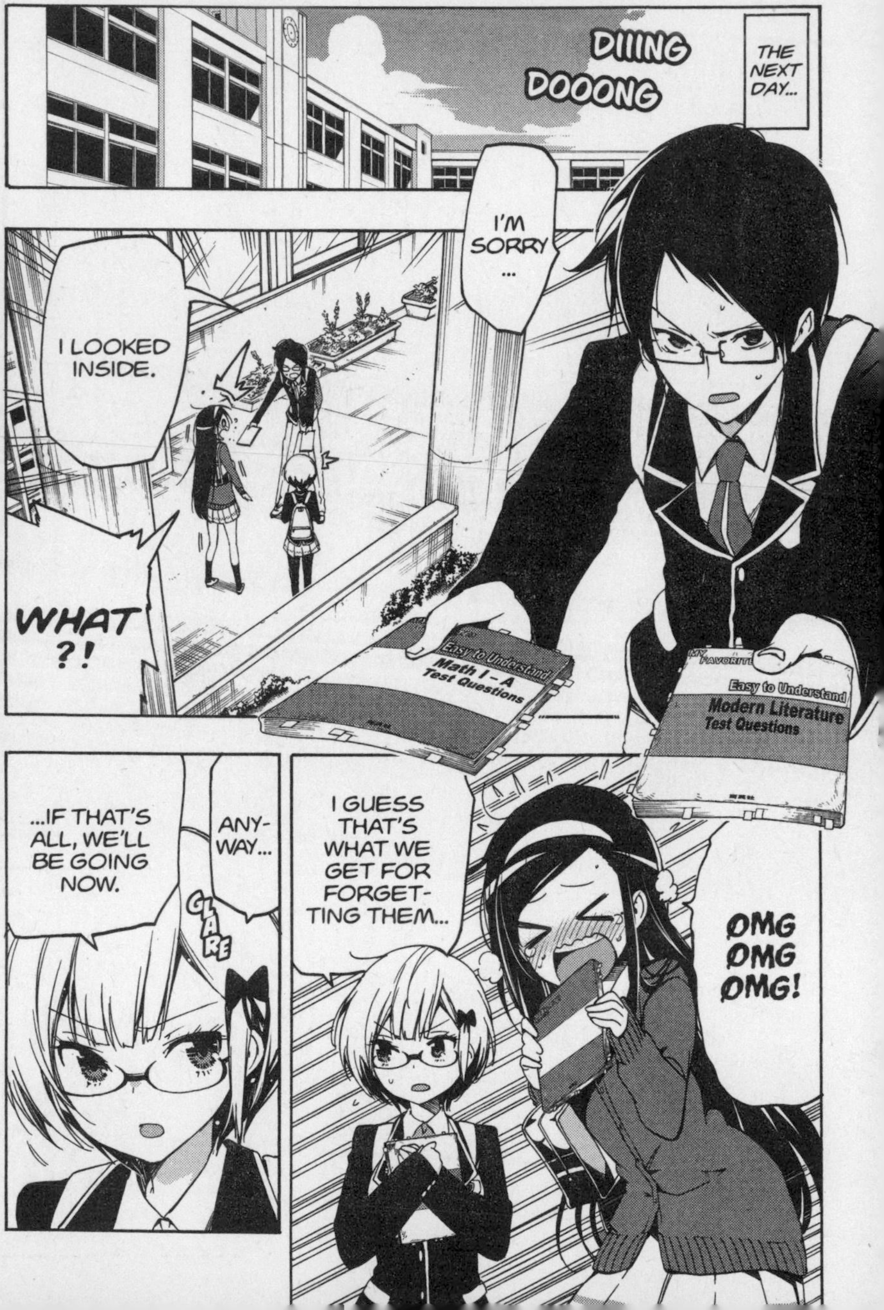
THE NEXT DAY...
DIIING DOOONG
I'M SORRY...
Easy to Understand Math I – A Test Questions
MY FAVORITE Easy to Understand Modern Literature Test Questions
I LOOKED INSIDE.
WHAT?!
OMG OMG OMG!
I GUESS THAT'S WHAT WE GET FOR FORGET-TING THEM...
ANY-WAY...
GLARE
...IF THAT'S ALL, WE'LL BE GOING NOW.

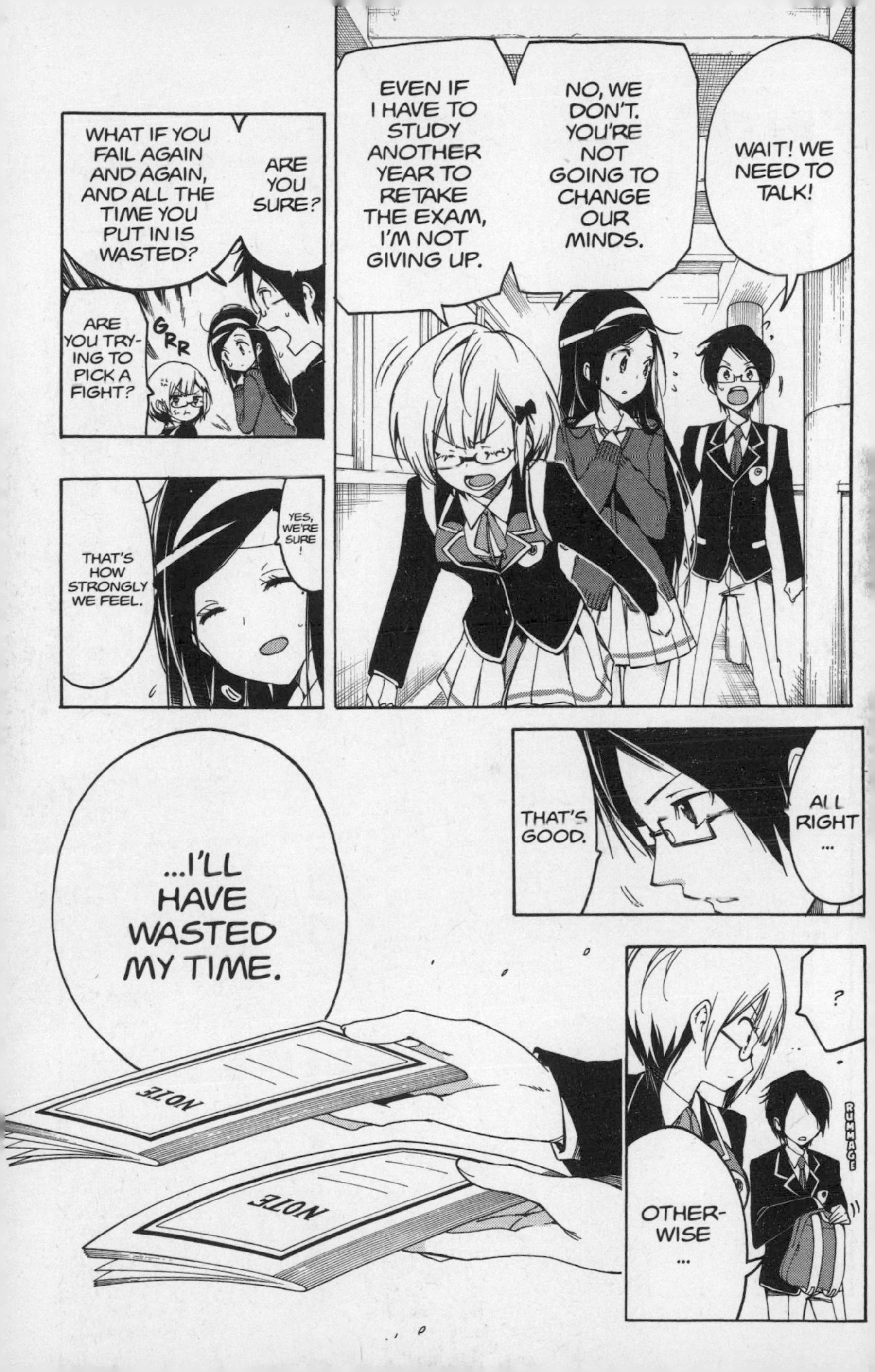
WAIT! WE NEED TO TALK!
NO, WE DON'T. YOU'RE NOT GOING TO CHANGE OUR MINDS.
EVEN IF I HAVE TO STUDY ANOTHER YEAR TO RETAKE THE EXAM, I'M NOT GIVING UP.
ARE YOU SURE?
WHAT IF YOU FAIL AGAIN AND AGAIN, AND ALL THE TIME YOU PUT IN IS WASTED?
GRR
ARE YOU TRYING TO PICK A FIGHT?
YES, WE'RE SURE!
THAT'S HOW STRONGLY WE FEEL.
ALL RIGHT...
THAT'S GOOD.
?
RUMMAGE
OTHERWISE...
...I'LL HAVE WASTED MY TIME.
NOTE
NOTE

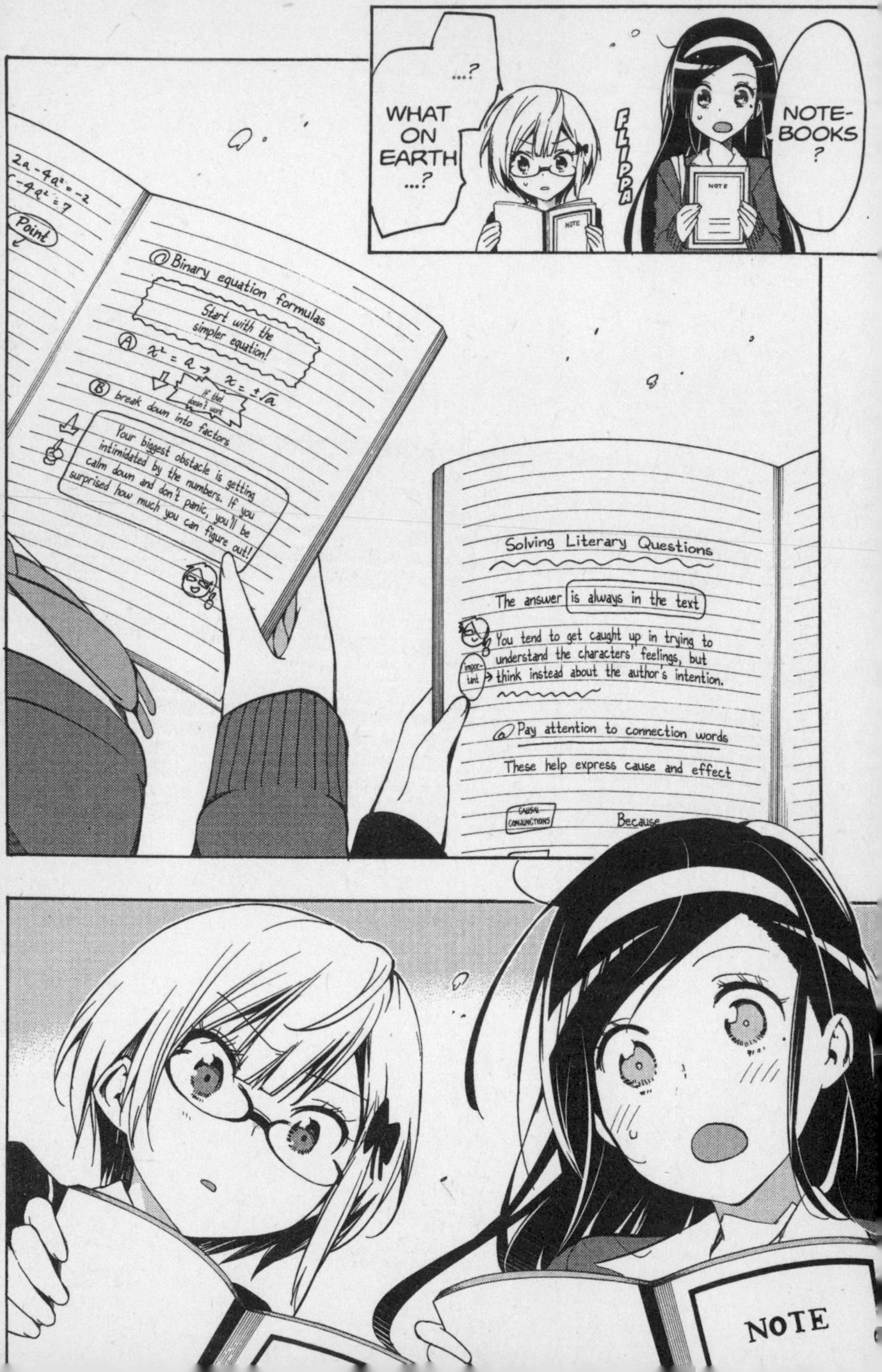
NOTE-BOOKS?
NOTE
FLIPPA
...?
WHAT ON EARTH...?
NOTE
Solving Literary Questions
The answer is always in the text
You tend to get caught up in trying to understand the characters' feelings, but think instead about the author's intention.
impor-tant
Pay attention to connection words
These help express cause and effect
CAUSAL CONJUNCTIONS
Because
2a - 4a² = -2
-4a² = 7
Point
Binary equation formulas
Start with the simpler equation!
A x² = a → x = ±√a
If that doesn't work
B break down into factors
Your biggest obstacle is getting intimidated by the numbers. If you calm down and don't panic, you'll be surprised how much you can figure out!
NOTE

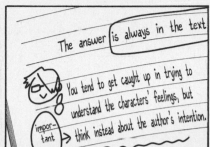

B
If that doesn't work
break down into factors
Your biggest obstacle is getting intimidated by the numbers. If you calm down and don't panic, you'll be surprised how much you
The answer is always in the text
You tend to get caught up in trying to understand the characters' feelings, but think instead about the author's intention.
impor-tant
WHA...
D-D-D-DID YOU WRITE ALL THIS FOR US?
OMG
YOU CREATED ...
...STUDY NOTES FOR US?
I LOOKED THROUGH YOUR BOOKS LAST NIGHT...
...AND GOT A BETTER IDEA OF YOUR STUMBLING BLOCKS.
SO...
YOU SPENT ALL NIGHT DOING THIS?
BUT... WHY ?!
I REMEMBERED THAT WHEN YOU DON'T UNDERSTAND SOMETHING...
...IF YOU JUST KEEP THROWING YOURSELF AT IT AND FAILING...
...YOU FEEL EVEN WORSE.

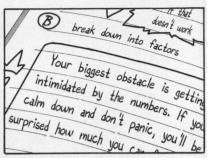

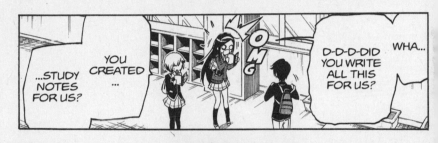

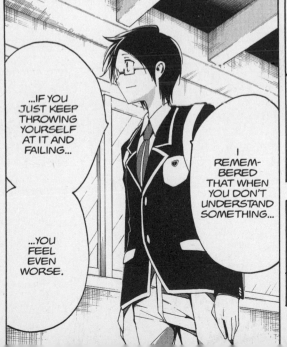

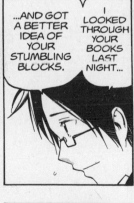

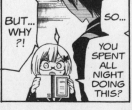

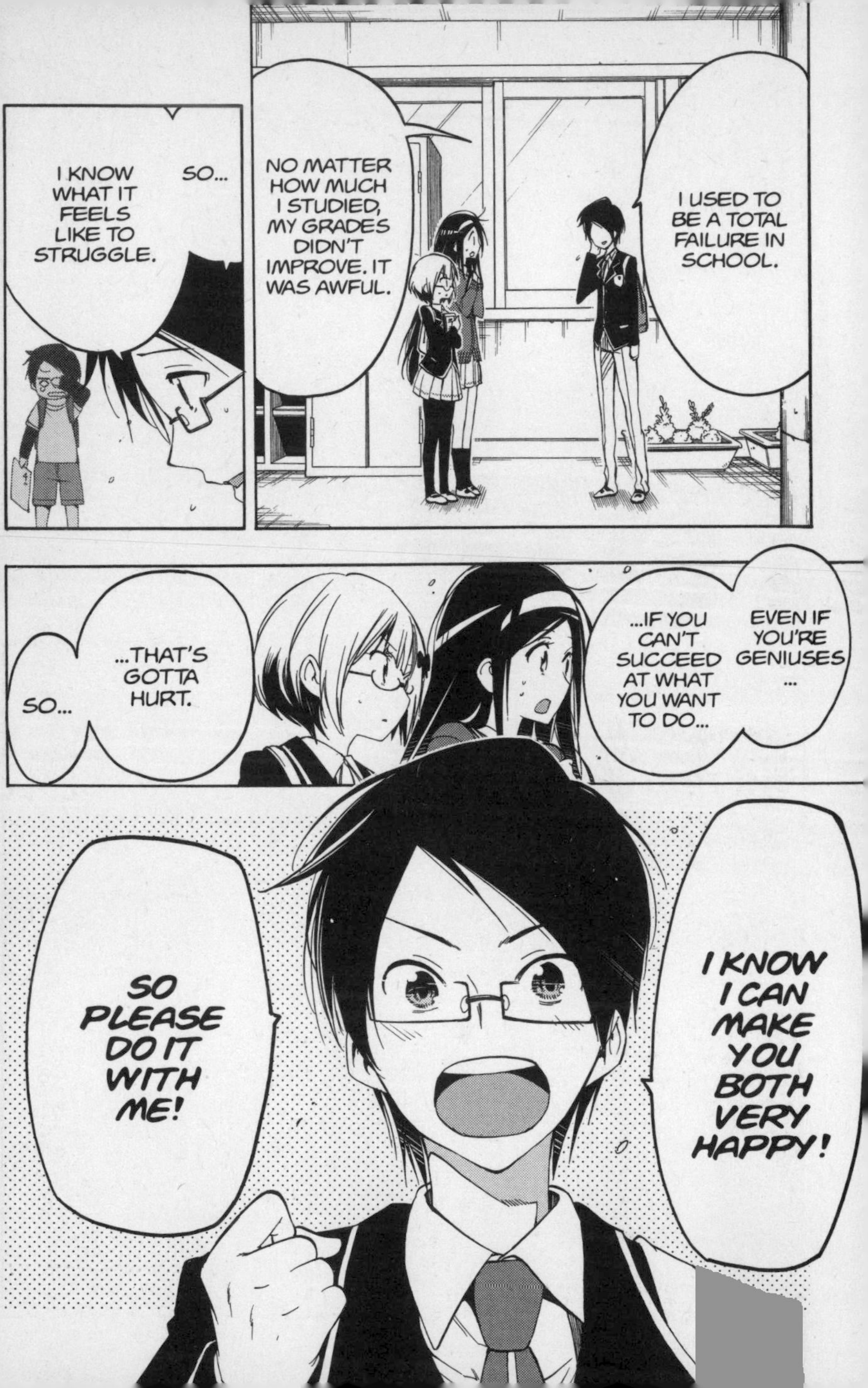
I USED TO BE A TOTAL FAILURE IN SCHOOL.
NO MATTER HOW MUCH I STUDIED, MY GRADES DIDN'T IMPROVE. IT WAS AWFUL.
SO...
I KNOW WHAT IT FEELS LIKE TO STRUGGLE.
EVEN IF YOU'RE GENIUSES...
...IF YOU CAN'T SUCCEED AT WHAT YOU WANT TO DO...
...THAT'S GOTTA HURT.
SO...
I KNOW I CAN MAKE YOU BOTH VERY HAPPY!
SO PLEASE DO IT WITH ME!

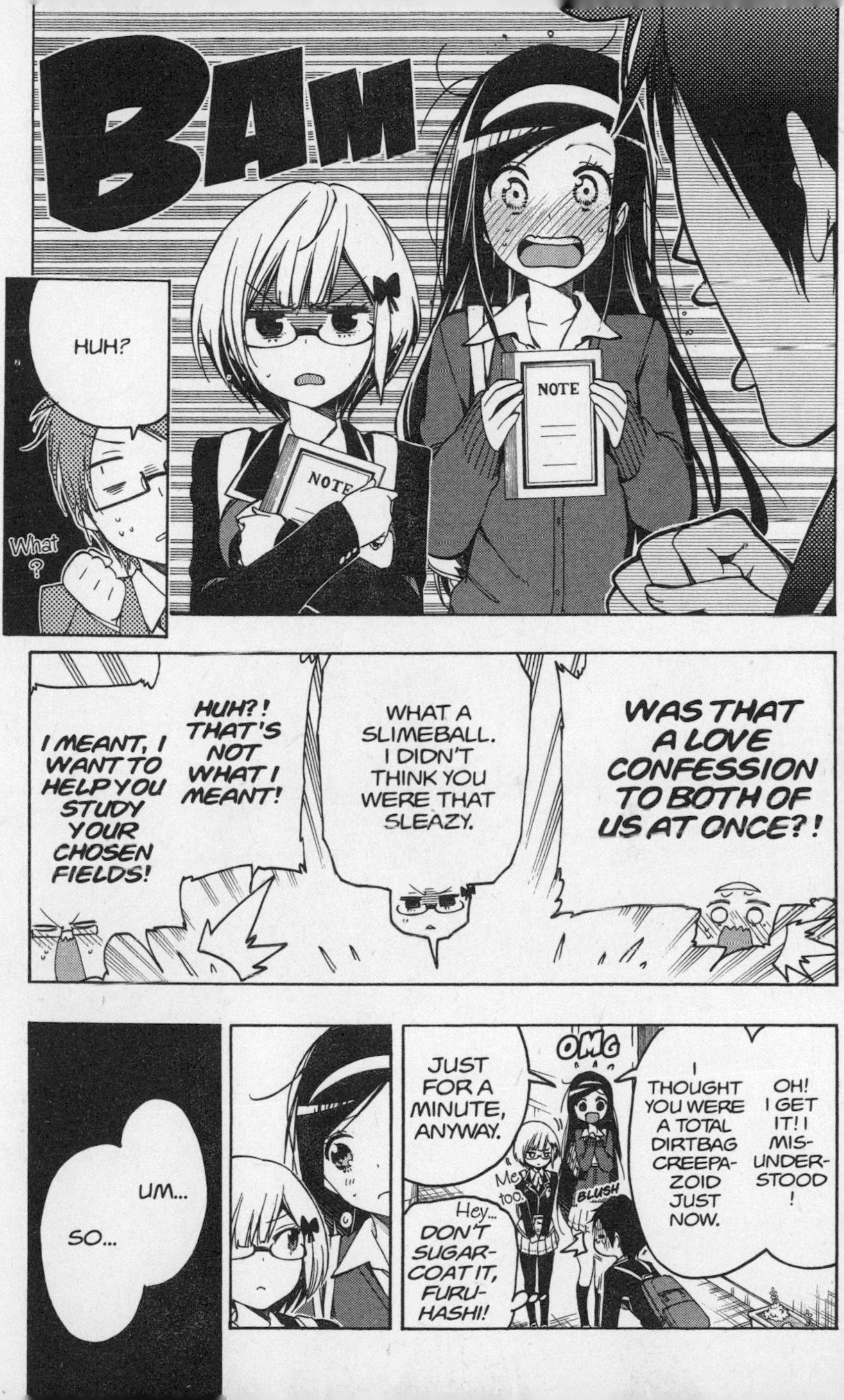
BAM
HUH?
What ?
WAS THAT A LOVE CONFESSION TO BOTH OF US AT ONCE?!
WHAT A SLIMEBALL. I DIDN'T THINK YOU WERE THAT SLEAZY.
HUH?! THAT'S NOT WHAT I MEANT!
I MEANT, I WANT TO HELP YOU STUDY YOUR CHOSEN FIELDS!
OH! I GET IT! I MIS-UNDER-STOOD!
I THOUGHT YOU WERE A TOTAL DIRTBAG CREEPA-ZOID JUST NOW.
OMG
JUST FOR A MINUTE, ANYWAY.
Me too.
BLUSH
Hey... DON'T SUGAR-COAT IT, FURU-HASHI!
UM...
SO...

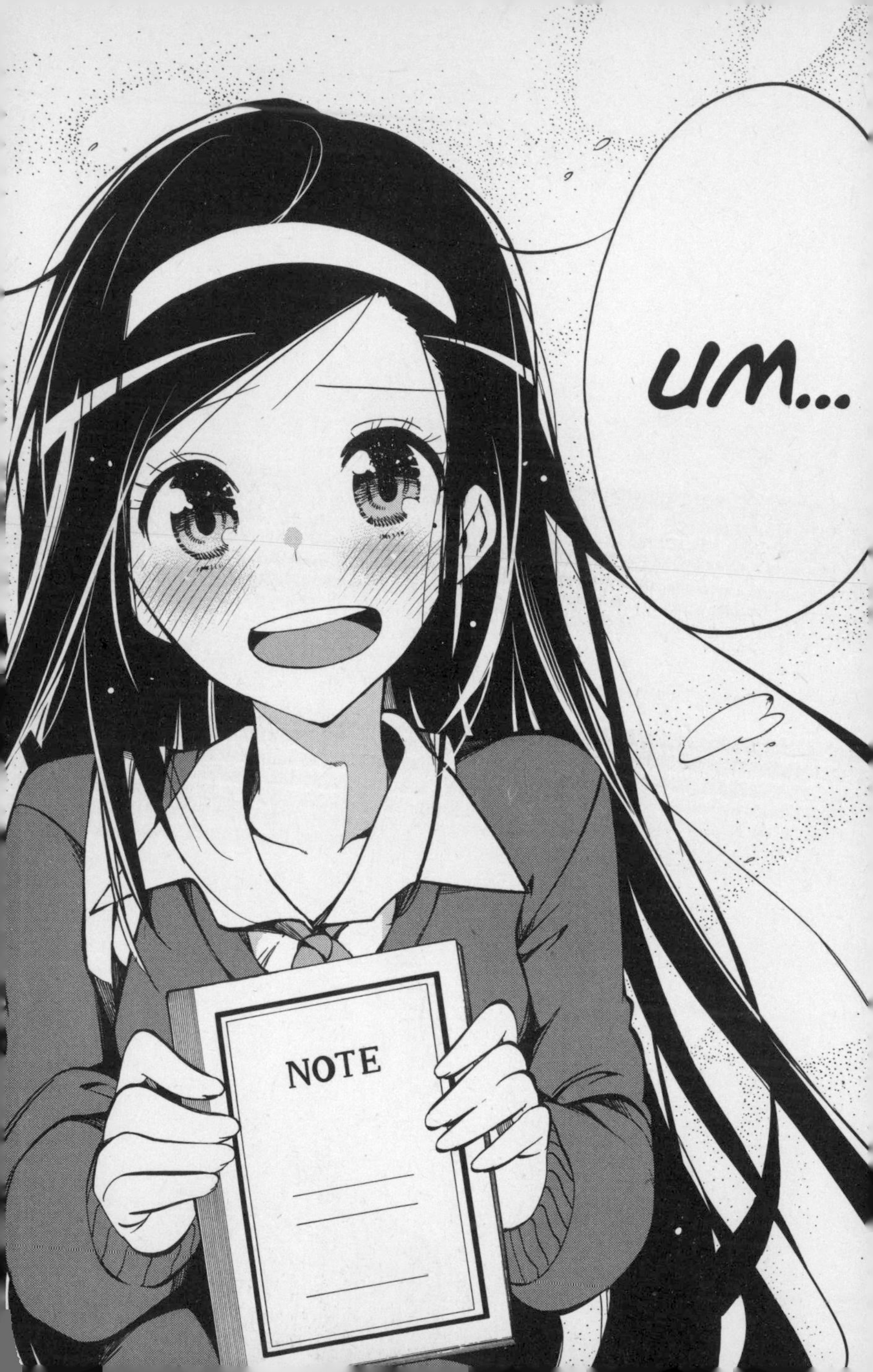
UM...
NOTE

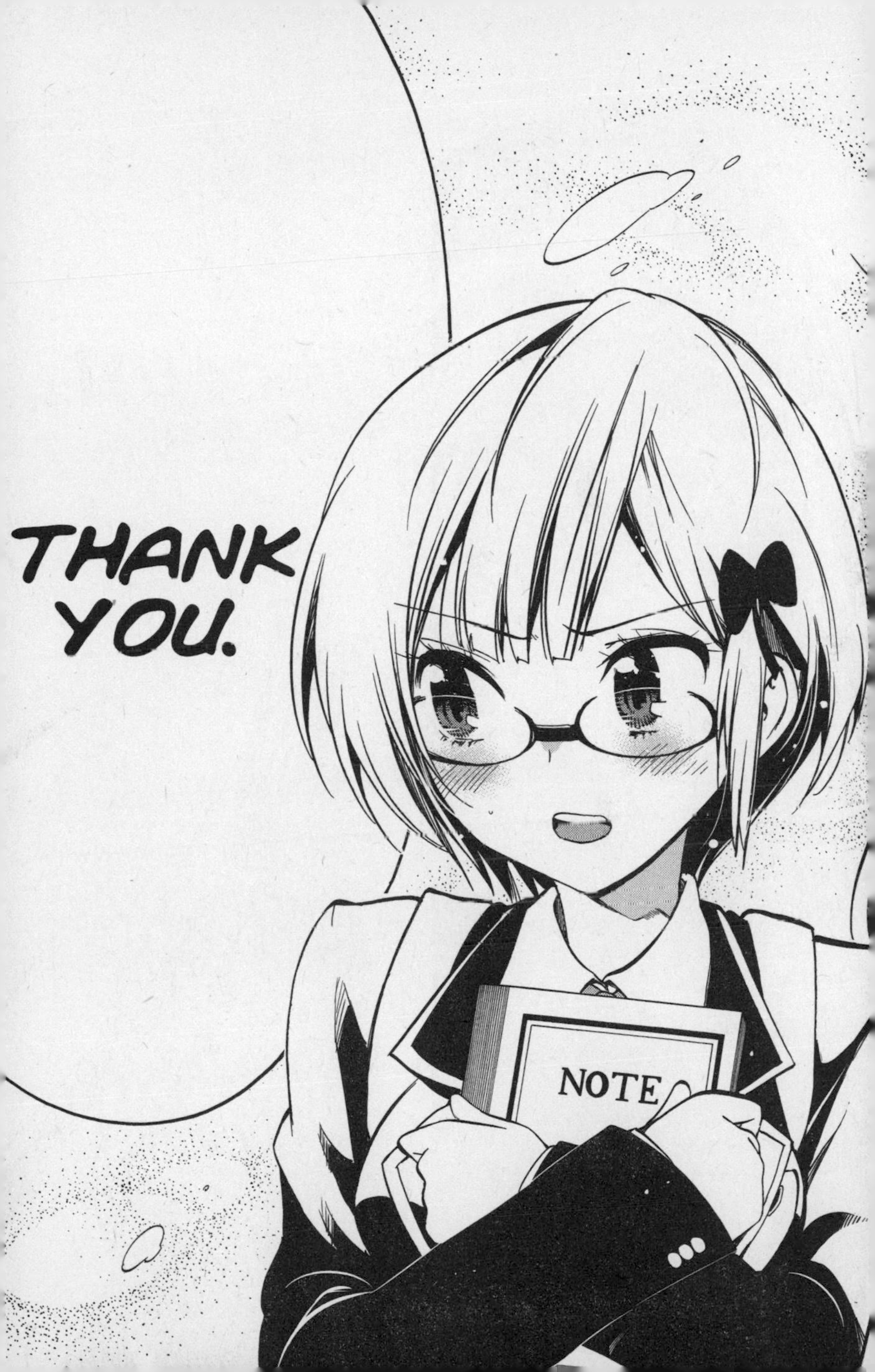
THANK YOU.
NOTE

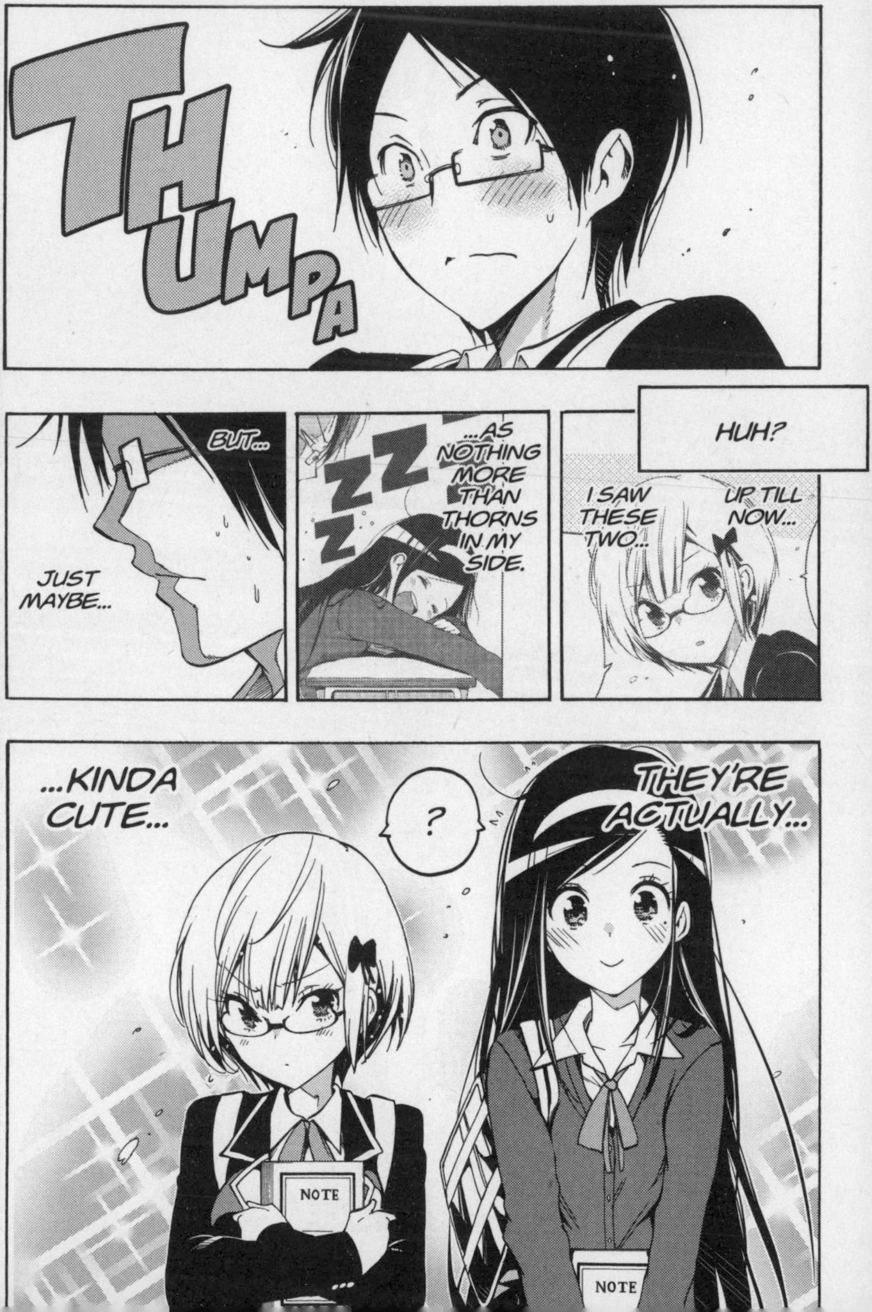
THUMPA
HUH?
UP TILL NOW...
I SAW THESE TWO...
...AS NOTHING MORE THAN THORNS IN MY SIDE.
ZZZ
BUT...
JUST MAYBE...
THEY'RE ACTUALLY...
?
...KINDA CUTE...
NOTE
NOTE

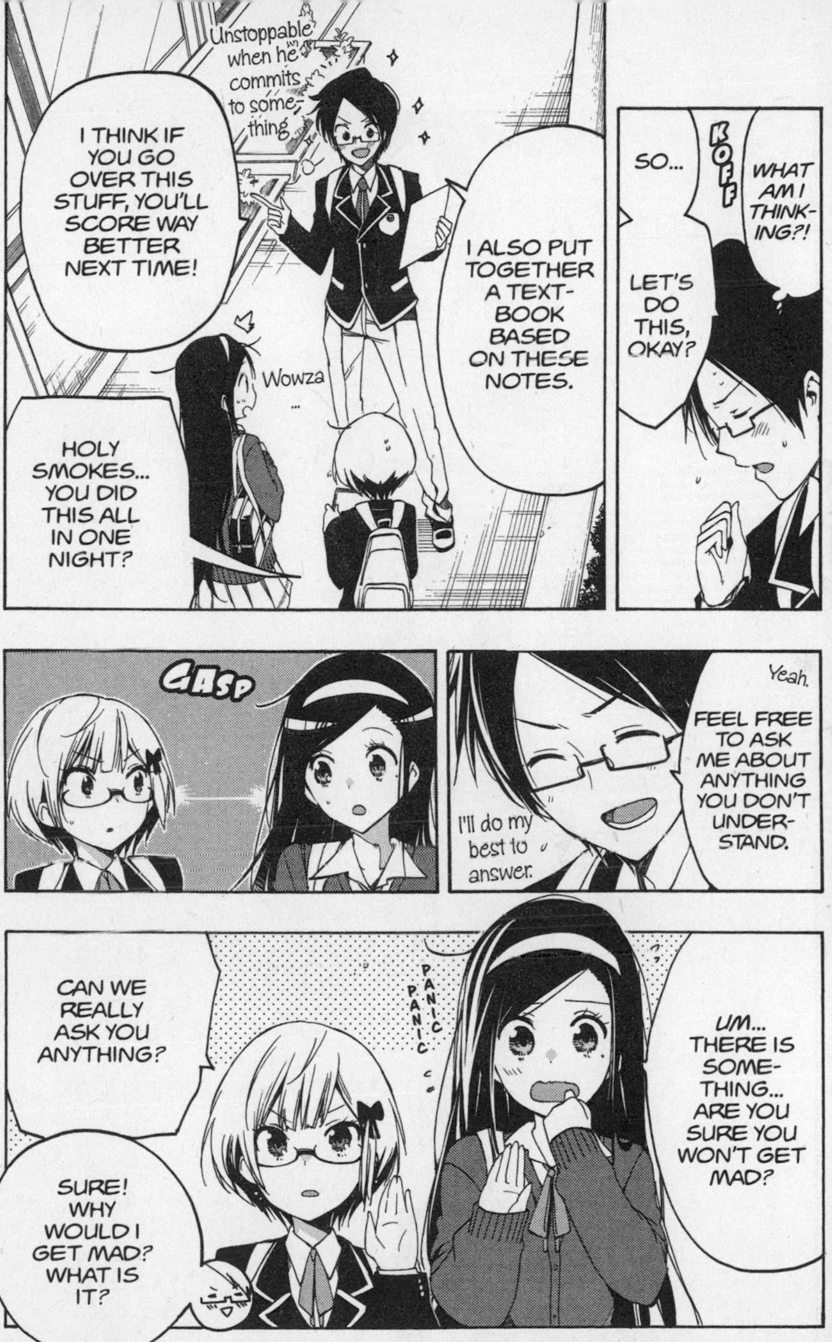
WHAT AM I THINKING?!
KOFF
SO...
LET'S DO THIS, OKAY?
I ALSO PUT TOGETHER A TEXTBOOK BASED ON THESE NOTES.
Unstoppable when he commits to something
I THINK IF YOU GO OVER THIS STUFF, YOU'LL SCORE WAY BETTER NEXT TIME!
Wowza...
HOLY SMOKES... YOU DID THIS ALL IN ONE NIGHT?
Yeah.
FEEL FREE TO ASK ME ABOUT ANYTHING YOU DON'T UNDERSTAND.
I'll do my best to answer.
GASP
UM... THERE IS SOMETHING... ARE YOU SURE YOU WON'T GET MAD?
PANIC PANIC
CAN WE REALLY ASK YOU ANYTHING?
SURE! WHY WOULD I GET MAD? WHAT IS IT?

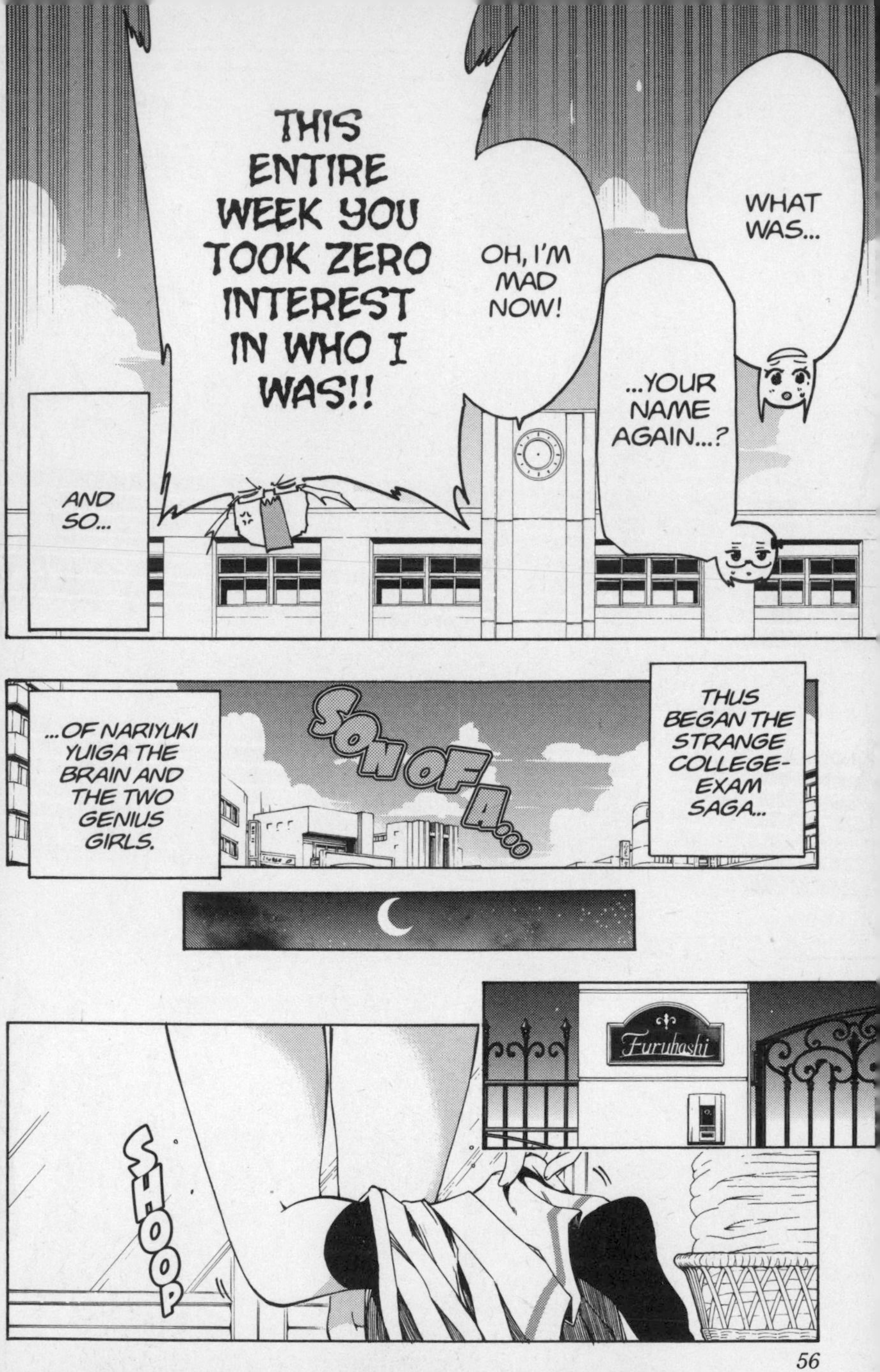
WHAT WAS...
...YOUR NAME AGAIN...?
OH, I'M MAD NOW!
THIS ENTIRE WEEK YOU TOOK ZERO INTEREST IN WHO I WAS!!
AND SO...
THUS BEGAN THE STRANGE COLLEGE-EXAM SAGA...
SON OF A...
...OF NARIYUKI YUIGA THE BRAIN AND THE TWO GENIUS GIRLS.
Furuhashi
SHOOP

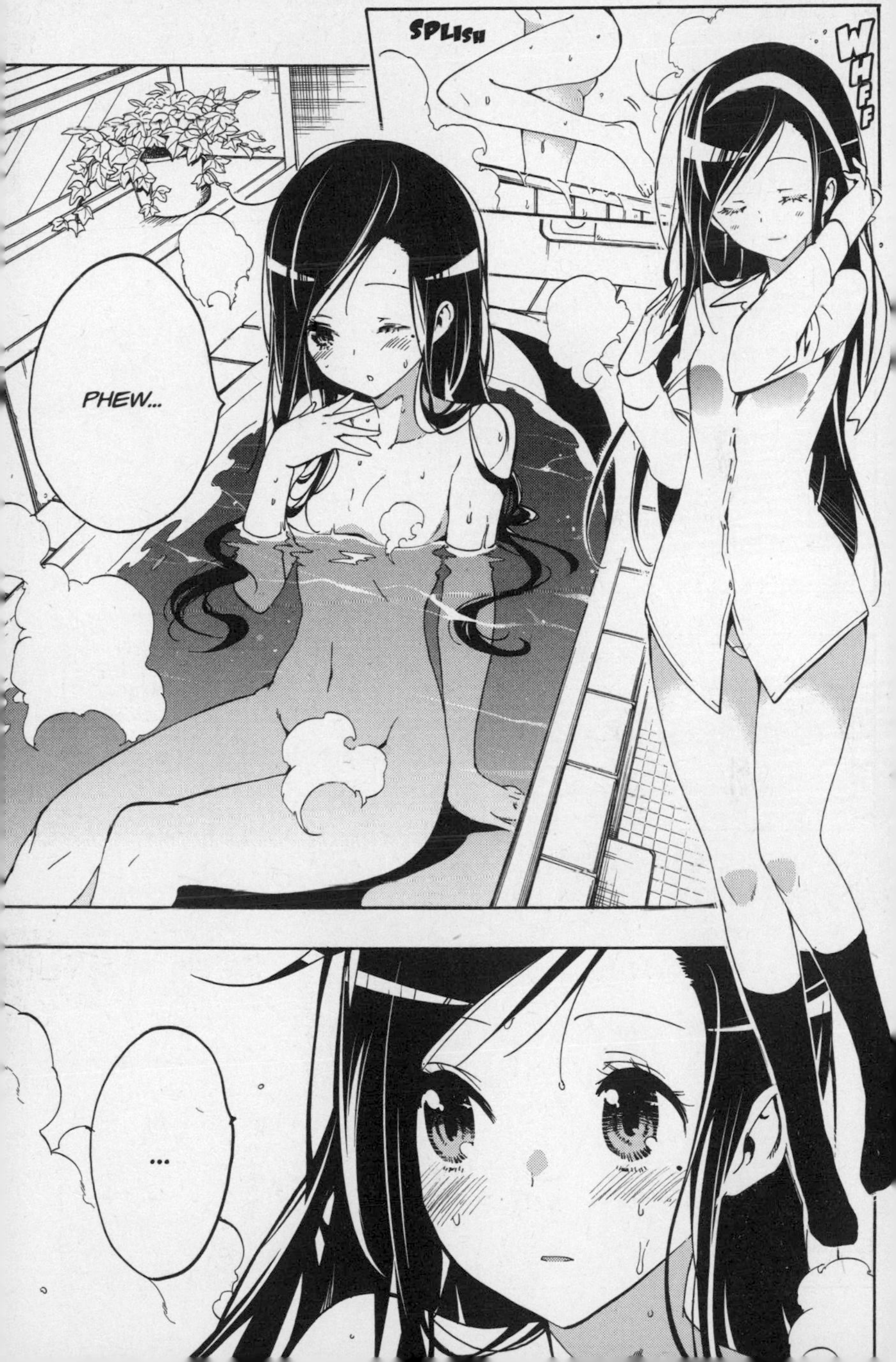
WHFF
SPLISH
PHEW...
...

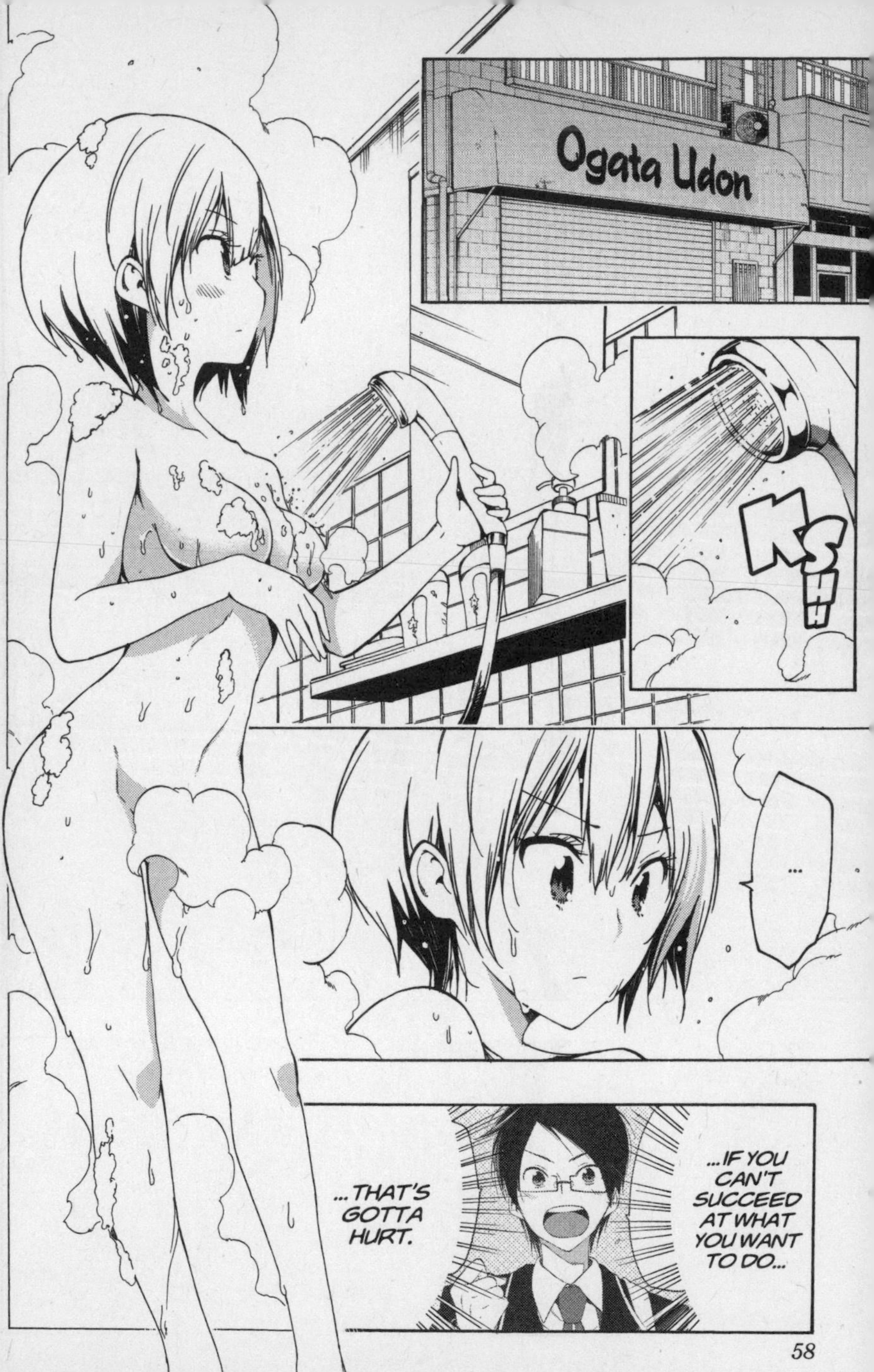
Ogata Udon
KSHH
...
...IF YOU CAN'T SUCCEED AT WHAT YOU WANT TO DO...
...THAT'S GOTTA HURT.

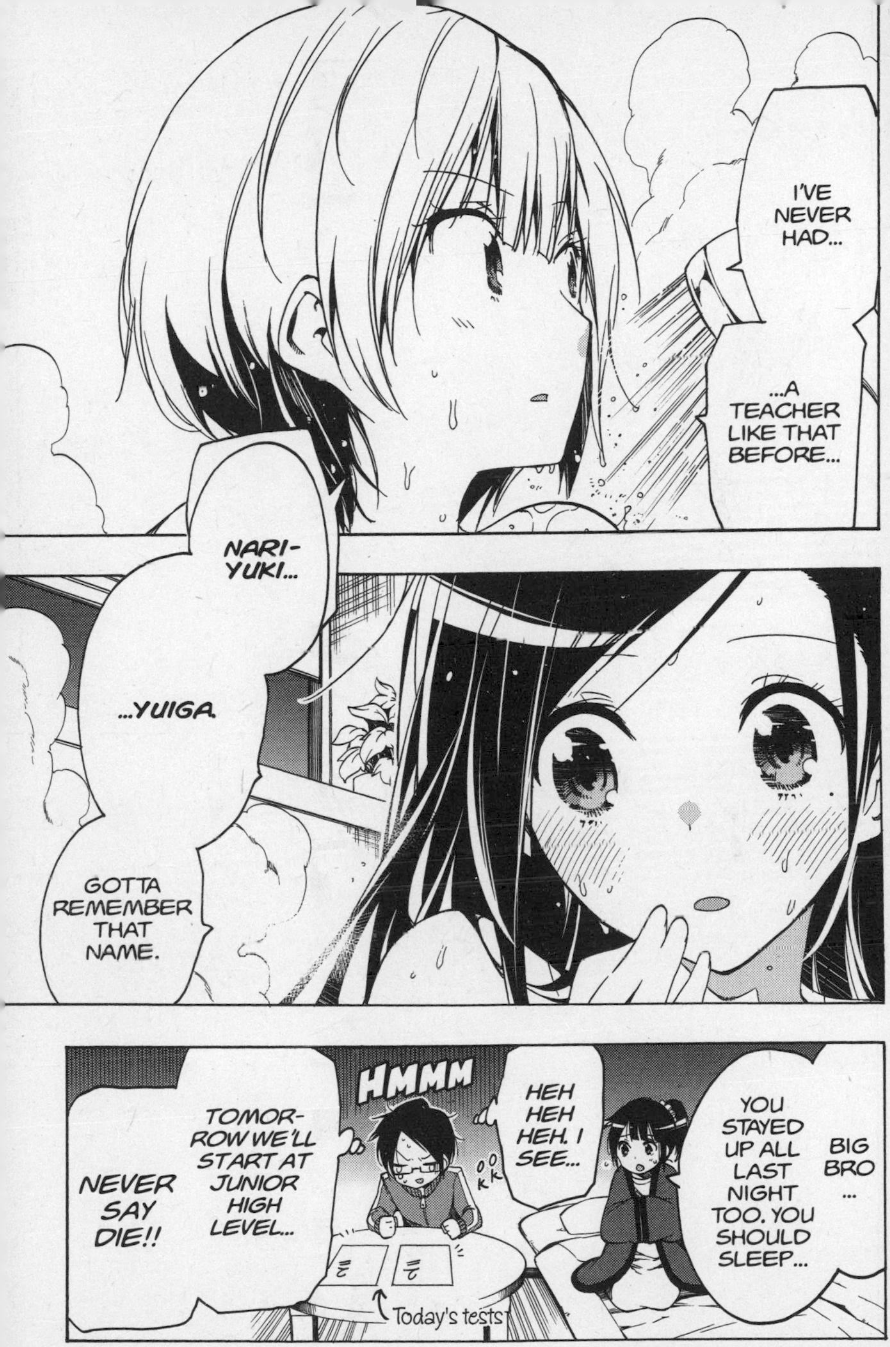
I'VE NEVER HAD...
...A TEACHER LIKE THAT BEFORE...
NARI-YUKI...
...YUIGA.
GOTTA REMEMBER THAT NAME.
BIG BRO ...
YOU STAYED UP ALL LAST NIGHT TOO. YOU SHOULD SLEEP...
HEH HEH HEH. I SEE...
KOK
HMMM
TOMORROW WE'LL START AT JUNIOR HIGH LEVEL...
NEVER SAY DIE!!
Today's tests

We're in the same classes for STEM and language arts, but we're in different sections.

3-B

3-F

3-A

A...

F...

That doesn't matter... right?

NO.
DATE

Question 2: A Genius's Yearning = [*X*]

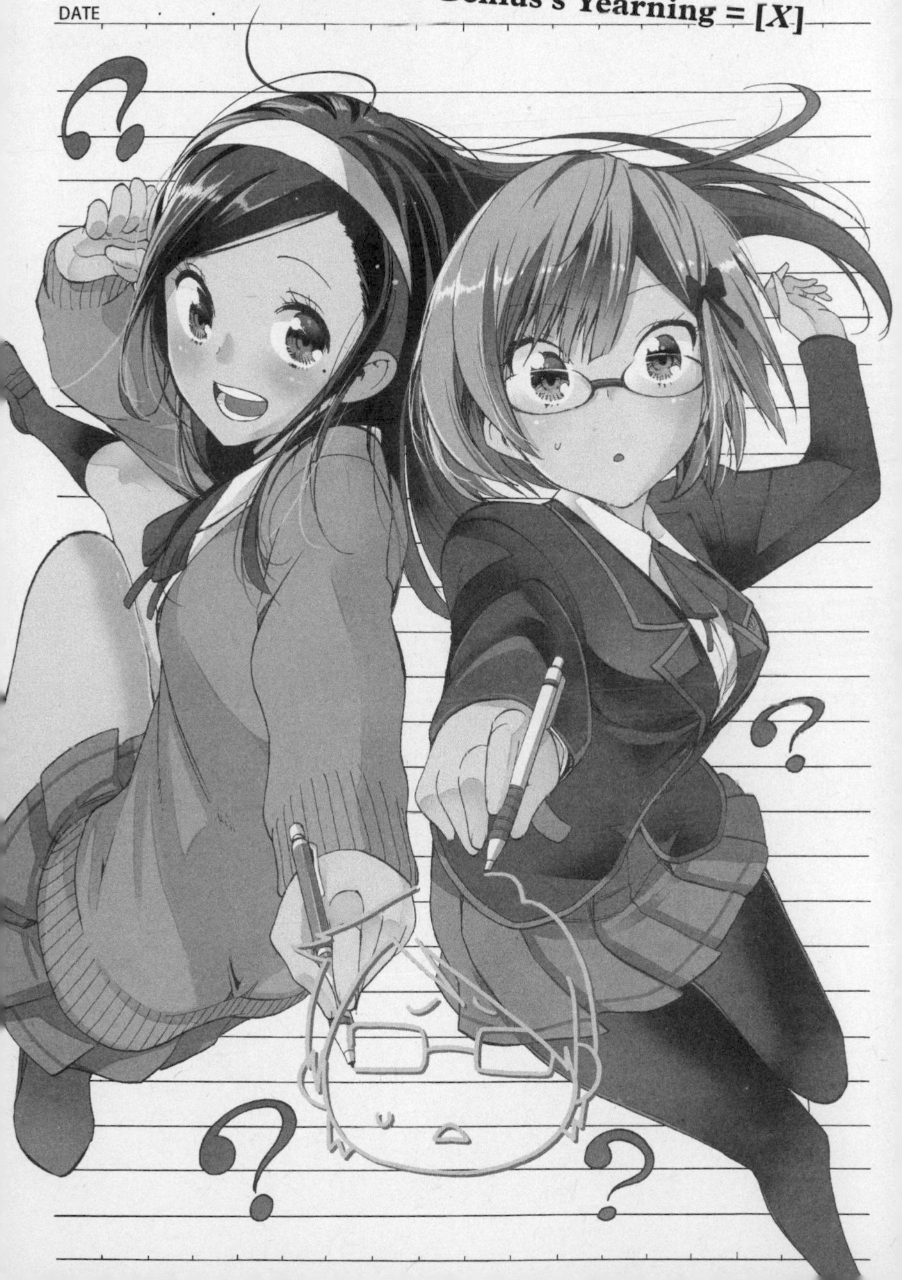

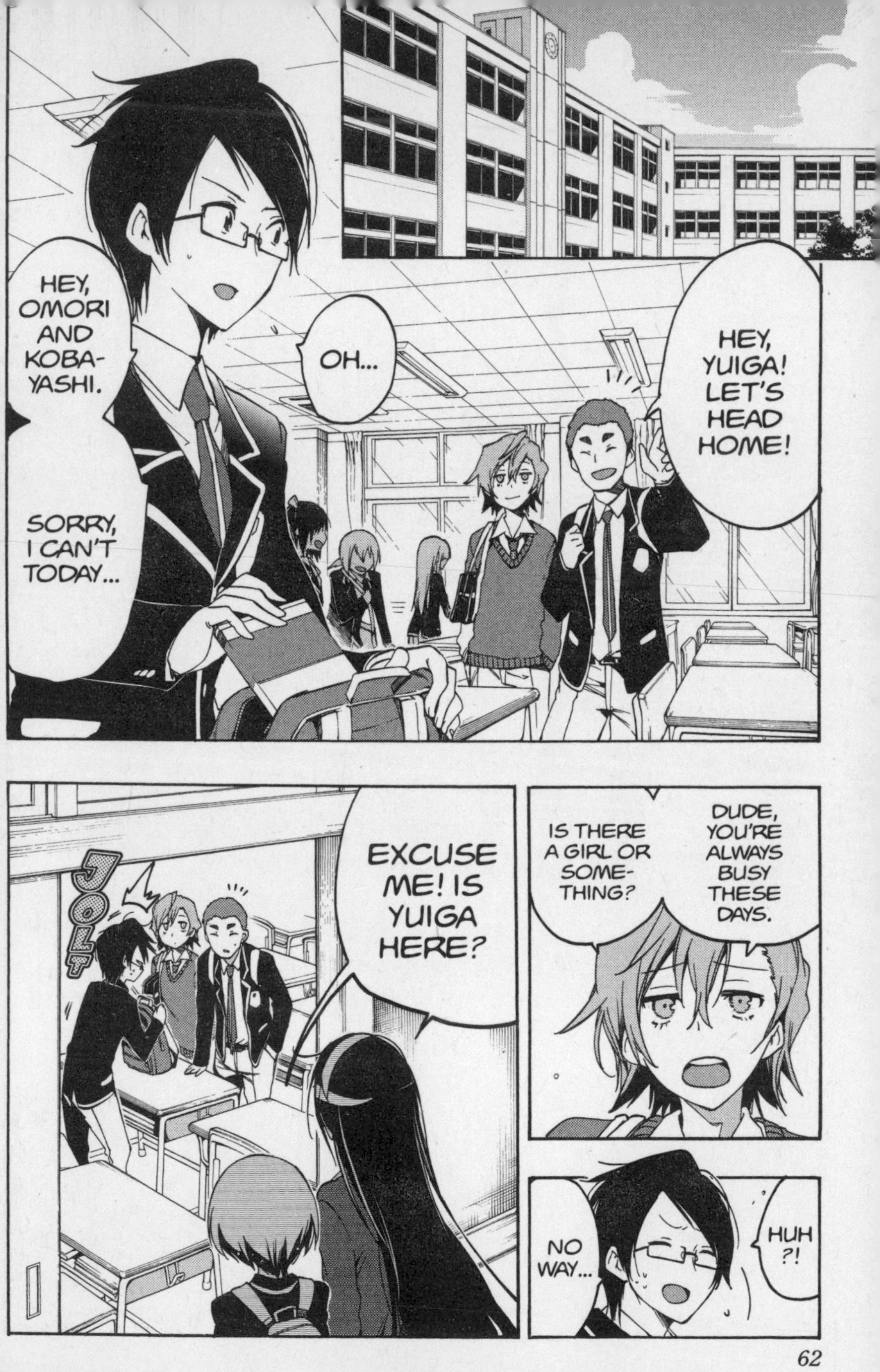
HEY, YUIGA! LET'S HEAD HOME!
OH...
HEY, OMORI AND KOBA-YASHI.
SORRY, I CAN'T TODAY...
DUDE, YOU'RE ALWAYS BUSY THESE DAYS.
IS THERE A GIRL OR SOME-THING?
HUH?!
NO WAY...
EXCUSE ME! IS YUIGA HERE?
JOLT

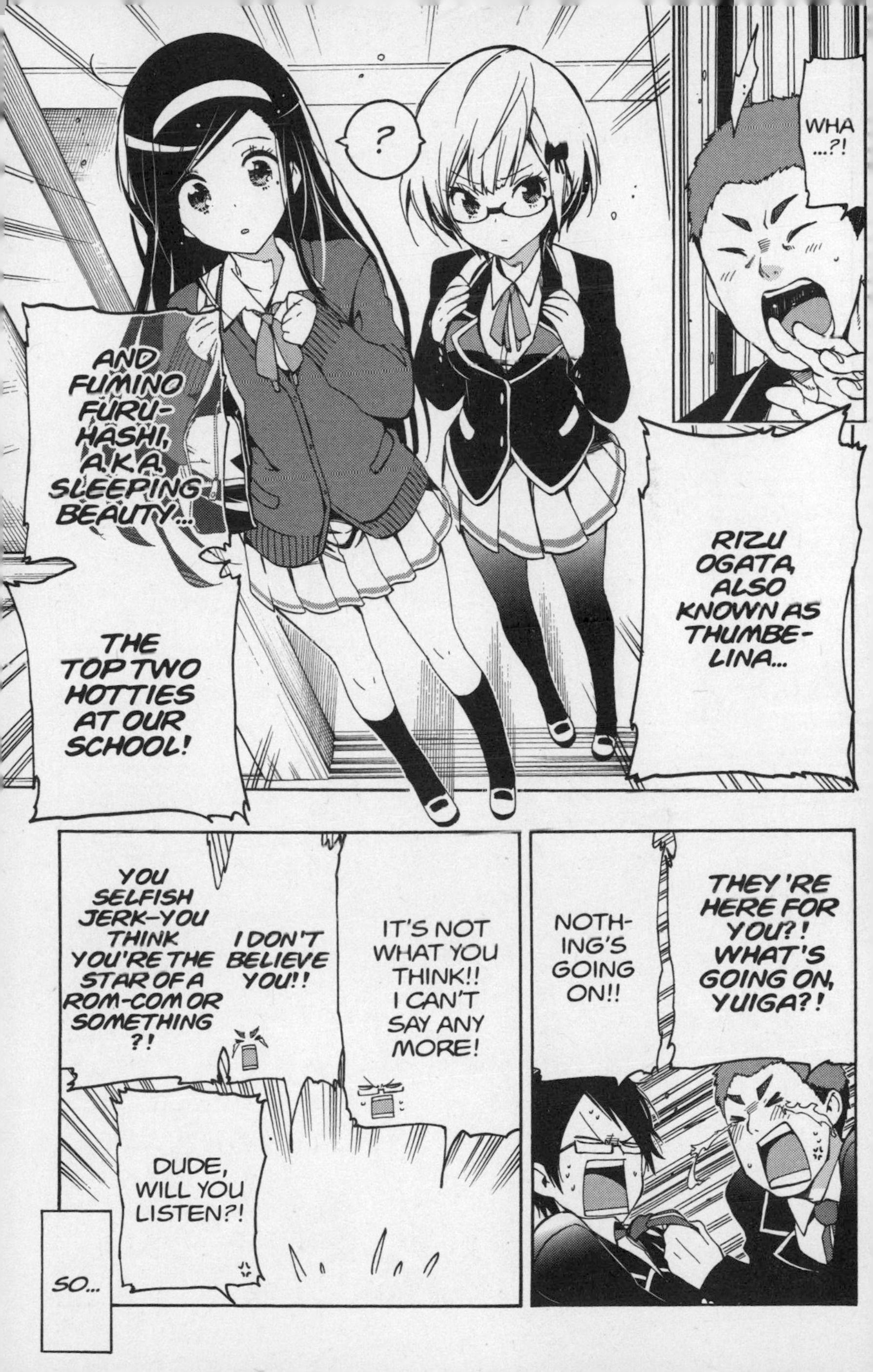

WHA ...?!
RIZU OGATA, ALSO KNOWN AS THUMBE-LINA...
?
AND FUMINO FURU-HASHI, A.K.A. SLEEPING BEAUTY...
THE TOP TWO HOTTIES AT OUR SCHOOL!
THEY'RE HERE FOR YOU?! WHAT'S GOING ON, YUIGA?!
NOTH-ING'S GOING ON!!
IT'S NOT WHAT YOU THINK!! I CAN'T SAY ANY MORE!
I DON'T BELIEVE YOU!!
YOU SELFISH JERK—YOU THINK YOU'RE THE STAR OF A ROM-COM OR SOMETHING?!
DUDE, WILL YOU LISTEN?!
SO...

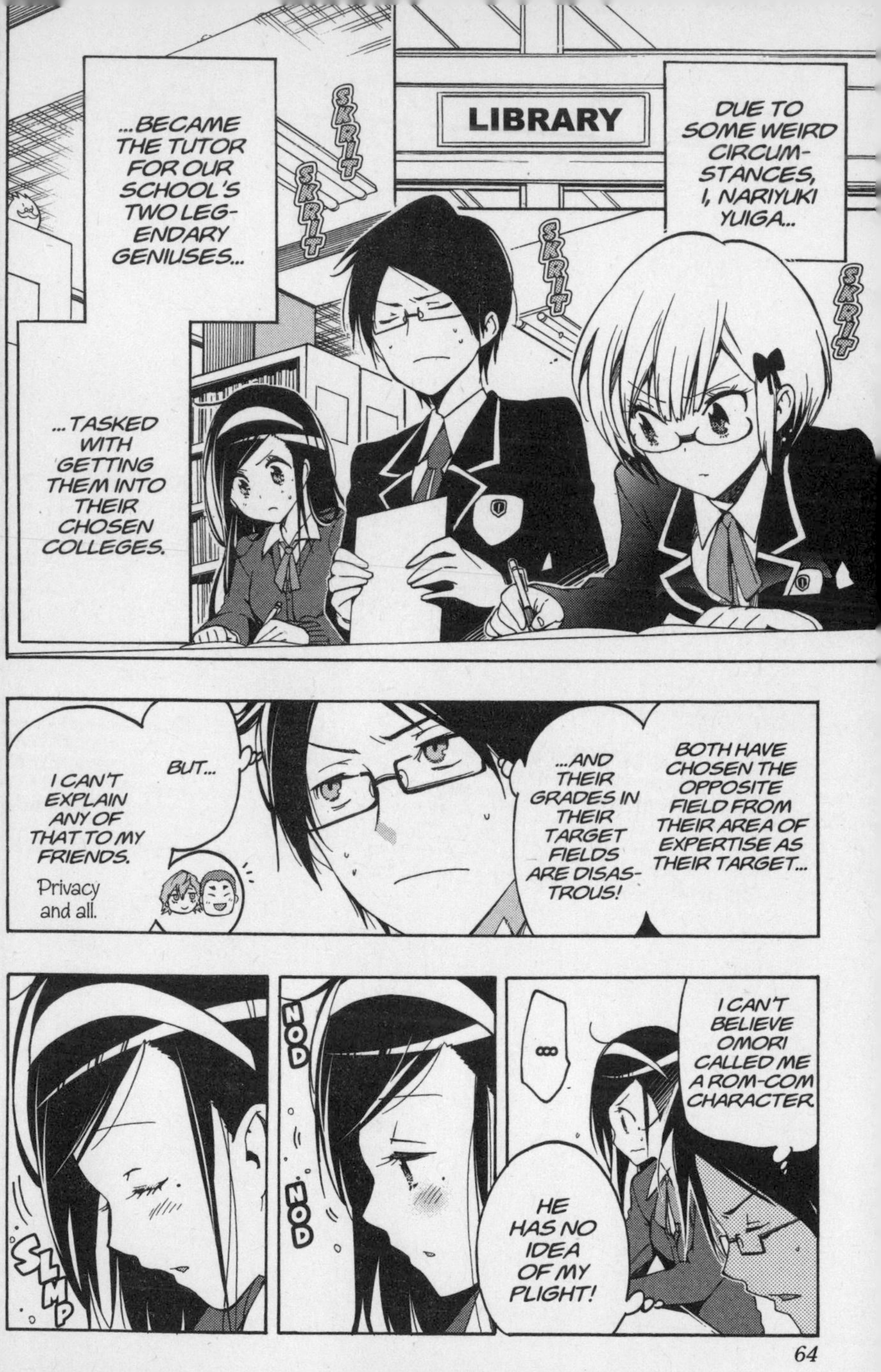
LIBRARY
DUE TO SOME WEIRD CIRCUMSTANCES, I, NARIYUKI YUIGA...
SKRIT
SKRIT
...BECAME THE TUTOR FOR OUR SCHOOL'S TWO LEGENDARY GENIUSES...
SKRIT
SKRIT
...TASKED WITH GETTING THEM INTO THEIR CHOSEN COLLEGES.
BOTH HAVE CHOSEN THE OPPOSITE FIELD FROM THEIR AREA OF EXPERTISE AS THEIR TARGET...
...AND THEIR GRADES IN THEIR TARGET FIELDS ARE DISASTROUS!
BUT...
I CAN'T EXPLAIN ANY OF THAT TO MY FRIENDS.
Privacy and all.
I CAN'T BELIEVE OMORI CALLED ME A ROM-COM CHARACTER.
...
HE HAS NO IDEA OF MY PLIGHT!
NOD
NOD
SLMP

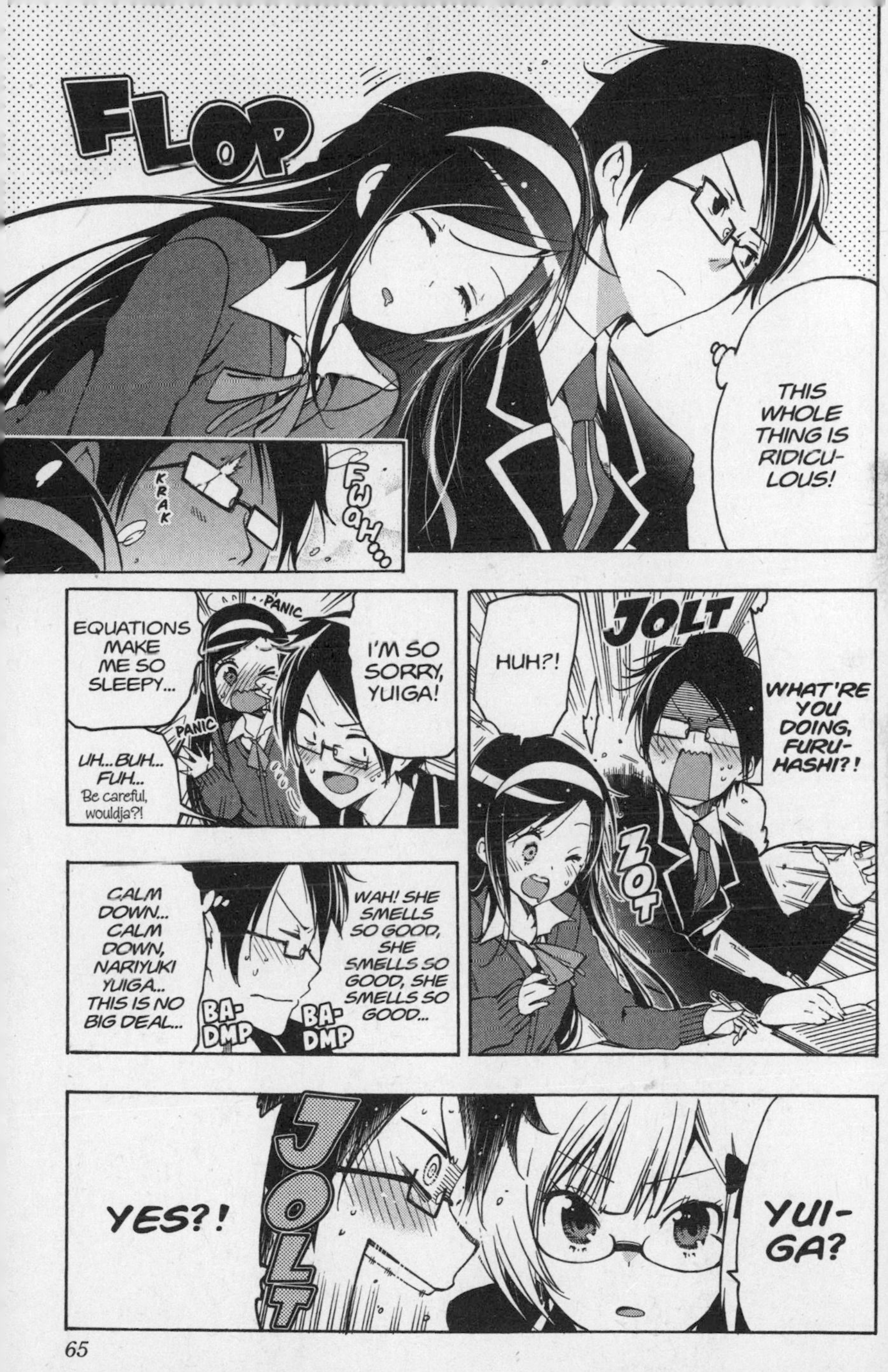
FLOP
THIS WHOLE THING IS RIDICULOUS!
FWOH...
KRAK
JOLT
HUH?!
WHAT'RE YOU DOING, FURU-HASHI?!
ZOT
I'M SO SORRY, YUIGA!
PANIC
EQUATIONS MAKE ME SO SLEEPY...
PANIC
UH...BUH... FUH...
Be careful, wouldja?!
WAH! SHE SMELLS SO GOOD, SHE SMELLS SO GOOD, SHE SMELLS SO GOOD...
BA-DMP
CALM DOWN... CALM DOWN, NARIYUKI YUIGA... THIS IS NO BIG DEAL...
BA-DMP
YUI-GA?
JOLT
YES?!

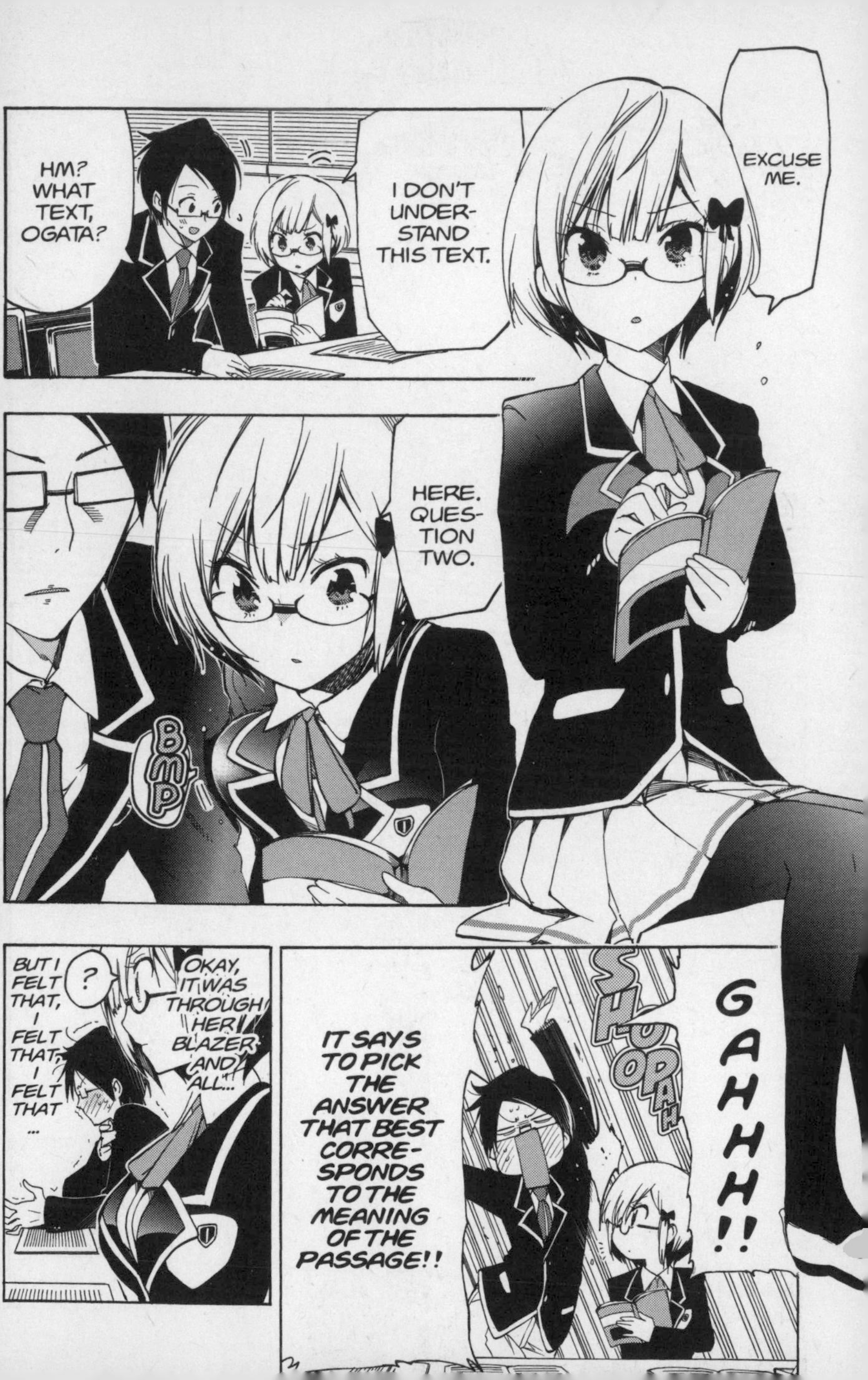
EXCUSE ME.
I DON'T UNDER-STAND THIS TEXT.
HM? WHAT TEXT, OGATA?
HERE. QUESTION TWO.
BMP
GAHHH!!
SHOOPAH
IT SAYS TO PICK THE ANSWER THAT BEST CORRE-SPONDS TO THE MEANING OF THE PASSAGE!!
OKAY, IT WAS THROUGH HER BLAZER AND ALL...
?
BUT I FELT THAT, I FELT THAT, I FELT THAT ...

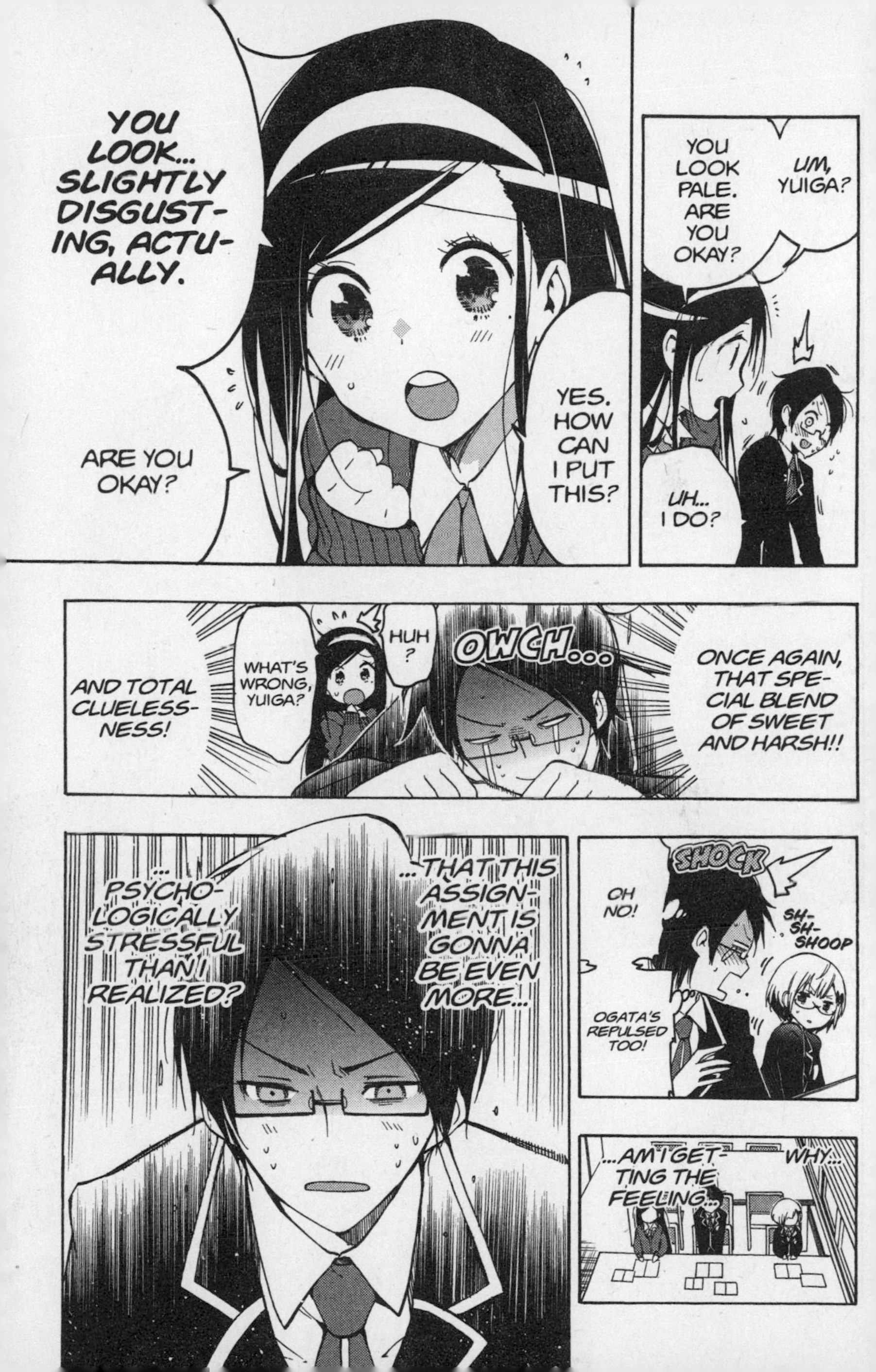
UM, YUIGA?
YOU LOOK PALE. ARE YOU OKAY?
UH... I DO?
YES. HOW CAN I PUT THIS?
YOU LOOK... SLIGHTLY DISGUST-ING, ACTU-ALLY.
ARE YOU OKAY?
ONCE AGAIN, THAT SPE-CIAL BLEND OF SWEET AND HARSH!!
OWCH...
HUH?
WHAT'S WRONG, YUIGA?
AND TOTAL CLUELESS-NESS!
SHOCK
SH-SH-SHOOP
OH NO!
OGATA'S REPULSED TOO!
WHY...
...AM I GET-TING THE FEELING...
...THAT THIS ASSIGN-MENT IS GONNA BE EVEN MORE...
...PSYCHO-LOGICALLY STRESSFUL THAN I REALIZED?

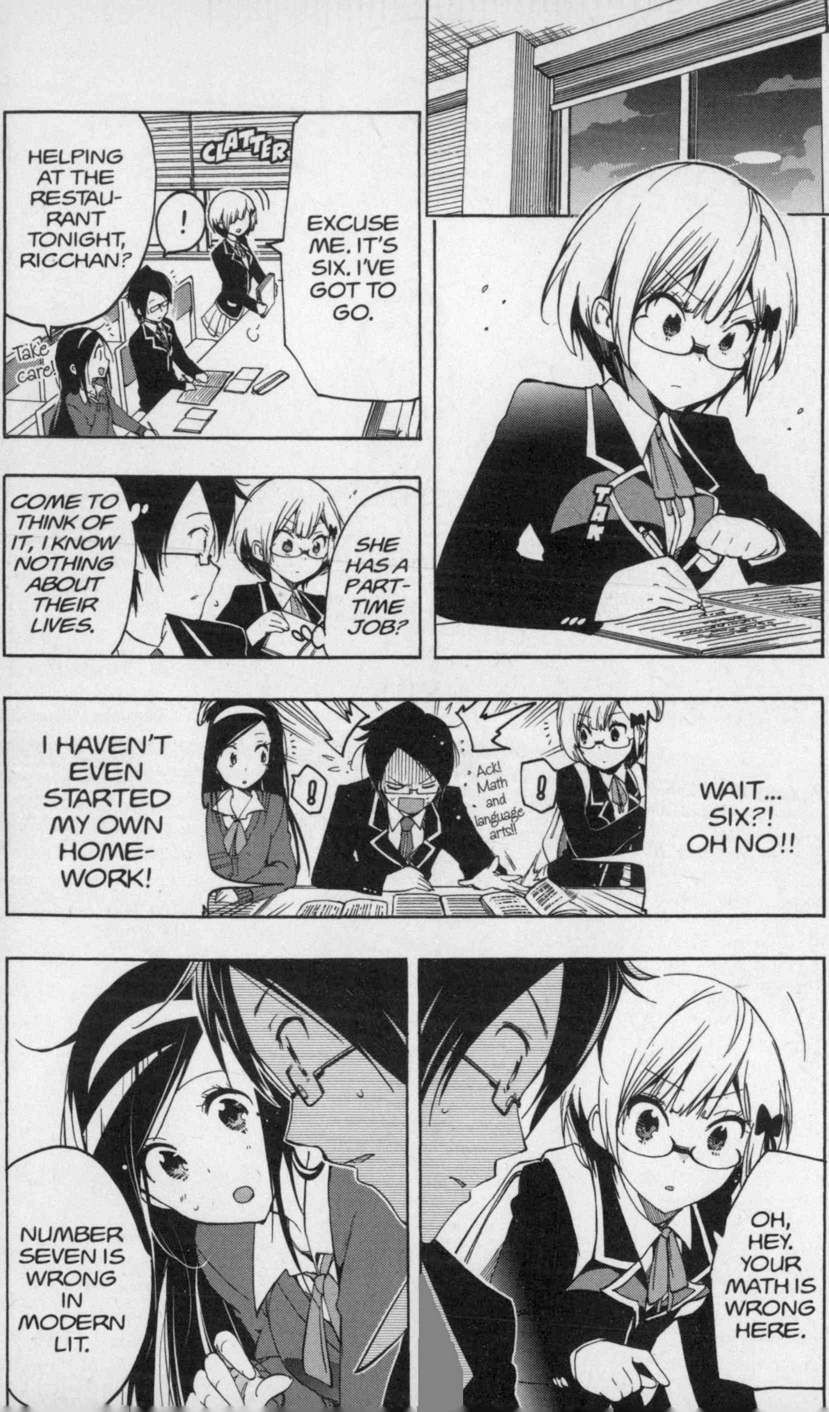
TAK
EXCUSE ME. IT'S SIX. I'VE GOT TO GO.
CLATTER
!
HELPING AT THE RESTAU-RANT TONIGHT, RICCHAN?
Take care!
SHE HAS A PART-TIME JOB?
COME TO THINK OF IT, I KNOW NOTHING ABOUT THEIR LIVES.
WAIT... SIX?! OH NO!!
!
Ack! Math and language arts!!
!
I HAVEN'T EVEN STARTED MY OWN HOME-WORK!
OH, HEY. YOUR MATH IS WRONG HERE.
NUMBER SEVEN IS WRONG IN MODERN LIT.

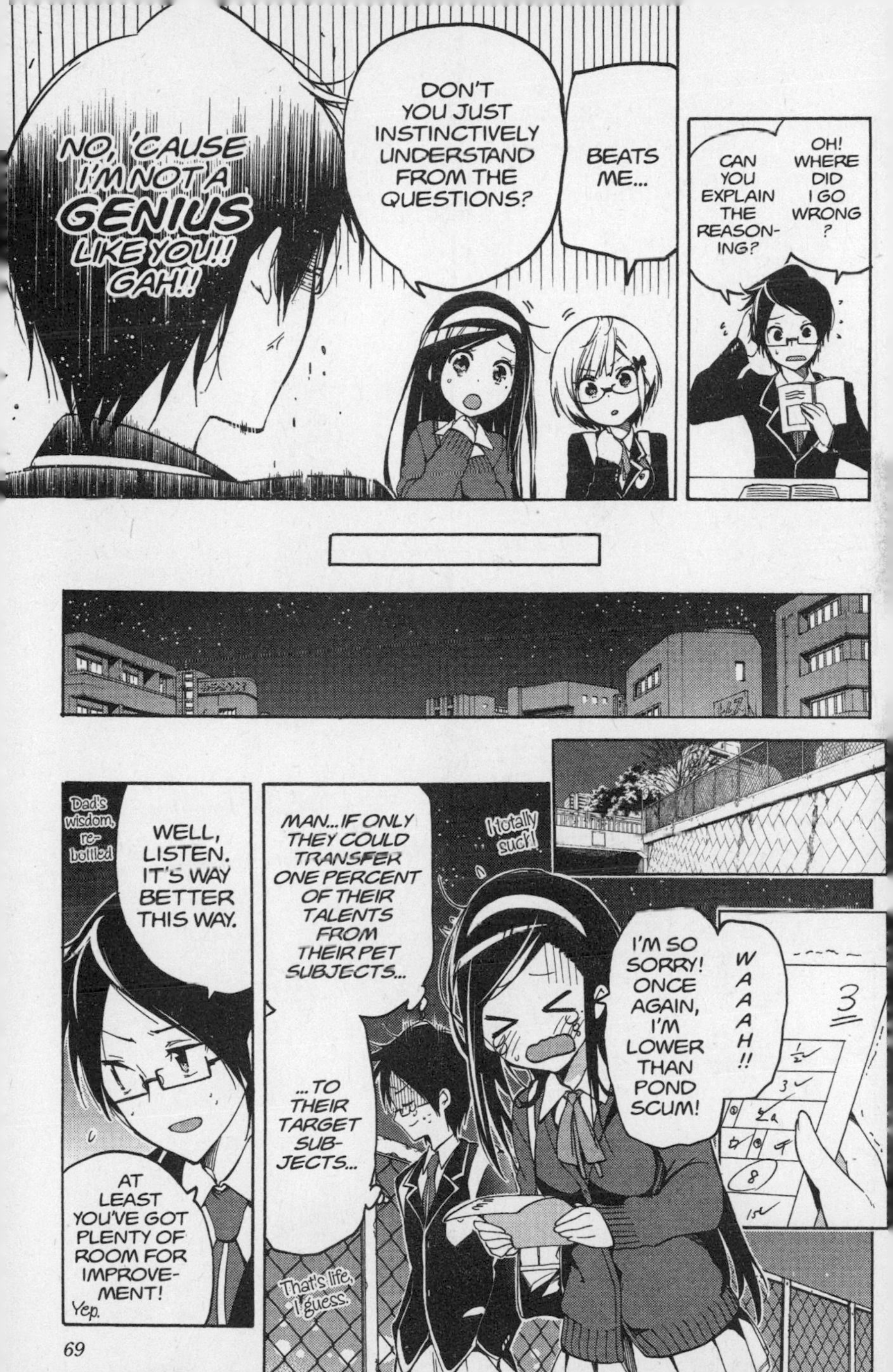
OH! WHERE DID I GO WRONG?
CAN YOU EXPLAIN THE REASONING?
BEATS ME...
DON'T YOU JUST INSTINCTIVELY UNDERSTAND FROM THE QUESTIONS?
NO, 'CAUSE I'M NOT A GENIUS LIKE YOU!! GAH!!
WAAAAH!!
I'M SO SORRY! ONCE AGAIN, I'M LOWER THAN POND SCUM!
I totally suck!
MAN... IF ONLY THEY COULD TRANSFER ONE PERCENT OF THEIR TALENTS FROM THEIR PET SUBJECTS...
...TO THEIR TARGET SUBJECTS...
That's life, I guess.
Dad's wisdom, re-boiled
WELL, LISTEN. IT'S WAY BETTER THIS WAY.
AT LEAST YOU'VE GOT PLENTY OF ROOM FOR IMPROVEMENT!
Yep.

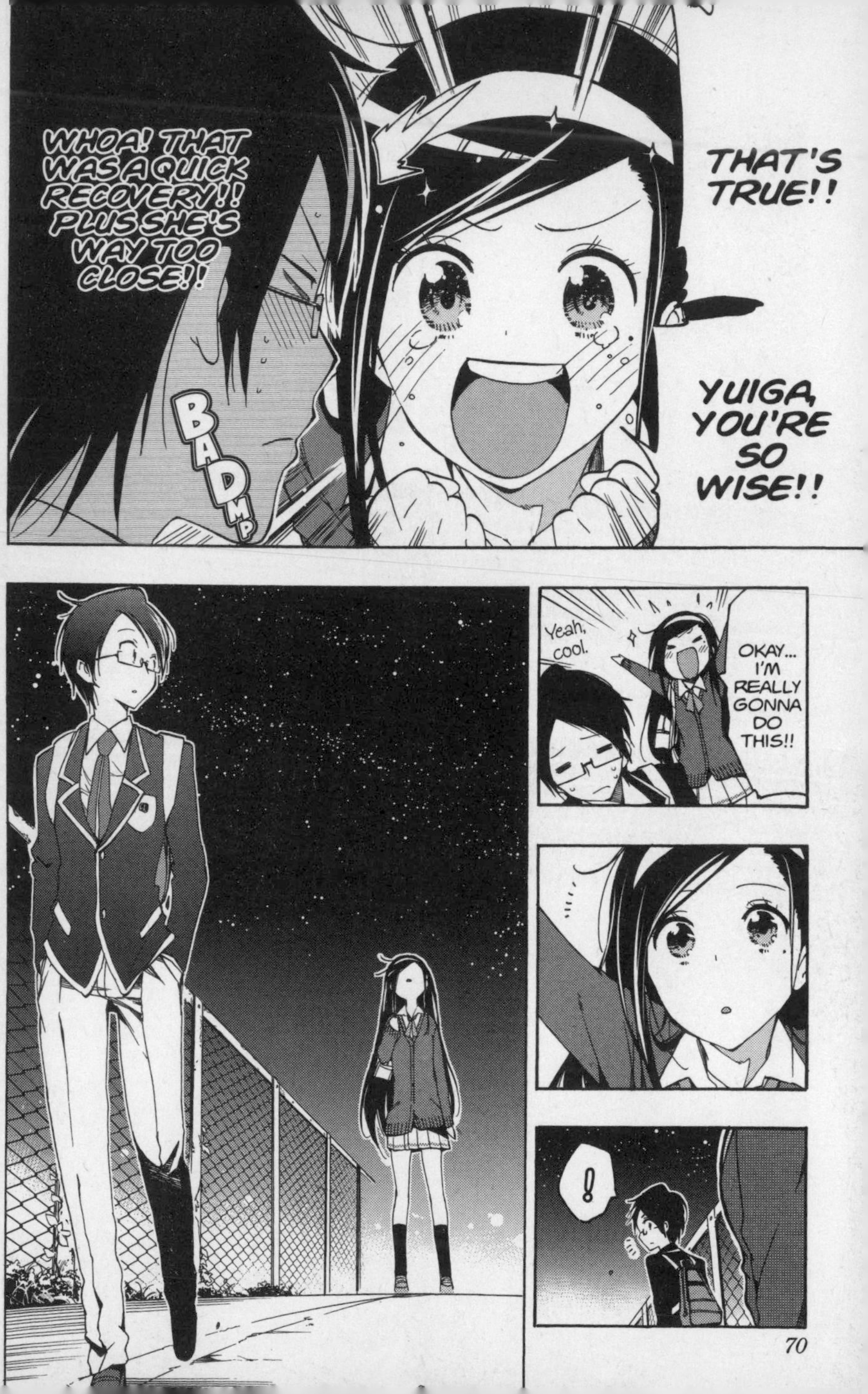
THAT'S TRUE!!
YUIGA, YOU'RE SO WISE!!
WHOA! THAT WAS A QUICK RECOVERY!! PLUS SHE'S WAY TOO CLOSE!!
BADMP
OKAY... I'M REALLY GONNA DO THIS!!
Yeah, cool.
!

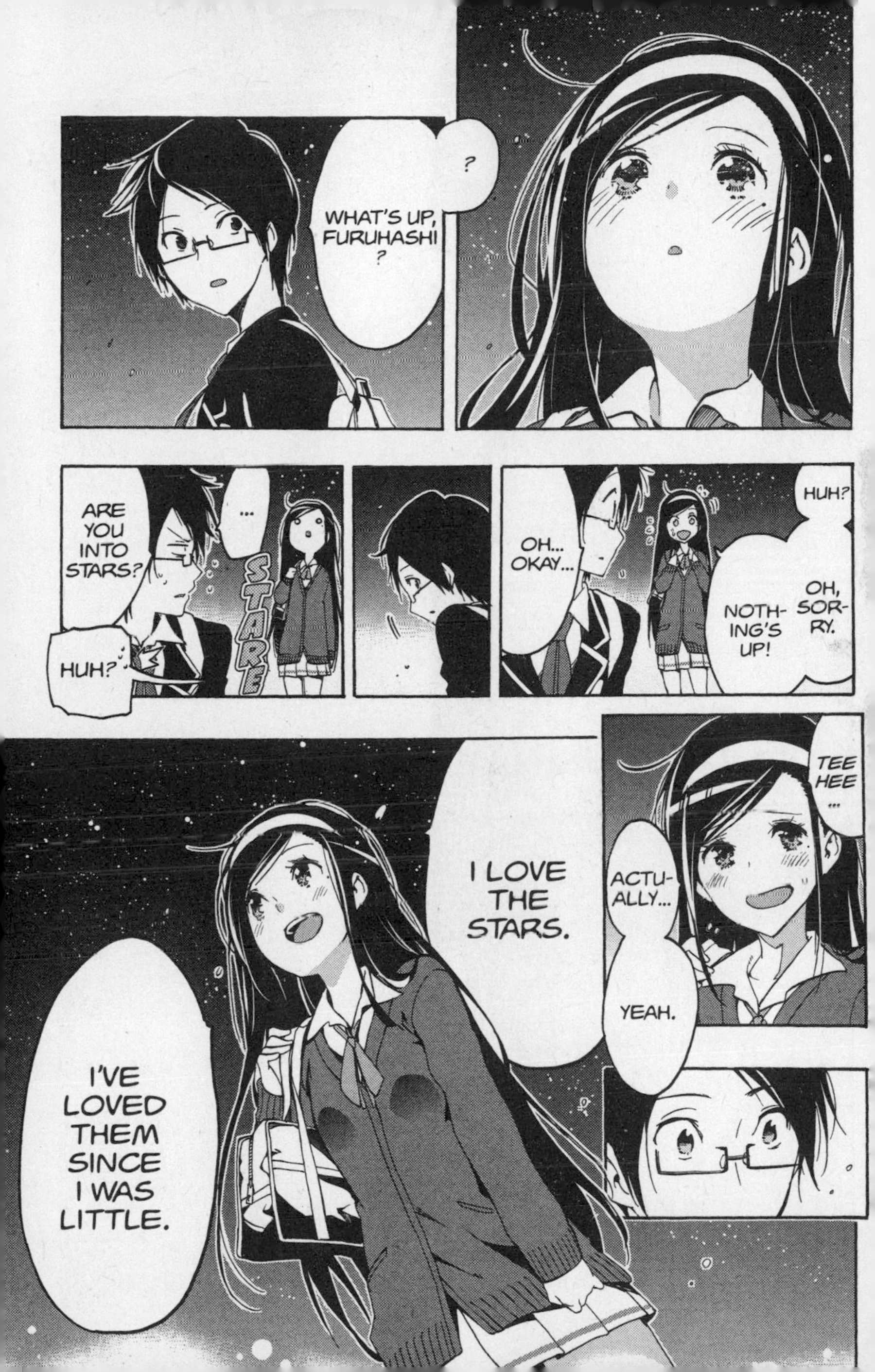
?
WHAT'S UP, FURUHASHI?
HUH?
OH, SORRY.
NOTHING'S UP!
OH... OKAY...
...
STARE
ARE YOU INTO STARS?
HUH?
TEE HEE...
ACTUALLY...
YEAH.
I LOVE THE STARS.
I'VE LOVED THEM SINCE I WAS LITTLE.

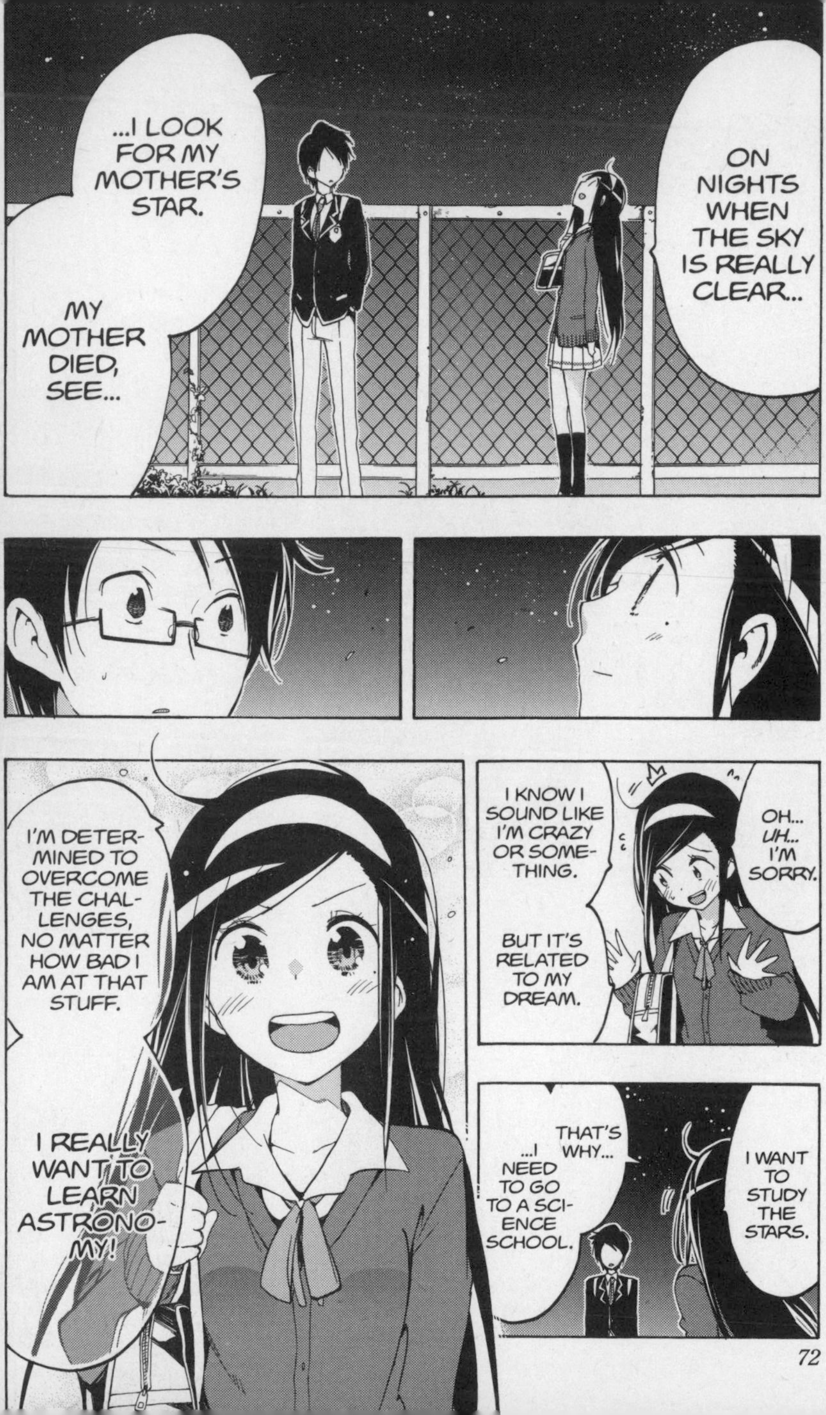
ON NIGHTS WHEN THE SKY IS REALLY CLEAR...
...I LOOK FOR MY MOTHER'S STAR.
MY MOTHER DIED, SEE...
OH... UH... I'M SORRY.
I KNOW I SOUND LIKE I'M CRAZY OR SOMETHING.
BUT IT'S RELATED TO MY DREAM.
I WANT TO STUDY THE STARS.
THAT'S WHY...
...I NEED TO GO TO A SCIENCE SCHOOL.
I'M DETERMINED TO OVERCOME THE CHALLENGES, NO MATTER HOW BAD I AM AT THAT STUFF.
I REALLY WANT TO LEARN ASTRONOMY!

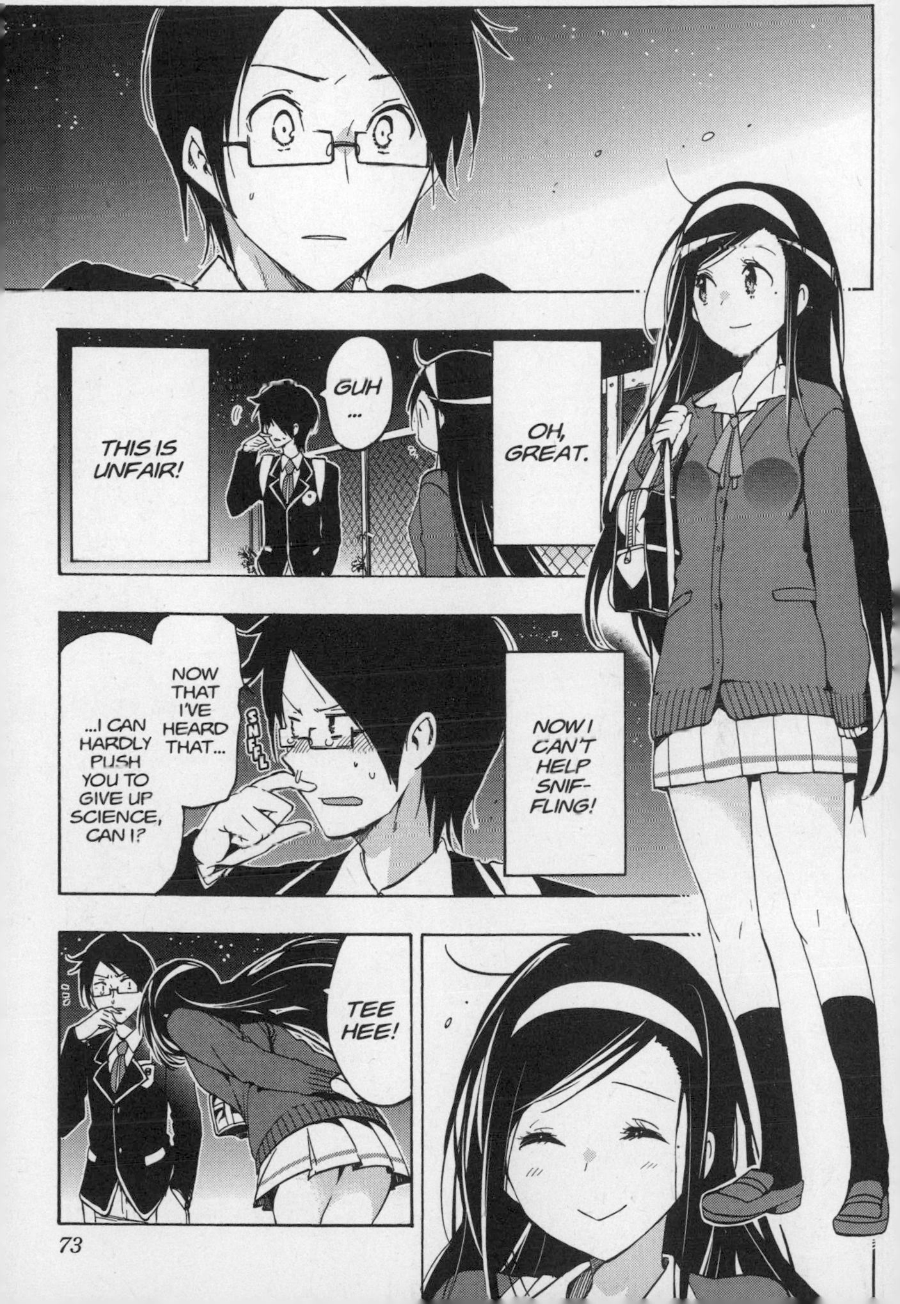
OH, GREAT.
GUH ...
THIS IS UNFAIR!
NOW I CAN'T HELP SNIF-FLING!
SNFFL
NOW THAT I'VE HEARD THAT...
...I CAN HARDLY PUSH YOU TO GIVE UP SCIENCE, CAN I?
TEE HEE!

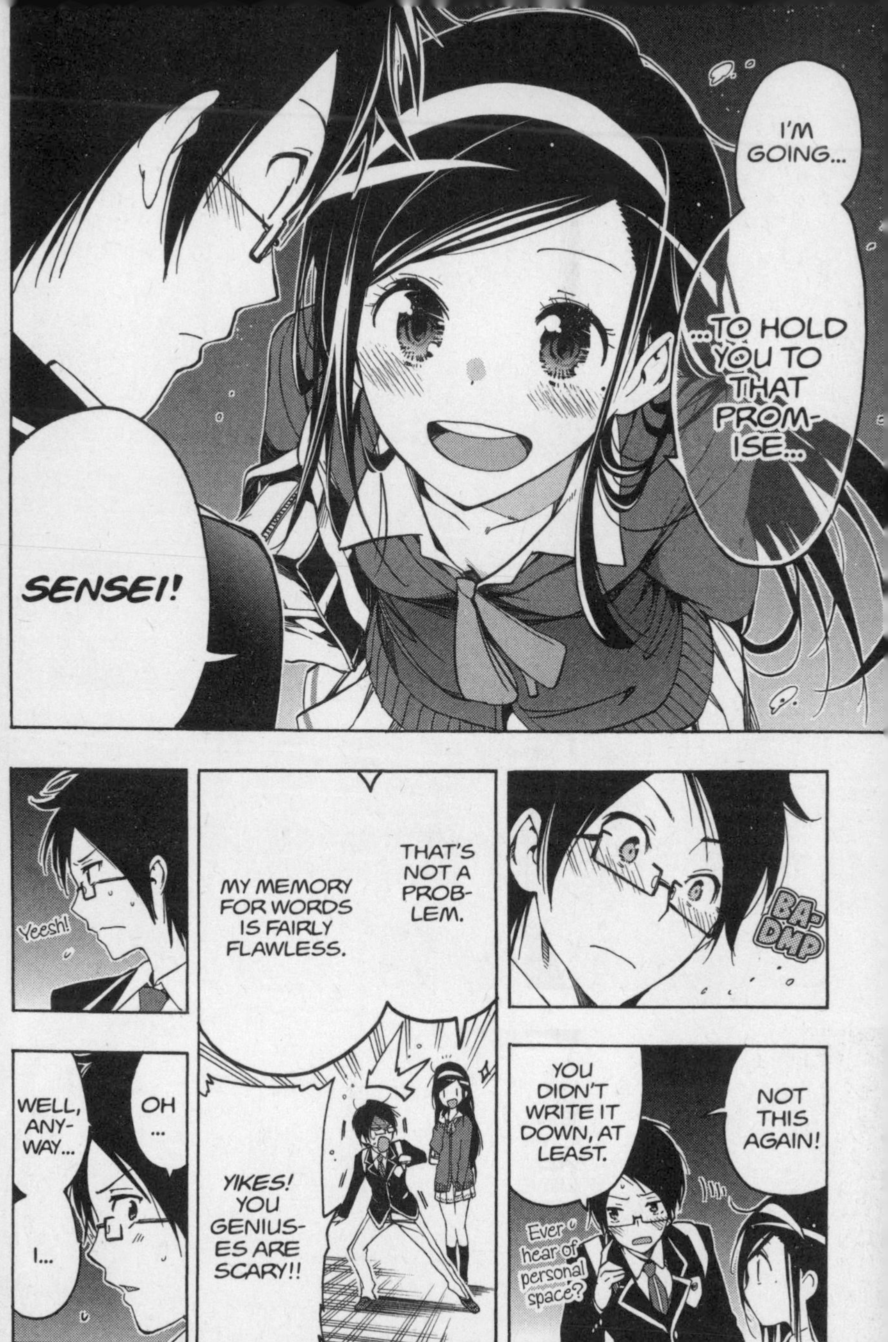
I'M GOING...
...TO HOLD YOU TO THAT PROMISE...
SENSEI!
BA-DMP
THAT'S NOT A PROBLEM.
MY MEMORY FOR WORDS IS FAIRLY FLAWLESS.
Yeesh!
NOT THIS AGAIN!
YOU DIDN'T WRITE IT DOWN, AT LEAST.
Ever hear of personal space?
YIKES! YOU GENIUSES ARE SCARY!!
OH...
WELL, ANYWAY...
I...

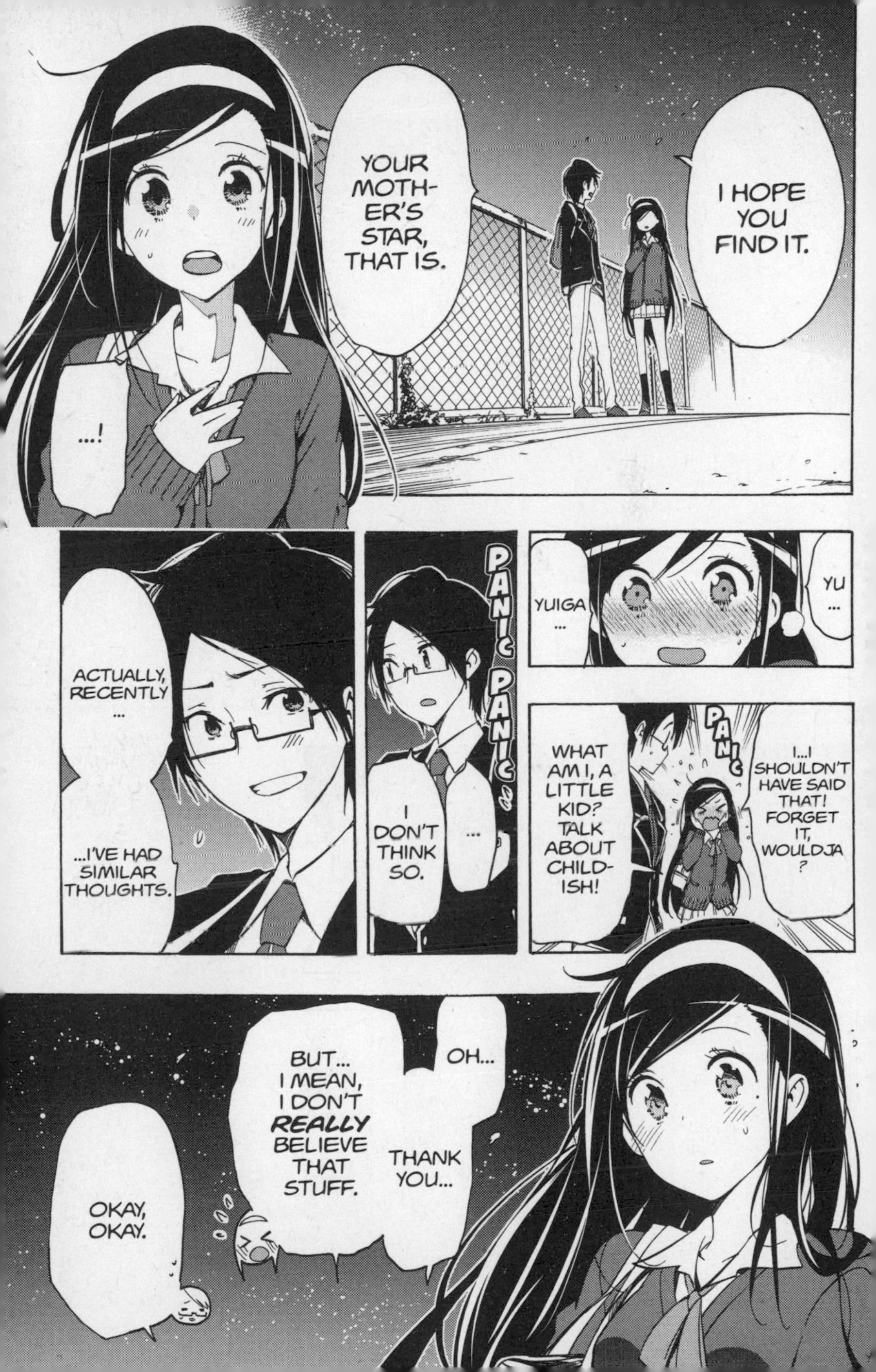
I HOPE YOU FIND IT.
YOUR MOTHER'S STAR, THAT IS.
...!
YU ...
YUIGA ...
I...I SHOULDN'T HAVE SAID THAT! FORGET IT, WOULDJA?
PANIC
WHAT AM I, A LITTLE KID? TALK ABOUT CHILDISH!
PANIC PANIC
...
I DON'T THINK SO.
ACTUALLY, RECENTLY ...
...I'VE HAD SIMILAR THOUGHTS.
OH...
THANK YOU...
BUT... I MEAN, I DON'T REALLY BELIEVE THAT STUFF.
OKAY, OKAY.

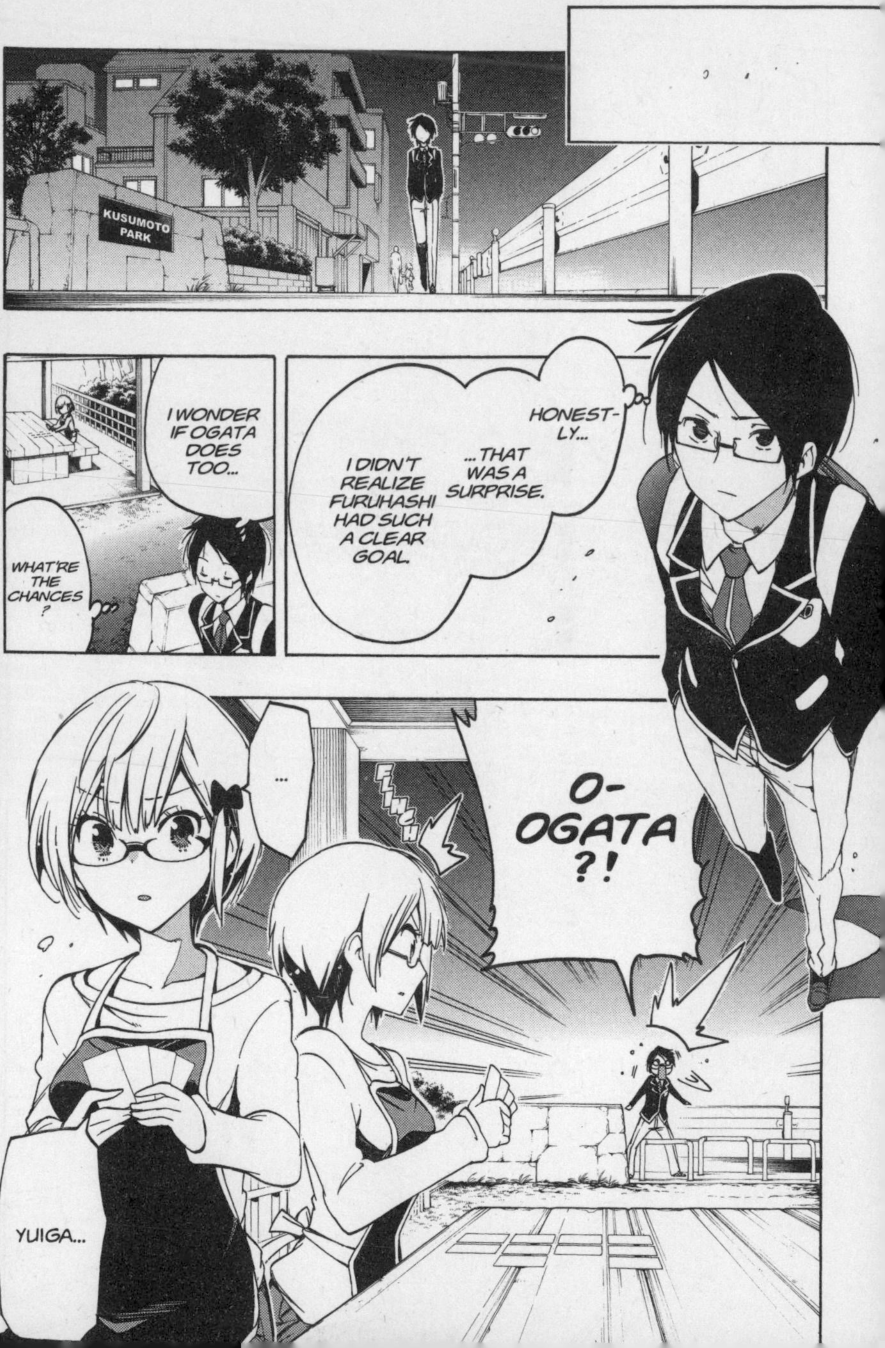
KUSUMOTO PARK
HONEST-LY...
...THAT WAS A SURPRISE.
I DIDN'T REALIZE FURUHASHI HAD SUCH A CLEAR GOAL.
I WONDER IF OGATA DOES TOO...
WHAT'RE THE CHANCES?
O-OGATA?!
FLINCH
...
YUIGA...

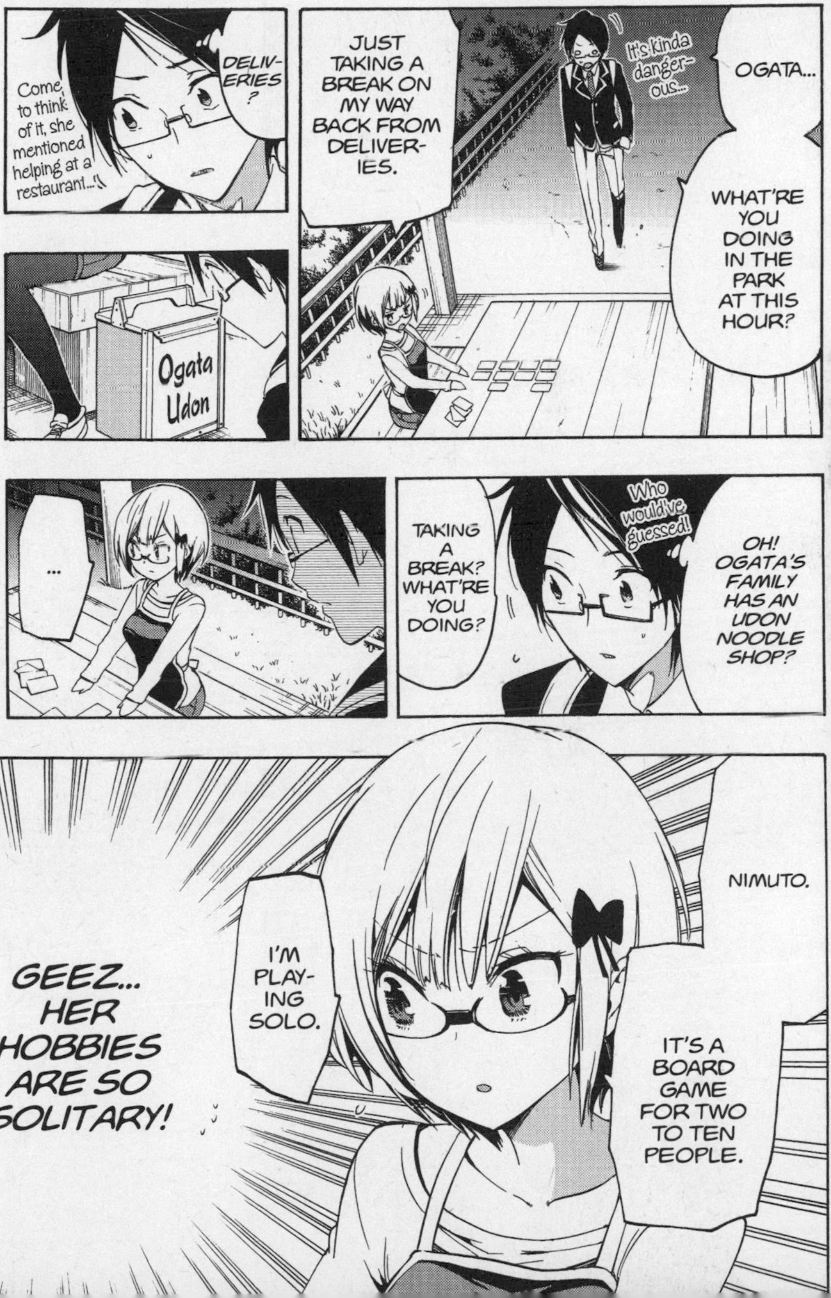
OGATA...
WHAT'RE YOU DOING IN THE PARK AT THIS HOUR?
It's kinda danger-ous...
JUST TAKING A BREAK ON MY WAY BACK FROM DELIVER-IES.
DELIV-ERIES?
Come to think of it, she mentioned helping at a restaurant...!!
Ogata Udon
OH! OGATA'S FAMILY HAS AN UDON NOODLE SHOP?
Who would've guessed!
TAKING A BREAK? WHAT'RE YOU DOING?
...
NIMUTO.
IT'S A BOARD GAME FOR TWO TO TEN PEOPLE.
I'M PLAY-ING SOLO.
GEEZ... HER HOBBIES ARE SO SOLITARY!

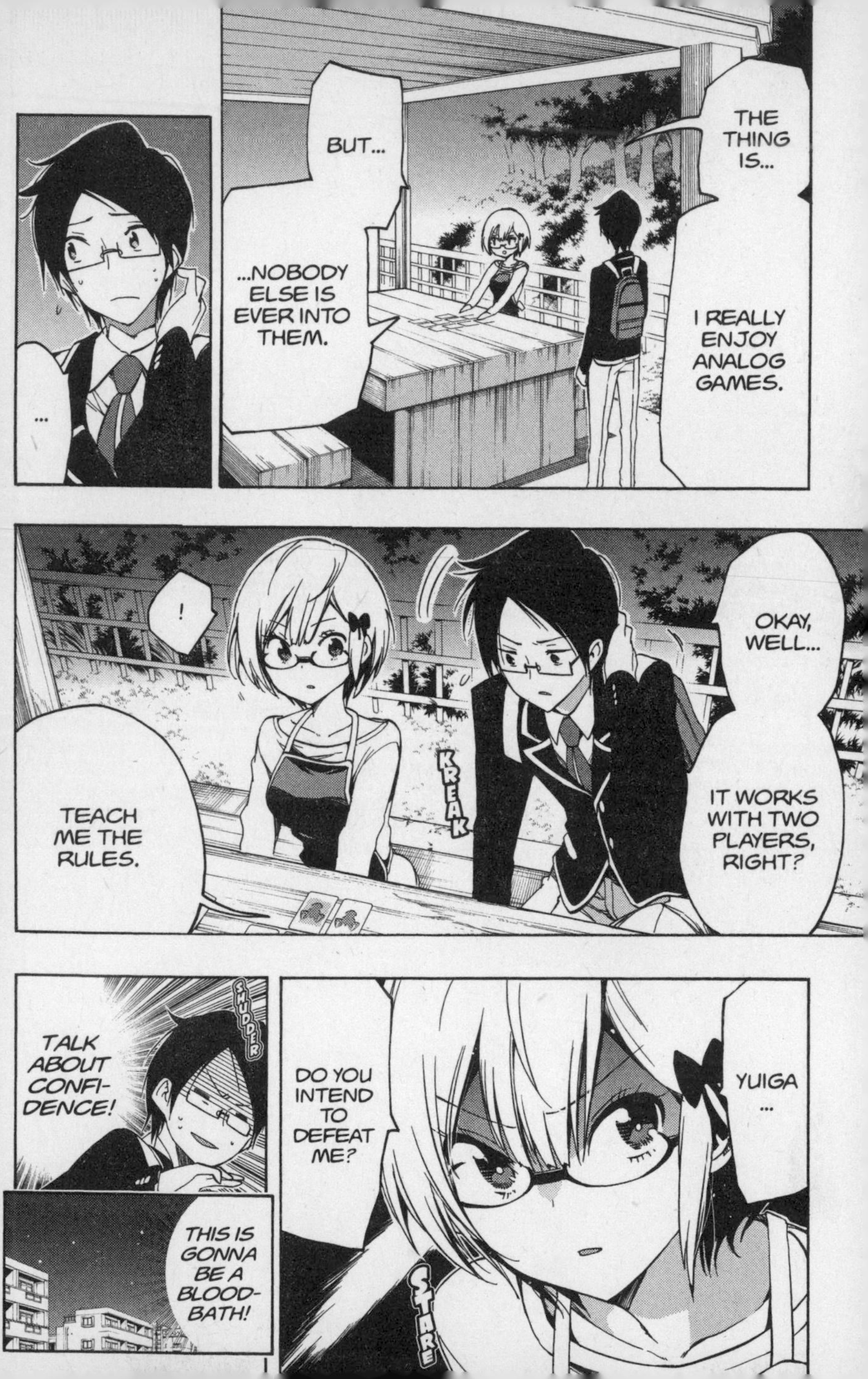

THE THING IS...
I REALLY ENJOY ANALOG GAMES.
BUT...
...NOBODY ELSE IS EVER INTO THEM.
...
OKAY, WELL...
IT WORKS WITH TWO PLAYERS, RIGHT?
KREAK
!
TEACH ME THE RULES.
YUIGA...
DO YOU INTEND TO DEFEAT ME?
STARE
SHUDDER
TALK ABOUT CONFI-DENCE!
THIS IS GONNA BE A BLOOD-BATH!

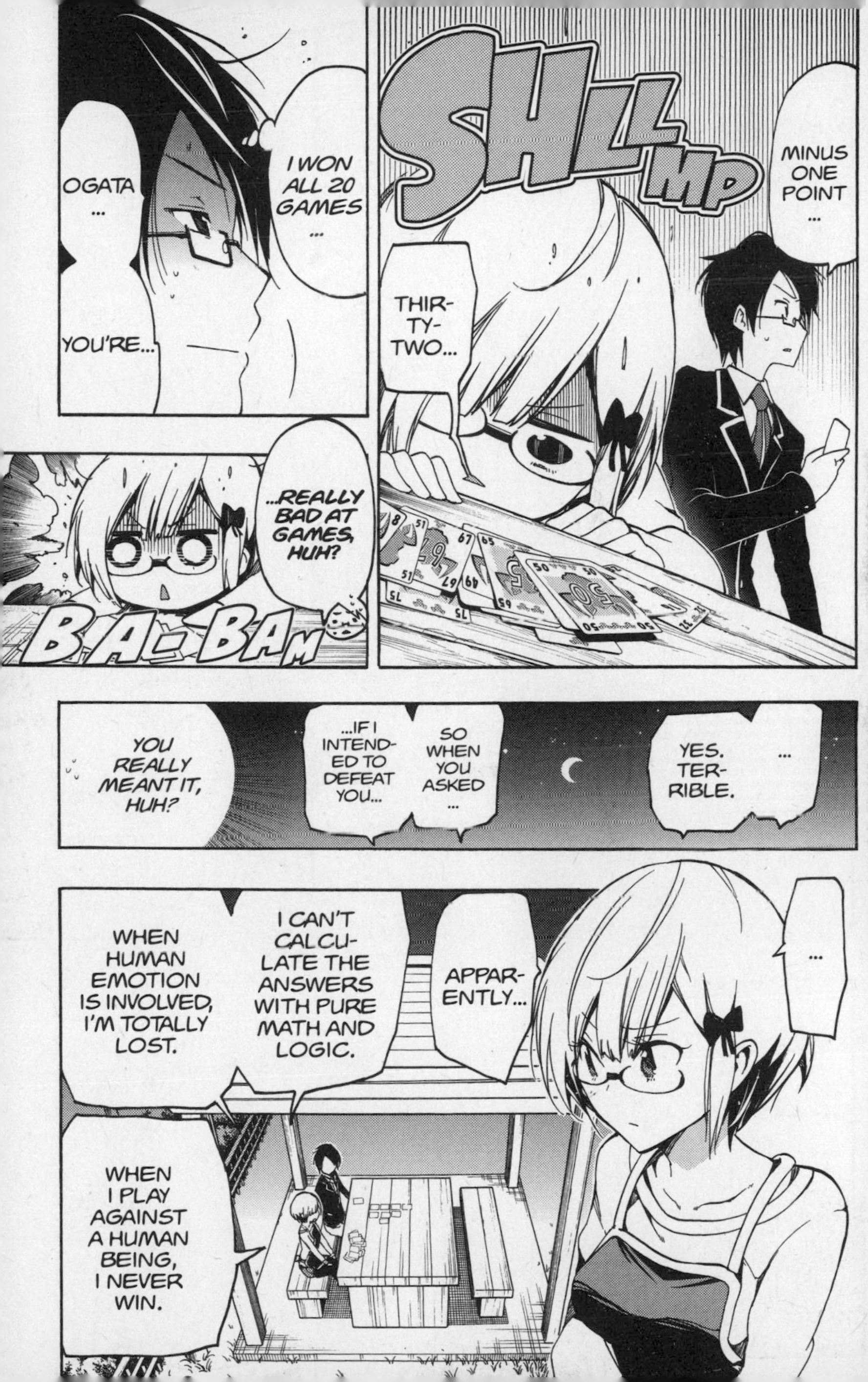
SHLLMP
MINUS ONE POINT...
THIRTY-TWO...
I WON ALL 20 GAMES...
OGATA... YOU'RE...
...REALLY BAD AT GAMES, HUH?
BA-BAM
...
YES. TERRIBLE.
SO WHEN YOU ASKED...
...IF I INTENDED TO DEFEAT YOU...
YOU REALLY MEANT IT, HUH?
...
APPARENTLY...
I CAN'T CALCULATE THE ANSWERS WITH PURE MATH AND LOGIC.
WHEN HUMAN EMOTION IS INVOLVED, I'M TOTALLY LOST.
WHEN I PLAY AGAINST A HUMAN BEING, I NEVER WIN.

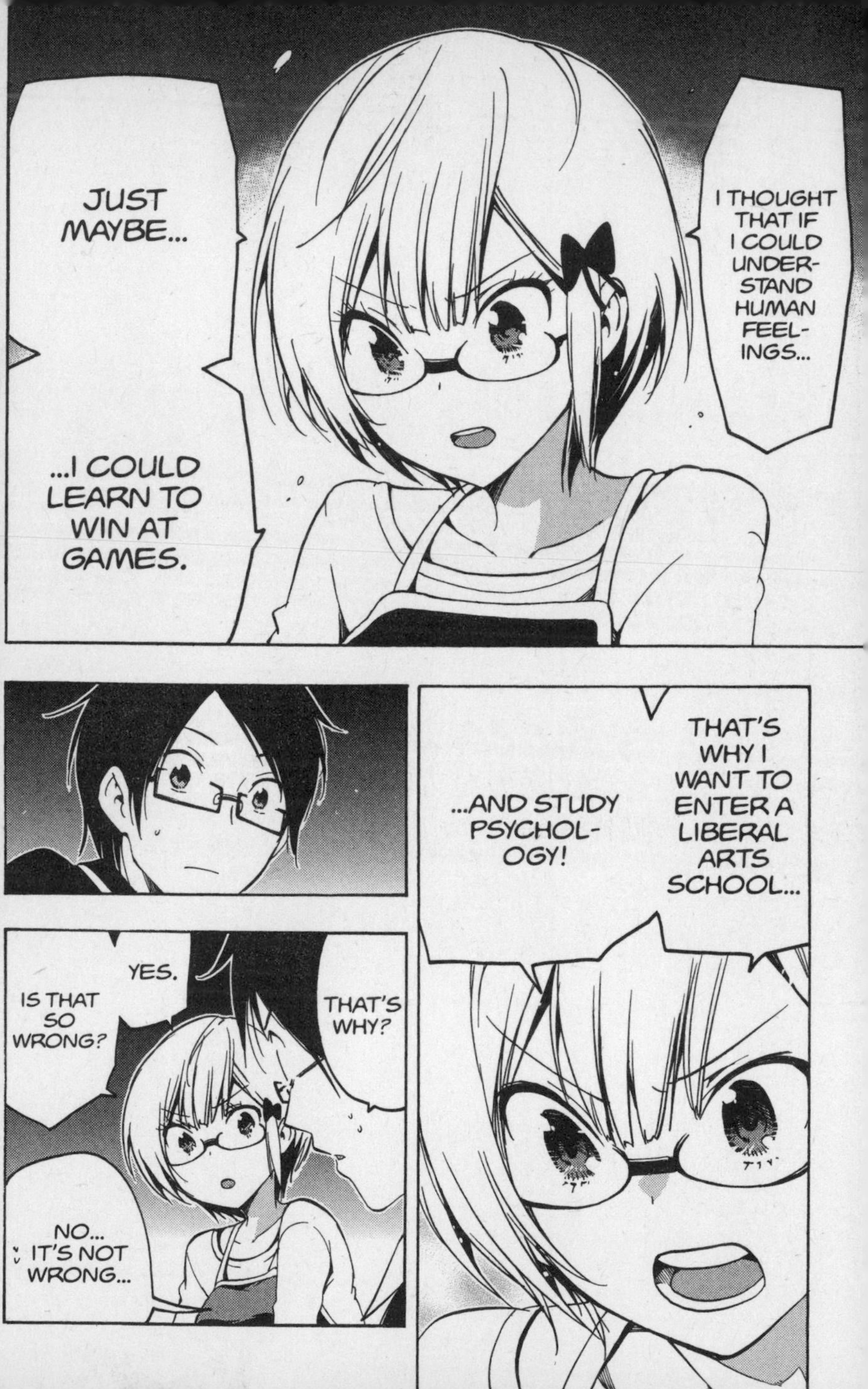
I THOUGHT THAT IF I COULD UNDERSTAND HUMAN FEELINGS...
JUST MAYBE...
...I COULD LEARN TO WIN AT GAMES.
THAT'S WHY I WANT TO ENTER A LIBERAL ARTS SCHOOL...
...AND STUDY PSYCHOLOGY!
THAT'S WHY?
YES.
IS THAT SO WRONG?
NO... IT'S NOT WRONG...

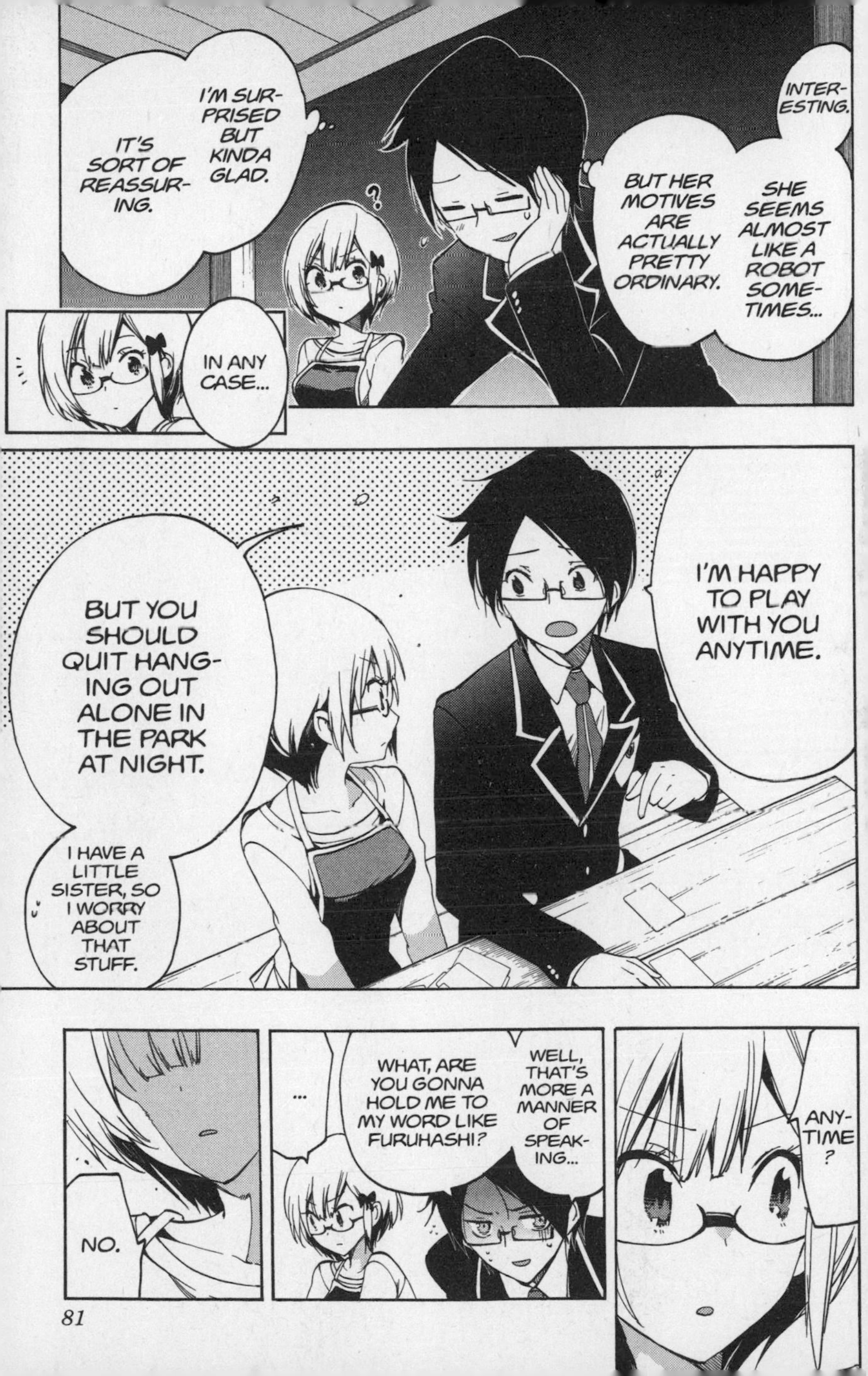
INTERESTING.
SHE SEEMS ALMOST LIKE A ROBOT SOMETIMES...
BUT HER MOTIVES ARE ACTUALLY PRETTY ORDINARY.
I'M SURPRISED BUT KINDA GLAD.
IT'S SORT OF REASSURING.
IN ANY CASE...
I'M HAPPY TO PLAY WITH YOU ANYTIME.
BUT YOU SHOULD QUIT HANGING OUT ALONE IN THE PARK AT NIGHT.
I HAVE A LITTLE SISTER, SO I WORRY ABOUT THAT STUFF.
ANYTIME?
WELL, THAT'S MORE A MANNER OF SPEAKING...
WHAT, ARE YOU GONNA HOLD ME TO MY WORD LIKE FURUHASHI?
...
NO.

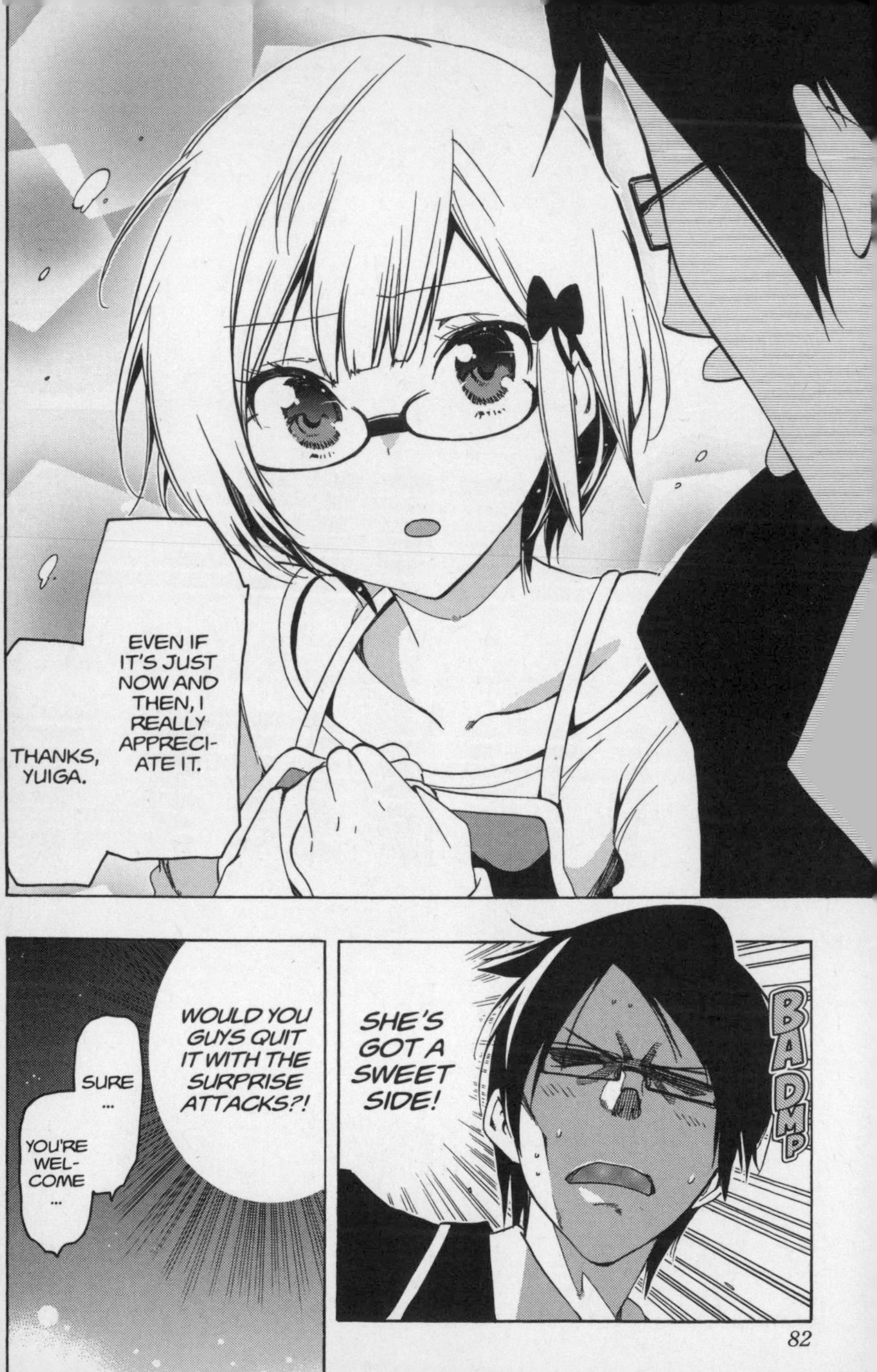
EVEN IF IT'S JUST NOW AND THEN, I REALLY APPRECIATE IT.
THANKS, YUIGA.
BADMP
SHE'S GOT A SWEET SIDE!
WOULD YOU GUYS QUIT IT WITH THE SURPRISE ATTACKS?!
SURE ... YOU'RE WELCOME ...

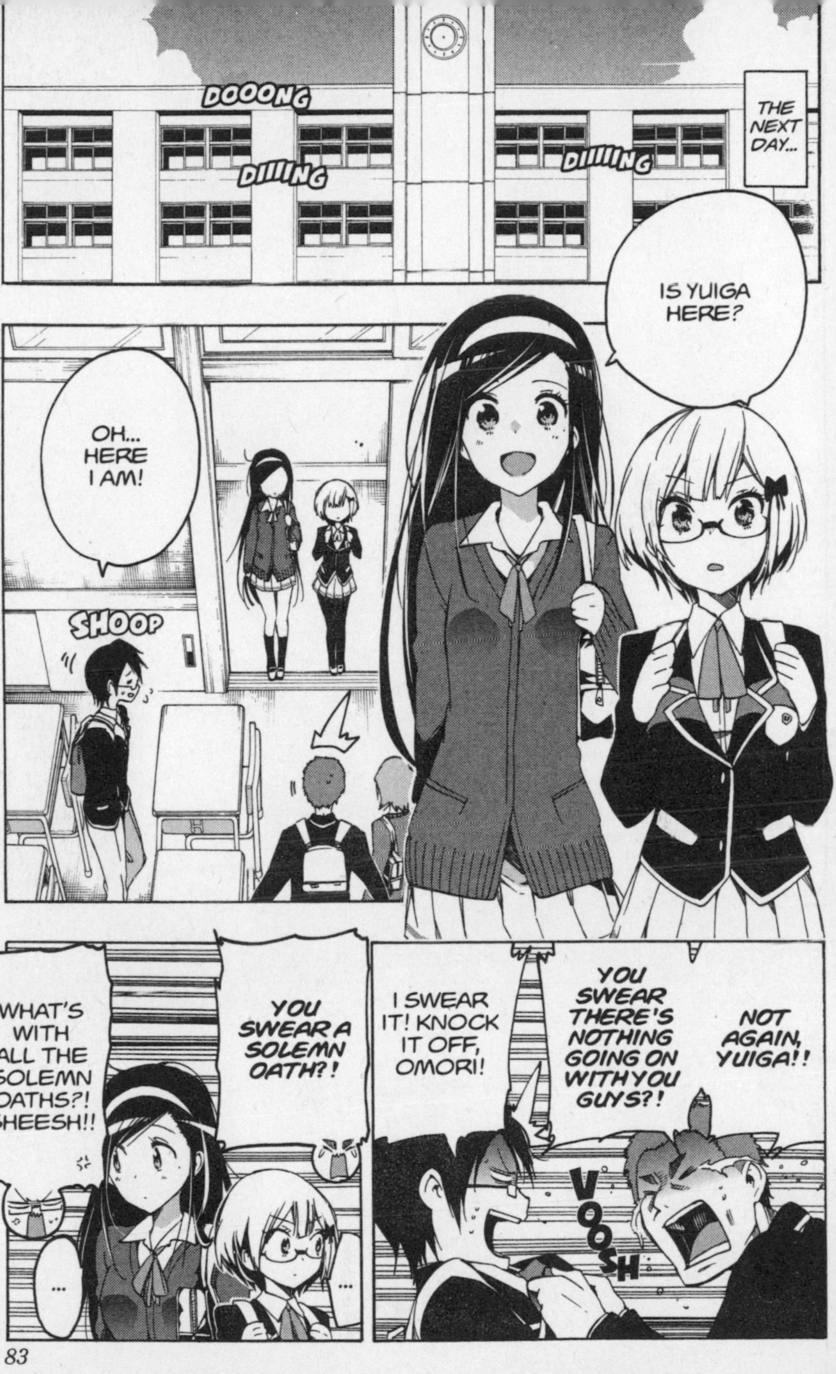
THE NEXT DAY...
DOOONG
DIIIING
DIIIING
IS YUIGA HERE?
OH... HERE I AM!
SHOOP
NOT AGAIN, YUIGA!!
YOU SWEAR THERE'S NOTHING GOING ON WITH YOU GUYS?!
I SWEAR IT! KNOCK IT OFF, OMORI!
VOOSH
YOU SWEAR A SOLEMN OATH?!
WHAT'S WITH ALL THE SOLEMN OATHS?! SHEESH!!
...
...

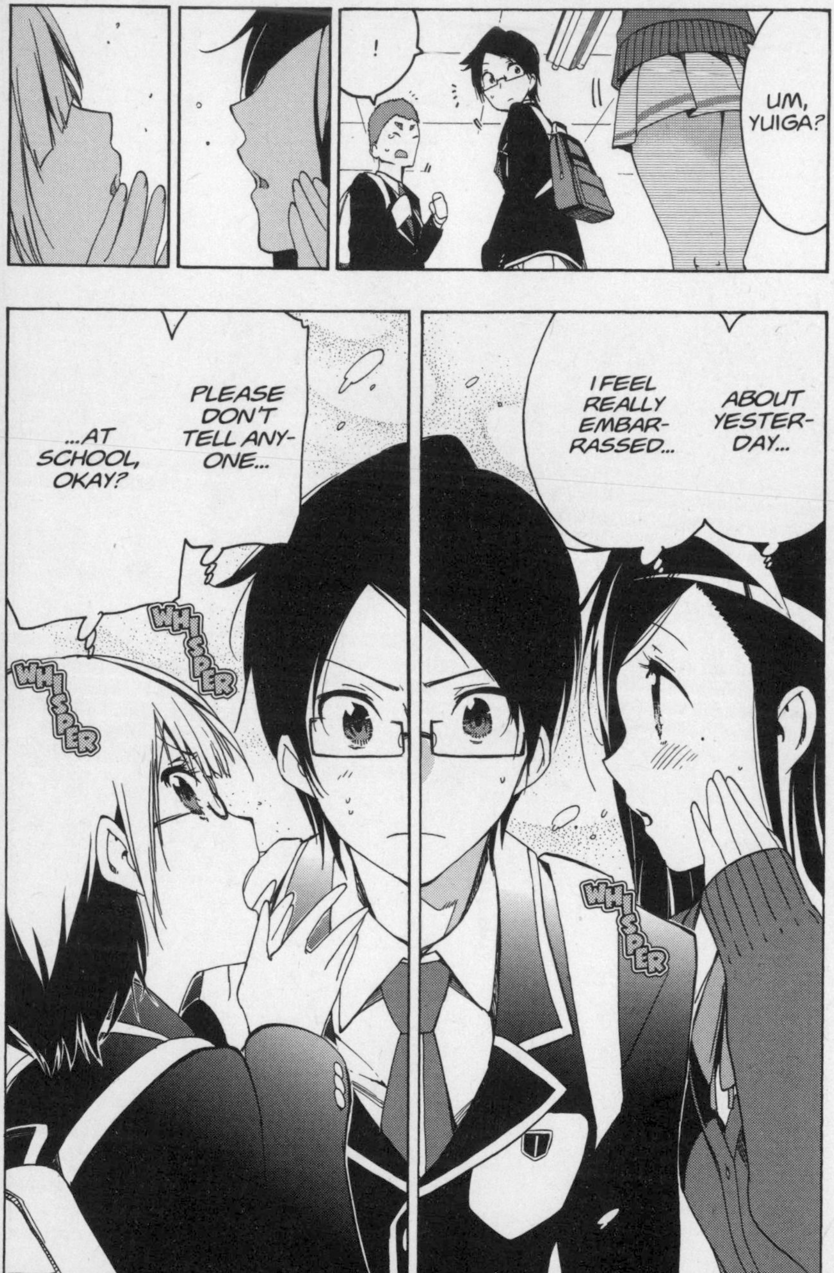
UM, YUIGA?
!
ABOUT YESTER-DAY...
I FEEL REALLY EMBAR-RASSED...
WHISPER
PLEASE DON'T TELL ANY-ONE...
...AT SCHOOL, OKAY?
WHISPER
WHISPER

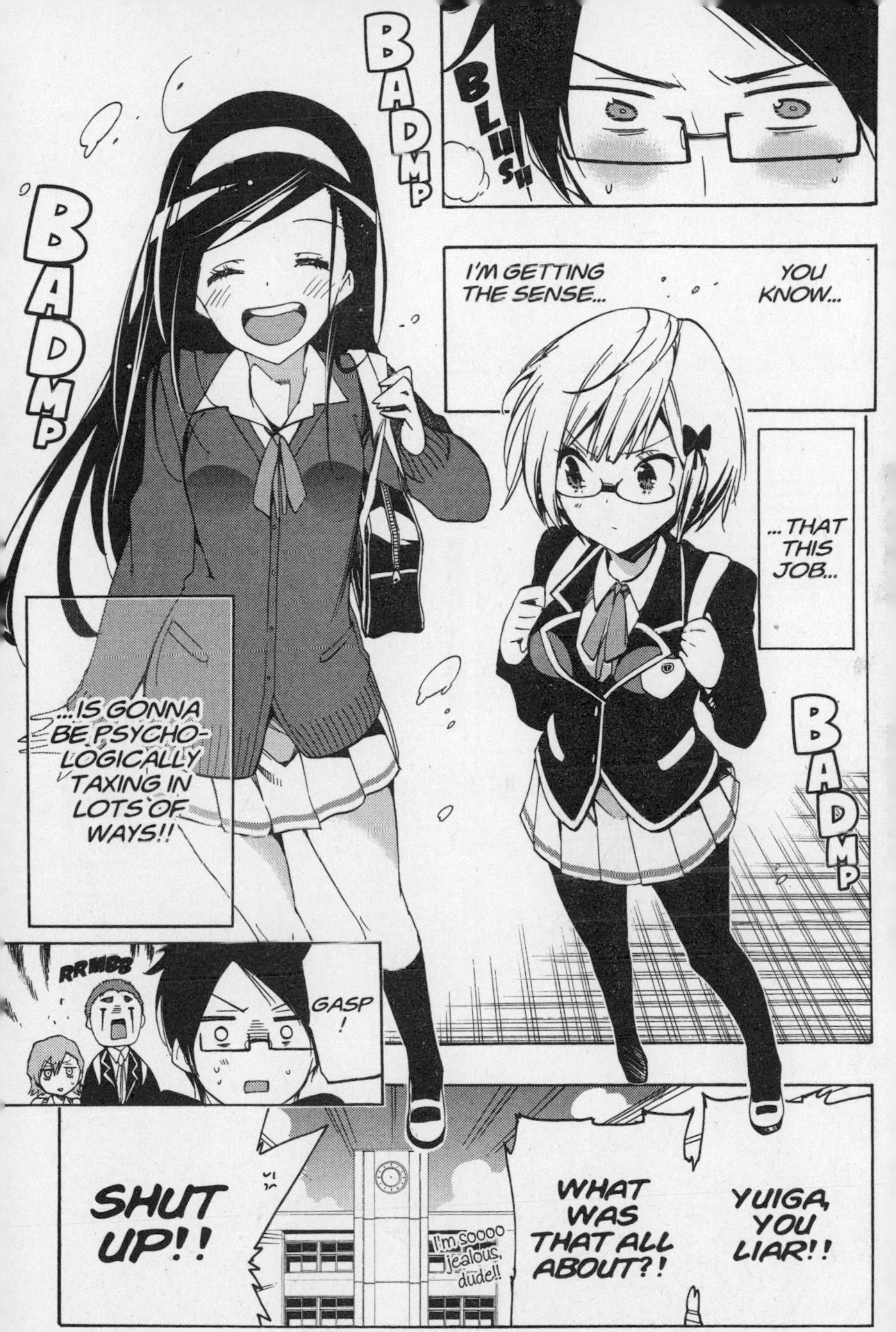
BLUSH
BADMP
I'M GETTING THE SENSE... YOU KNOW...
...THAT THIS JOB...
BADMP
...IS GONNA BE PSYCHO-LOGICALLY TAXING IN LOTS OF WAYS!!
BADMP
GASP!
RRMBB
YUIGA, YOU LIAR!!
WHAT WAS THAT ALL ABOUT?!
I'm soooo jealous, dude!!
SHUT UP!!

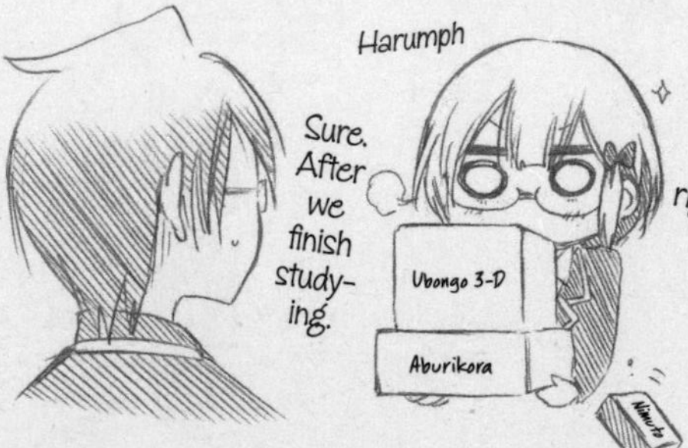
Harumph
Let's get right to it.
Sure. After we finish study-ing.
Ubongo 3-D
Aburikora
Nimuto

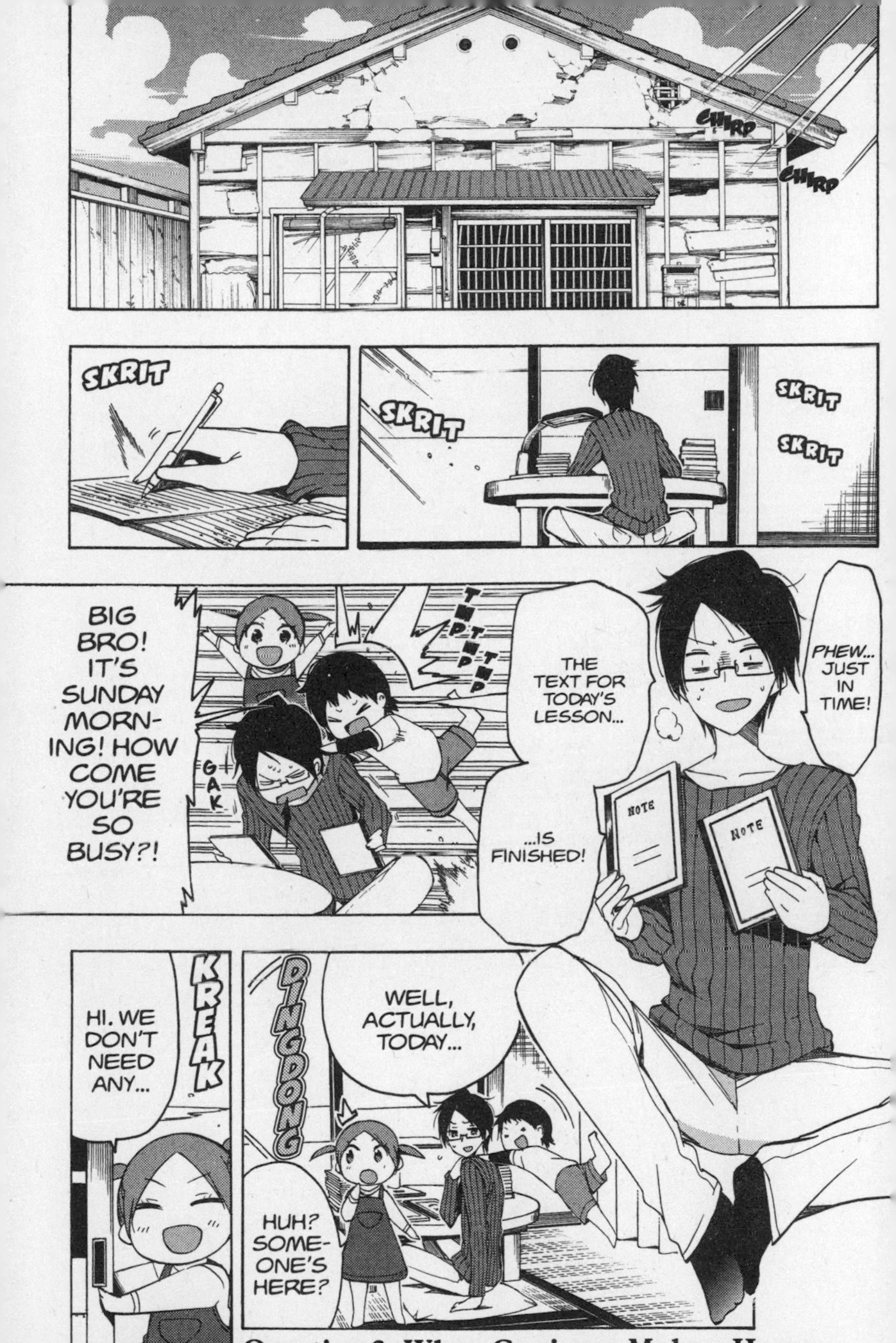
CHIRP
CHIRP
SKRIT
SKRIT
SKRIT
SKRIT
PHEW... JUST IN TIME!
THE TEXT FOR TODAY'S LESSON...
...IS FINISHED!
TMP TMP TMP TMP
BIG BRO! IT'S SUNDAY MORN-ING! HOW COME YOU'RE SO BUSY?!
GAK
DINGDONG
WELL, ACTUALLY, TODAY...
HUH? SOME-ONE'S HERE?
KREAK
HI. WE DON'T NEED ANY...

Question 3: When Geniuses Make a House Call, [X] Is of Utmost Importance

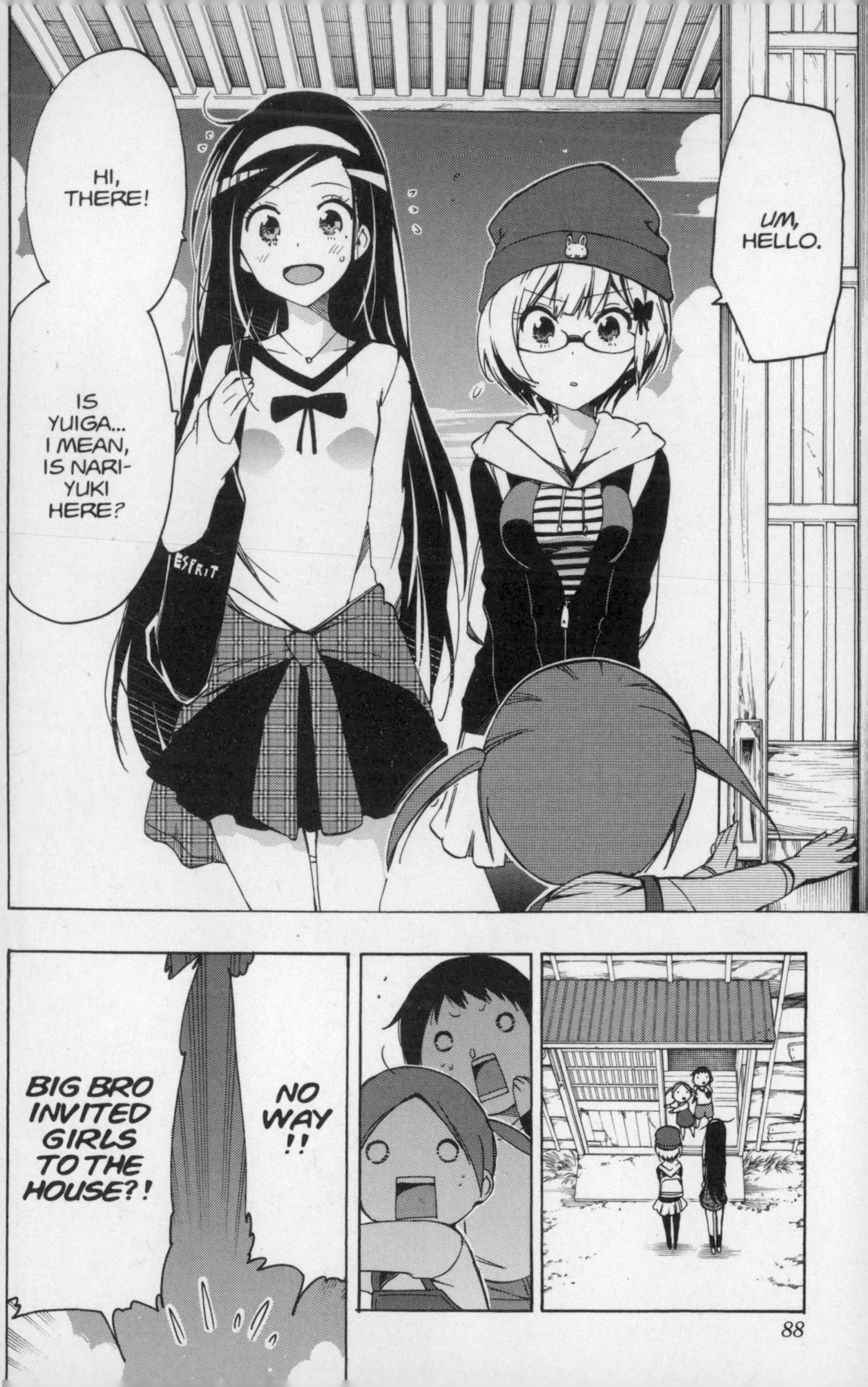
UM, HELLO.
HI, THERE!
IS YUIGA... I MEAN, IS NARI-YUKI HERE?
ESPRIT
NO WAY!!
BIG BRO INVITED GIRLS TO THE HOUSE?!

Question 3:
When Geniuses Make a House Call,
[*X*] Is of Utmost Importance

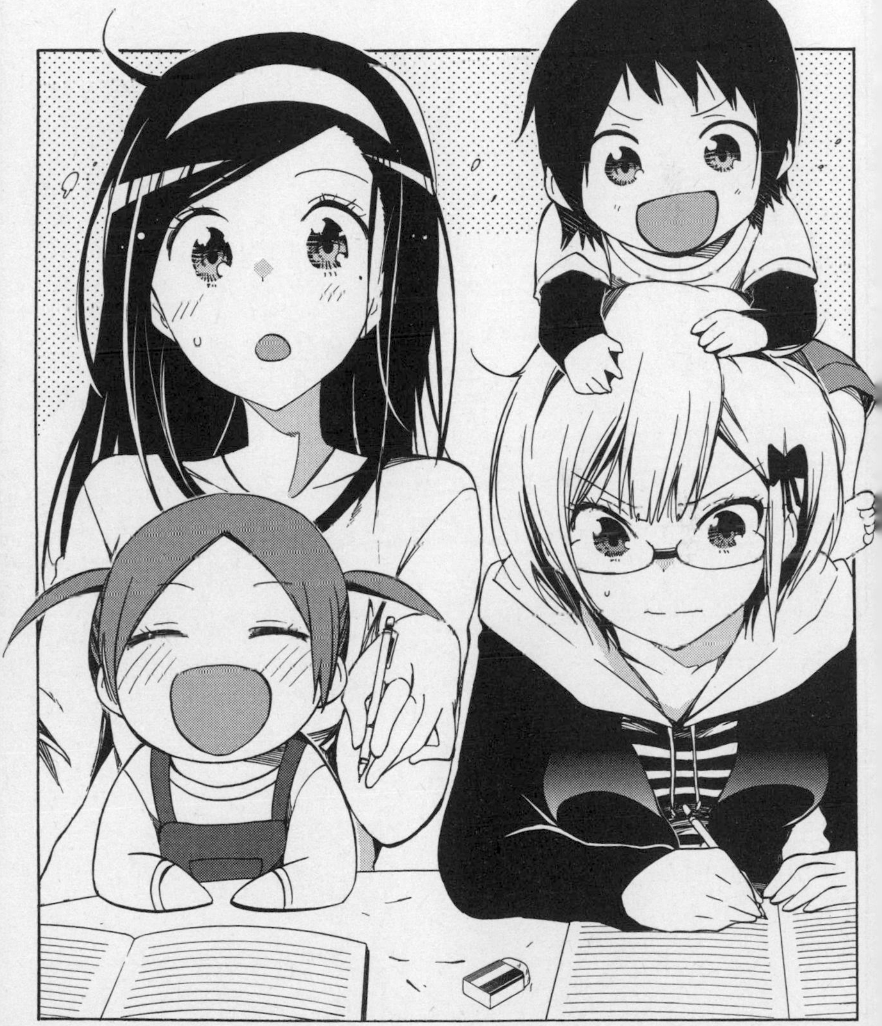

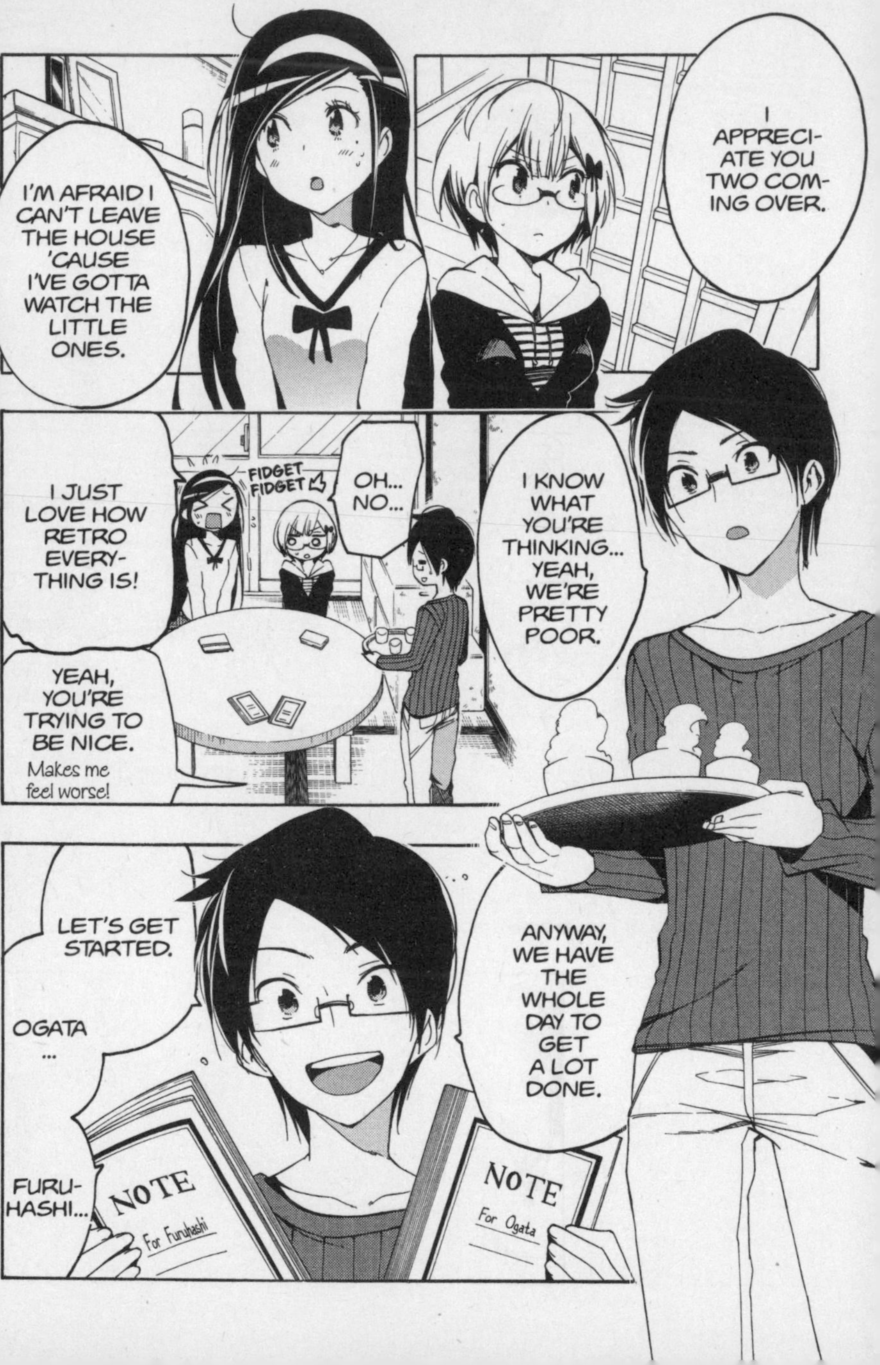
I APPRECIATE YOU TWO COMING OVER.
I'M AFRAID I CAN'T LEAVE THE HOUSE 'CAUSE I'VE GOTTA WATCH THE LITTLE ONES.
I KNOW WHAT YOU'RE THINKING... YEAH, WE'RE PRETTY POOR.
OH... NO...
FIDGET FIDGET
I JUST LOVE HOW RETRO EVERYTHING IS!
YEAH, YOU'RE TRYING TO BE NICE.
Makes me feel worse!
ANYWAY, WE HAVE THE WHOLE DAY TO GET A LOT DONE.
LET'S GET STARTED.
OGATA ...
NOTE
For Ogata
FURUHASHI...
NOTE
For Furuhashi

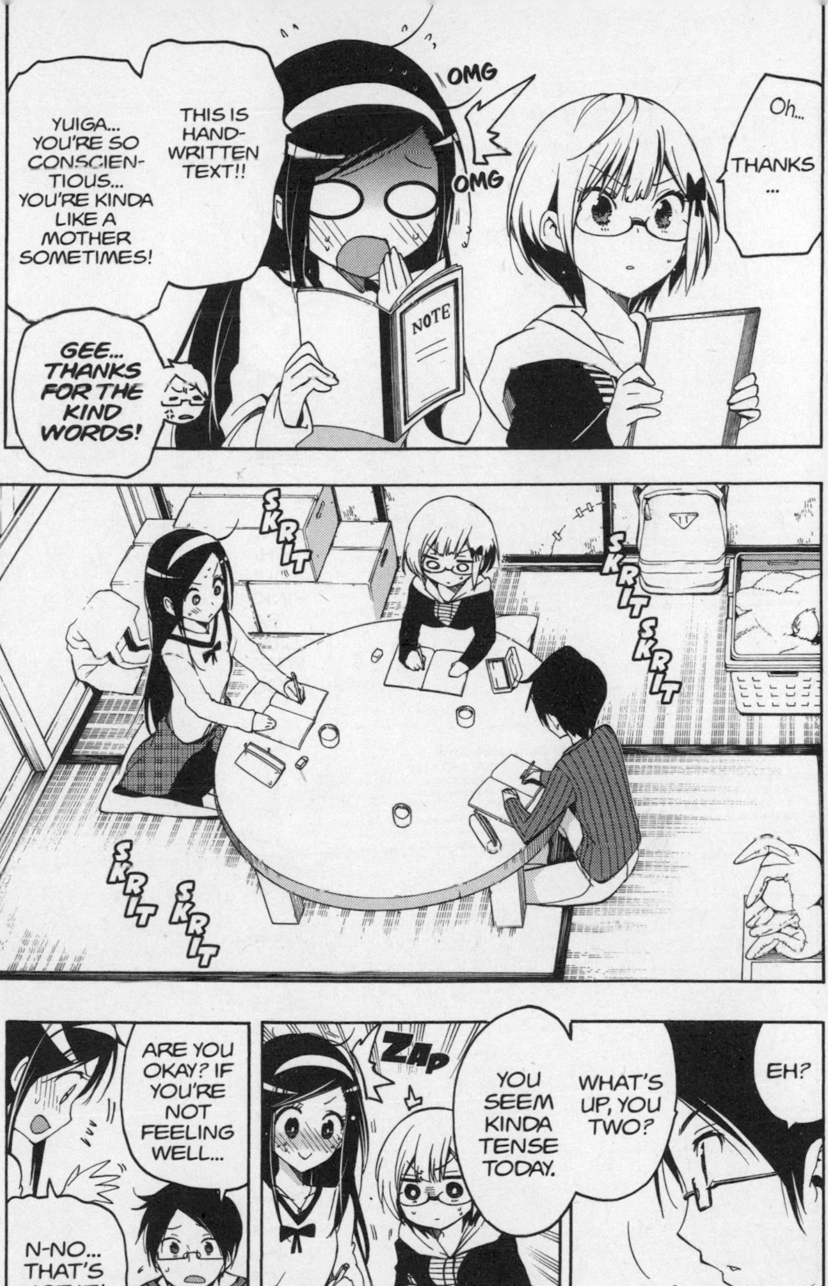
Oh... THANKS...
OMG
OMG
THIS IS HAND-WRITTEN TEXT!!
YUIGA... YOU'RE SO CONSCIENTIOUS... YOU'RE KINDA LIKE A MOTHER SOMETIMES!
GEE... THANKS FOR THE KIND WORDS!
NOTE
SKRIT
SKRIT SKRIT
SKRIT SKRIT
EH?
WHAT'S UP, YOU TWO?
YOU SEEM KINDA TENSE TODAY.
ZAP
ARE YOU OKAY? IF YOU'RE NOT FEELING WELL...
N-NO... THAT'S NOT IT!

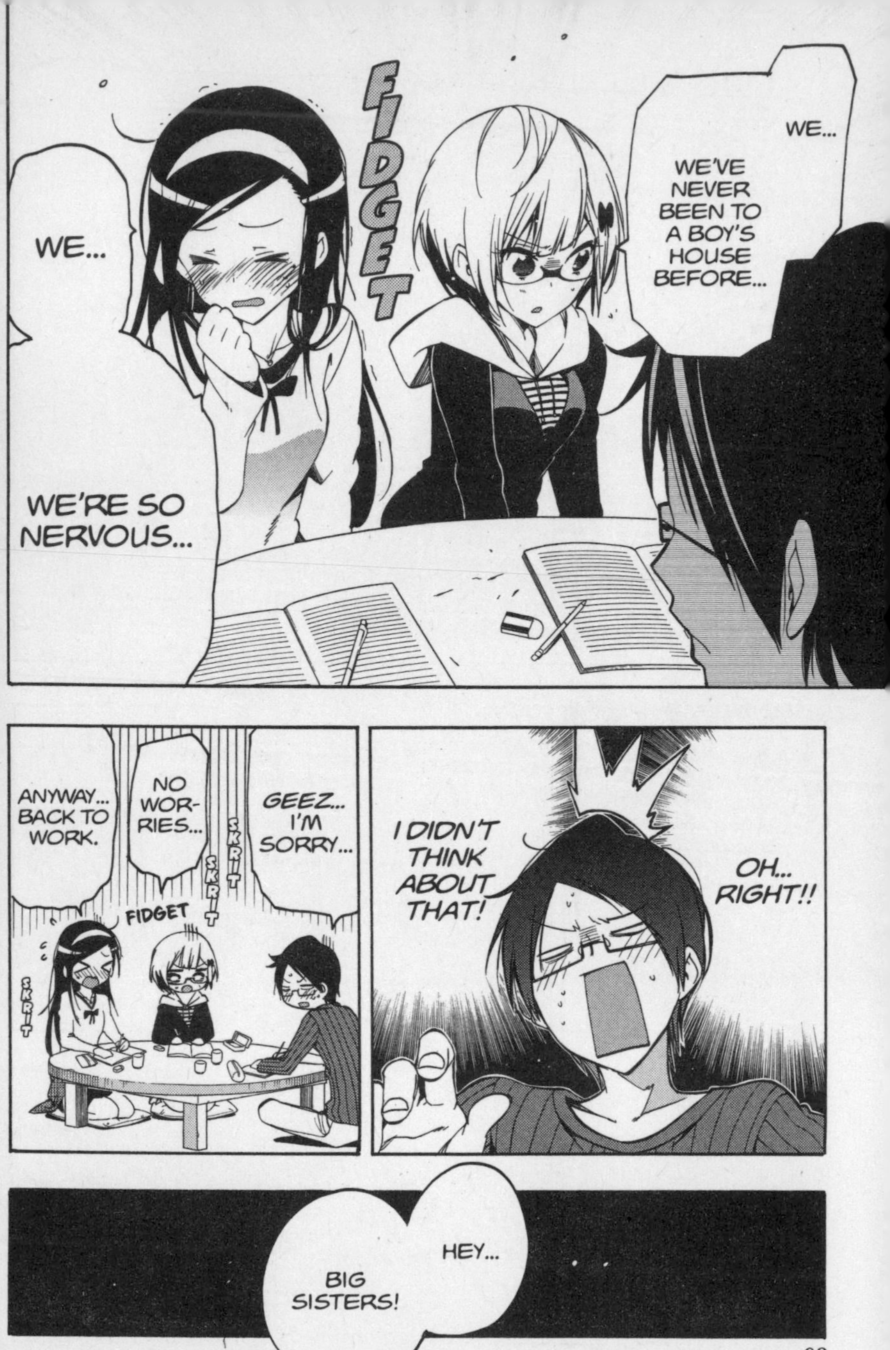
WE...
WE'VE NEVER BEEN TO A BOY'S HOUSE BEFORE...
FIDGET
WE...
WE'RE SO NERVOUS...
OH... RIGHT!!
I DIDN'T THINK ABOUT THAT!
GEEZ... I'M SORRY...
SKRIT
NO WORRIES...
SKRIT
ANYWAY... BACK TO WORK.
FIDGET
SKRIT
HEY...
BIG SISTERS!

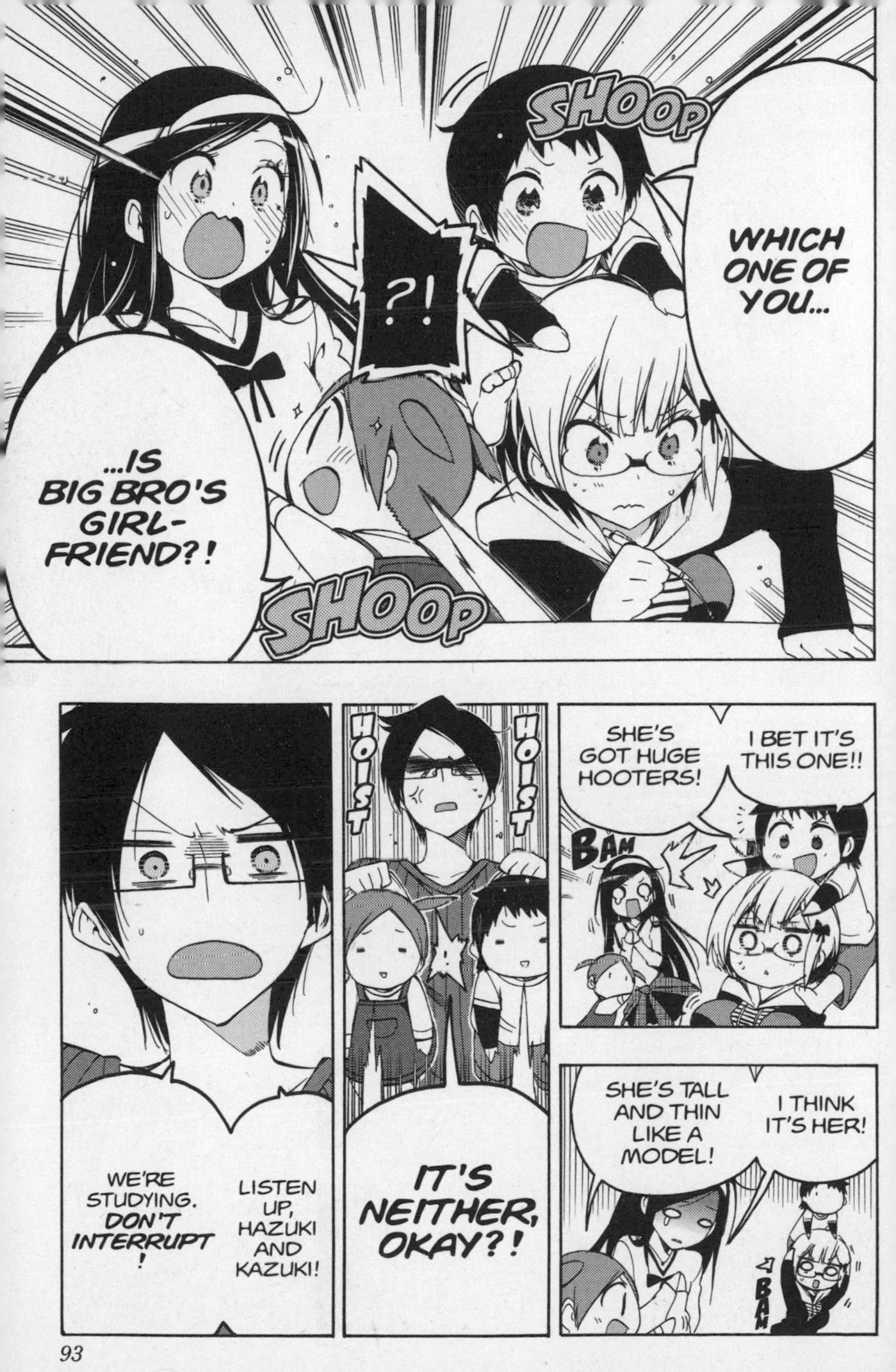
SHOOP
WHICH ONE OF YOU...
?!
...IS BIG BRO'S GIRL-FRIEND?!
SHOOP
I BET IT'S THIS ONE!!
SHE'S GOT HUGE HOOTERS!
BAM
I THINK IT'S HER!
SHE'S TALL AND THIN LIKE A MODEL!
BAM
HOIST
HOIST
IT'S NEITHER, OKAY?!
LISTEN UP, HAZUKI AND KAZUKI!
WE'RE STUDYING. DON'T INTERRUPT!

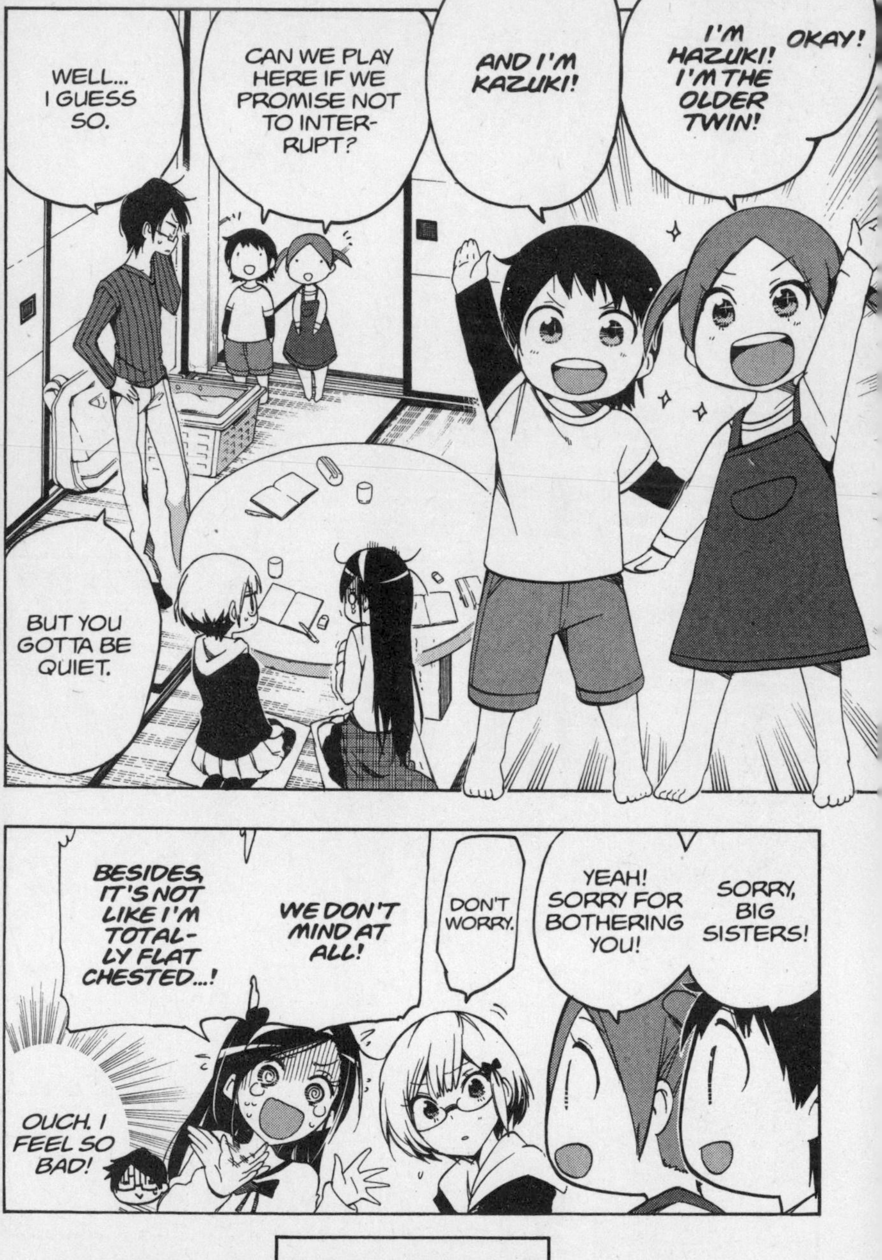
OKAY!
I'M HAZUKI! I'M THE OLDER TWIN!
AND I'M KAZUKI!
CAN WE PLAY HERE IF WE PROMISE NOT TO INTER-RUPT?
WELL... I GUESS SO.
BUT YOU GOTTA BE QUIET.
SORRY, BIG SISTERS!
YEAH! SORRY FOR BOTHERING YOU!
DON'T WORRY.
WE DON'T MIND AT ALL!
BESIDES, IT'S NOT LIKE I'M TOTAL-LY FLAT CHESTED...!
OUCH. I FEEL SO BAD!

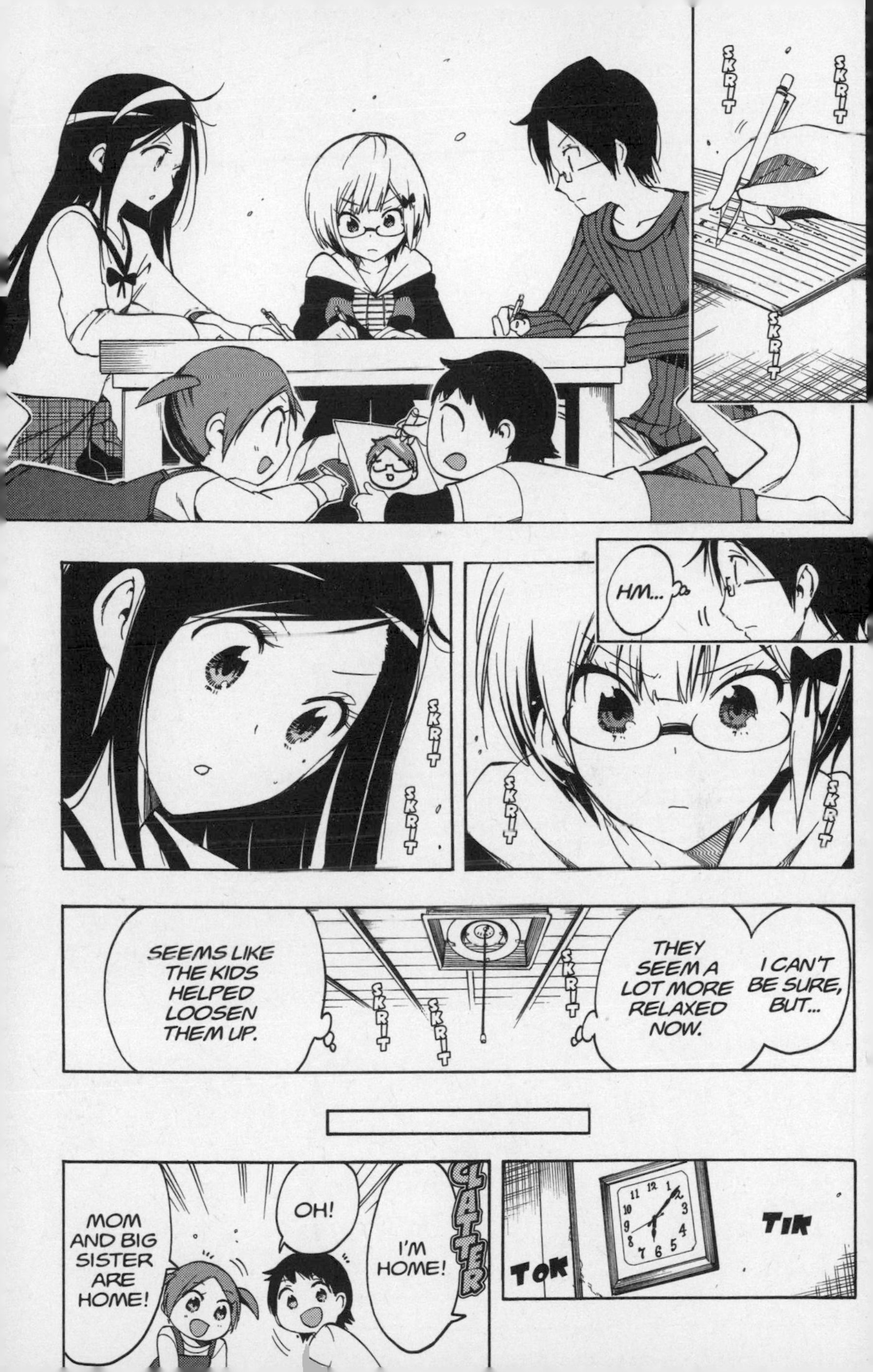
SKRIT
SKRIT
SKRIT
HM...
SKRIT
SKRIT
SKRIT
SKRIT
I CAN'T BE SURE, BUT...
THEY SEEM A LOT MORE RELAXED NOW.
SKRIT
SKRIT
SKRIT
SEEMS LIKE THE KIDS HELPED LOOSEN THEM UP.
TIK
TOK
CLATTER
I'M HOME!
OH!
MOM AND BIG SISTER ARE HOME!

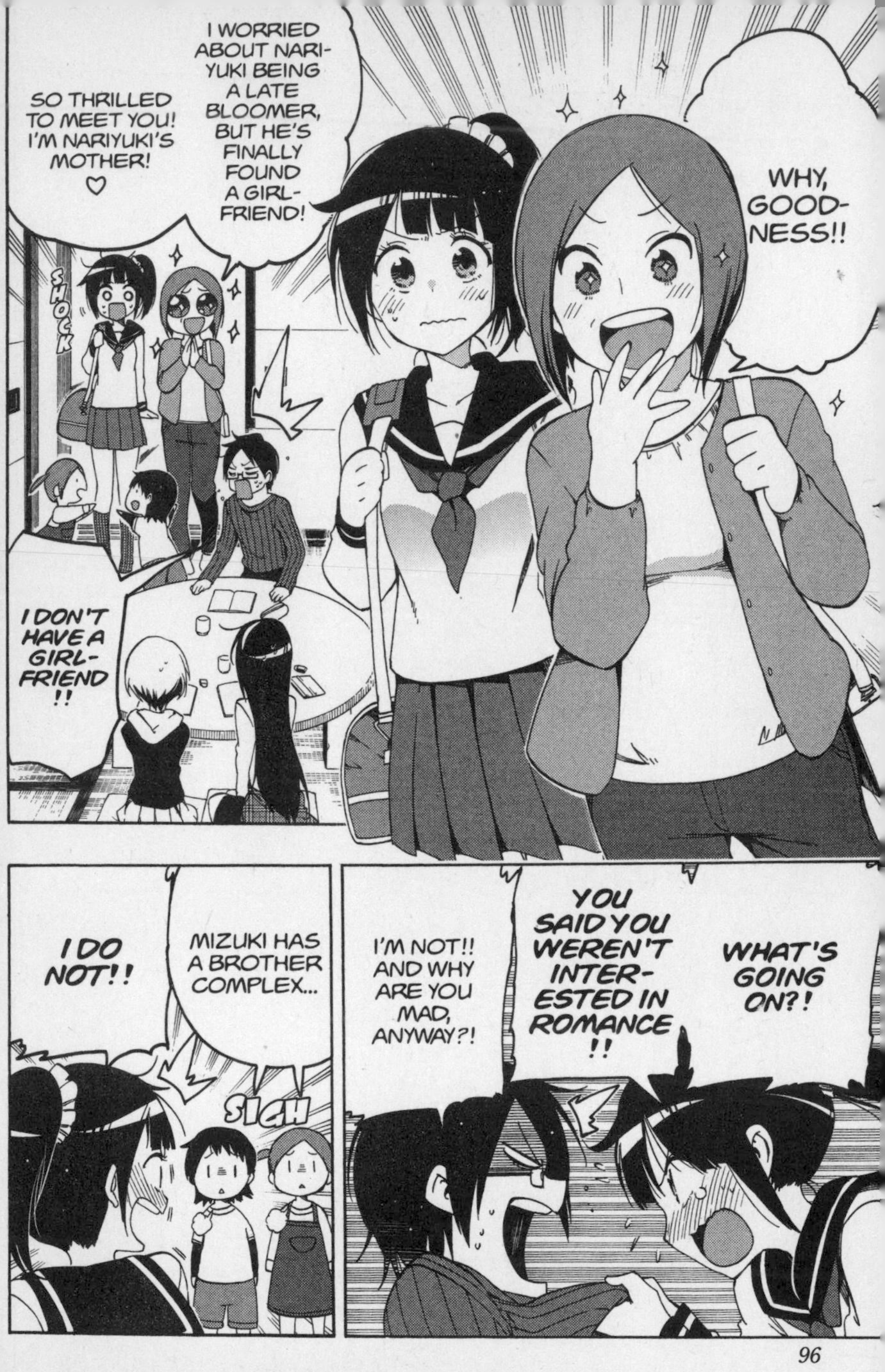
WHY, GOODNESS!!
I WORRIED ABOUT NARIYUKI BEING A LATE BLOOMER, BUT HE'S FINALLY FOUND A GIRLFRIEND!
SO THRILLED TO MEET YOU! I'M NARIYUKI'S MOTHER! ♡
SHOCK
I DON'T HAVE A GIRLFRIEND!!
WHAT'S GOING ON?!
YOU SAID YOU WEREN'T INTERESTED IN ROMANCE!!
I'M NOT!! AND WHY ARE YOU MAD, ANYWAY?!
MIZUKI HAS A BROTHER COMPLEX...
SIGH
I DO NOT!!

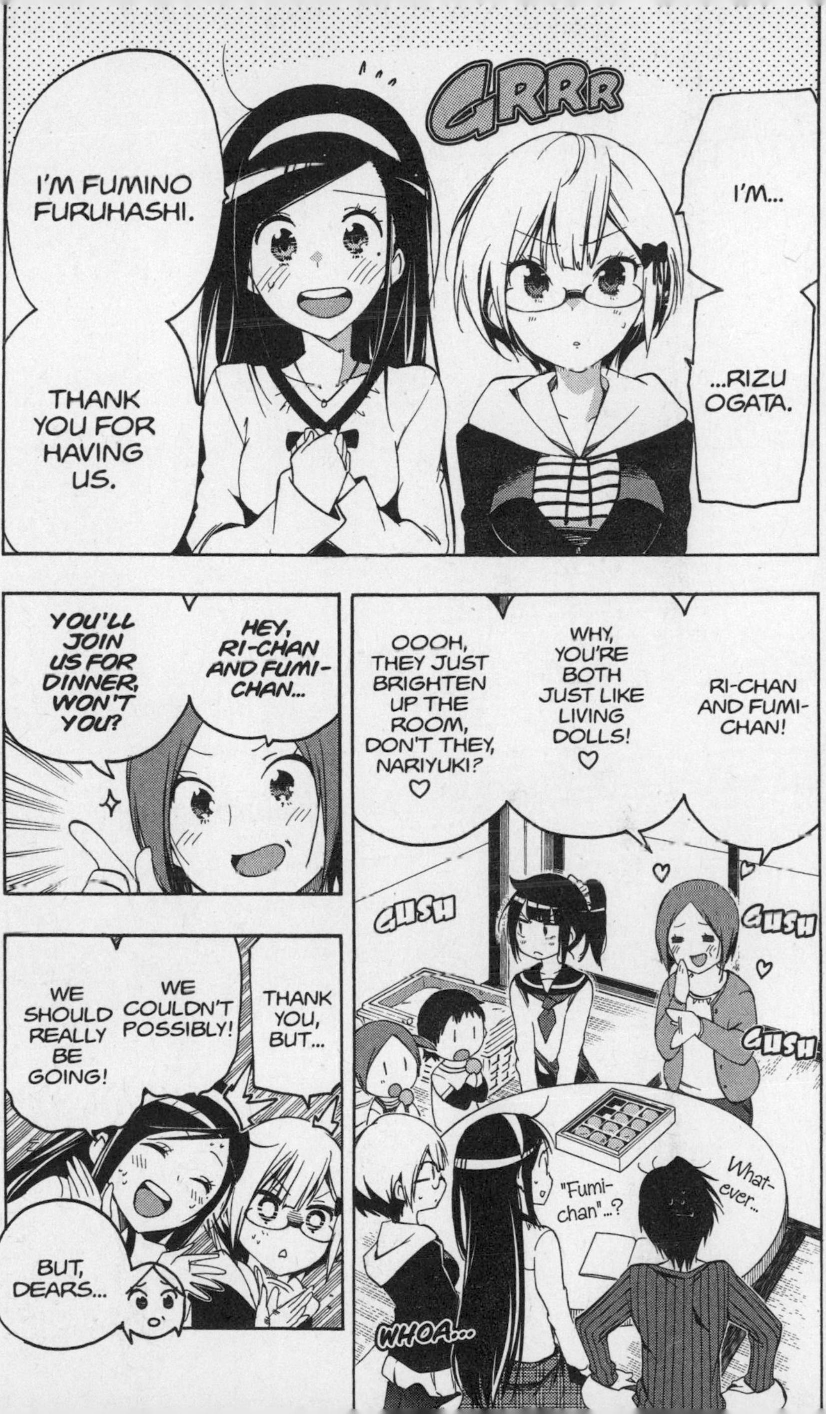
I'M...
...RIZU OGATA.
GRRR
I'M FUMINO FURUHASHI.
THANK YOU FOR HAVING US.
RI-CHAN AND FUMI-CHAN!
WHY, YOU'RE BOTH JUST LIKE LIVING DOLLS! ♡
OOOH, THEY JUST BRIGHTEN UP THE ROOM, DON'T THEY, NARIYUKI? ♡
GUSH
GUSH
GUSH
What-ever...
"Fumi-chan"...?
WHOA...
HEY, RI-CHAN AND FUMI-CHAN...
YOU'LL JOIN US FOR DINNER, WON'T YOU?
THANK YOU, BUT...
WE COULDN'T POSSIBLY!
WE SHOULD REALLY BE GOING!
BUT, DEARS...

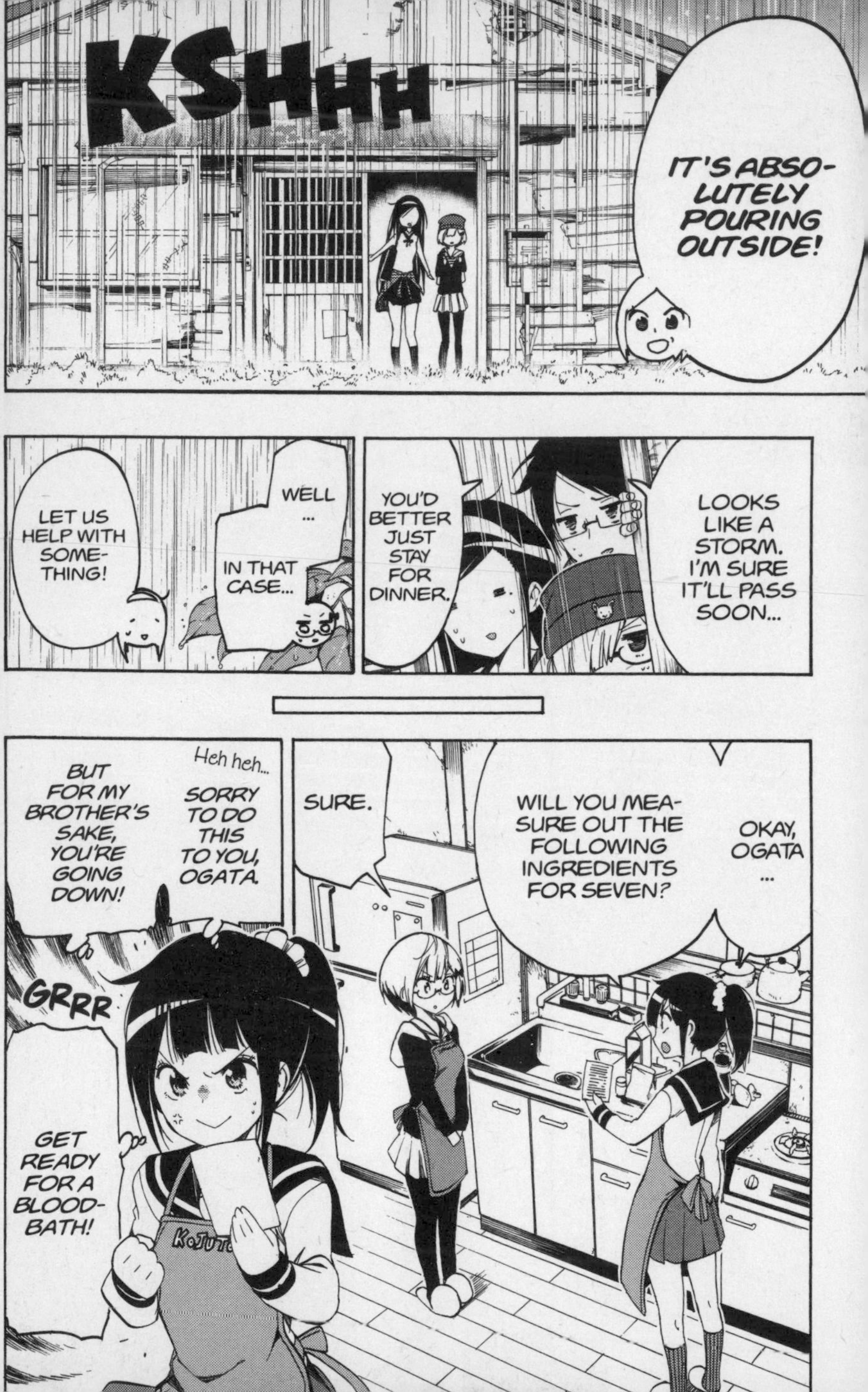
IT'S ABSOLUTELY POURING OUTSIDE!
KSHHH
LOOKS LIKE A STORM. I'M SURE IT'LL PASS SOON...
YOU'D BETTER JUST STAY FOR DINNER.
WELL... IN THAT CASE...
LET US HELP WITH SOMETHING!
OKAY, OGATA...
WILL YOU MEASURE OUT THE FOLLOWING INGREDIENTS FOR SEVEN?
SURE.
Heh heh...
SORRY TO DO THIS TO YOU, OGATA.
BUT FOR MY BROTHER'S SAKE, YOU'RE GOING DOWN!
GRRR
GET READY FOR A BLOODBATH!

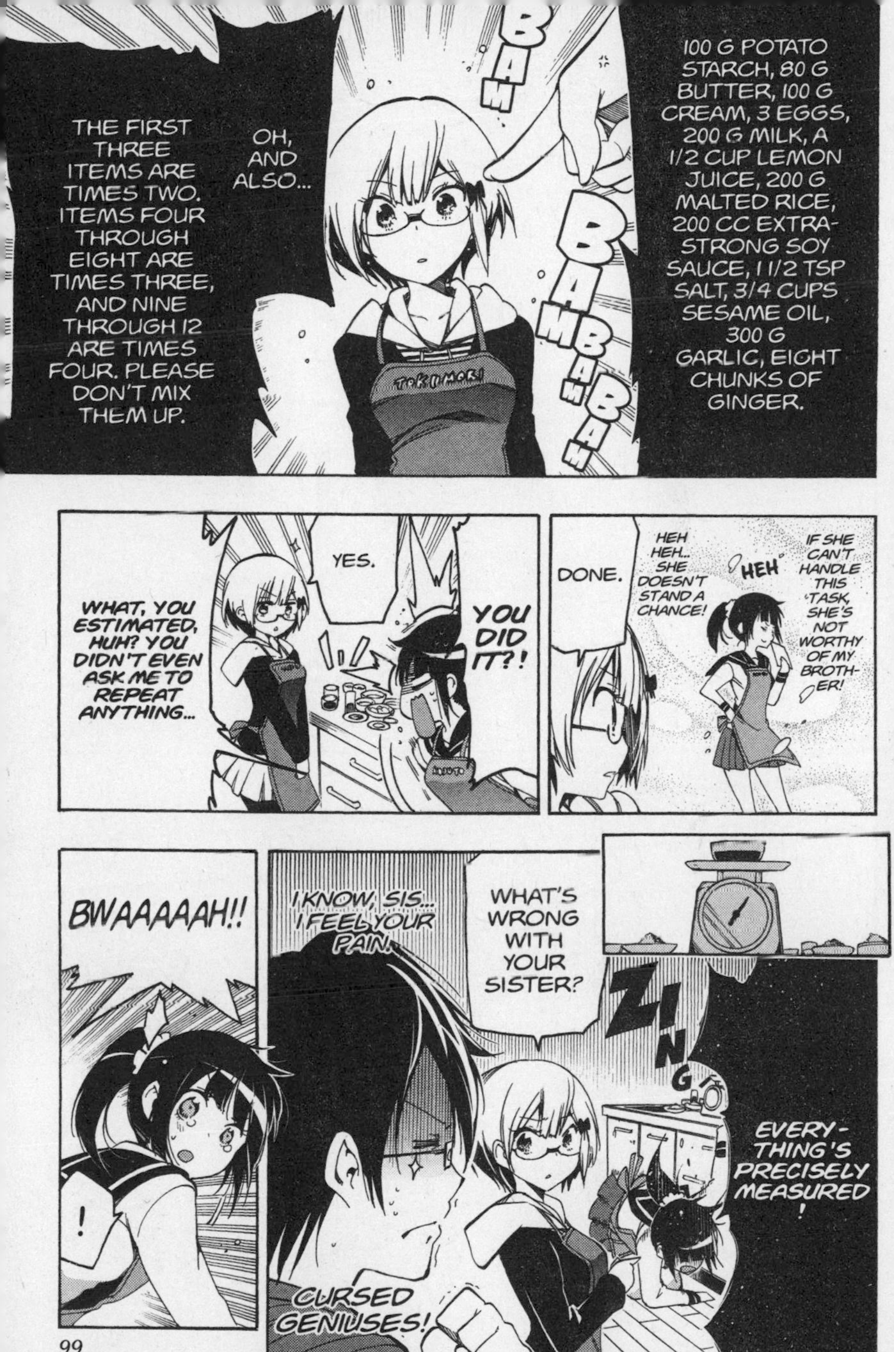
100 G POTATO STARCH, 80 G BUTTER, 100 G CREAM, 3 EGGS, 200 G MILK, A 1/2 CUP LEMON JUICE, 200 G MALTED RICE, 200 CC EXTRA-STRONG SOY SAUCE, 1 1/2 TSP SALT, 3/4 CUPS SESAME OIL, 300 G GARLIC, EIGHT CHUNKS OF GINGER.
BAM
BAM
BAM
BAM
OH, AND ALSO...
THE FIRST THREE ITEMS ARE TIMES TWO. ITEMS FOUR THROUGH EIGHT ARE TIMES THREE, AND NINE THROUGH 12 ARE TIMES FOUR. PLEASE DON'T MIX THEM UP.
IF SHE CAN'T HANDLE THIS TASK, SHE'S NOT WORTHY OF MY BROTHER!
HEH
HEH HEH... SHE DOESN'T STAND A CHANCE!
DONE.
YOU DID IT?!
YES.
WHAT, YOU ESTIMATED, HUH? YOU DIDN'T EVEN ASK ME TO REPEAT ANYTHING...
ZING
WHAT'S WRONG WITH YOUR SISTER?
I KNOW, SIS... I FEEL YOUR PAIN.
EVERY-THING'S PRECISELY MEASURED!
CURSED GENIUSES!
BWAAAAAH!!
!

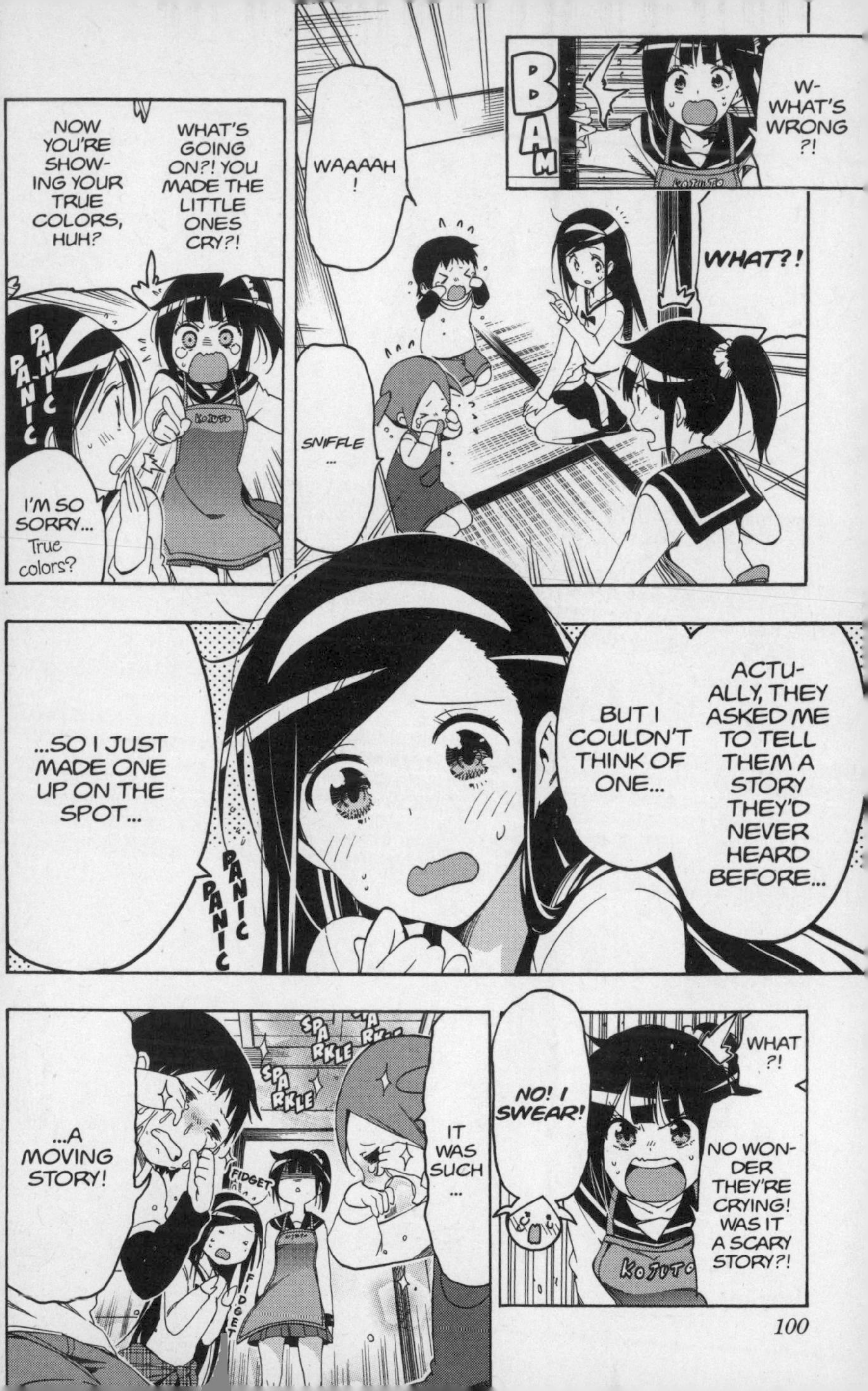
BAM
W- WHAT'S WRONG ?!
WAAAAH !
WHAT?!
SNIFFLE ...
WHAT'S GOING ON?! YOU MADE THE LITTLE ONES CRY?!
NOW YOU'RE SHOW- ING YOUR TRUE COLORS, HUH?
PANIC PANIC
I'M SO SORRY...
True colors?
ACTU- ALLY, THEY ASKED ME TO TELL THEM A STORY THEY'D NEVER HEARD BEFORE...
BUT I COULDN'T THINK OF ONE...
...SO I JUST MADE ONE UP ON THE SPOT...
PANIC PANIC
WHAT ?!
NO WON- DER THEY'RE CRYING! WAS IT A SCARY STORY?!
NO! I SWEAR!
SPARKLE SPARKLE
IT WAS SUCH ...
SPARKLE
...A MOVING STORY!
FIDGET
FIDGET

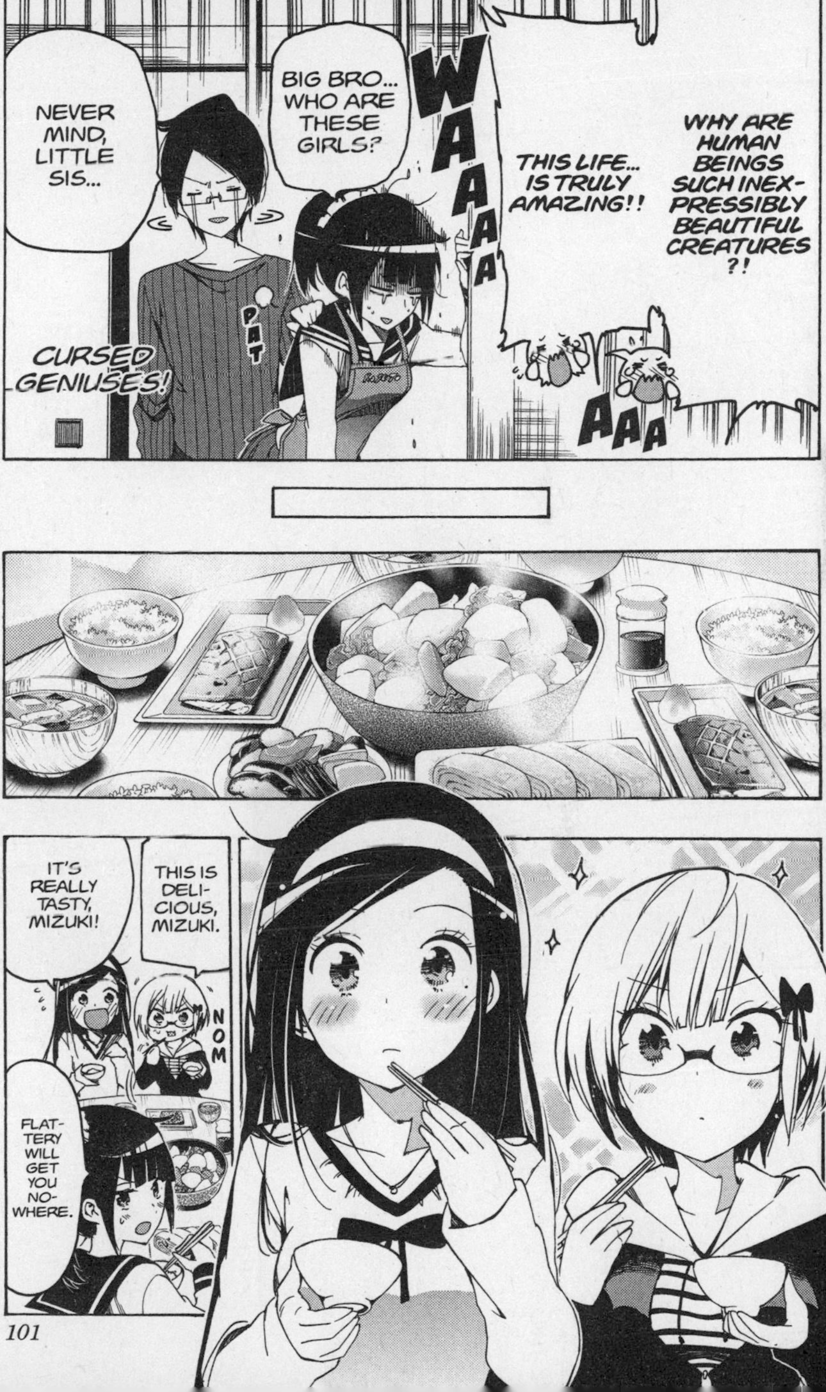
WHY ARE HUMAN BEINGS SUCH INEXPRESSIBLY BEAUTIFUL CREATURES?!
THIS LIFE... IS TRULY AMAZING!!
WAAAAAAAA
BIG BRO... WHO ARE THESE GIRLS?
NEVER MIND, LITTLE SIS...
PAT
CURSED GENIUSES!
THIS IS DELICIOUS, MIZUKI.
IT'S REALLY TASTY, MIZUKI!
NOM
FLATTERY WILL GET YOU NOWHERE.

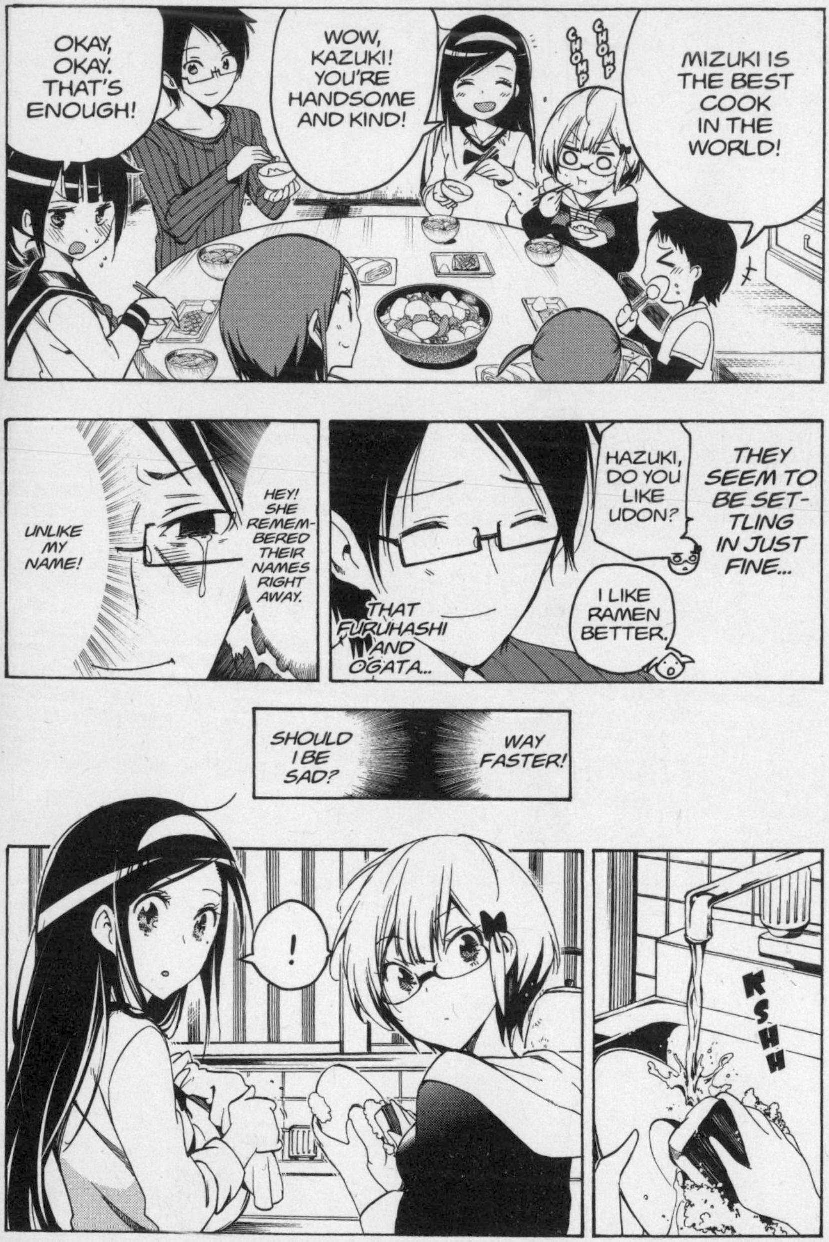
MIZUKI IS THE BEST COOK IN THE WORLD!
CHOMP CHOMP
WOW, KAZUKI! YOU'RE HANDSOME AND KIND!
OKAY, OKAY. THAT'S ENOUGH!
THEY SEEM TO BE SET-TLING IN JUST FINE...
HAZUKI, DO YOU LIKE UDON?
I LIKE RAMEN BETTER.
THAT FURUHASHI AND OGATA...
HEY! SHE REMEM-BERED THEIR NAMES RIGHT AWAY.
UNLIKE MY NAME!
WAY FASTER!
SHOULD I BE SAD?
KSHH
!

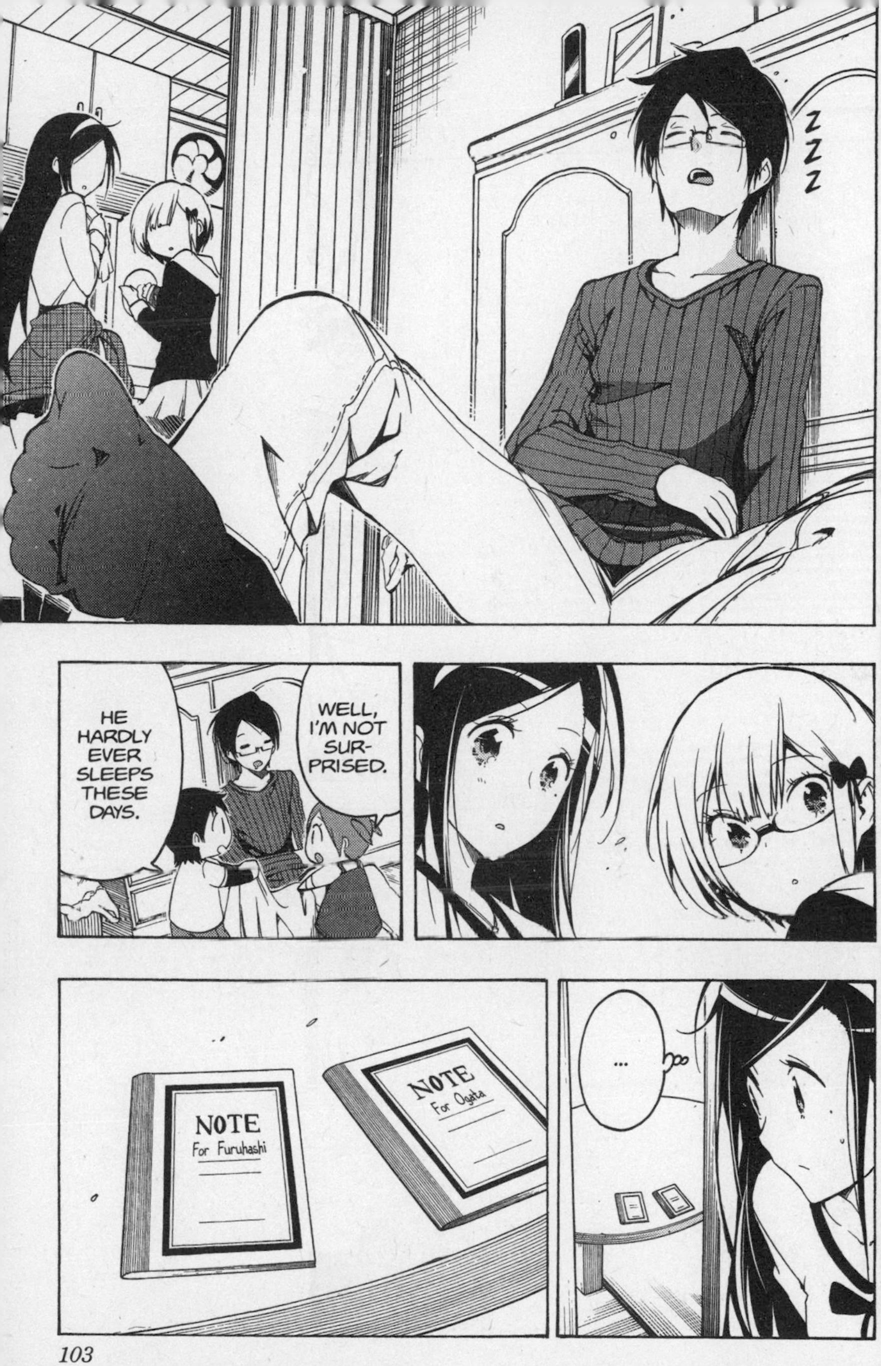
ZZZ
WELL, I'M NOT SUR-PRISED.
HE HARDLY EVER SLEEPS THESE DAYS.
...
NOTE For Ogata
NOTE For Furuhashi

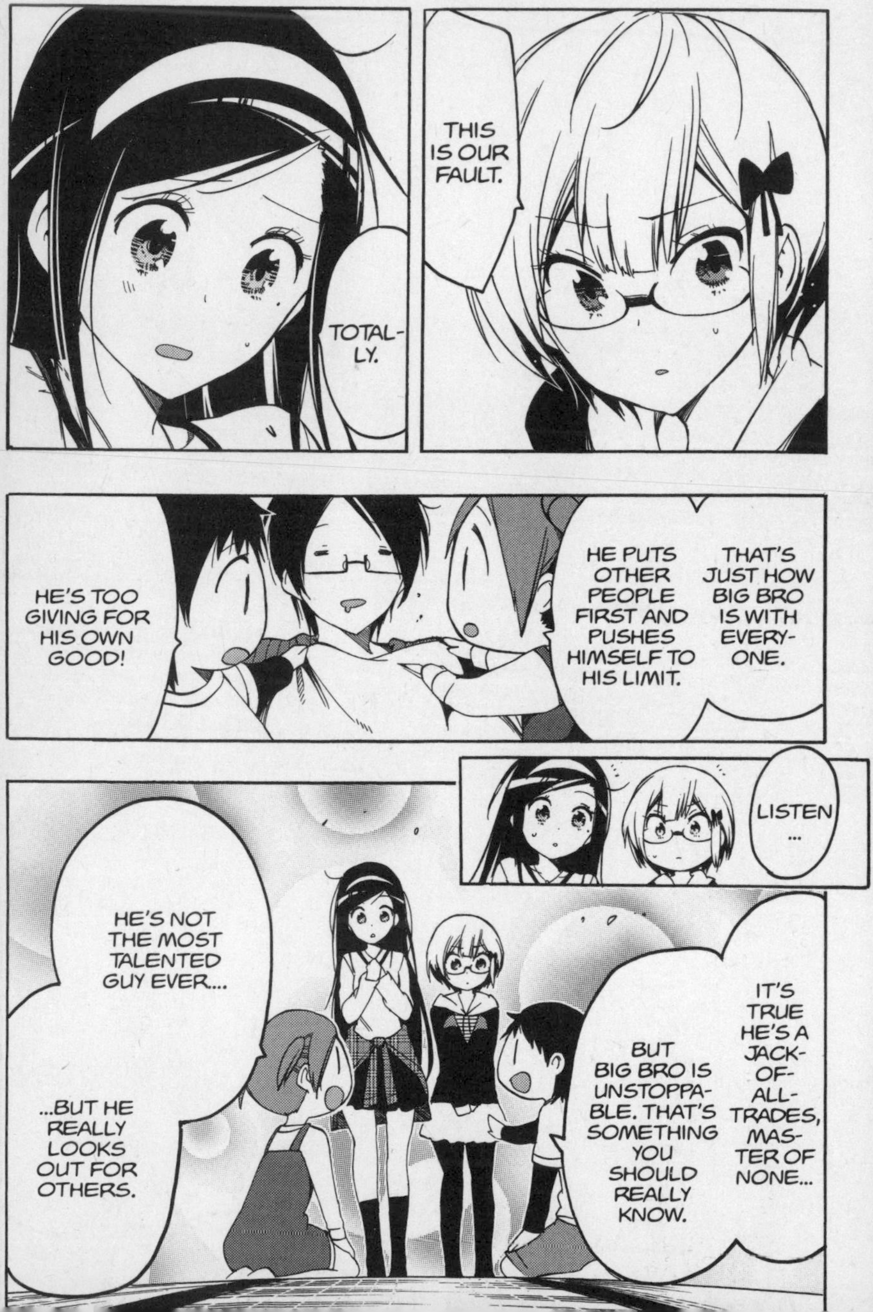
THIS IS OUR FAULT.
TOTAL-LY.
THAT'S JUST HOW BIG BRO IS WITH EVERY-ONE.
HE PUTS OTHER PEOPLE FIRST AND PUSHES HIMSELF TO HIS LIMIT.
HE'S TOO GIVING FOR HIS OWN GOOD!
LISTEN ...
IT'S TRUE HE'S A JACK-OF-ALL-TRADES, MAS-TER OF NONE...
BUT BIG BRO IS UNSTOPPA-BLE. THAT'S SOMETHING YOU SHOULD REALLY KNOW.
HE'S NOT THE MOST TALENTED GUY EVER....
...BUT HE REALLY LOOKS OUT FOR OTHERS.

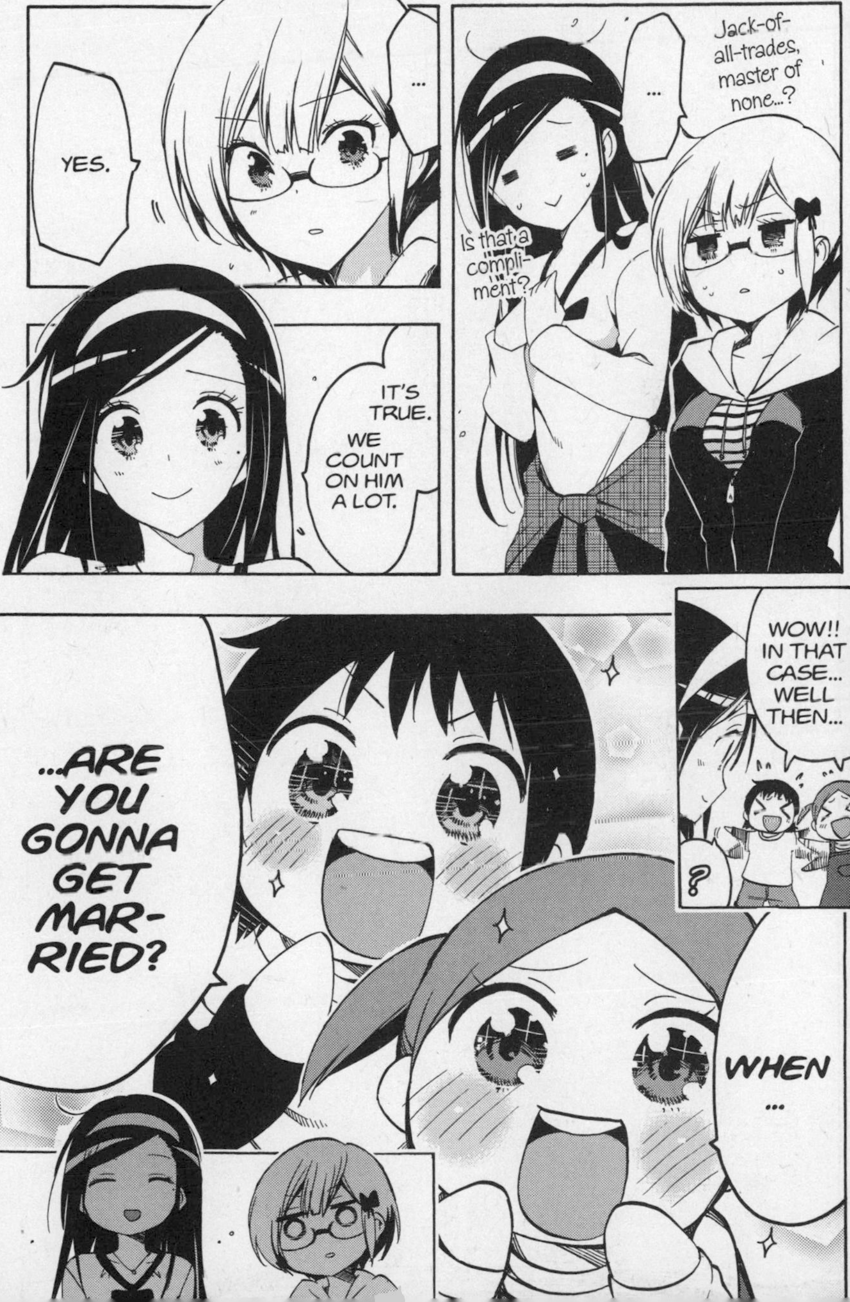
Jack-of-all-trades, master of none...?
...
Is that a compliment?
...
YES.
IT'S TRUE. WE COUNT ON HIM A LOT.
WOW!! IN THAT CASE... WELL THEN...
?
WHEN ...
...ARE YOU GONNA GET MARRIED?

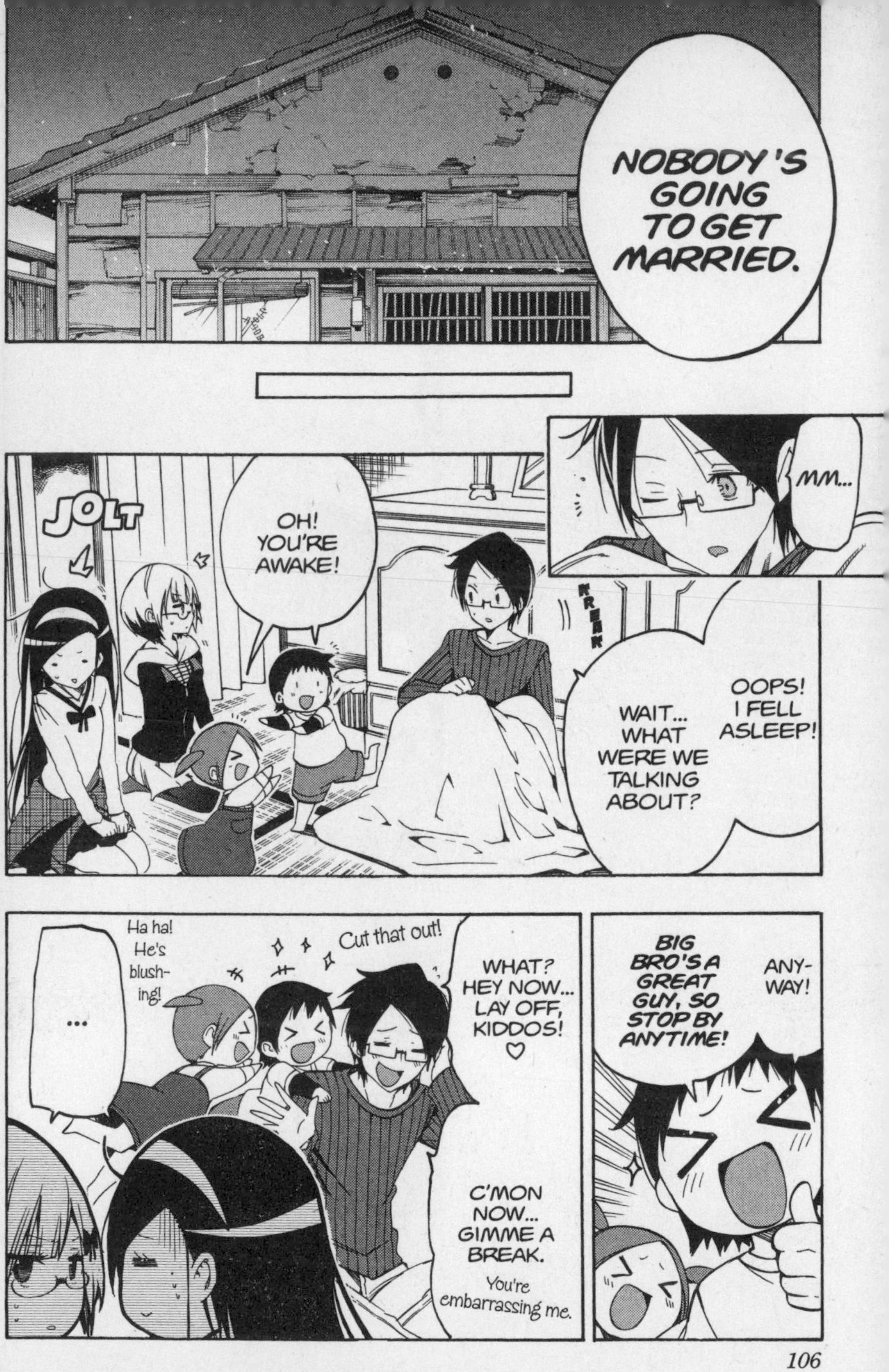
NOBODY'S GOING TO GET MARRIED.
MM...
OOPS! I FELL ASLEEP!
WAIT... WHAT WERE WE TALKING ABOUT?
OH! YOU'RE AWAKE!
JOLT
ANY-WAY!
BIG BRO'S A GREAT GUY, SO STOP BY ANYTIME!
WHAT? HEY NOW... LAY OFF, KIDDOS! ♡
Cut that out!
Ha ha! He's blush-ing!
...
C'MON NOW... GIMME A BREAK.
You're embarrassing me.

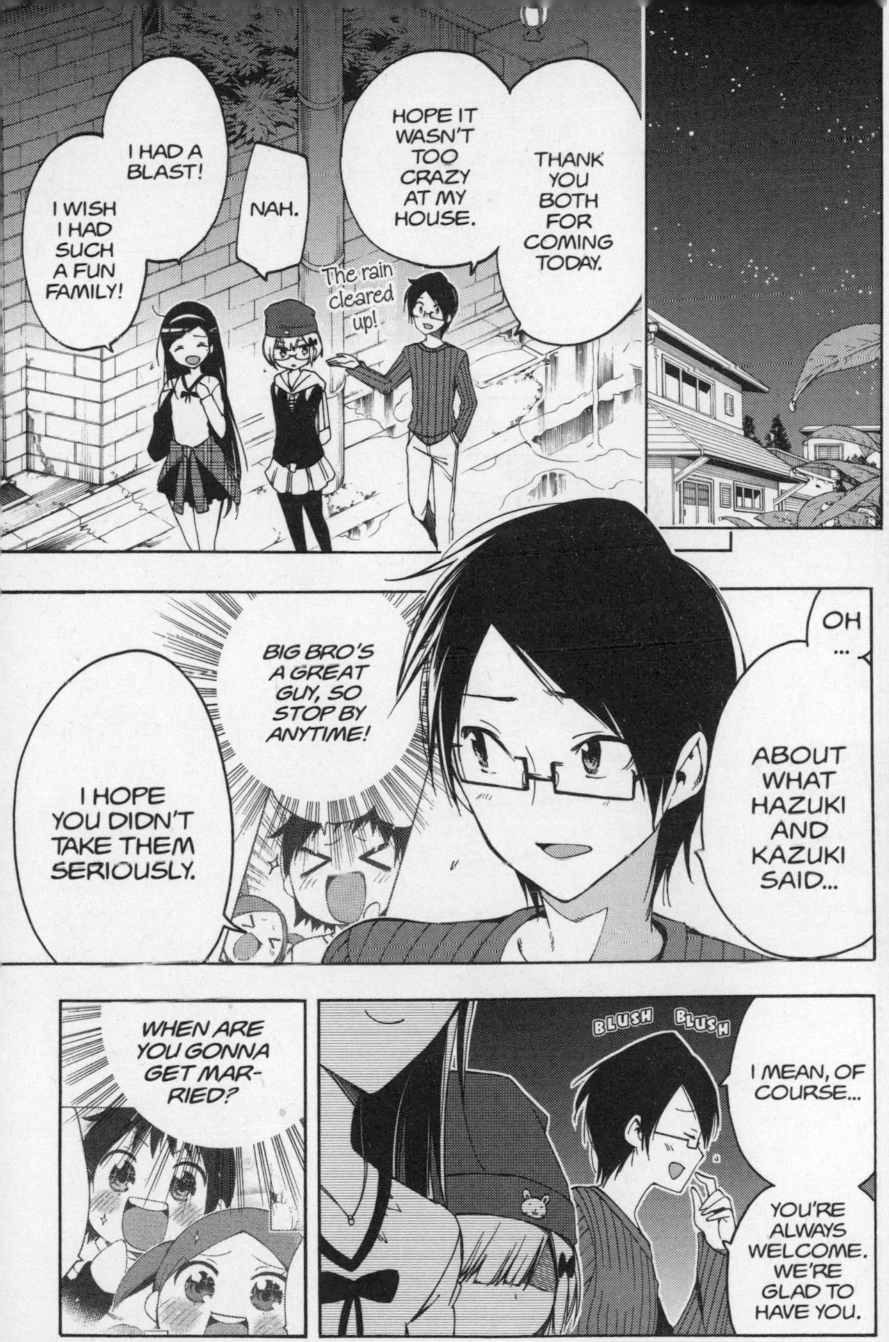
THANK YOU BOTH FOR COMING TODAY.
HOPE IT WASN'T TOO CRAZY AT MY HOUSE.
The rain cleared up!
NAH.
I HAD A BLAST!
I WISH I HAD SUCH A FUN FAMILY!
OH ...
ABOUT WHAT HAZUKI AND KAZUKI SAID...
BIG BRO'S A GREAT GUY, SO STOP BY ANYTIME!
I HOPE YOU DIDN'T TAKE THEM SERIOUSLY.
BLUSH BLUSH
I MEAN, OF COURSE...
YOU'RE ALWAYS WELCOME. WE'RE GLAD TO HAVE YOU.
WHEN ARE YOU GONNA GET MAR-RIED?

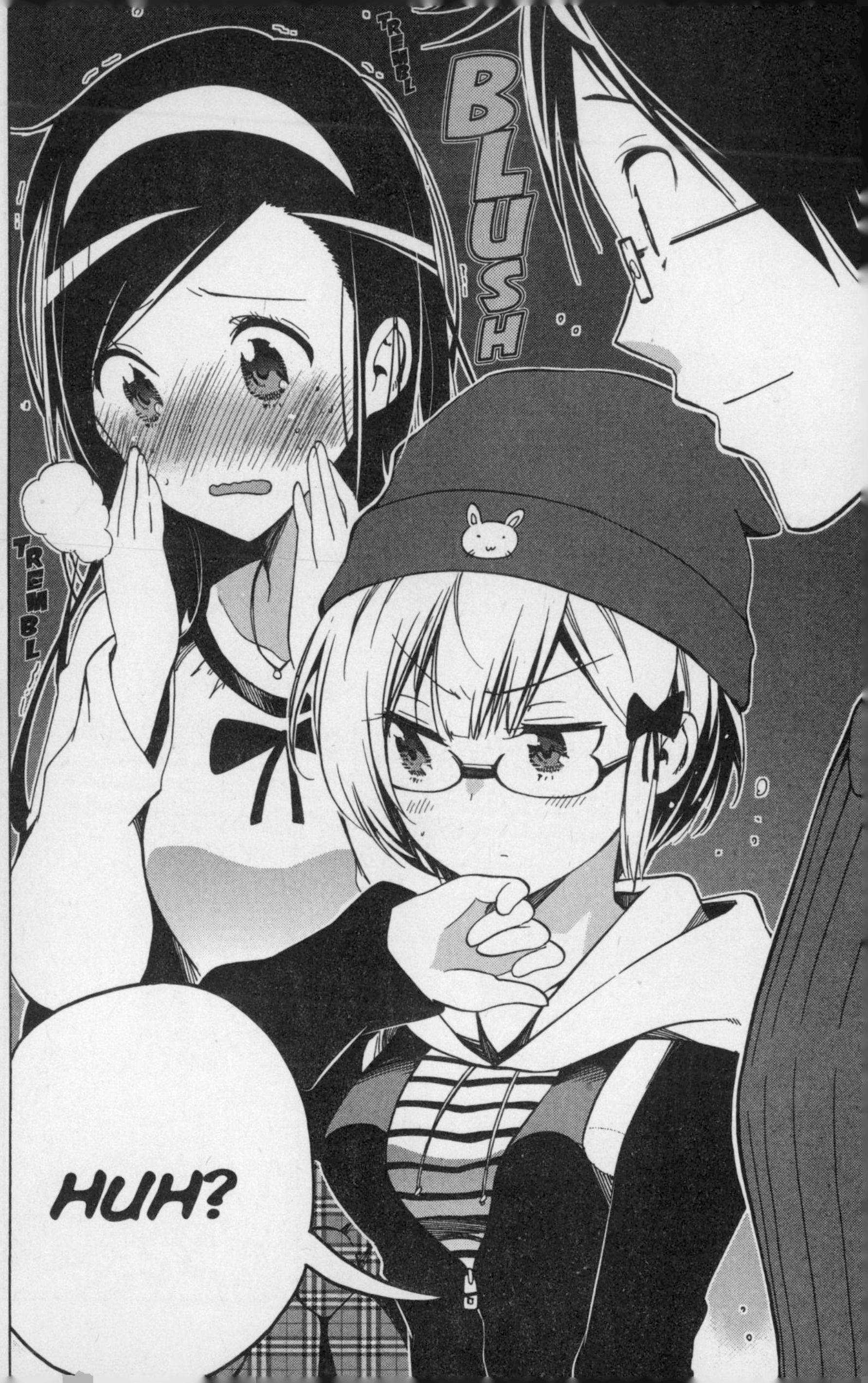
BLUSH
TREMBL
TREMBL
HUH?

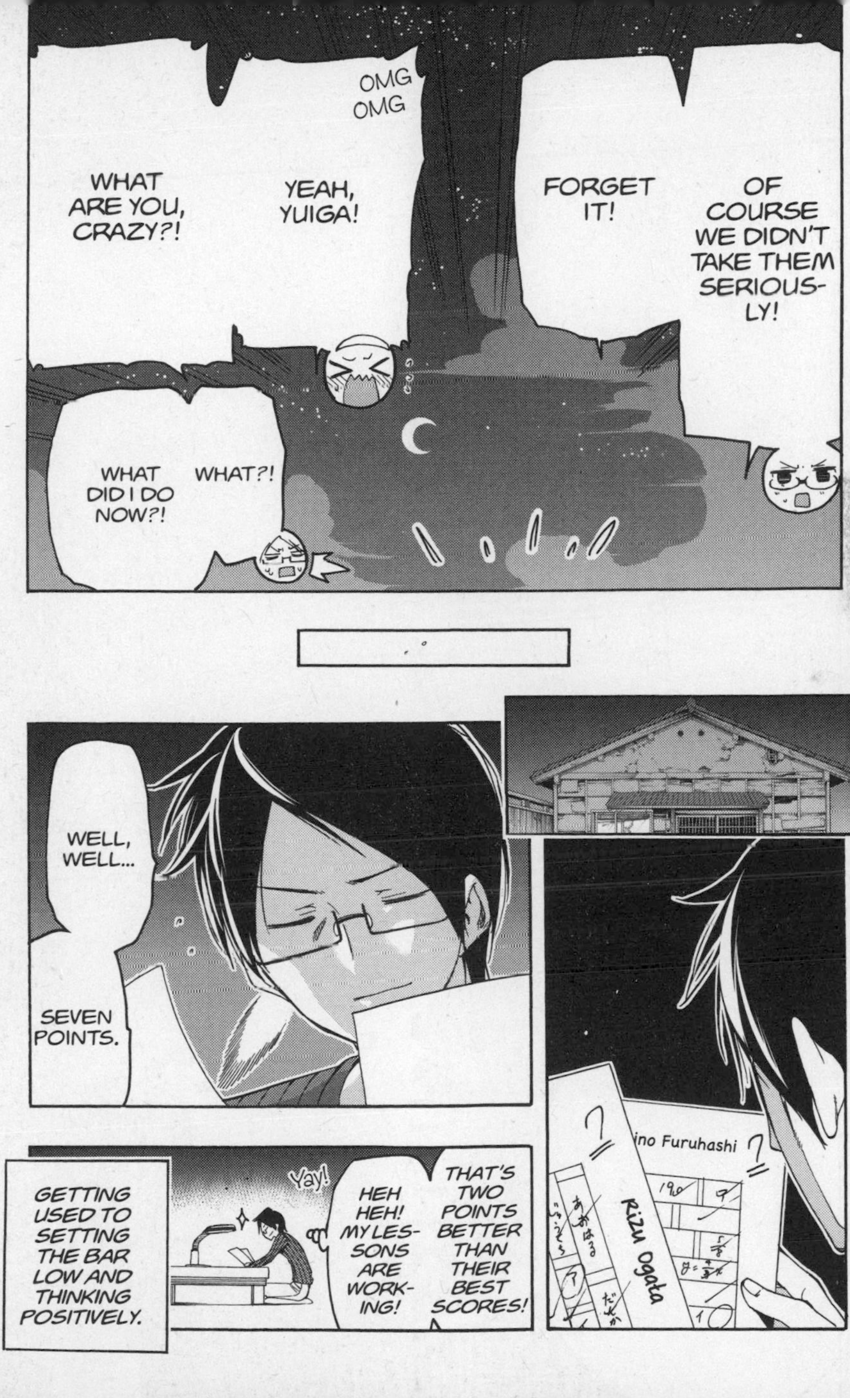
OF COURSE WE DIDN'T TAKE THEM SERIOUS-LY!
FORGET IT!
OMG OMG
YEAH, YUIGA!
WHAT ARE YOU, CRAZY?!
WHAT?!
WHAT DID I DO NOW?!
ino Furuhashi
Rizu Ogata
WELL, WELL...
SEVEN POINTS.
THAT'S TWO POINTS BETTER THAN THEIR BEST SCORES!
HEH HEH! MY LES-SONS ARE WORK-ING!
Yay!
GETTING USED TO SETTING THE BAR LOW AND THINKING POSITIVELY.

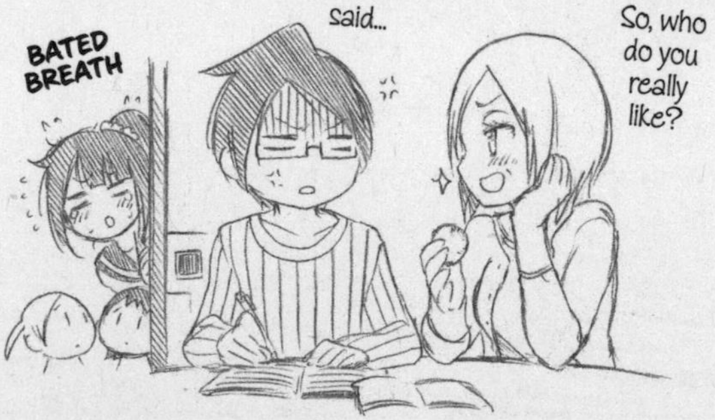
So, who do you really like?
Like I said...
BATED BREATH

Question 4:
A Fish Is to Water as a Genius Is to [X]

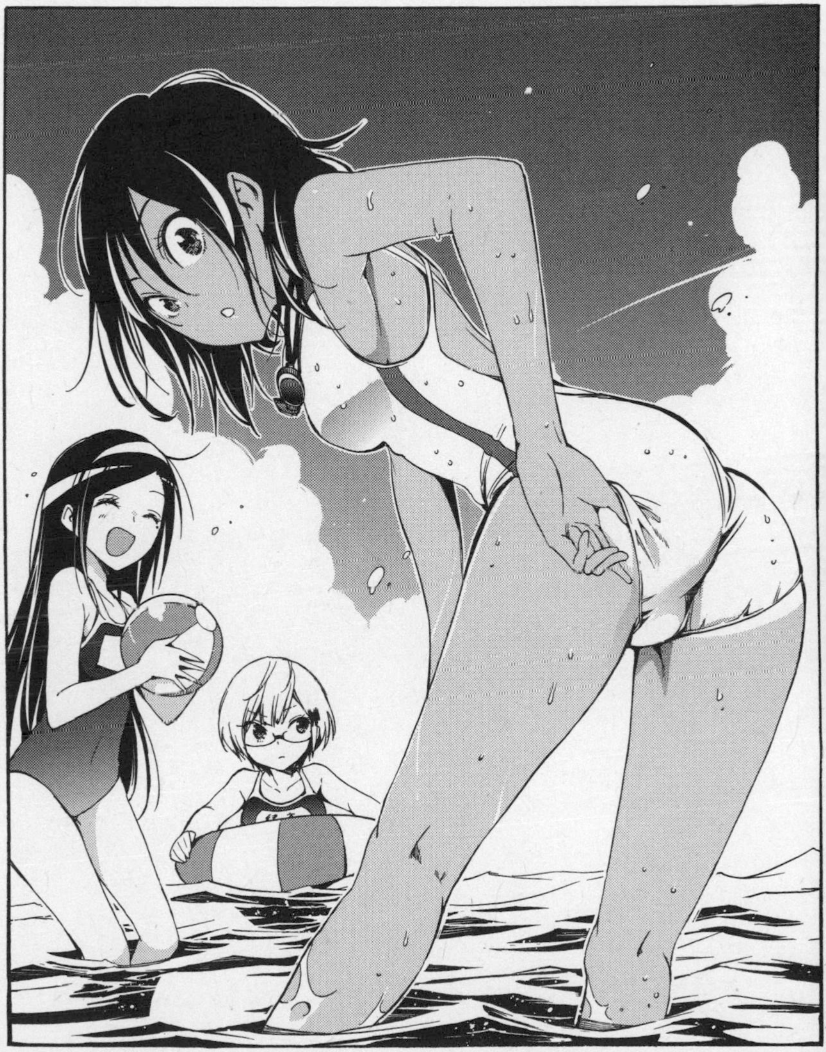

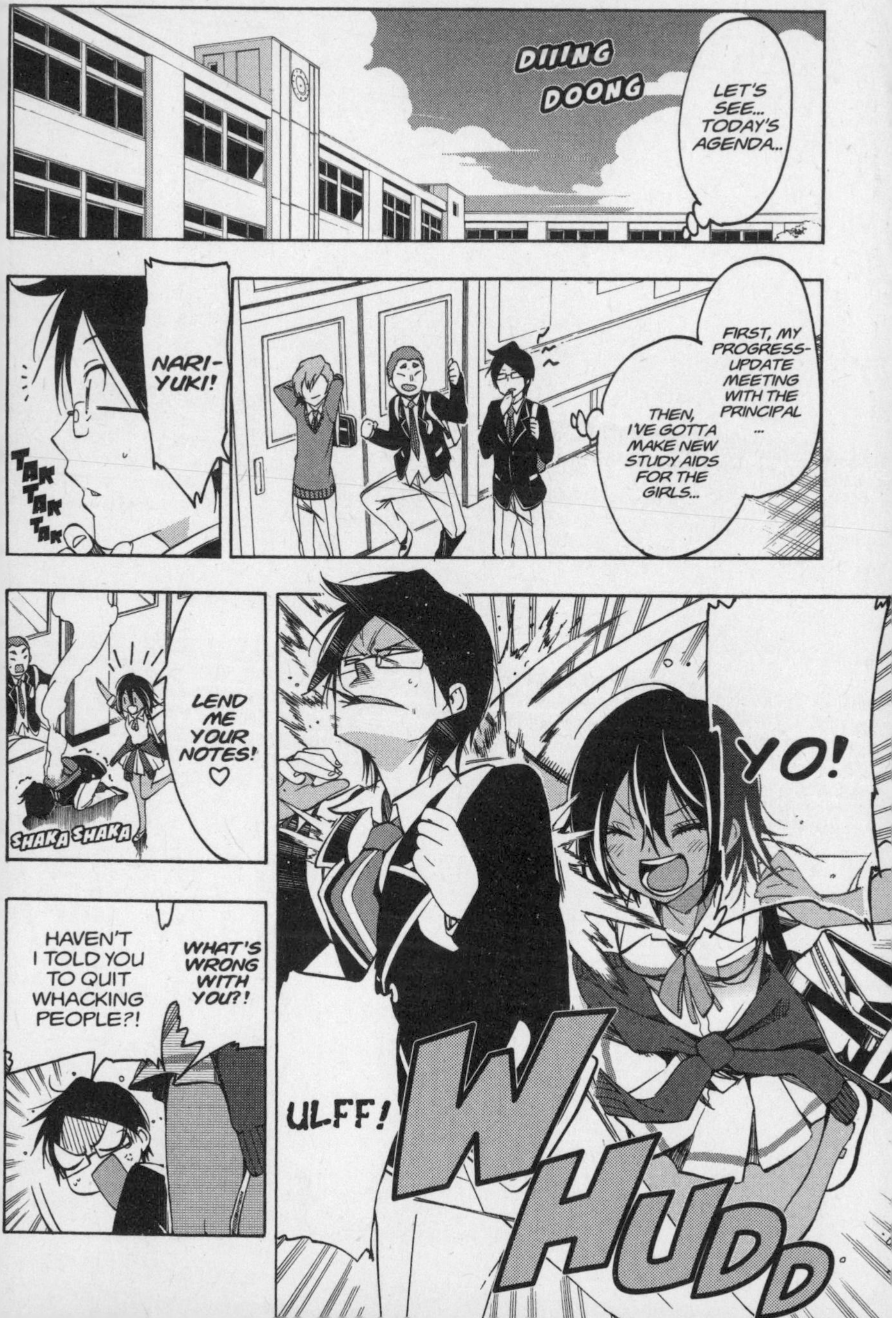
DIIING
DOONG
LET'S SEE... TODAY'S AGENDA...
FIRST, MY PROGRESS-UPDATE MEETING WITH THE PRINCIPAL ...
THEN, I'VE GOTTA MAKE NEW STUDY AIDS FOR THE GIRLS...
NARI-YUKI!
TAK TAK TAK
YO!
WHUDD
ULFF!
LEND ME YOUR NOTES! ♡
SHAKA SHAKA
WHAT'S WRONG WITH YOU?!
HAVEN'T I TOLD YOU TO QUIT WHACKING PEOPLE?!

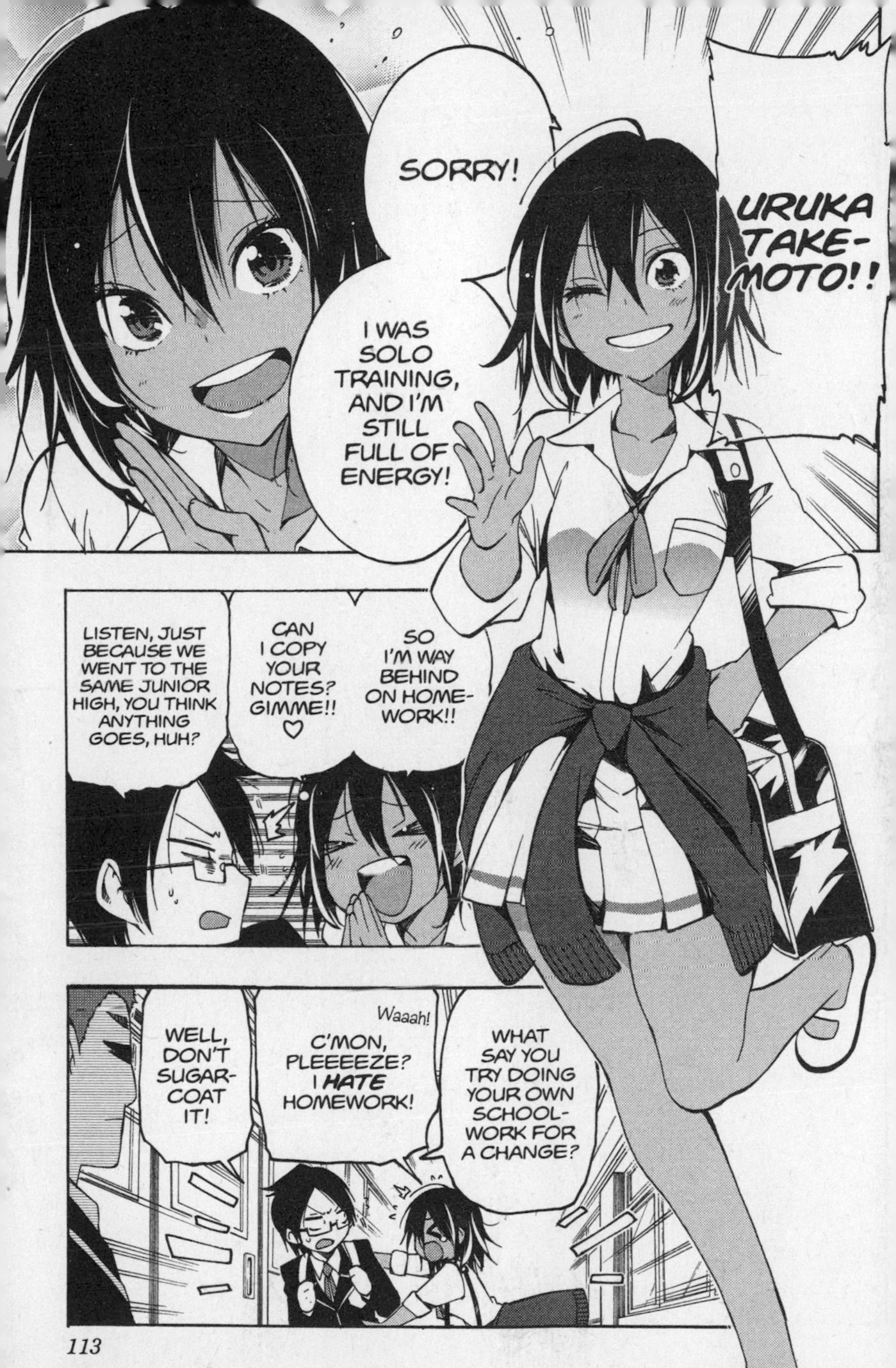
URUKA TAKE-MOTO!!
SORRY!
I WAS SOLO TRAINING, AND I'M STILL FULL OF ENERGY!
SO I'M WAY BEHIND ON HOME-WORK!!
CAN I COPY YOUR NOTES? GIMME!! ♡
LISTEN, JUST BECAUSE WE WENT TO THE SAME JUNIOR HIGH, YOU THINK ANYTHING GOES, HUH?
WHAT SAY YOU TRY DOING YOUR OWN SCHOOL-WORK FOR A CHANGE?
Waaah!
C'MON, PLEEEEZE? I ***HATE*** HOMEWORK!
WELL, DON'T SUGAR-COAT IT!

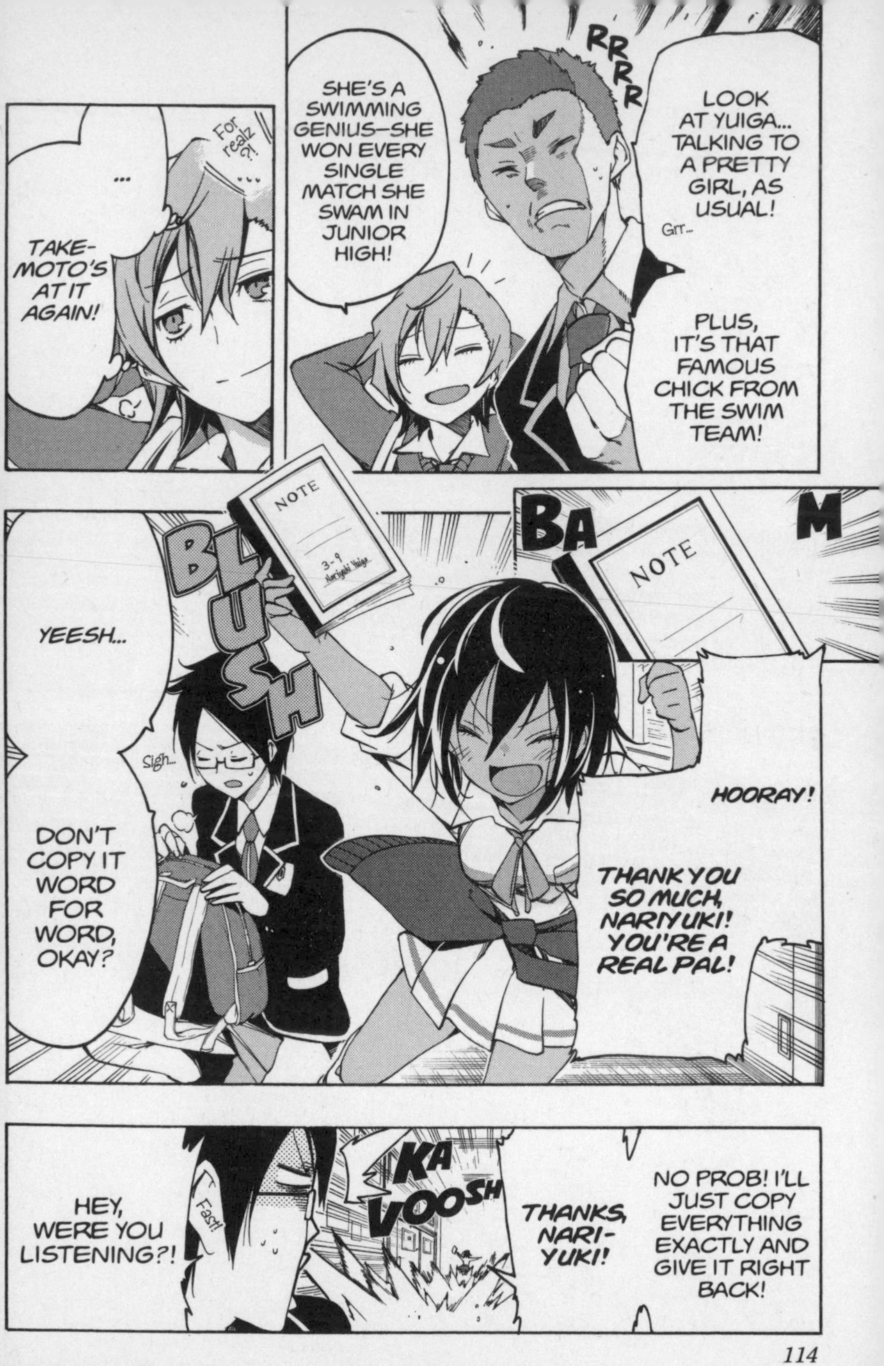
RRRR
LOOK AT YUIGA... TALKING TO A PRETTY GIRL, AS USUAL!
Grr...
PLUS, IT'S THAT FAMOUS CHICK FROM THE SWIM TEAM!
SHE'S A SWIMMING GENIUS—SHE WON EVERY SINGLE MATCH SHE SWAM IN JUNIOR HIGH!
For realz?!
...
...
TAKE-MOTO'S AT IT AGAIN!
BAM
NOTE
HOORAY!
THANK YOU SO MUCH, NARIYUKI! YOU'RE A REAL PAL!
NOTE
3-9
BLUSH
YEESH...
Sigh...
DON'T COPY IT WORD FOR WORD, OKAY?
NO PROB! I'LL JUST COPY EVERYTHING EXACTLY AND GIVE IT RIGHT BACK!
THANKS, NARI-YUKI!
KA VOOSH
Fast!
HEY, WERE YOU LISTENING?!

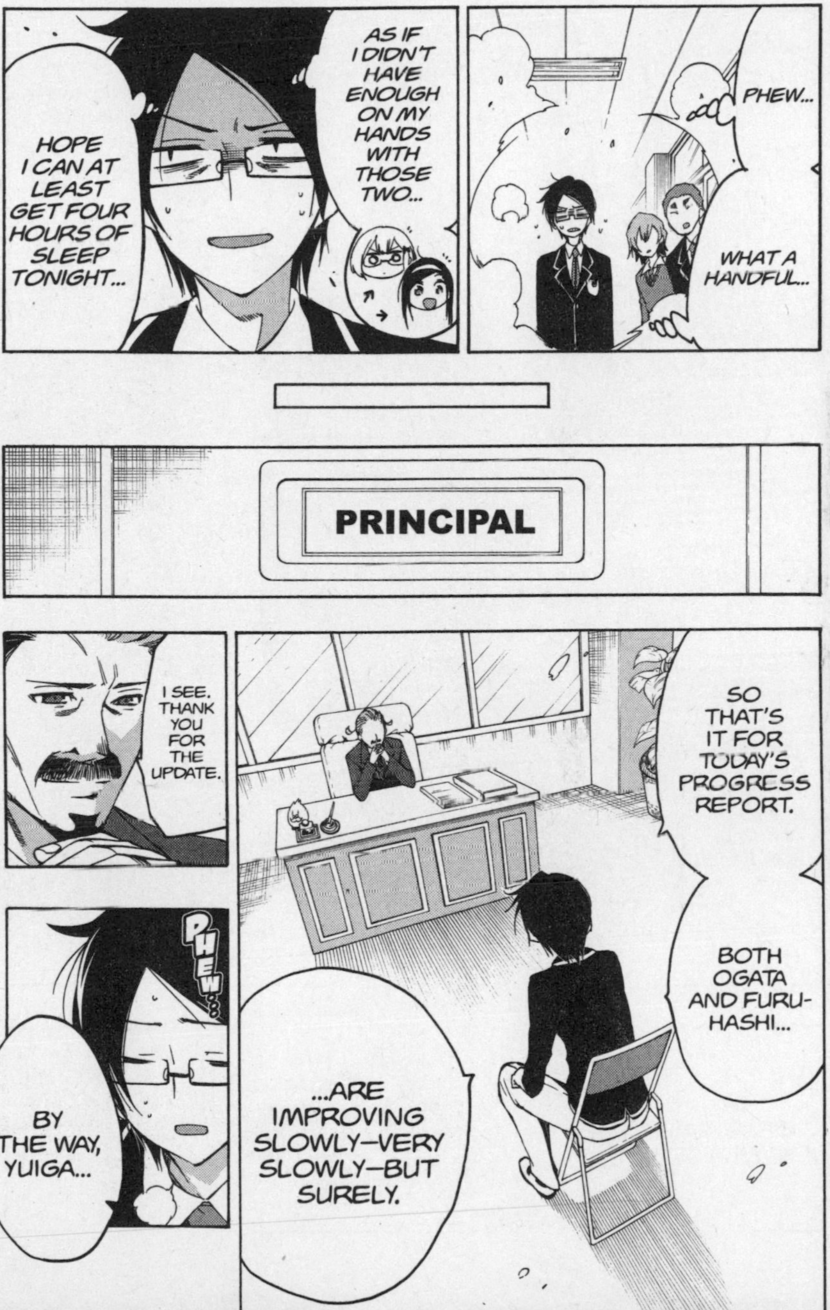
PHEW...
WHAT A HANDFUL...
AS IF I DIDN'T HAVE ENOUGH ON MY HANDS WITH THOSE TWO...
HOPE I CAN AT LEAST GET FOUR HOURS OF SLEEP TONIGHT...
PRINCIPAL
SO THAT'S IT FOR TODAY'S PROGRESS REPORT.
BOTH OGATA AND FURU-HASHI...
...ARE IMPROVING SLOWLY—VERY SLOWLY—BUT SURELY.
I SEE. THANK YOU FOR THE UPDATE.
PHEW...
BY THE WAY, YUIGA...

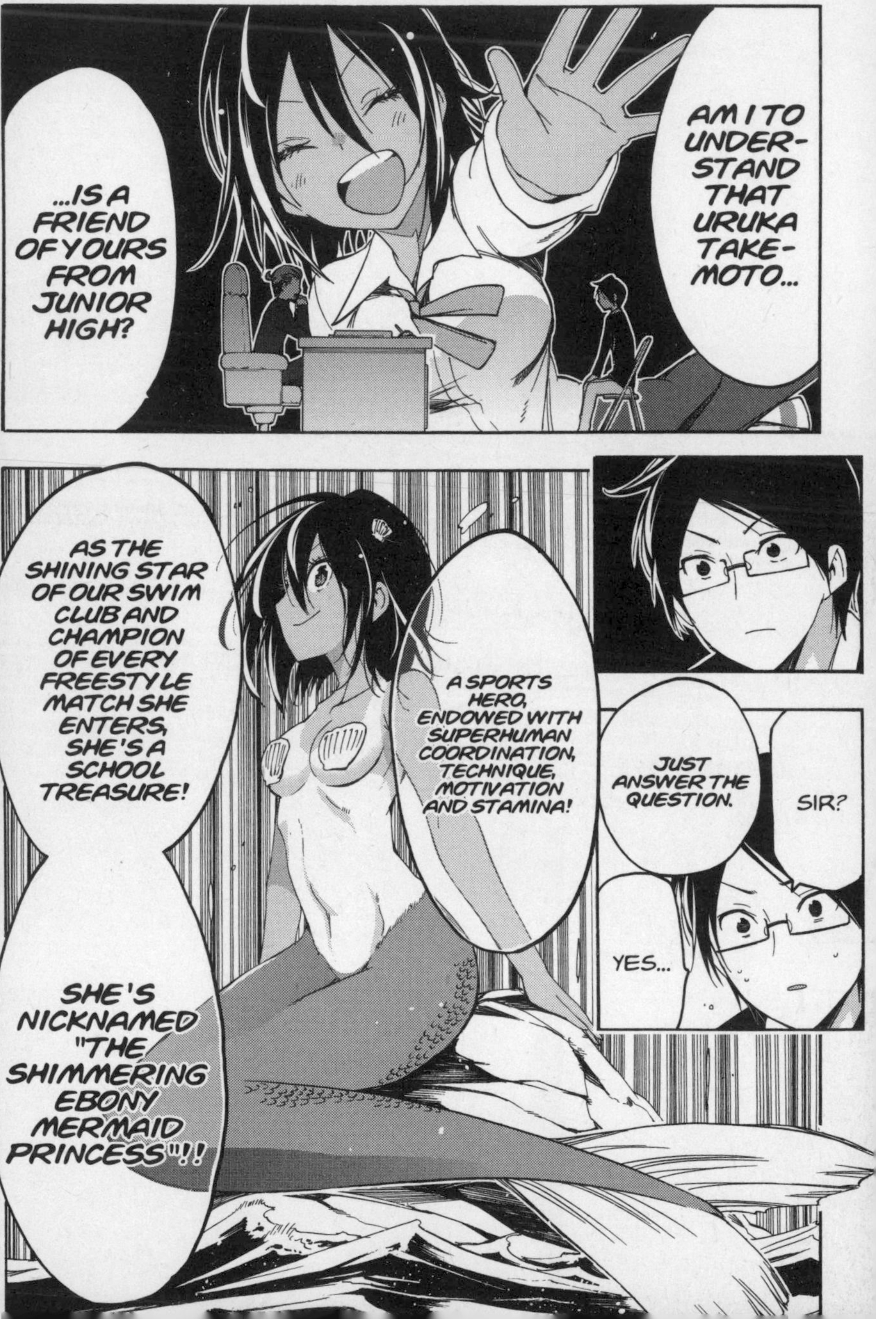
AM I TO UNDERSTAND THAT URUKA TAKEMOTO...
...IS A FRIEND OF YOURS FROM JUNIOR HIGH?
SIR?
JUST ANSWER THE QUESTION.
YES...
A SPORTS HERO, ENDOWED WITH SUPERHUMAN COORDINATION, TECHNIQUE, MOTIVATION AND STAMINA!
AS THE SHINING STAR OF OUR SWIM CLUB AND CHAMPION OF EVERY FREESTYLE MATCH SHE ENTERS, SHE'S A SCHOOL TREASURE!
SHE'S NICKNAMED "THE SHIMMERING EBONY MERMAID PRINCESS"!!

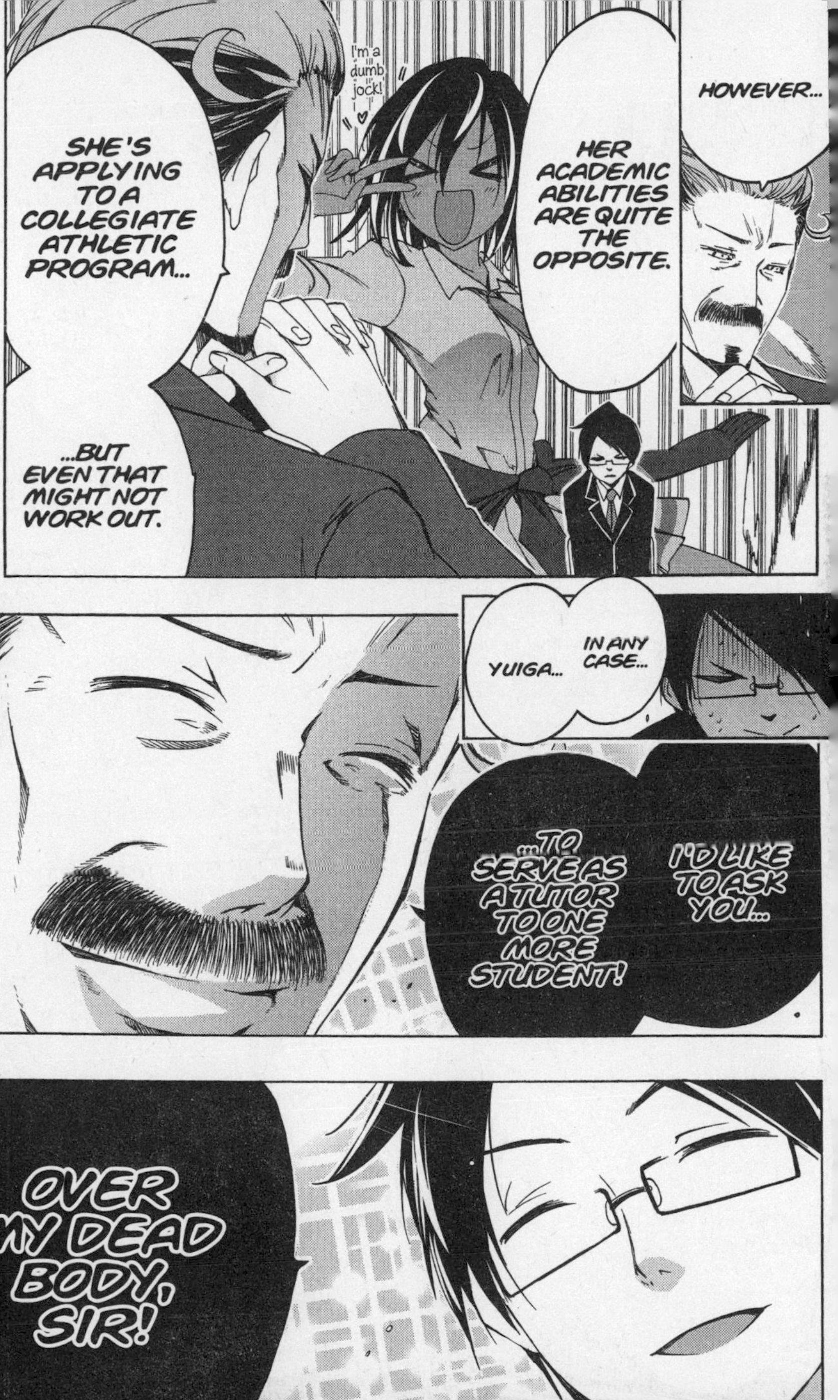
HOWEVER...
HER ACADEMIC ABILITIES ARE QUITE THE OPPOSITE.
I'm a dumb jock!
SHE'S APPLYING TO A COLLEGIATE ATHLETIC PROGRAM...
...BUT EVEN THAT MIGHT NOT WORK OUT.
IN ANY CASE...
YUIGA...
I'D LIKE TO ASK YOU...
...TO SERVE AS A TUTOR TO ONE MORE STUDENT!
OVER MY DEAD BODY, SIR!

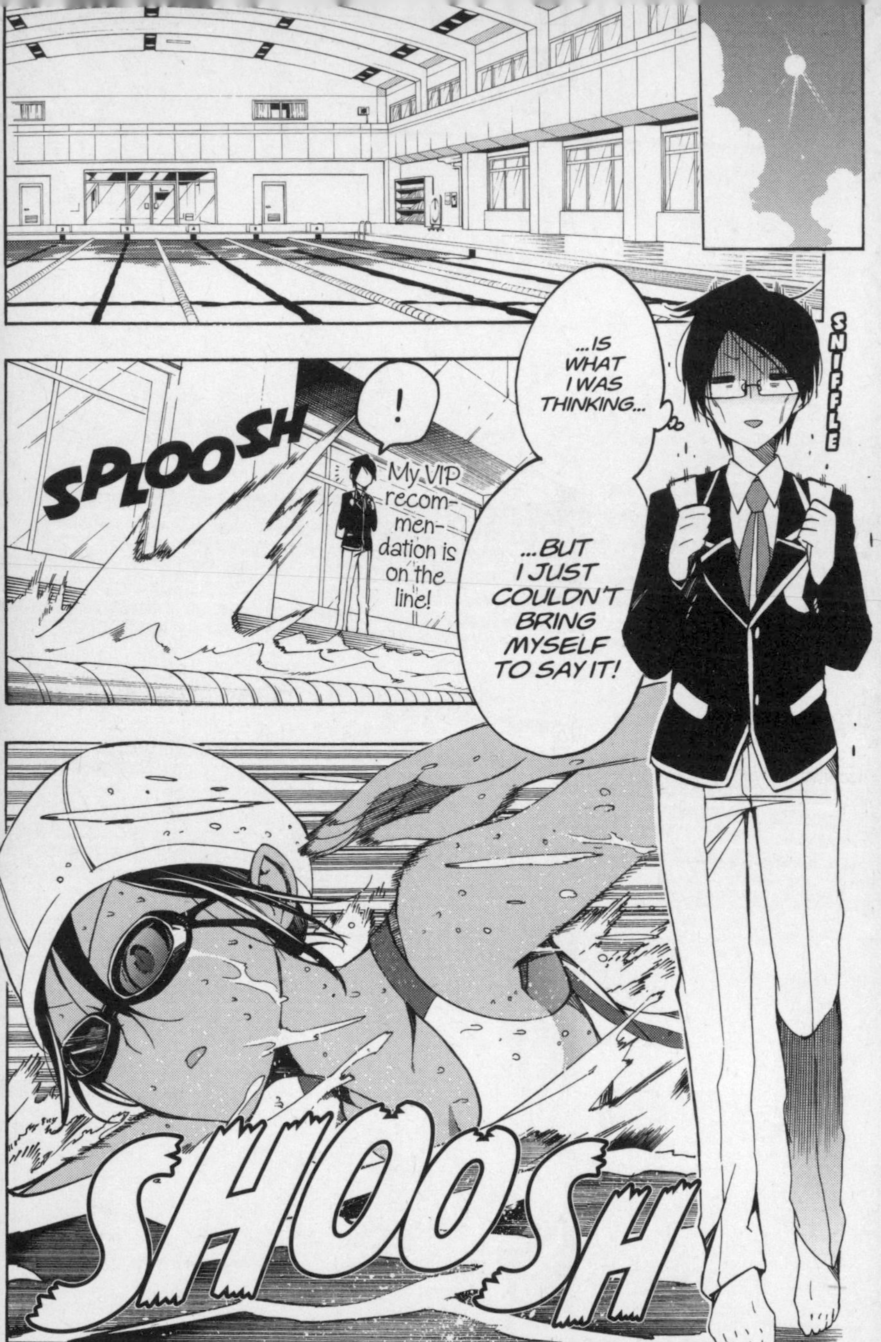

SPLOOSH
!
My VIP recommendation is on the line!
...IS WHAT I WAS THINKING...
...BUT I JUST COULDN'T BRING MYSELF TO SAY IT!
SNIFFLE
SHOOSH

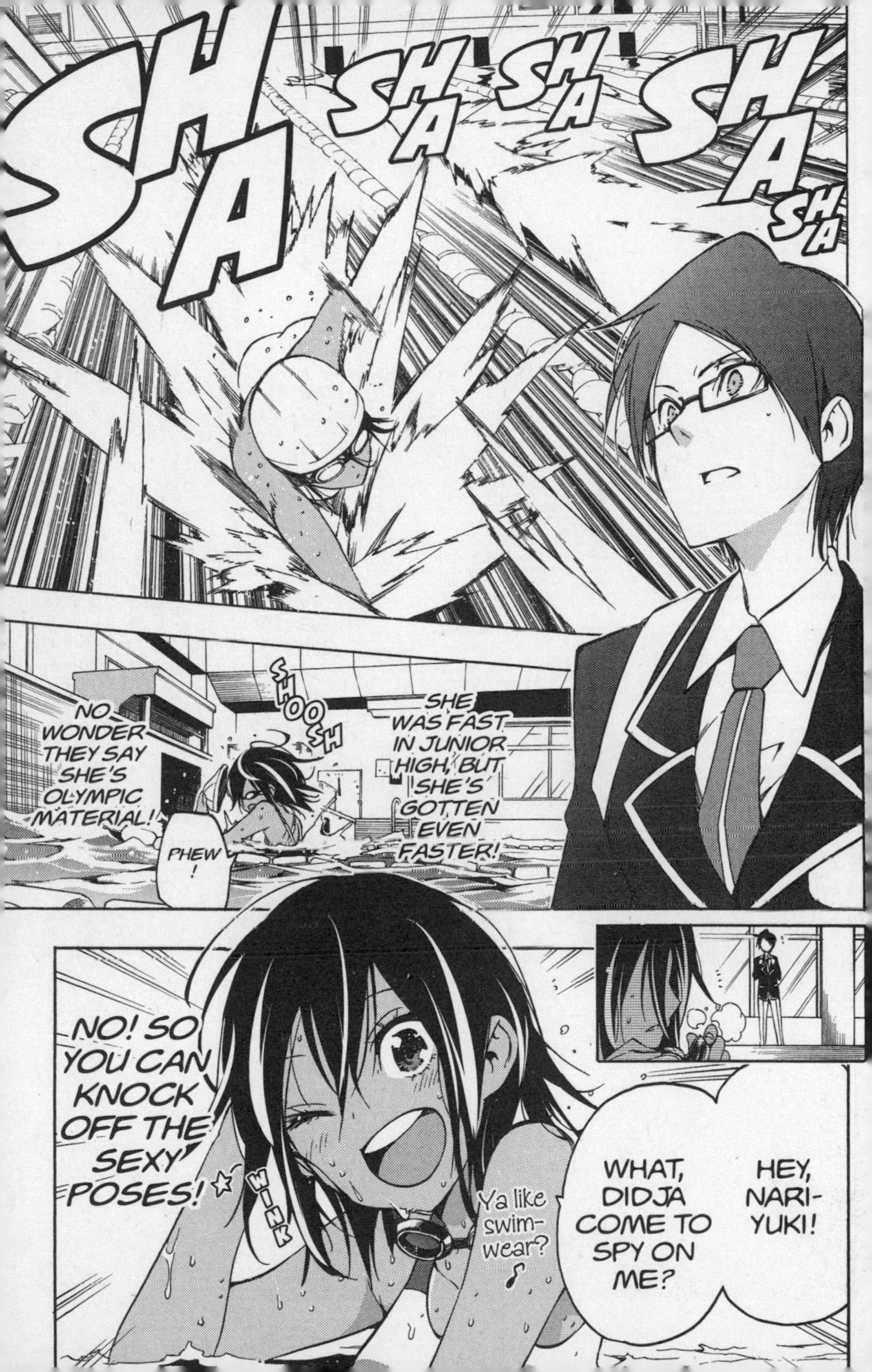
SHA SHA SHA SHA SHA SHA
SHE WAS FAST IN JUNIOR HIGH, BUT SHE'S GOTTEN EVEN FASTER!
SHOOSH
NO WONDER THEY SAY SHE'S OLYMPIC MATERIAL!
PHEW!
HEY, NARI-YUKI!
WHAT, DIDJA COME TO SPY ON ME?
Ya like swim-wear?
WINK
NO! SO YOU CAN KNOCK OFF THE SEXY POSES!

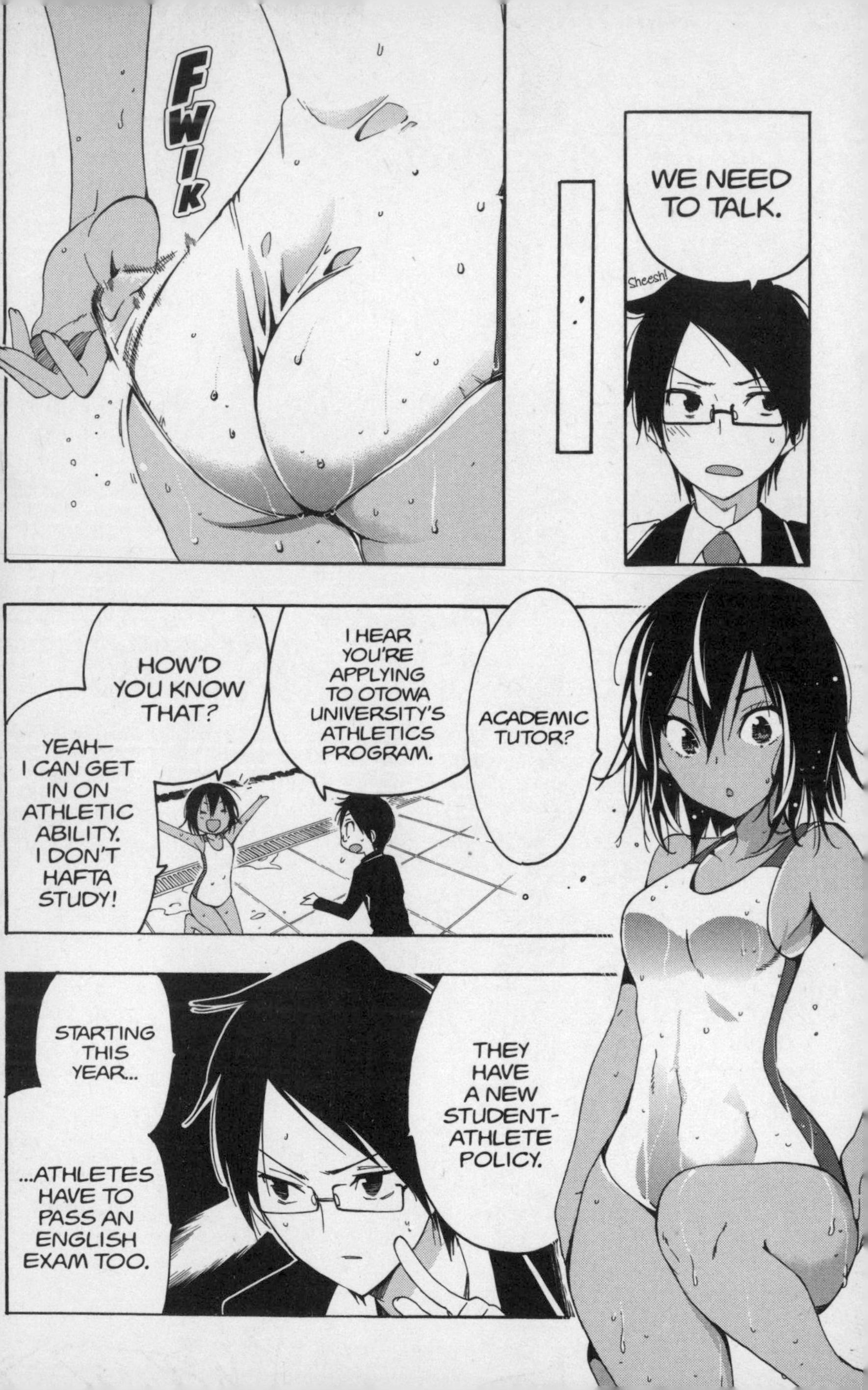
WE NEED TO TALK.
Sheesh!
FWIK
ACADEMIC TUTOR?
I HEAR YOU'RE APPLYING TO OTOWA UNIVERSITY'S ATHLETICS PROGRAM.
HOW'D YOU KNOW THAT?
YEAH— I CAN GET IN ON ATHLETIC ABILITY. I DON'T HAFTA STUDY!
THEY HAVE A NEW STUDENT-ATHLETE POLICY.
STARTING THIS YEAR...
...ATHLETES HAVE TO PASS AN ENGLISH EXAM TOO.

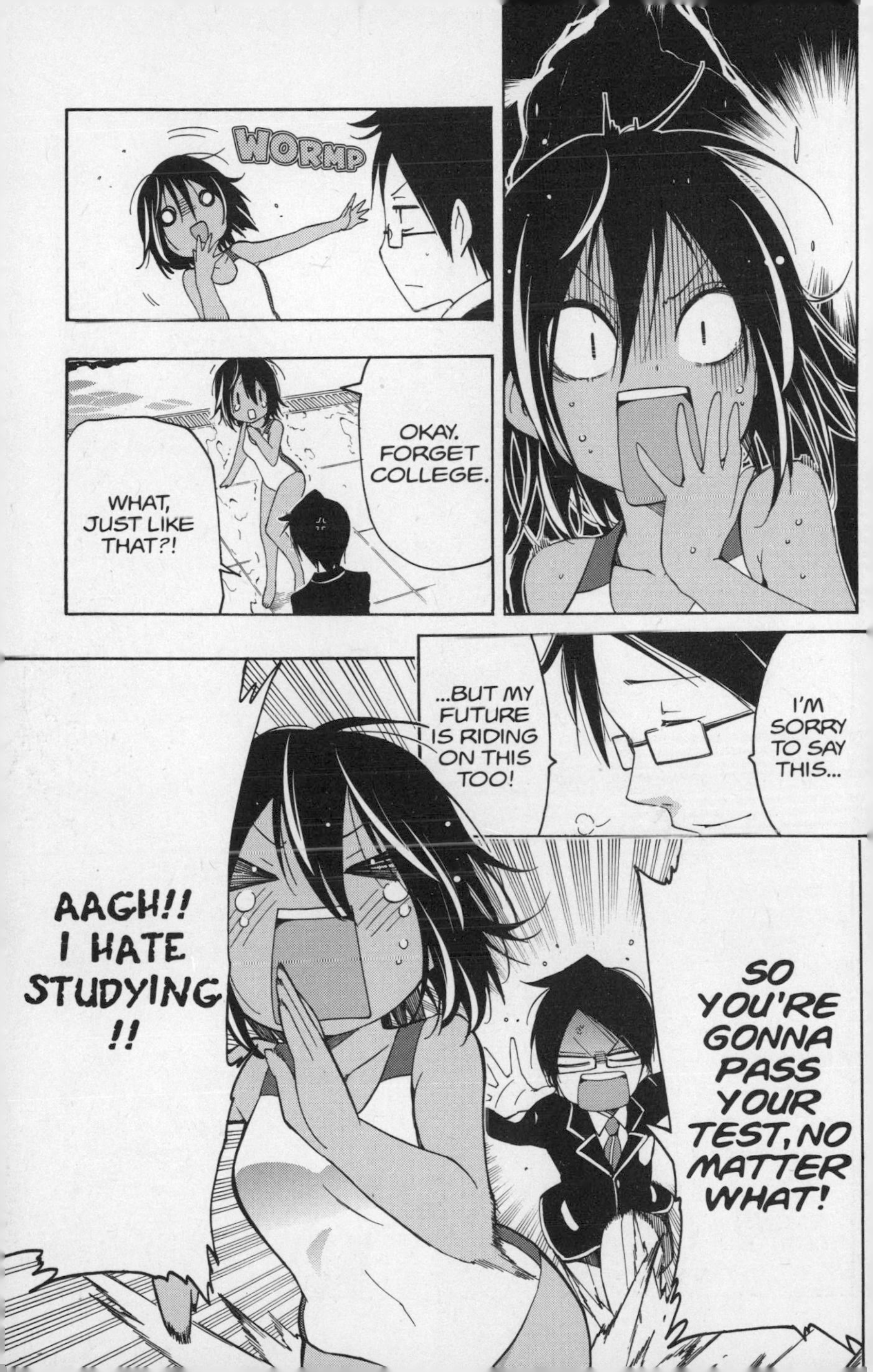
WORMP
OKAY. FORGET COLLEGE.
WHAT, JUST LIKE THAT?!
I'M SORRY TO SAY THIS...
...BUT MY FUTURE IS RIDING ON THIS TOO!
SO YOU'RE GONNA PASS YOUR TEST, NO MATTER WHAT!
AAGH!! I HATE STUDYING!!

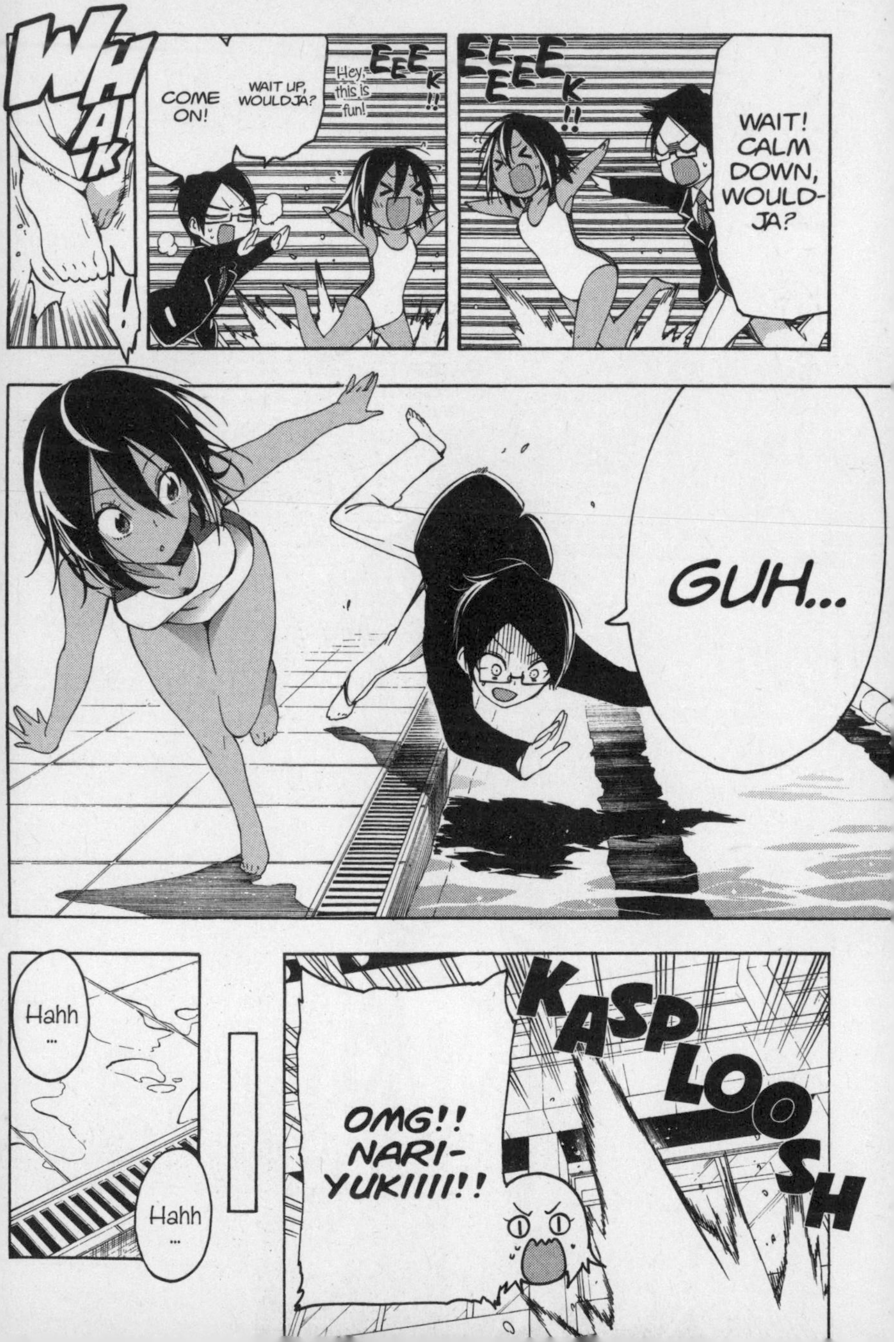
WAIT! CALM DOWN, WOULD-JA?
EEEEEEK!!
EEEEK!!
Hey, this is fun!
WAIT UP, WOULDJA?
COME ON!
WHAK!
GUH...
KASPLOOSH
OMG!! NARI-YUKIIII!!
Hahh ...
Hahh ...

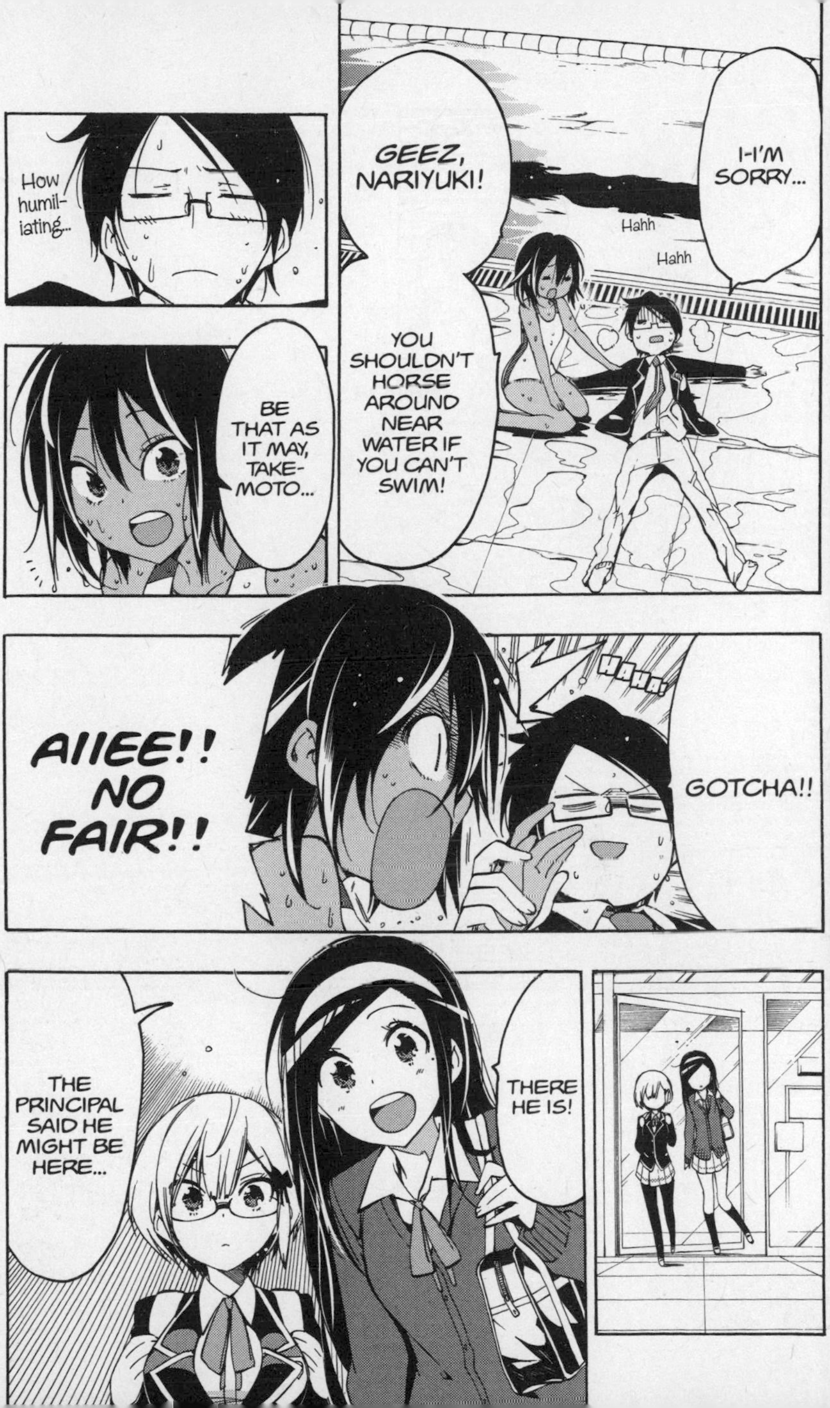
I-I'M SORRY...
Hahh
Hahh
GEEZ, NARIYUKI!
YOU SHOULDN'T HORSE AROUND NEAR WATER IF YOU CAN'T SWIM!
How humil-iating...
BE THAT AS IT MAY, TAKE-MOTO...
GOTCHA!!
HAHA!
AIIEE!! NO FAIR!!
THERE HE IS!
THE PRINCIPAL SAID HE MIGHT BE HERE...

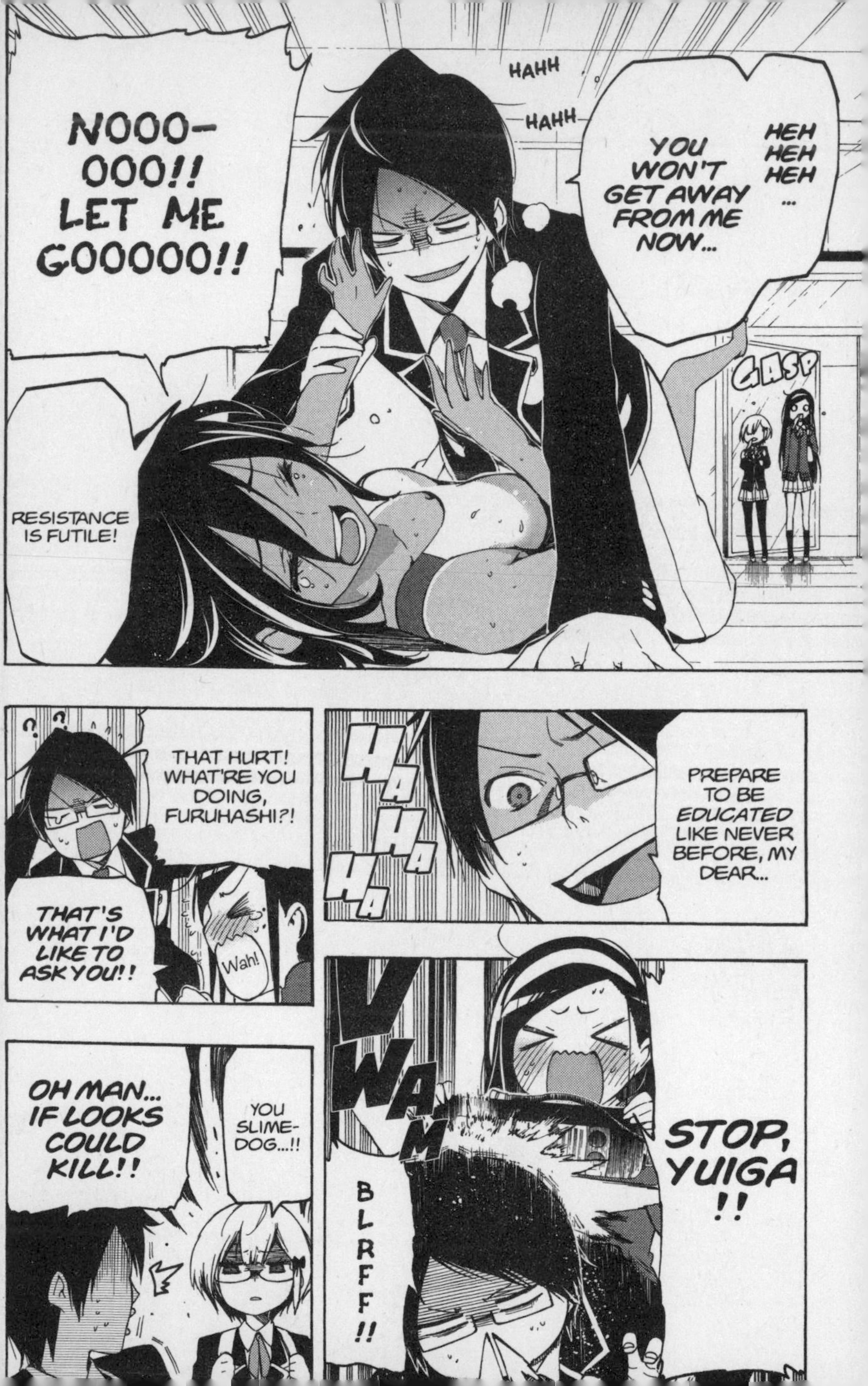

HEH HEH HEH ...
YOU WON'T GET AWAY FROM ME NOW...
HAHH
HAHH
GASP
NOOO-OOO!! LET ME GOOOOO!!
RESISTANCE IS FUTILE!
PREPARE TO BE EDUCATED LIKE NEVER BEFORE, MY DEAR...
HAHAHAHA
THAT HURT! WHAT'RE YOU DOING, FURUHASHI?!
Wah!
THAT'S WHAT I'D LIKE TO ASK YOU!!
STOP, YUIGA!!
WAM
BLRFF!!
YOU SLIME-DOG...!!
OH MAN... IF LOOKS COULD KILL!!

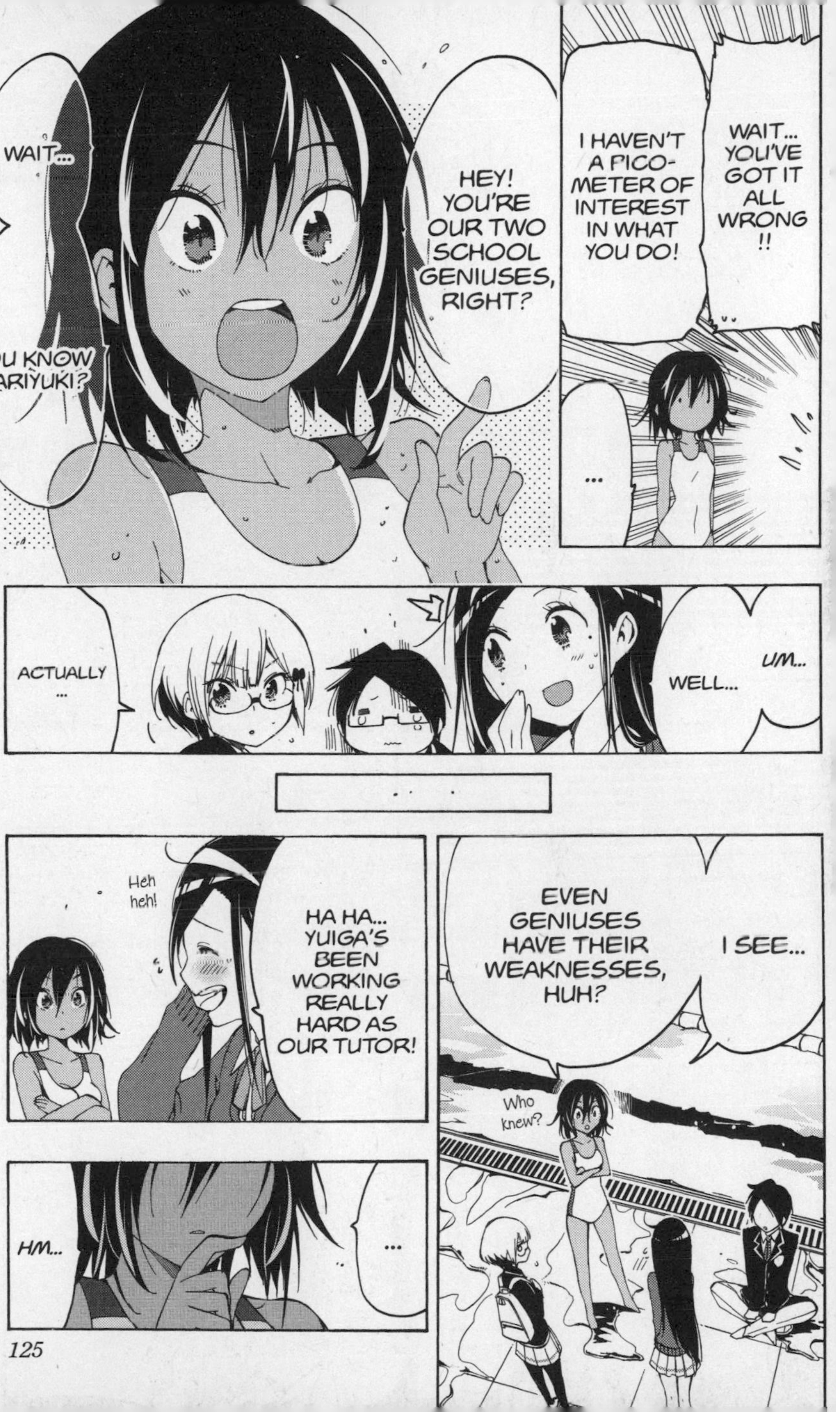
WAIT... YOU'VE GOT IT ALL WRONG !!
I HAVEN'T A PICO-METER OF INTEREST IN WHAT YOU DO!
...
HEY! YOU'RE OUR TWO SCHOOL GENIUSES, RIGHT?
WAIT...
YOU KNOW NARIYUKI?
UM... WELL...
ACTUALLY ...
I SEE...
EVEN GENIUSES HAVE THEIR WEAKNESSES, HUH?
Who knew?
HA HA... YUIGA'S BEEN WORKING REALLY HARD AS OUR TUTOR!
Heh heh!
...
HM...

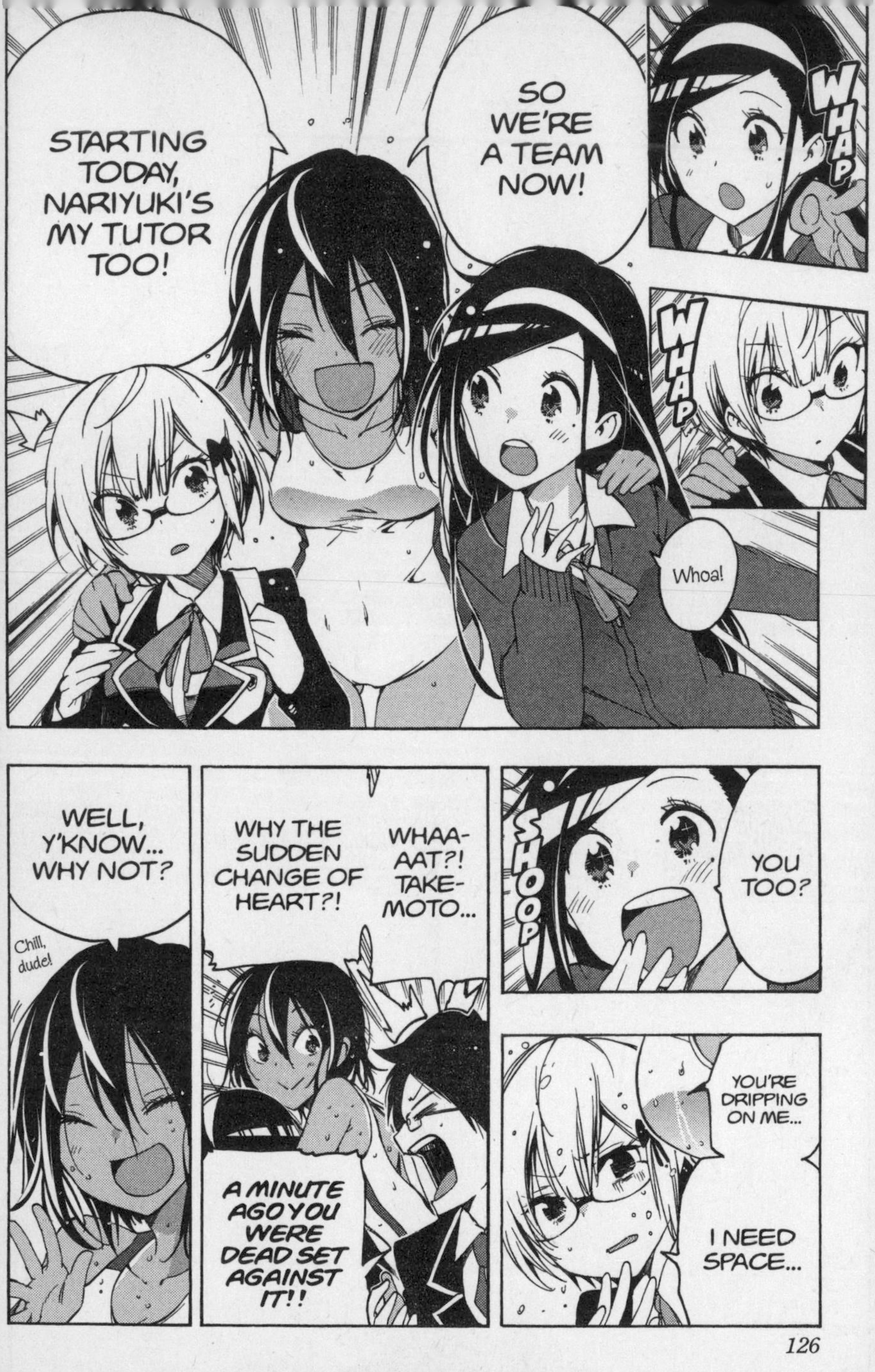
WHAP
WHAP WHAP
STARTING TODAY, NARIYUKI'S MY TUTOR TOO!
SO WE'RE A TEAM NOW!
Whoa!
SHOOP
YOU TOO?
YOU'RE DRIPPING ON ME...
I NEED SPACE...
WHAA-AAT?! TAKE-MOTO...
WHY THE SUDDEN CHANGE OF HEART?!
A MINUTE AGO YOU WERE DEAD SET AGAINST IT!!
WELL, Y'KNOW... WHY NOT?
Chill, dude!

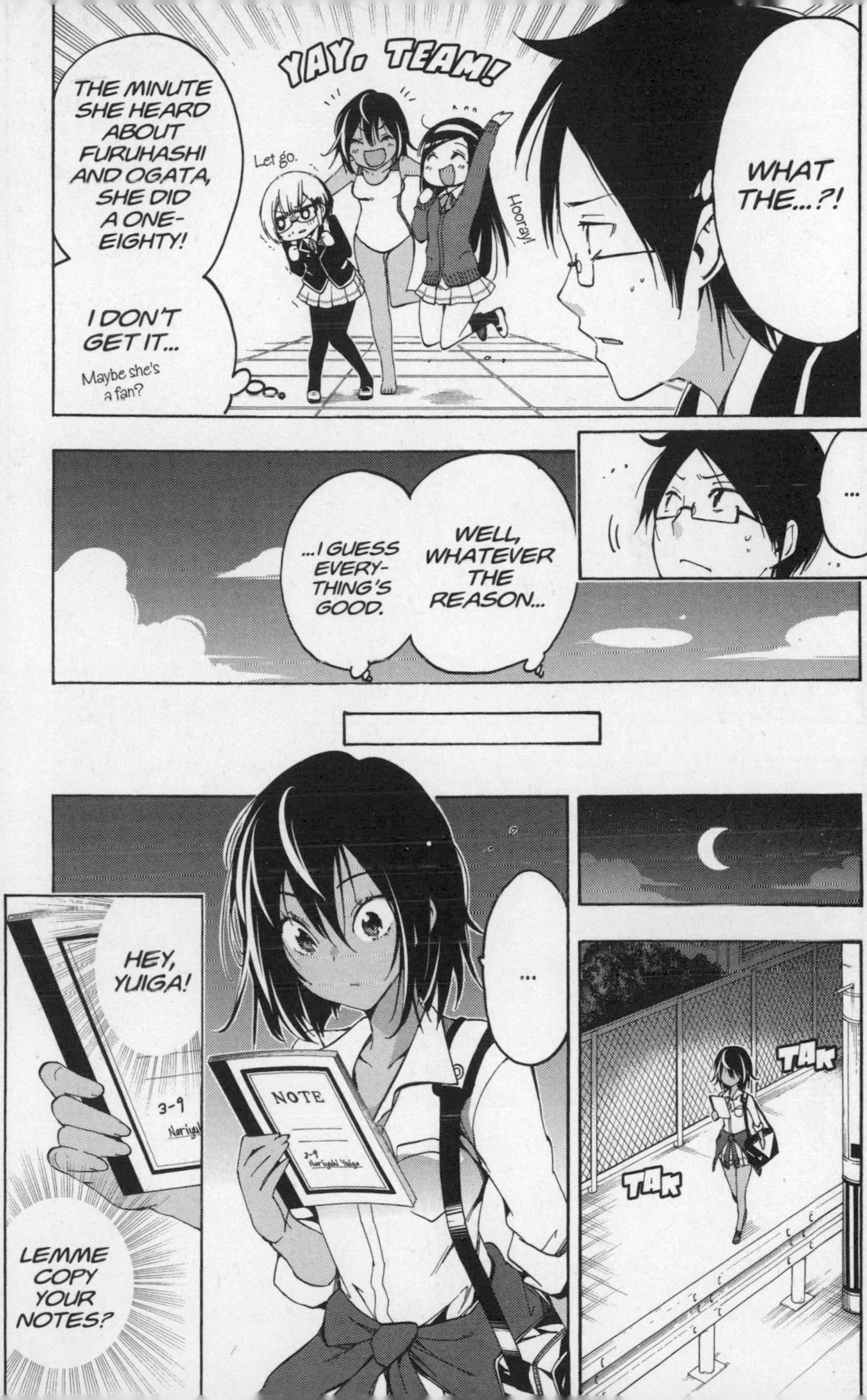
WHAT THE...?!
YAY, TEAM!
Hooray!
Let go.
THE MINUTE SHE HEARD ABOUT FURUHASHI AND OGATA, SHE DID A ONE-EIGHTY!
I DON'T GET IT...
Maybe she's a fan?
...
WELL, WHATEVER THE REASON...
...I GUESS EVERY-THING'S GOOD.
TAK
TAK
...
NOTE
3-9
HEY, YUIGA!
LEMME COPY YOUR NOTES?

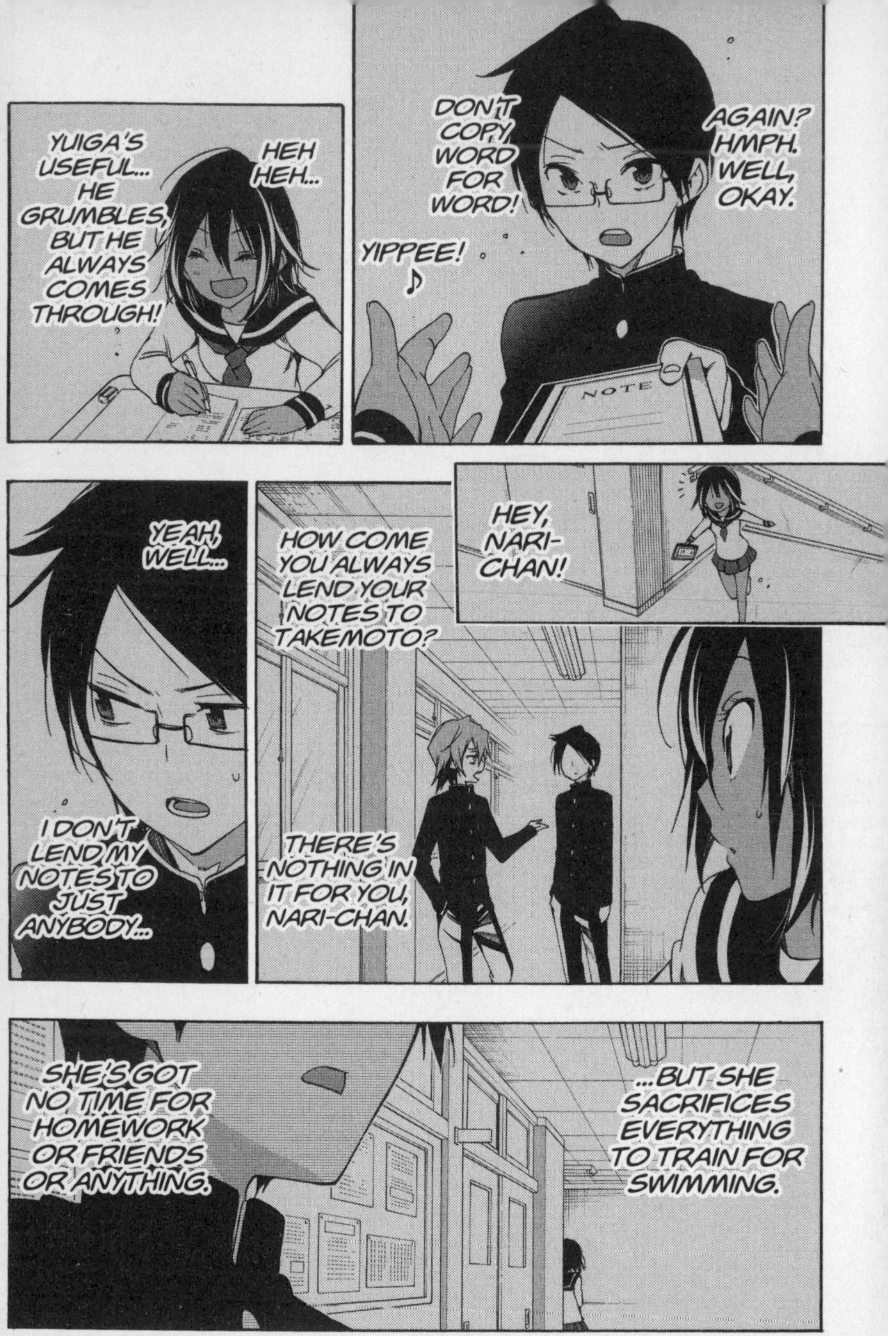
AGAIN? HMPH. WELL, OKAY.
DON'T COPY WORD FOR WORD!
YIPPEE! ♪
HEH HEH...
YUIGA'S USEFUL... HE GRUMBLES, BUT HE ALWAYS COMES THROUGH!
HEY, NARI-CHAN!
HOW COME YOU ALWAYS LEND YOUR NOTES TO TAKEMOTO?
THERE'S NOTHING IN IT FOR YOU, NARI-CHAN.
YEAH, WELL...
I DON'T LEND MY NOTES TO JUST ANYBODY...
SHE'S GOT NO TIME FOR HOMEWORK OR FRIENDS OR ANYTHING.
...BUT SHE SACRIFICES EVERYTHING TO TRAIN FOR SWIMMING.

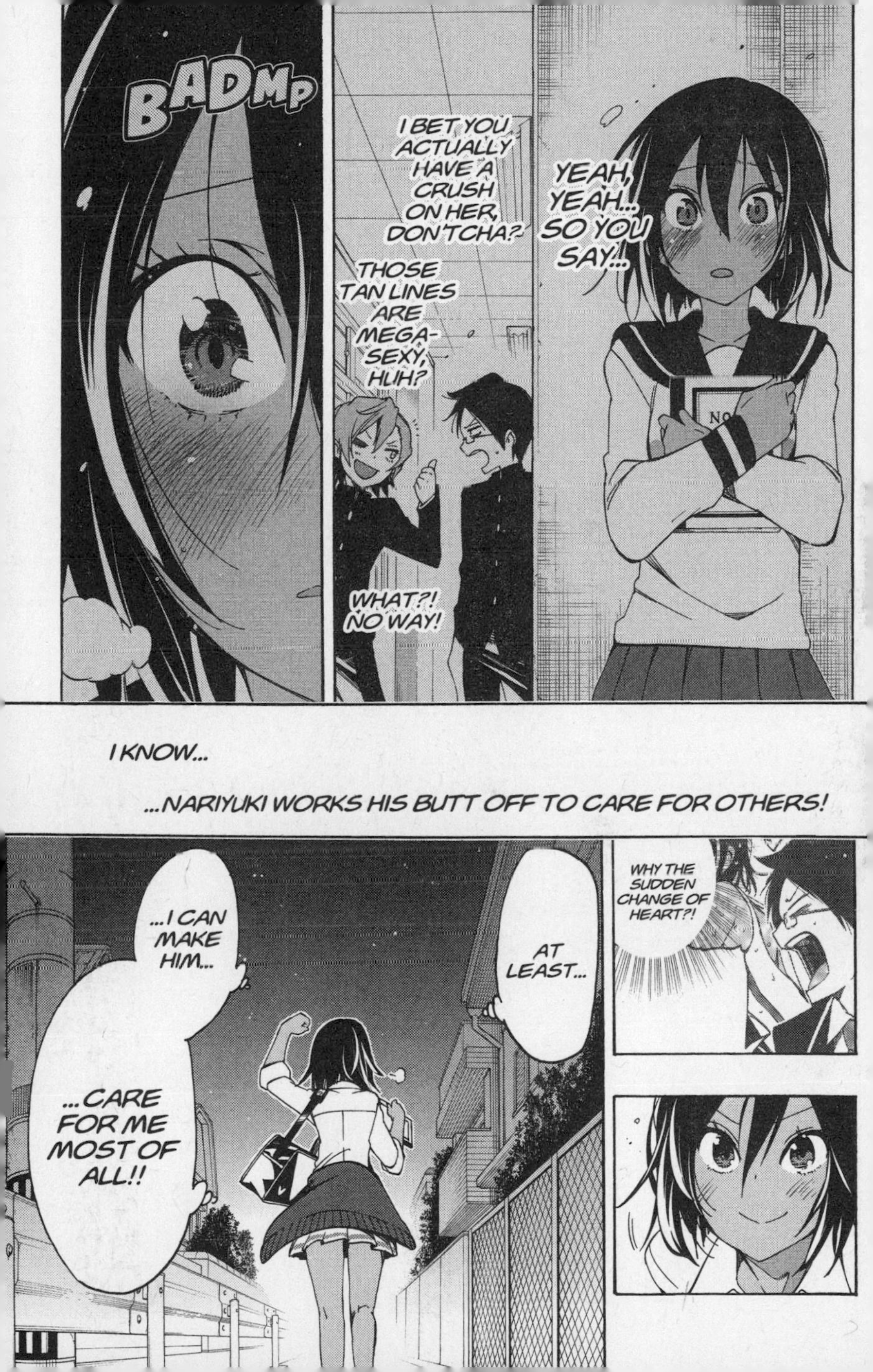
YEAH, YEAH... SO YOU SAY...
I BET YOU ACTUALLY HAVE A CRUSH ON HER, DON'TCHA?
THOSE TAN LINES ARE MEGA-SEXY, HUH?
WHAT?! NO WAY!
BADMP
I KNOW...
...NARIYUKI WORKS HIS BUTT OFF TO CARE FOR OTHERS!
WHY THE SUDDEN CHANGE OF HEART?!
AT LEAST...
...I CAN MAKE HIM...
...CARE FOR ME MOST OF ALL!!

Behind the scenes...

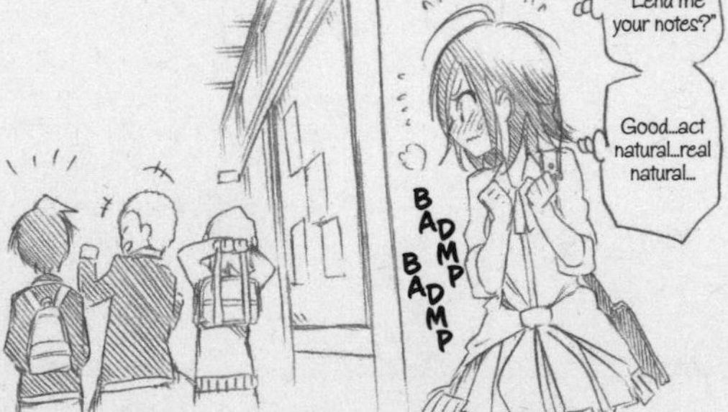
"Lend me your notes?" "Lend me your notes?"
Good...act natural...real natural...
BADMP BADMP

Question 5:
The Pathos of a Celebrated Genius = [*X*]

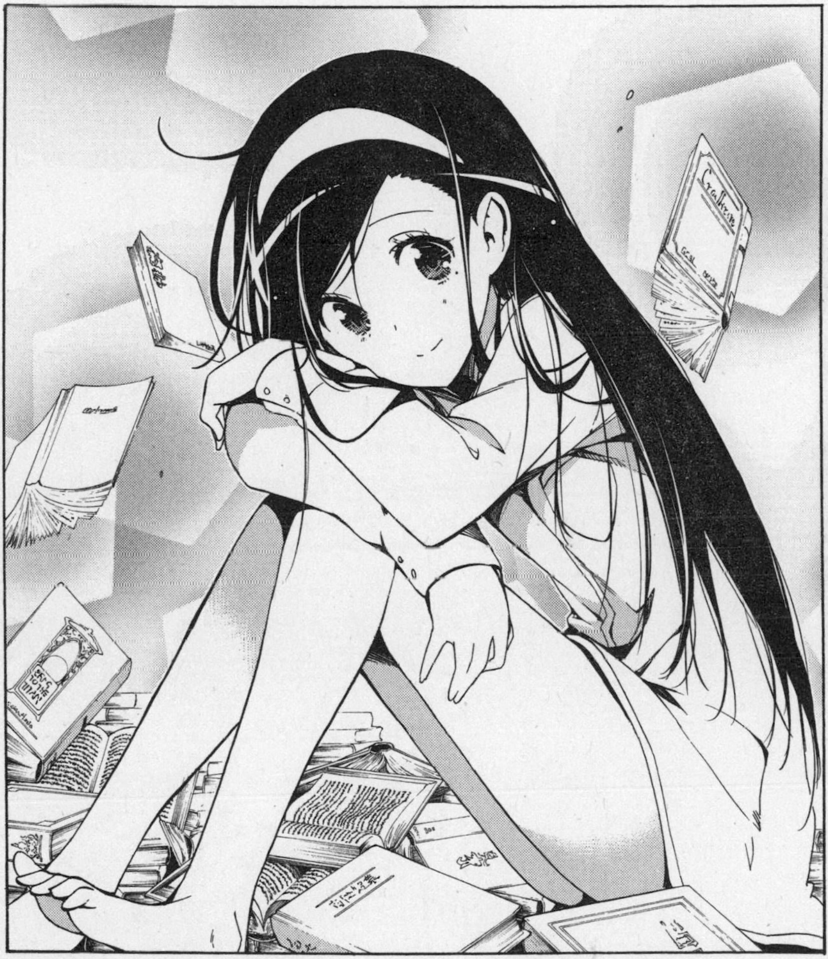

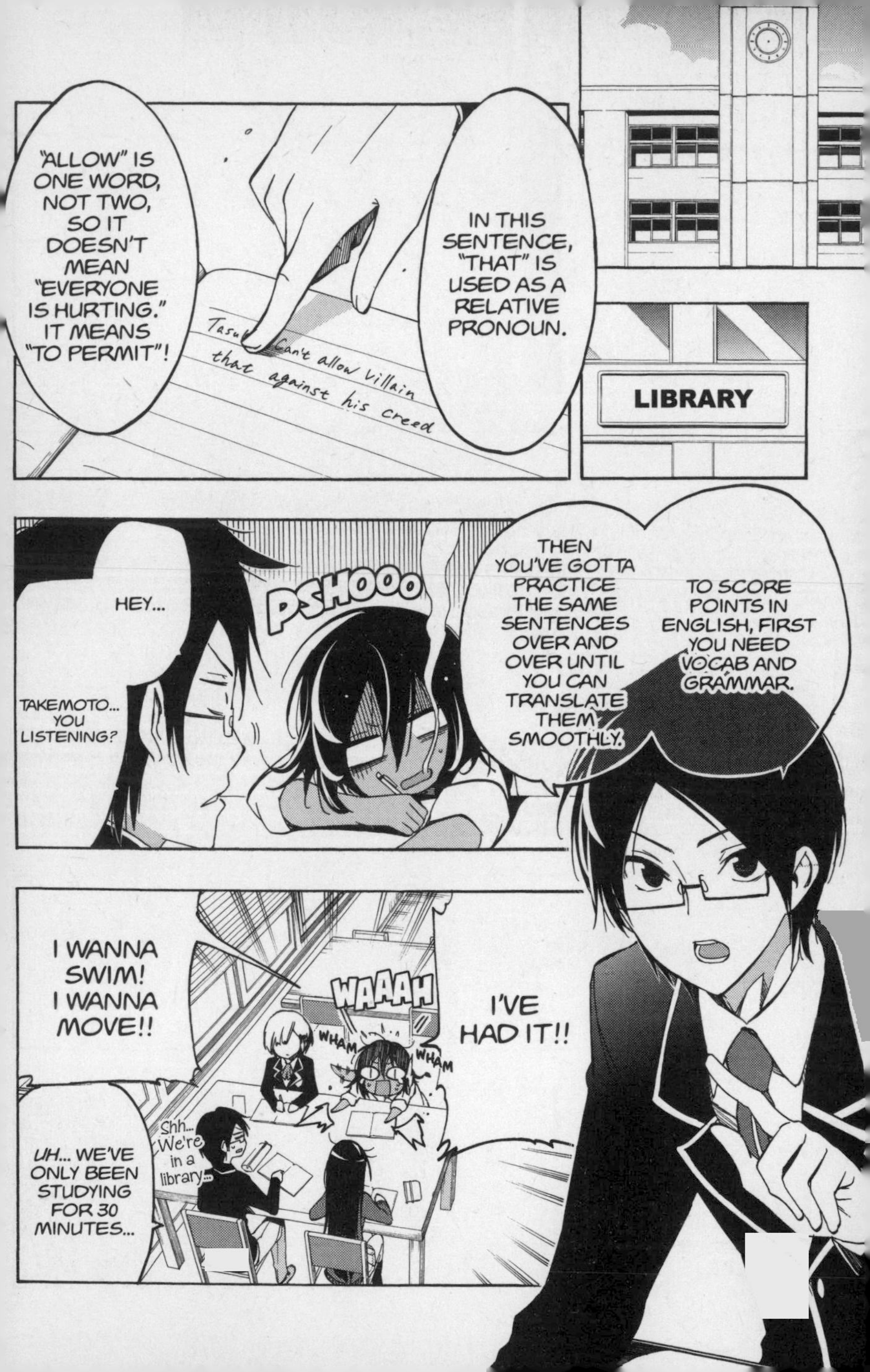
LIBRARY
IN THIS SENTENCE, "THAT" IS USED AS A RELATIVE PRONOUN.
"ALLOW" IS ONE WORD, NOT TWO, SO IT DOESN'T MEAN "EVERYONE IS HURTING." IT MEANS "TO PERMIT"!
Can't allow villain
that against his creed
TO SCORE POINTS IN ENGLISH, FIRST YOU NEED VOCAB AND GRAMMAR.
THEN YOU'VE GOTTA PRACTICE THE SAME SENTENCES OVER AND OVER UNTIL YOU CAN TRANSLATE THEM SMOOTHLY.
PSHOOO
HEY...
TAKEMOTO... YOU LISTENING?
I'VE HAD IT!!
WAAAH
WHAM
WHAM
I WANNA SWIM! I WANNA MOVE!!
Shh... We're in a library...
UH... WE'VE ONLY BEEN STUDYING FOR 30 MINUTES...

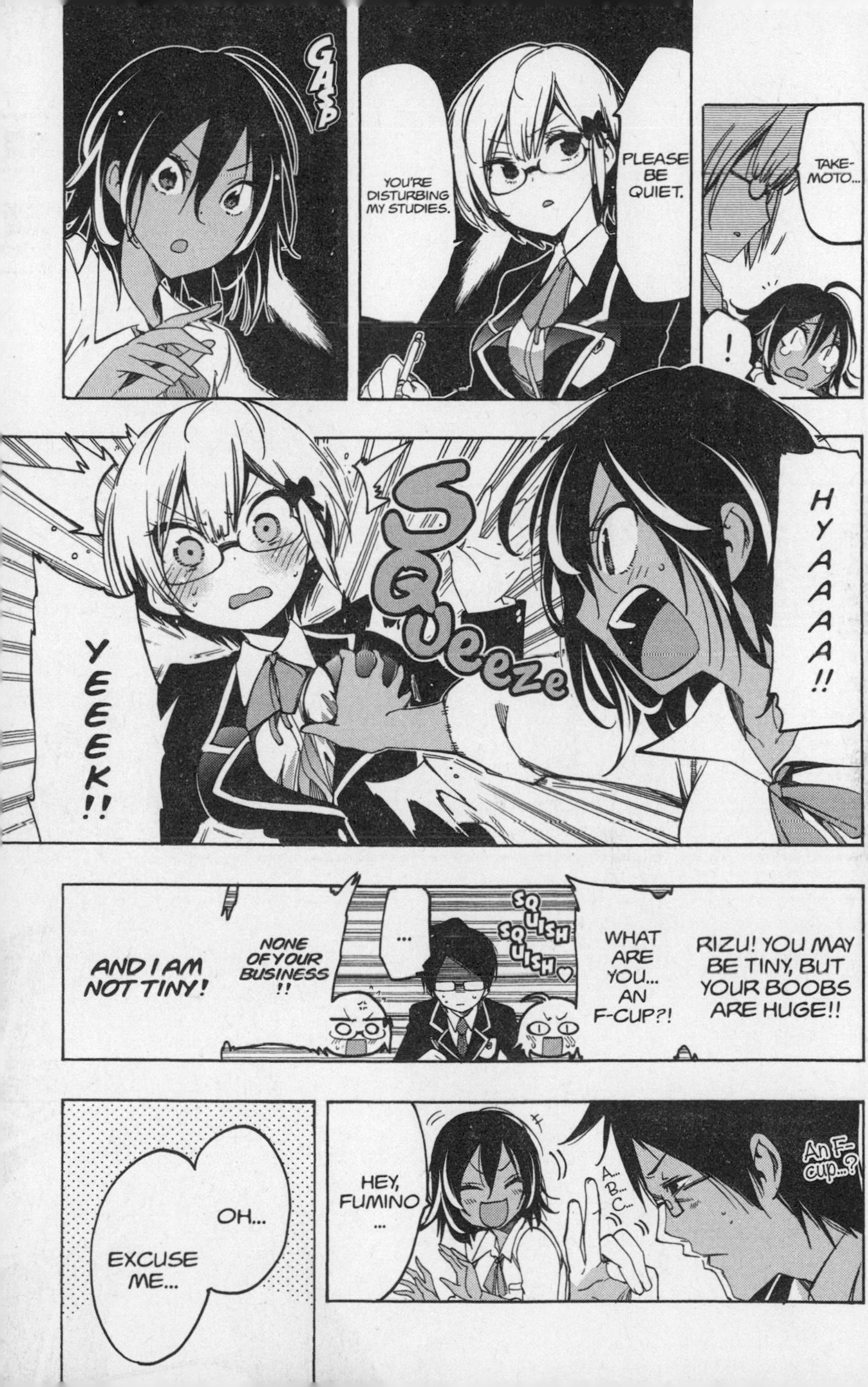
TAKE-MOTO...
!
PLEASE BE QUIET.
YOU'RE DISTURBING MY STUDIES.
GASP
HYAAAAA!!
SQUEEZE
YEEEEK!!
RIZU! YOU MAY BE TINY, BUT YOUR BOOBS ARE HUGE!!
WHAT ARE YOU... AN F-CUP?!
SQUISH SQUISH ♡
...
NONE OF YOUR BUSINESS!!
AND I AM NOT TINY!
An F-cup...?
A... B... C...
HEY, FUMINO...
OH... EXCUSE ME...

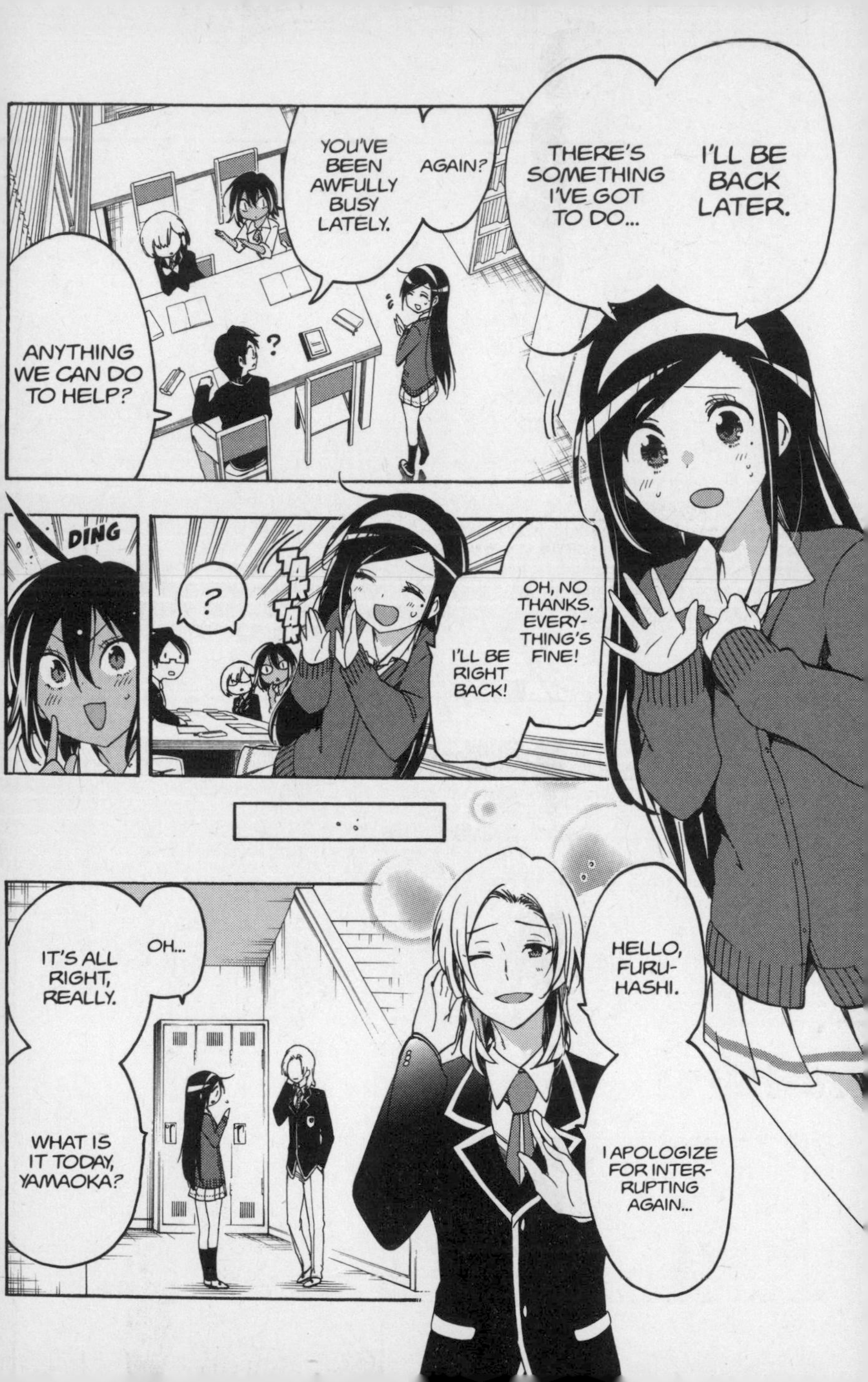

THERE'S SOMETHING I'VE GOT TO DO...
I'LL BE BACK LATER.
AGAIN?
YOU'VE BEEN AWFULLY BUSY LATELY.
ANYTHING WE CAN DO TO HELP?
OH, NO THANKS. EVERYTHING'S FINE!
I'LL BE RIGHT BACK!
TAK TAK
?
DING
..
HELLO, FURUHASHI.
I APOLOGIZE FOR INTERRUPTING AGAIN...
OH...
IT'S ALL RIGHT, REALLY.
WHAT IS IT TODAY, YAMAOKA?

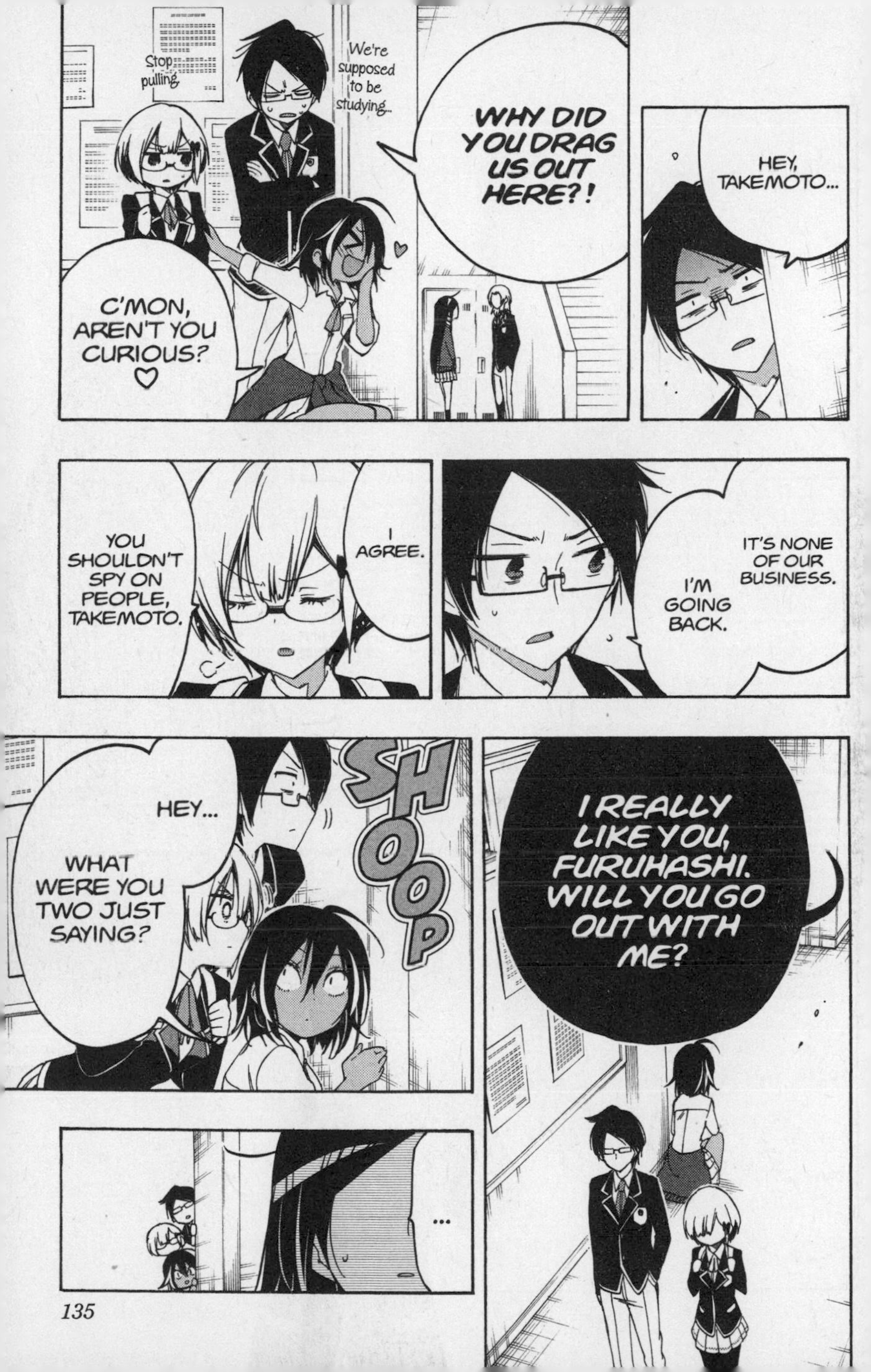
HEY, TAKEMOTO...
WHY DID YOU DRAG US OUT HERE?!
We're supposed to be studying...
Stop pulling
C'MON, AREN'T YOU CURIOUS? ♡
IT'S NONE OF OUR BUSINESS.
I'M GOING BACK.
I AGREE.
YOU SHOULDN'T SPY ON PEOPLE, TAKEMOTO.
I REALLY LIKE YOU, FURUHASHI. WILL YOU GO OUT WITH ME?
SHOOP
HEY...
WHAT WERE YOU TWO JUST SAYING?
...

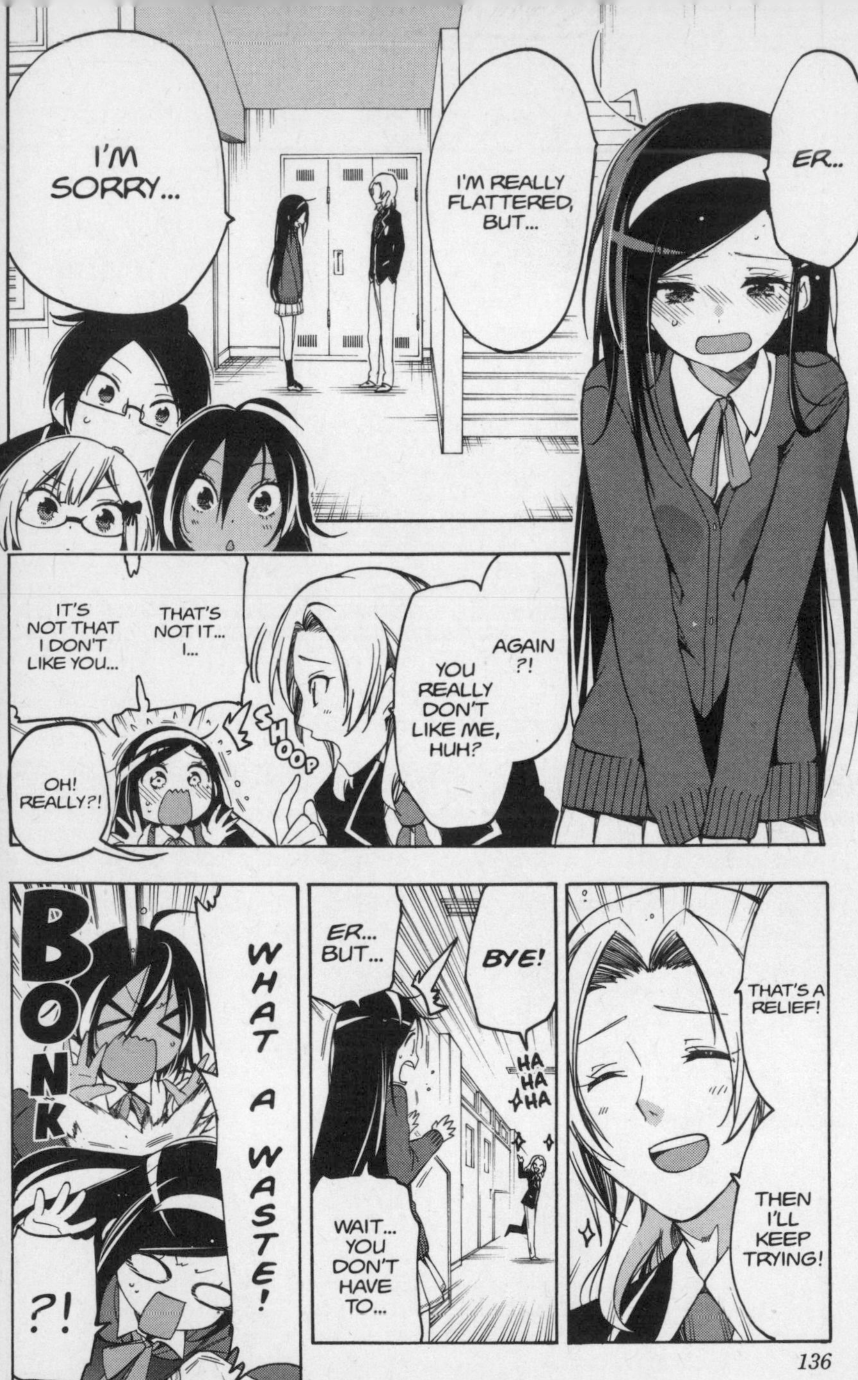
ER...
I'M REALLY FLATTERED, BUT...
I'M SORRY...
AGAIN?!
YOU REALLY DON'T LIKE ME, HUH?
SHOOP
THAT'S NOT IT... I...
IT'S NOT THAT I DON'T LIKE YOU...
OH! REALLY?!
THAT'S A RELIEF!
THEN I'LL KEEP TRYING!
BYE!
HA HA HA
ER... BUT...
WAIT... YOU DON'T HAVE TO...
WHAT A WASTE!
BONK
?!

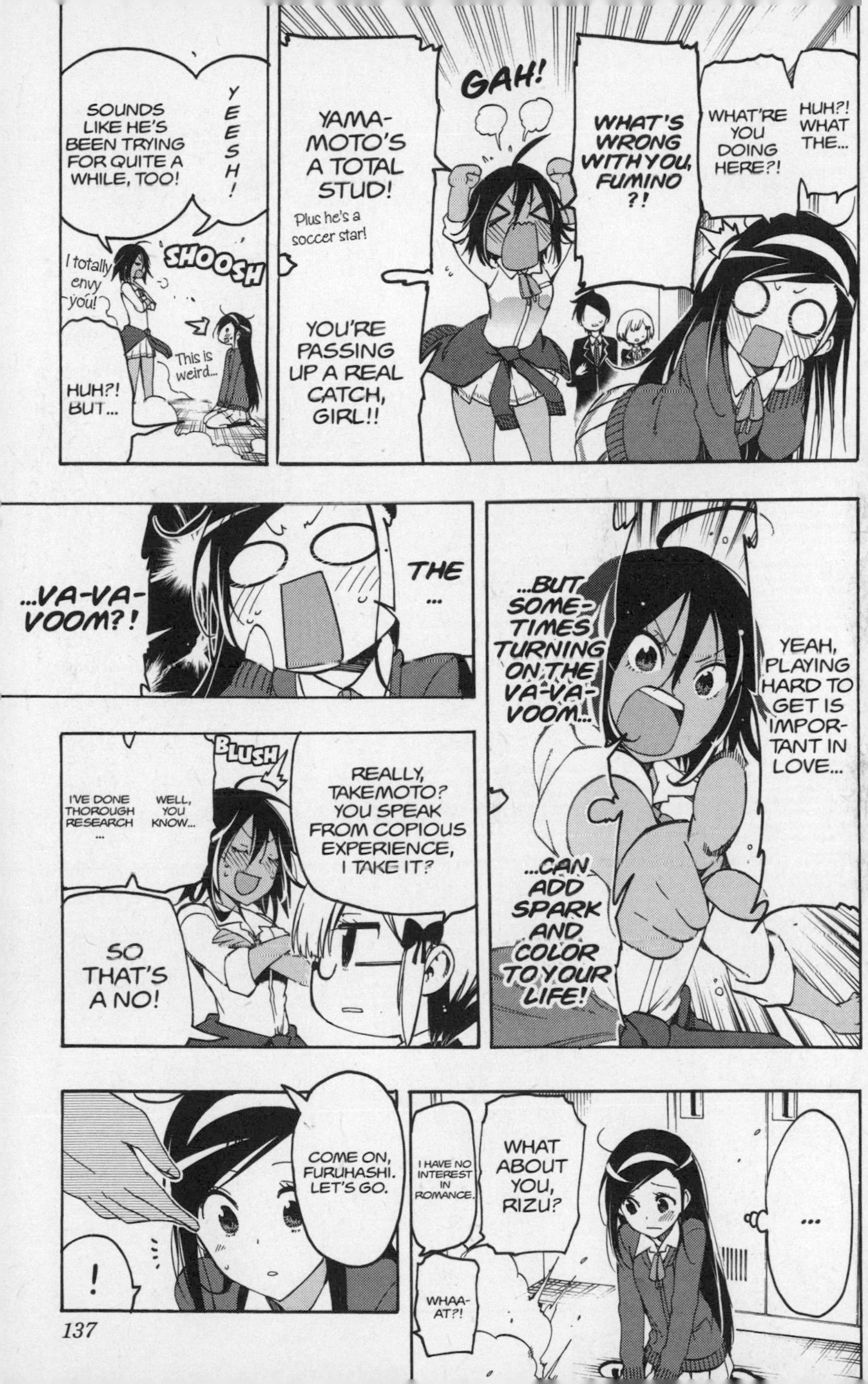
HUH?! WHAT THE...
WHAT'RE YOU DOING HERE?!
GAH!
WHAT'S WRONG WITH YOU, FUMINO?!
YAMA-MOTO'S A TOTAL STUD!
Plus he's a soccer star!
YOU'RE PASSING UP A REAL CATCH, GIRL!!
YEESH!
SOUNDS LIKE HE'S BEEN TRYING FOR QUITE A WHILE, TOO!
SHOOSH
This is weird...
I totally envy you!
HUH?! BUT...
YEAH, PLAYING HARD TO GET IS IMPORTANT IN LOVE...
...BUT SOME-TIMES TURNING ON THE VA-VA-VOOM...
...CAN ADD SPARK AND COLOR TO YOUR LIFE!
THE...
...VA-VA-VOOM?!
REALLY, TAKEMOTO? YOU SPEAK FROM COPIOUS EXPERIENCE, I TAKE IT?
BLUSH
WELL, YOU KNOW...
I'VE DONE THOROUGH RESEARCH...
SO THAT'S A NO!
...
WHAT ABOUT YOU, RIZU?
I HAVE NO INTEREST IN ROMANCE.
WHAA-AT?!
COME ON, FURUHASHI. LET'S GO.
!

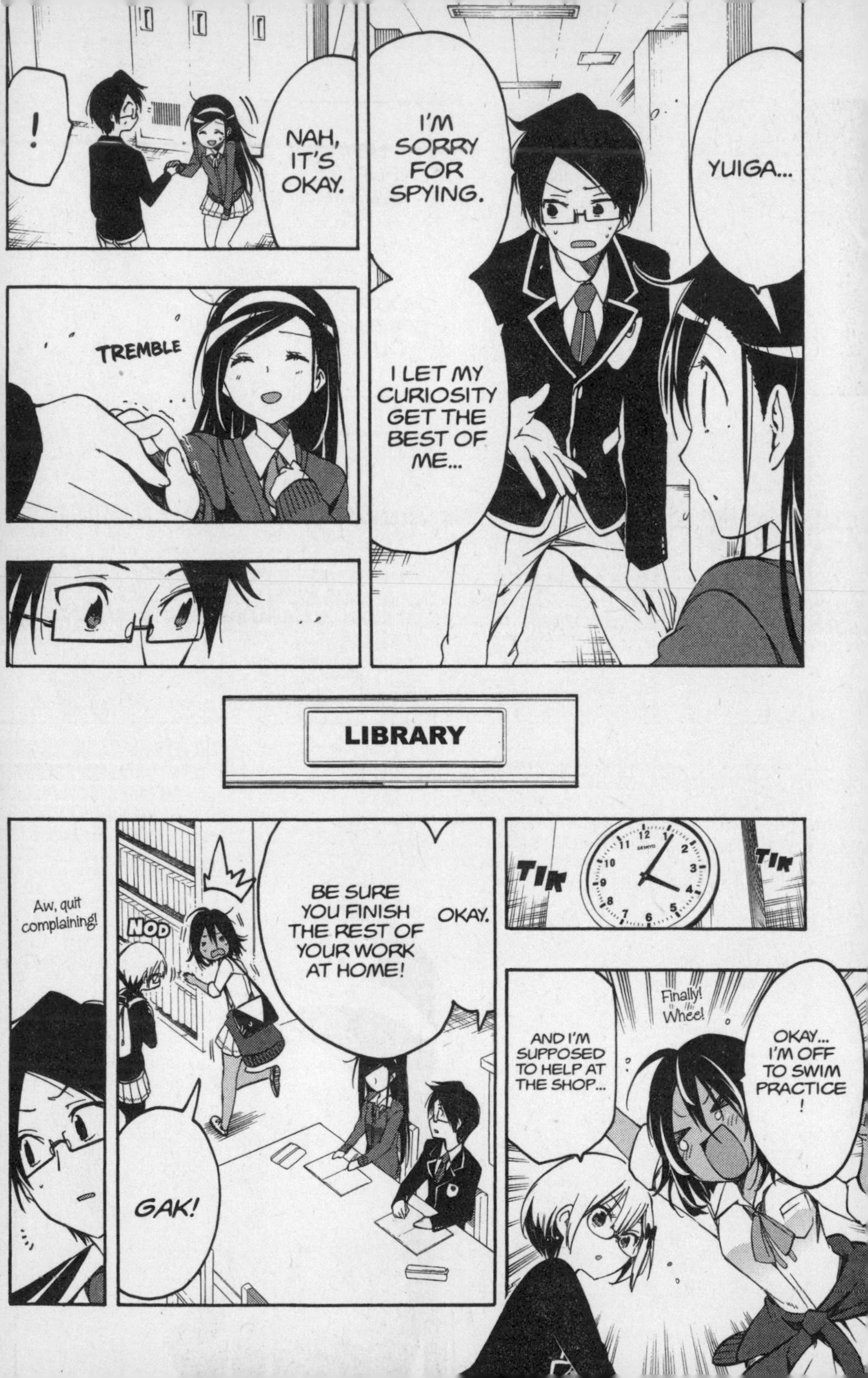
YUIGA...
I'M SORRY FOR SPYING.
I LET MY CURIOSITY GET THE BEST OF ME...
NAH, IT'S OKAY.
!
TREMBLE
LIBRARY
TIK
TIK
OKAY... I'M OFF TO SWIM PRACTICE!
Finally! Whee!
AND I'M SUPPOSED TO HELP AT THE SHOP...
OKAY.
BE SURE YOU FINISH THE REST OF YOUR WORK AT HOME!
NOD
GAK!
Aw, quit complaining!

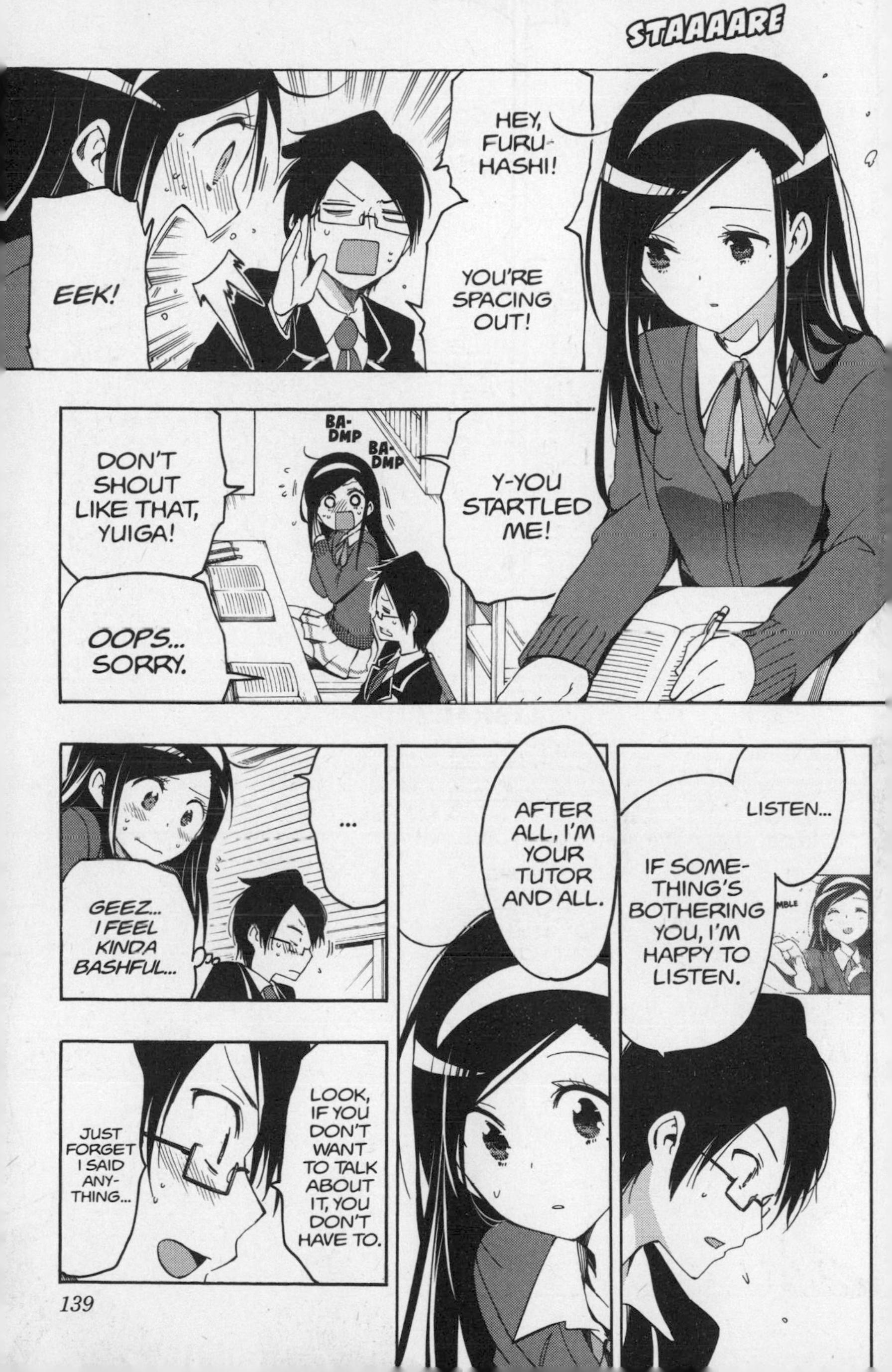
STAAAARE
HEY, FURUHASHI!
YOU'RE SPACING OUT!
EEK!
Y-YOU STARTLED ME!
BA-DMP
BA-DMP
DON'T SHOUT LIKE THAT, YUIGA!
OOPS... SORRY.
LISTEN...
IF SOMETHING'S BOTHERING YOU, I'M HAPPY TO LISTEN.
AFTER ALL, I'M YOUR TUTOR AND ALL.
...
GEEZ... I FEEL KINDA BASHFUL...
LOOK, IF YOU DON'T WANT TO TALK ABOUT IT, YOU DON'T HAVE TO.
JUST FORGET I SAID ANYTHING...

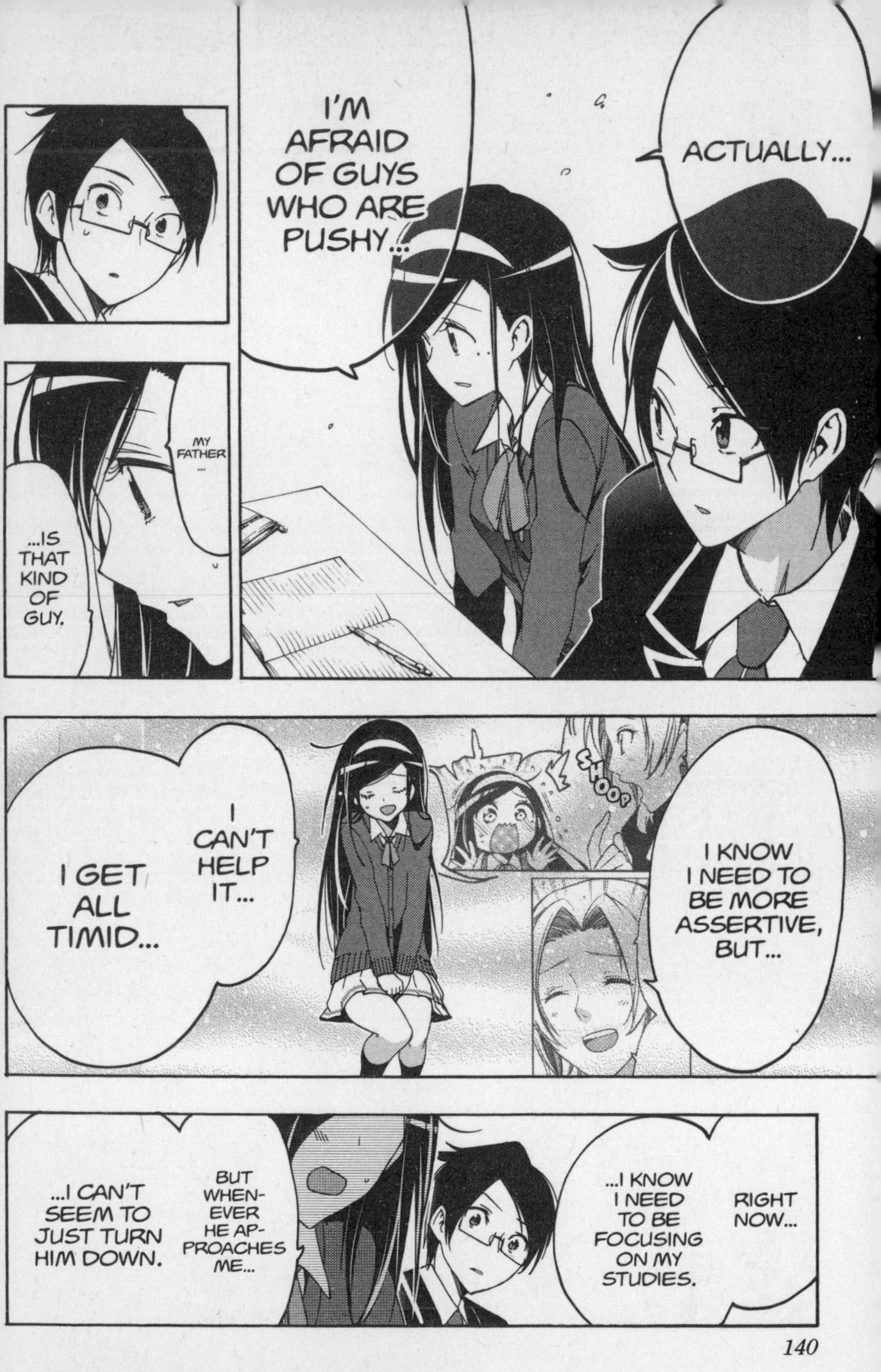
ACTUALLY...
I'M AFRAID OF GUYS WHO ARE PUSHY...
MY FATHER...
...IS THAT KIND OF GUY.
I KNOW I NEED TO BE MORE ASSERTIVE, BUT...
SHOOP
I CAN'T HELP IT...
I GET ALL TIMID...
RIGHT NOW...
...I KNOW I NEED TO BE FOCUSING ON MY STUDIES.
BUT WHENEVER HE APPROACHES ME...
...I CAN'T SEEM TO JUST TURN HIM DOWN.

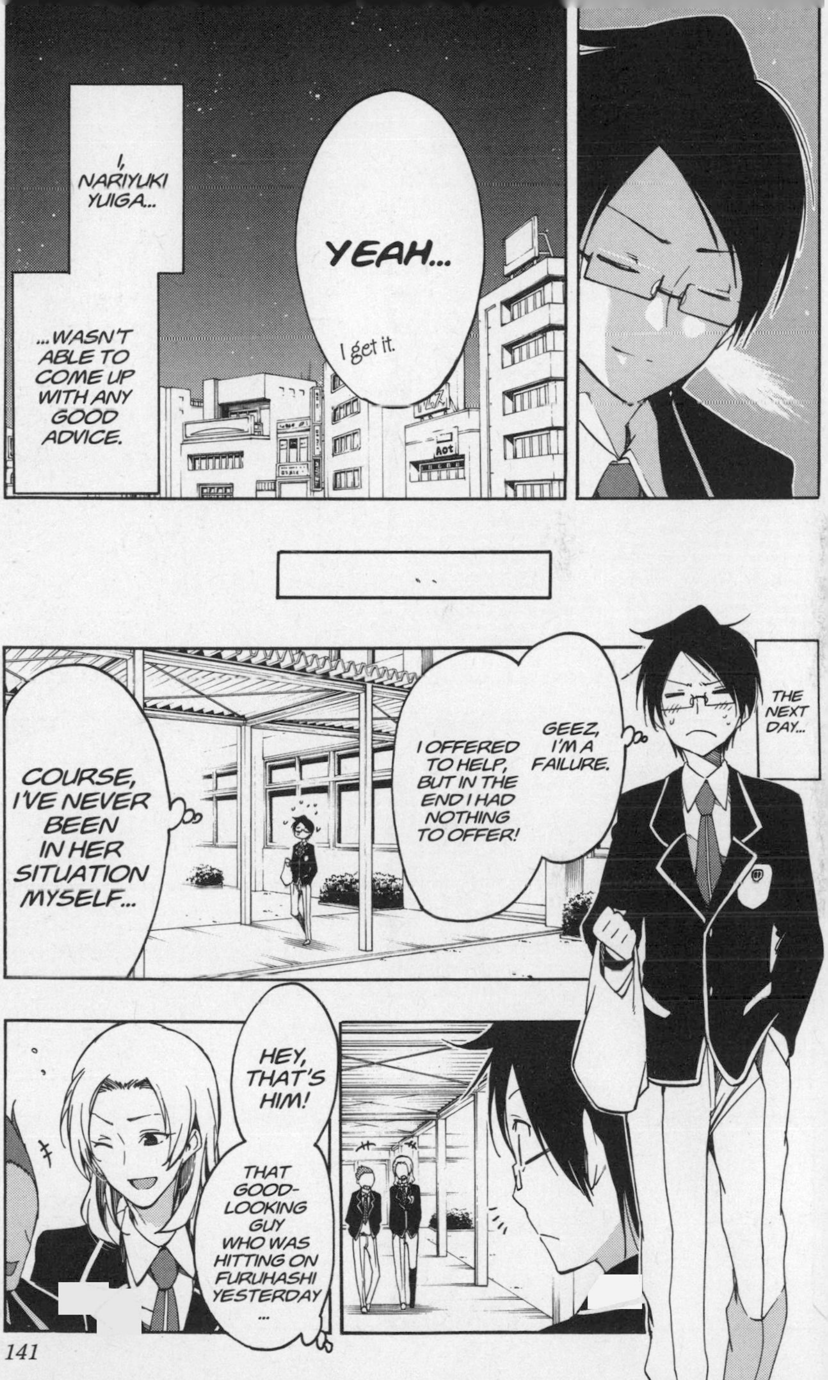
YEAH...
I get it.
I, NARIYUKI YUIGA...
...WASN'T ABLE TO COME UP WITH ANY GOOD ADVICE.
THE NEXT DAY...
GEEZ, I'M A FAILURE.
I OFFERED TO HELP, BUT IN THE END I HAD NOTHING TO OFFER!
COURSE, I'VE NEVER BEEN IN HER SITUATION MYSELF...
HEY, THAT'S HIM!
THAT GOOD-LOOKING GUY WHO WAS HITTING ON FURUHASHI YESTERDAY...

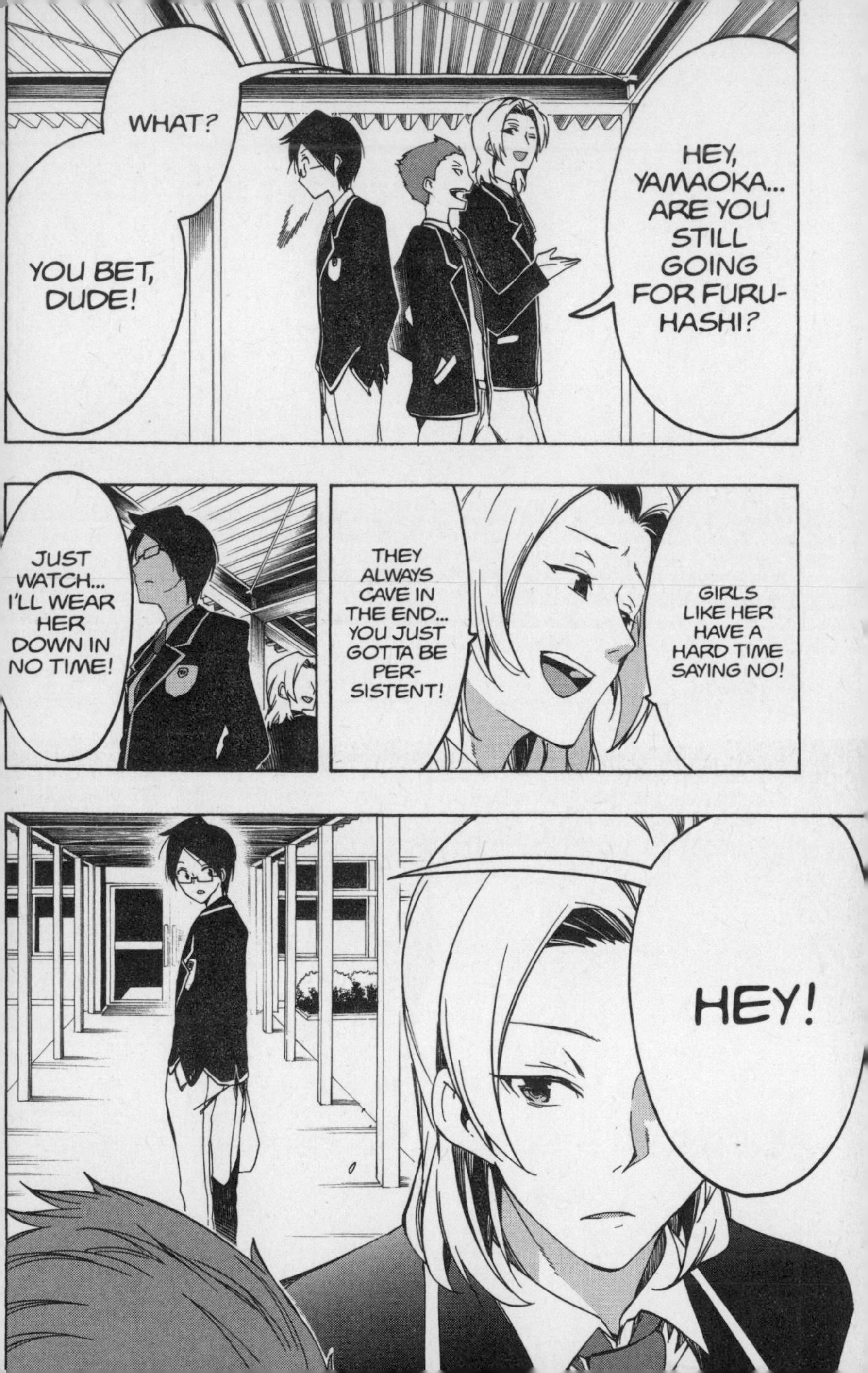
HEY, YAMAOKA... ARE YOU STILL GOING FOR FURU-HASHI?
WHAT?
YOU BET, DUDE!
GIRLS LIKE HER HAVE A HARD TIME SAYING NO!
THEY ALWAYS CAVE IN THE END... YOU JUST GOTTA BE PER-SISTENT!
JUST WATCH... I'LL WEAR HER DOWN IN NO TIME!
HEY!

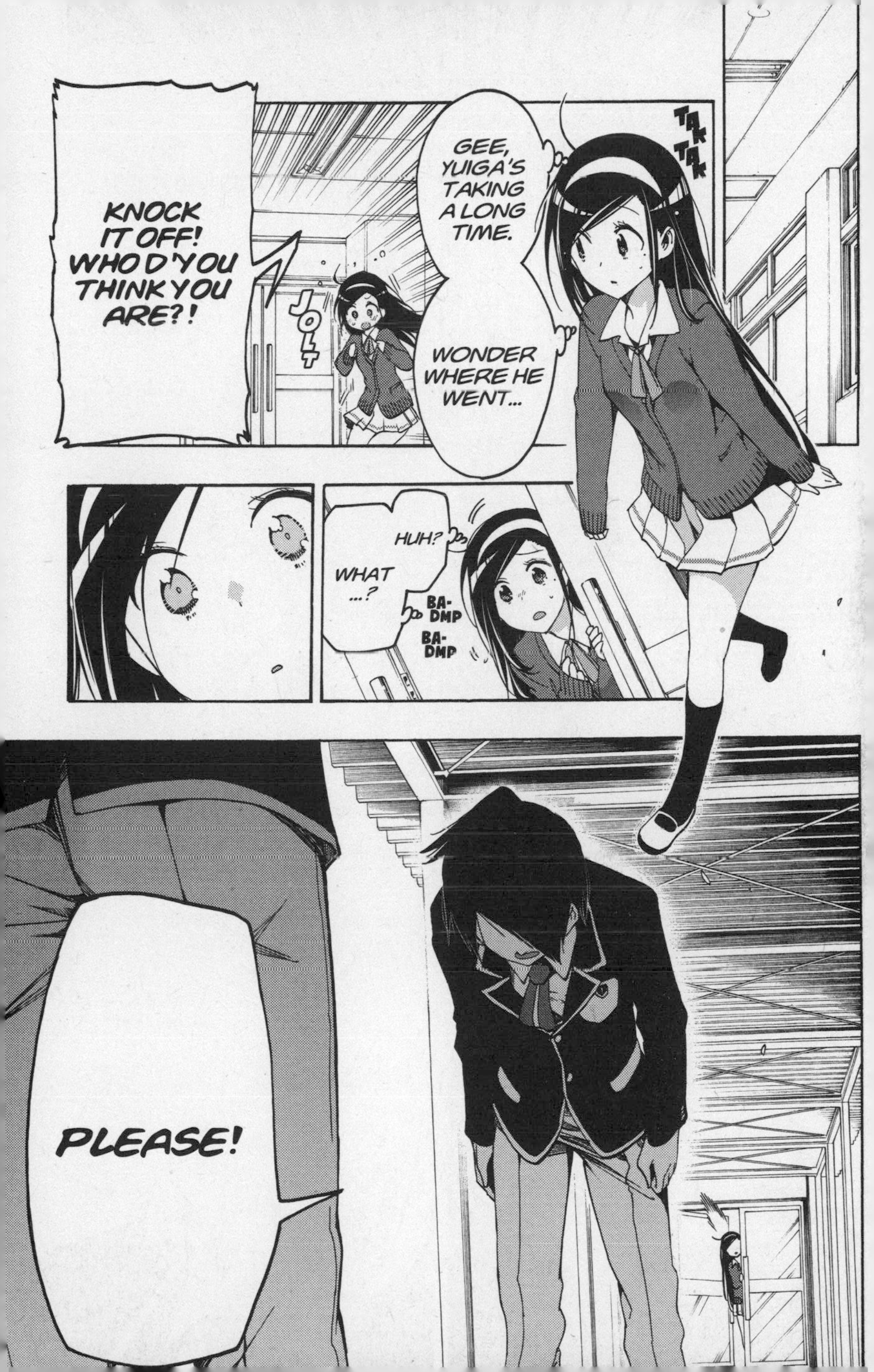
TAK TAK
GEE, YUIGA'S TAKING A LONG TIME.
WONDER WHERE HE WENT...
KNOCK IT OFF! WHO D'YOU THINK YOU ARE?!
JOLT
HUH?
WHAT ...?
BA-DMP BA-DMP
PLEASE!

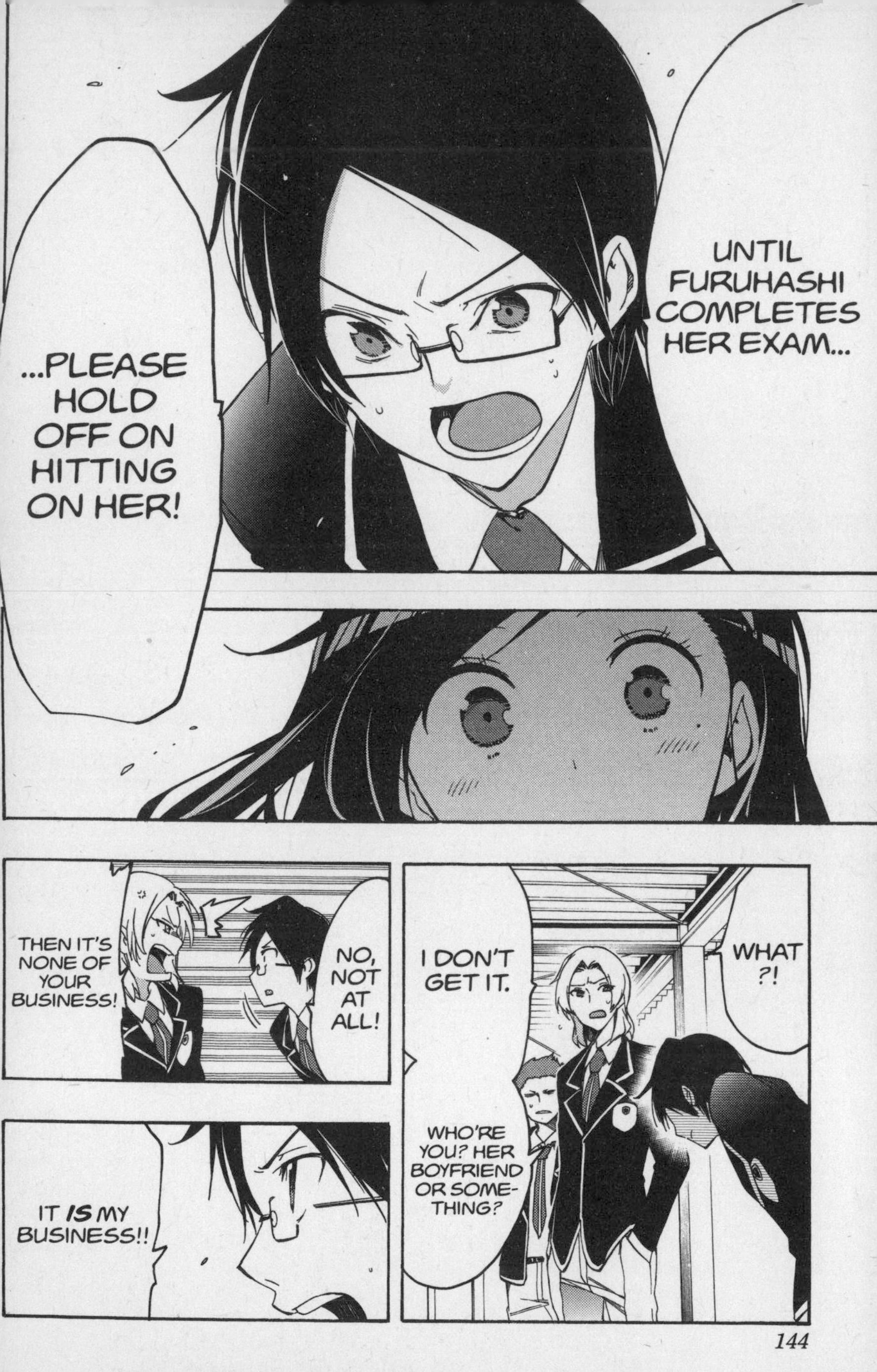
UNTIL FURUHASHI COMPLETES HER EXAM...
...PLEASE HOLD OFF ON HITTING ON HER!
WHAT?!
I DON'T GET IT.
WHO'RE YOU? HER BOYFRIEND OR SOMETHING?
NO, NOT AT ALL!
THEN IT'S NONE OF YOUR BUSINESS!
IT *IS* MY BUSINESS!!

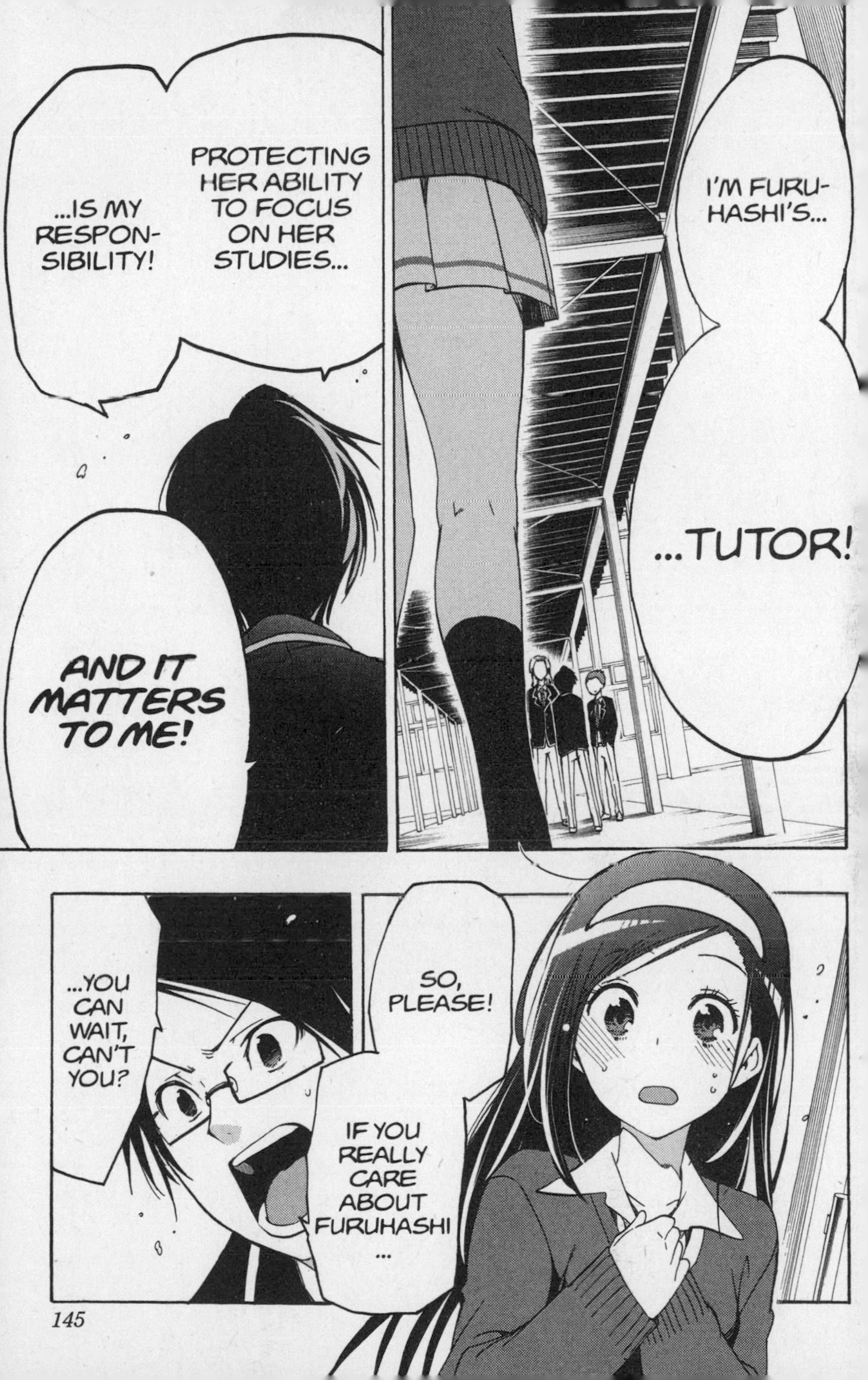
I'M FURU-HASHI'S...
...TUTOR!
PROTECTING HER ABILITY TO FOCUS ON HER STUDIES...
...IS MY RESPON-SIBILITY!
AND IT MATTERS TO ME!
SO, PLEASE!
IF YOU REALLY CARE ABOUT FURUHASHI ...
...YOU CAN WAIT, CAN'T YOU?

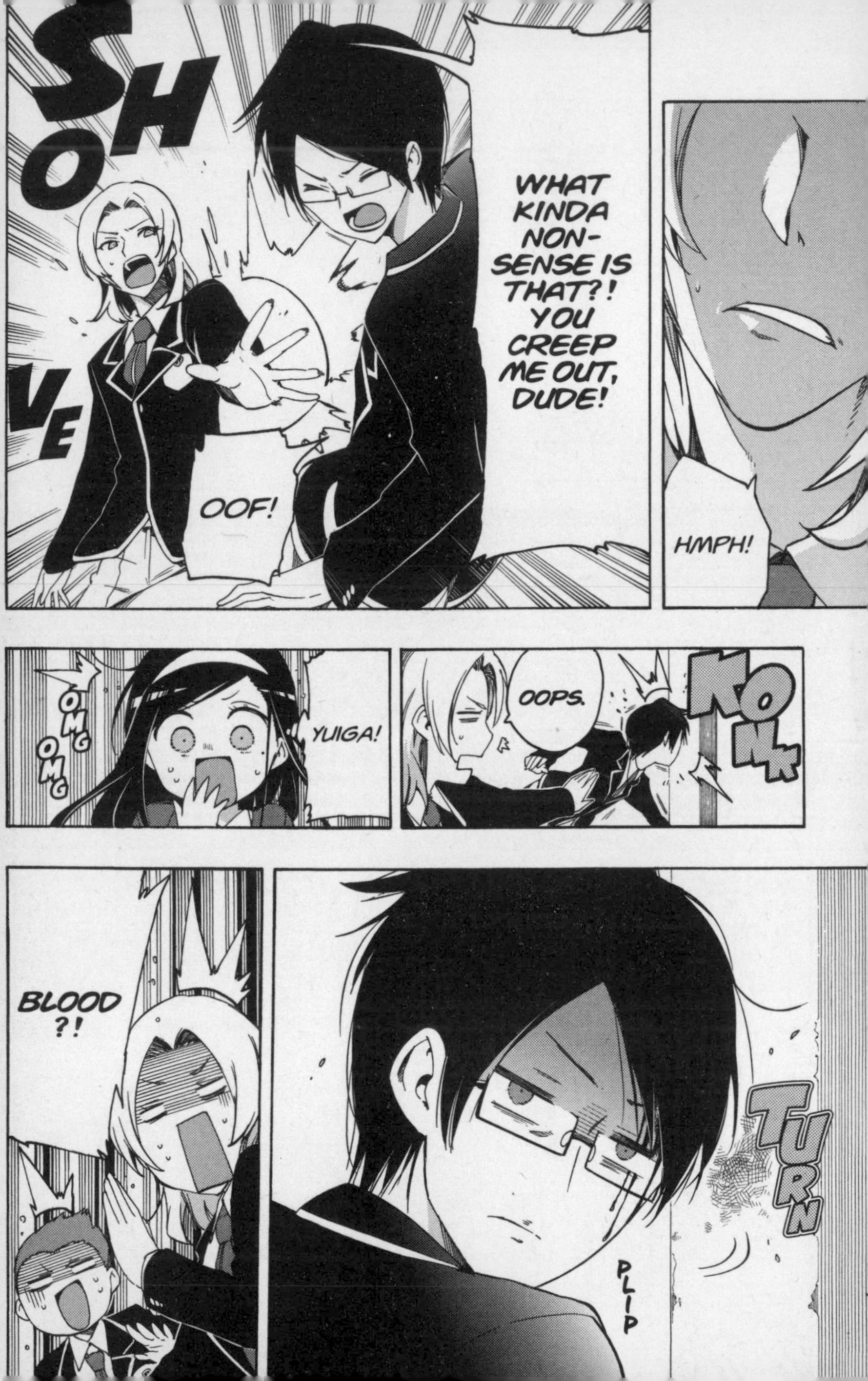
HMPH!
WHAT KINDA NON-SENSE IS THAT?! YOU CREEP ME OUT, DUDE!
SHOVE
OOF!
KONK
OOPS.
YUIGA!
OMG OMG
TURN
PLIP
BLOOD?!

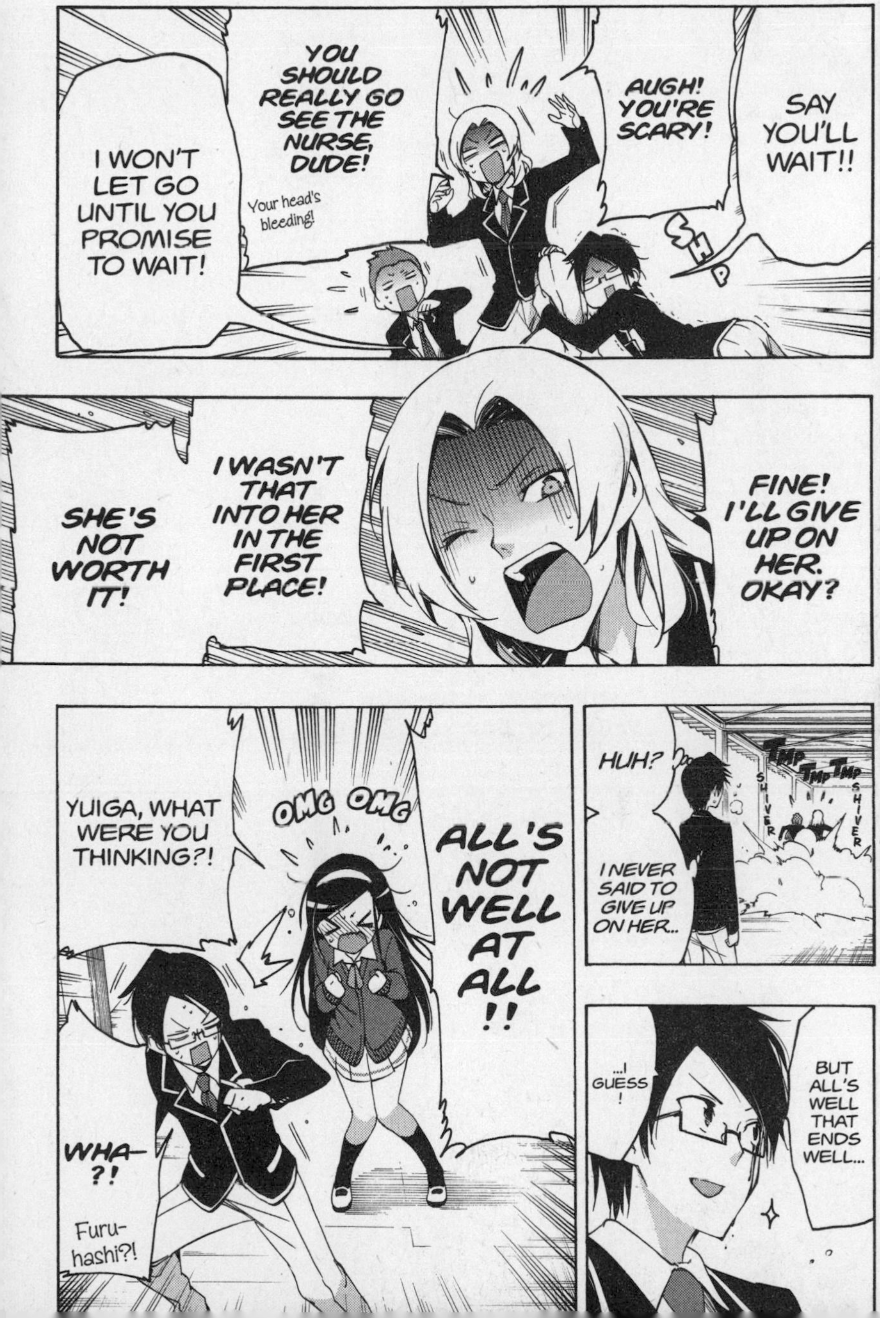
SAY YOU'LL WAIT!!
AUGH! YOU'RE SCARY!
SHP
YOU SHOULD REALLY GO SEE THE NURSE, DUDE!
Your head's bleeding!
I WON'T LET GO UNTIL YOU PROMISE TO WAIT!
FINE! I'LL GIVE UP ON HER. OKAY?
I WASN'T THAT INTO HER IN THE FIRST PLACE!
SHE'S NOT WORTH IT!
TMP TMP TMP
SHIVER
SHIVER
HUH?
I NEVER SAID TO GIVE UP ON HER...
BUT ALL'S WELL THAT ENDS WELL...
...I GUESS!
ALL'S NOT WELL AT ALL!!
OMG OMG
YUIGA, WHAT WERE YOU THINKING?!
WHA- ?!
Furu-hashi?!

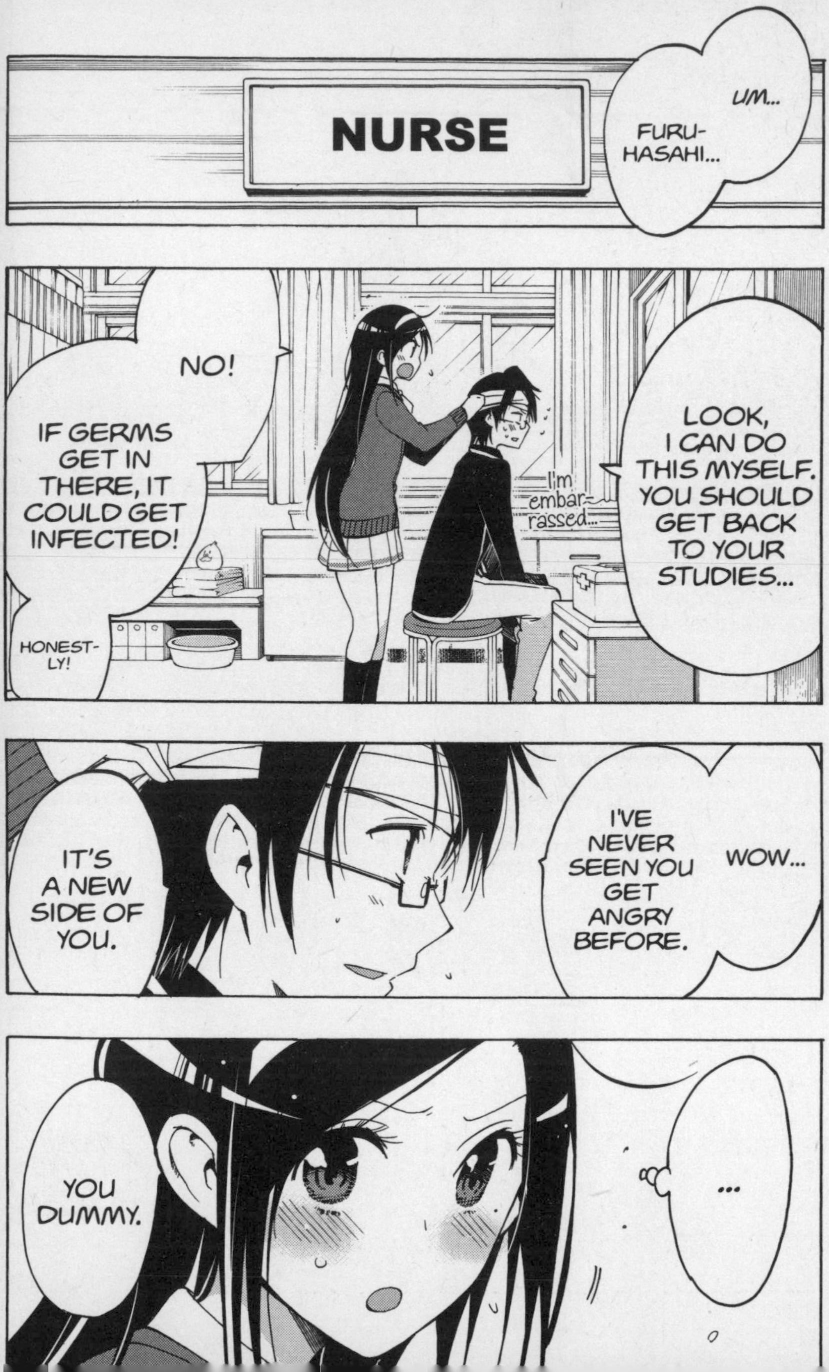
UM... FURU-HASAHI...
NURSE
LOOK, I CAN DO THIS MYSELF. YOU SHOULD GET BACK TO YOUR STUDIES...
I'm embarrassed...
NO! IF GERMS GET IN THERE, IT COULD GET INFECTED!
HONESTLY!
WOW...
I'VE NEVER SEEN YOU GET ANGRY BEFORE.
IT'S A NEW SIDE OF YOU.
...
YOU DUMMY.

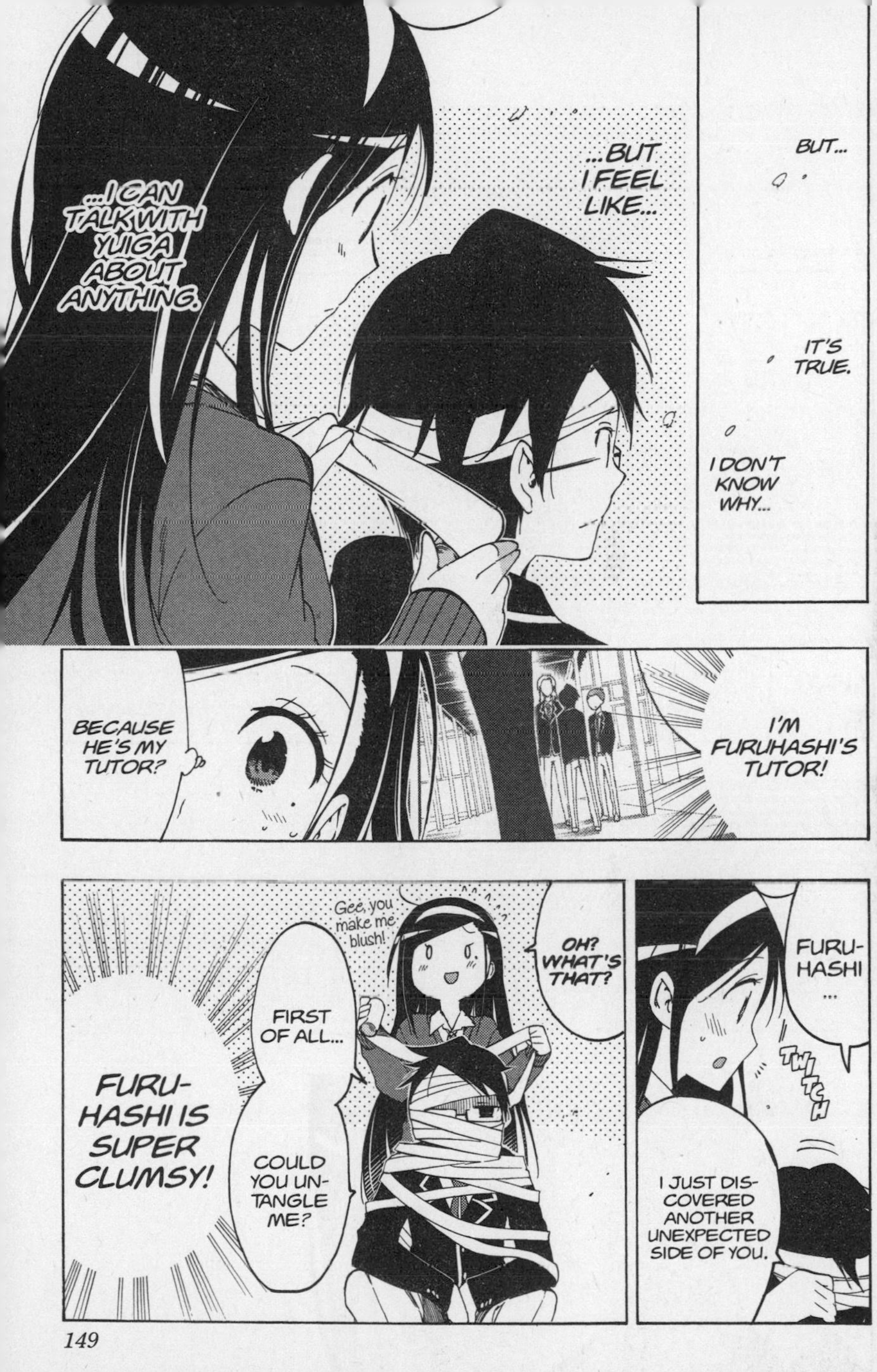
BUT...
IT'S TRUE.
I DON'T KNOW WHY...
...BUT I FEEL LIKE...
...I CAN TALK WITH YUIGA ABOUT ANYTHING.
I'M FURUHASHI'S TUTOR!
BECAUSE HE'S MY TUTOR?
FURU-HASHI...
TWITCH
I JUST DIS-COVERED ANOTHER UNEXPECTED SIDE OF YOU.
OH? WHAT'S THAT?
Gee, you make me blush!
FIRST OF ALL...
COULD YOU UN-TANGLE ME?
FURU-HASHI IS SUPER CLUMSY!

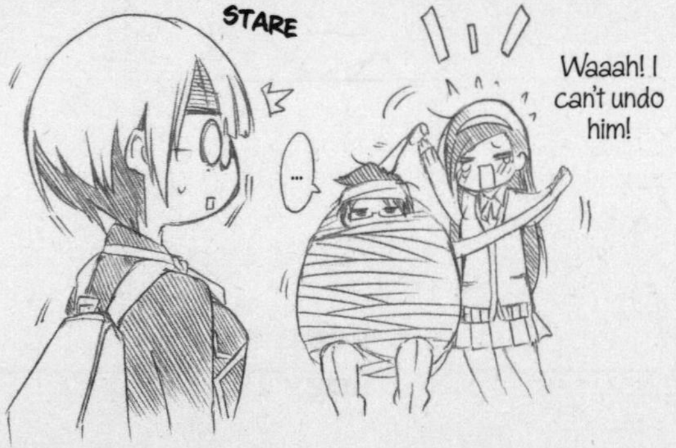
Waaah! I can't undo him!
...
STARE

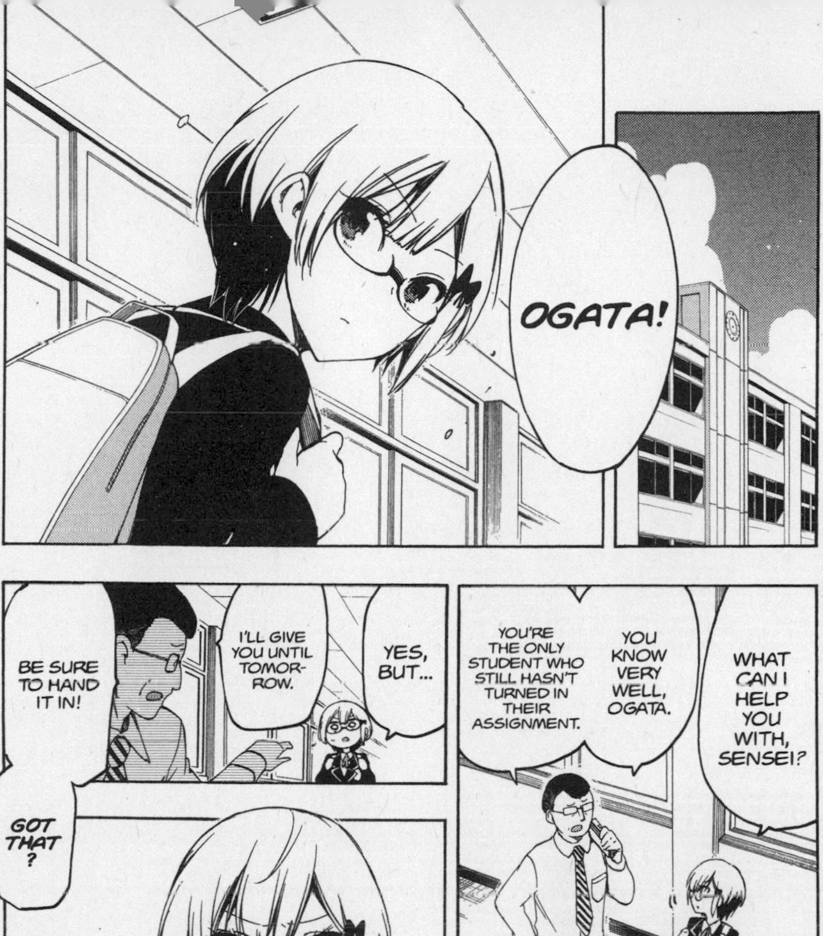
OGATA!
WHAT CAN I HELP YOU WITH, SENSEI?
YOU KNOW VERY WELL, OGATA.
YOU'RE THE ONLY STUDENT WHO STILL HASN'T TURNED IN THEIR ASSIGNMENT.
YES, BUT...
I'LL GIVE YOU UNTIL TOMOR-ROW.
BE SURE TO HAND IT IN!
GOT THAT?

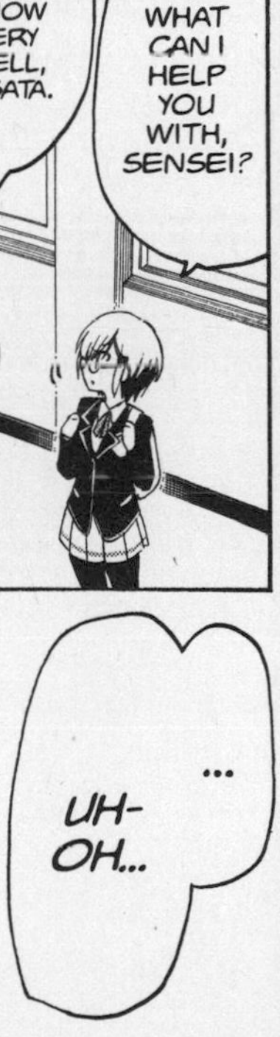
...
UH-OH...

Question 6:
A Genius's Conception of Modern Technology Is [*X*]

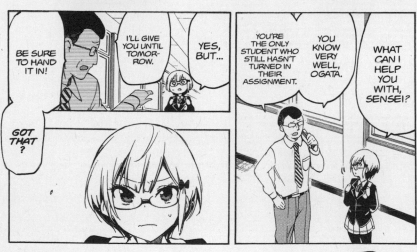

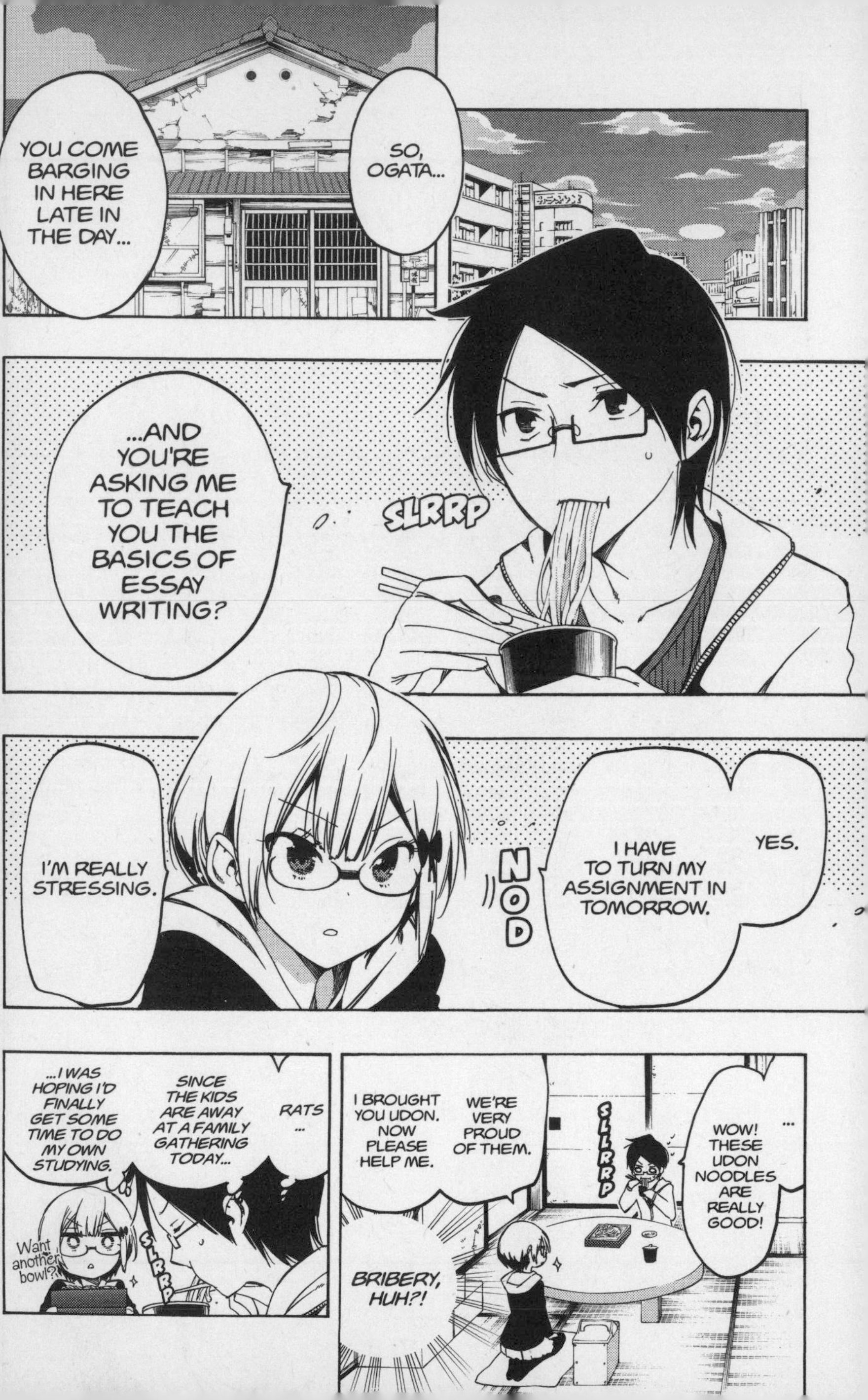
SO, OGATA...
YOU COME BARGING IN HERE LATE IN THE DAY...
...AND YOU'RE ASKING ME TO TEACH YOU THE BASICS OF ESSAY WRITING?
SLRRP
YES.
I HAVE TO TURN MY ASSIGNMENT IN TOMORROW.
NOD
I'M REALLY STRESSING.
...
WOW! THESE UDON NOODLES ARE REALLY GOOD!
SLLRRP
WE'RE VERY PROUD OF THEM.
I BROUGHT YOU UDON. NOW PLEASE HELP ME.
BRIBERY, HUH?!
RATS...
SINCE THE KIDS ARE AWAY AT A FAMILY GATHERING TODAY...
...I WAS HOPING I'D FINALLY GET SOME TIME TO DO MY OWN STUDYING.
SLRRP
Want another bowl?

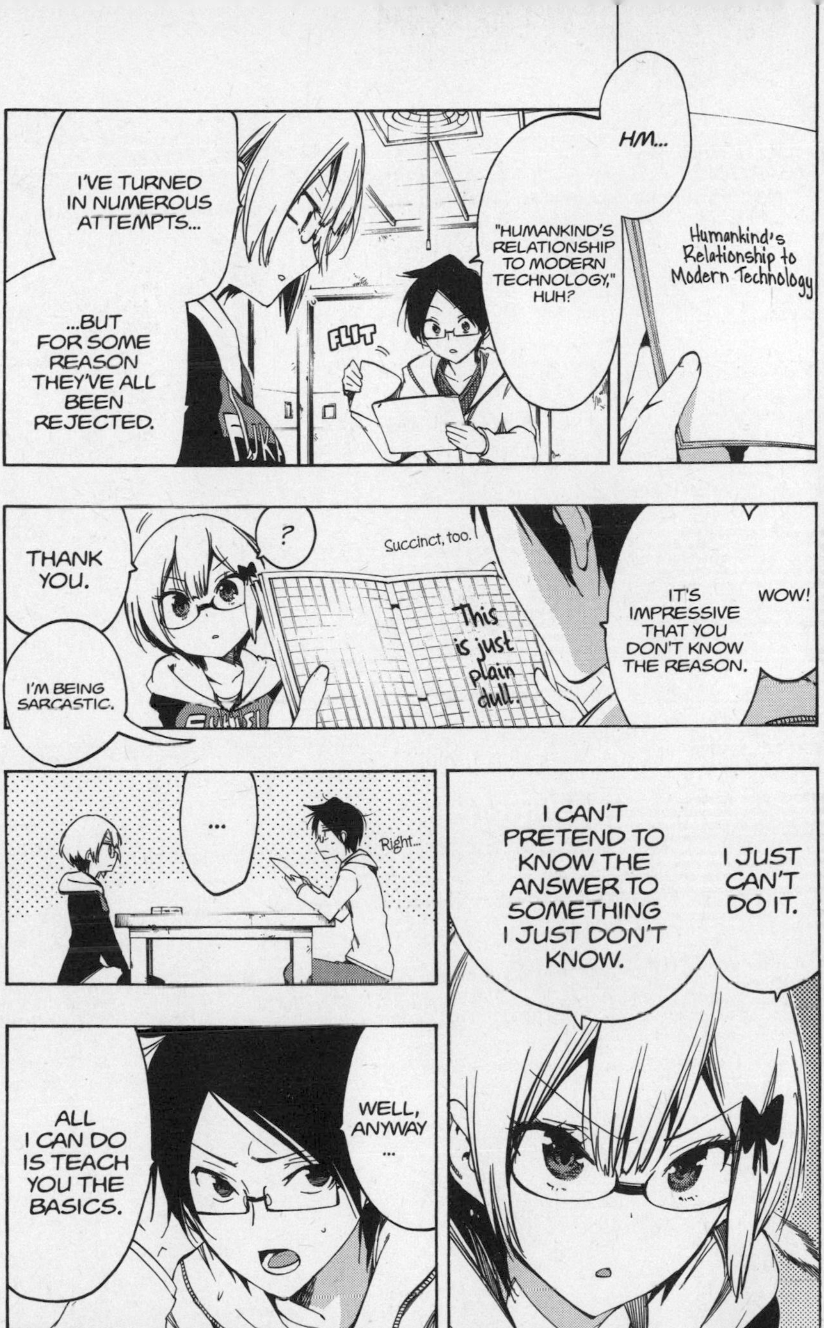
HM...
Humankind's Relationship to Modern Technology
"HUMANKIND'S RELATIONSHIP TO MODERN TECHNOLOGY," HUH?
FLIT
I'VE TURNED IN NUMEROUS ATTEMPTS...
...BUT FOR SOME REASON THEY'VE ALL BEEN REJECTED.
WOW!
IT'S IMPRESSIVE THAT YOU DON'T KNOW THE REASON.
This is just plain dull.
Succinct, too.
?
THANK YOU.
I'M BEING SARCASTIC.
I JUST CAN'T DO IT.
I CAN'T PRETEND TO KNOW THE ANSWER TO SOMETHING I JUST DON'T KNOW.
...
Right...
WELL, ANYWAY...
ALL I CAN DO IS TEACH YOU THE BASICS.

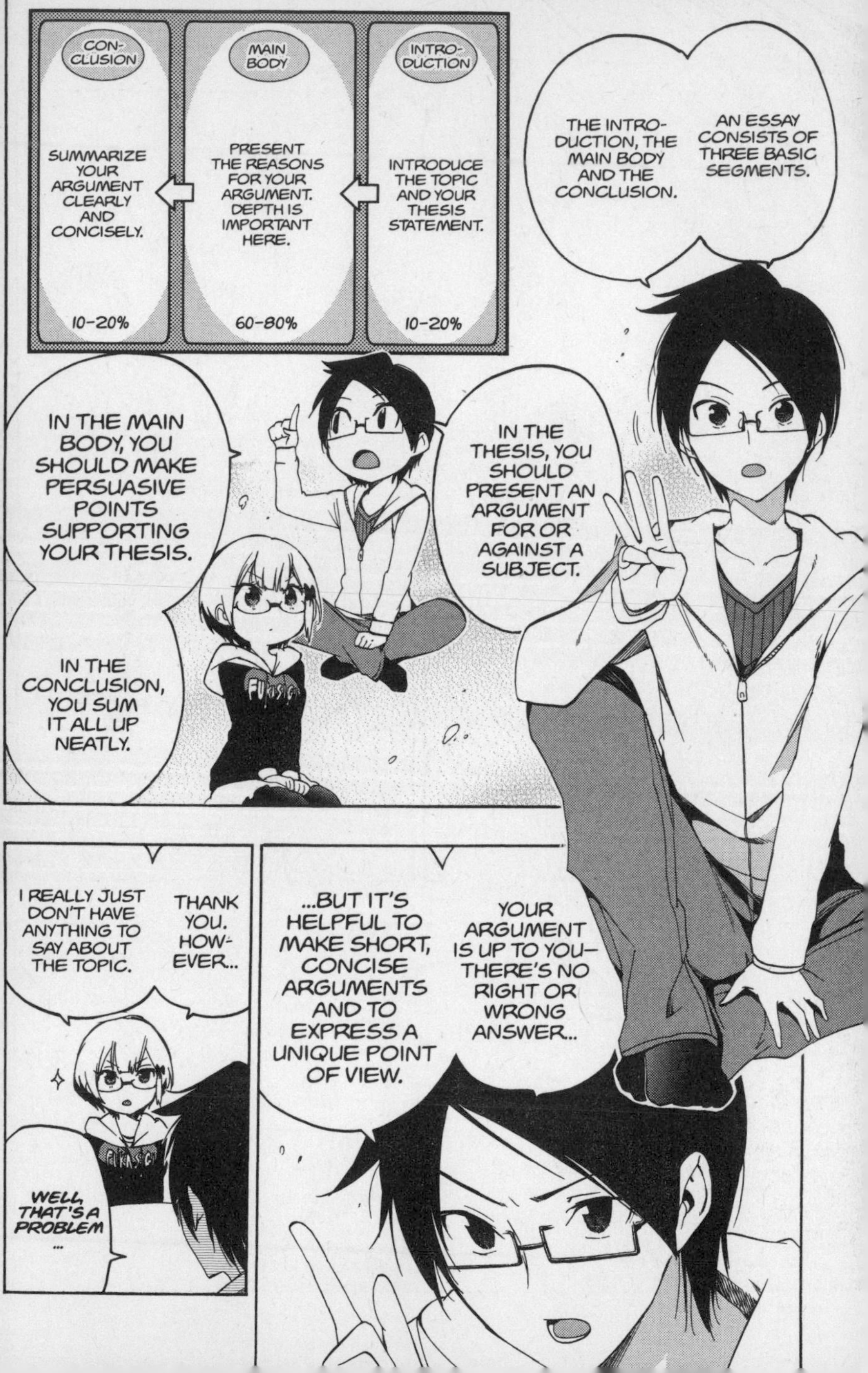
AN ESSAY CONSISTS OF THREE BASIC SEGMENTS.
THE INTRO-DUCTION, THE MAIN BODY AND THE CONCLUSION.
INTRO-DUCTION
INTRODUCE THE TOPIC AND YOUR THESIS STATEMENT.
10-20%
MAIN BODY
PRESENT THE REASONS FOR YOUR ARGUMENT. DEPTH IS IMPORTANT HERE.
60-80%
CON-CLUSION
SUMMARIZE YOUR ARGUMENT CLEARLY AND CONCISELY.
10-20%
IN THE THESIS, YOU SHOULD PRESENT AN ARGUMENT FOR OR AGAINST A SUBJECT.
IN THE MAIN BODY, YOU SHOULD MAKE PERSUASIVE POINTS SUPPORTING YOUR THESIS.
IN THE CONCLUSION, YOU SUM IT ALL UP NEATLY.
YOUR ARGUMENT IS UP TO YOU—THERE'S NO RIGHT OR WRONG ANSWER...
...BUT IT'S HELPFUL TO MAKE SHORT, CONCISE ARGUMENTS AND TO EXPRESS A UNIQUE POINT OF VIEW.
THANK YOU. HOW-EVER...
I REALLY JUST DON'T HAVE ANYTHING TO SAY ABOUT THE TOPIC.
WELL, THAT'S A PROBLEM...

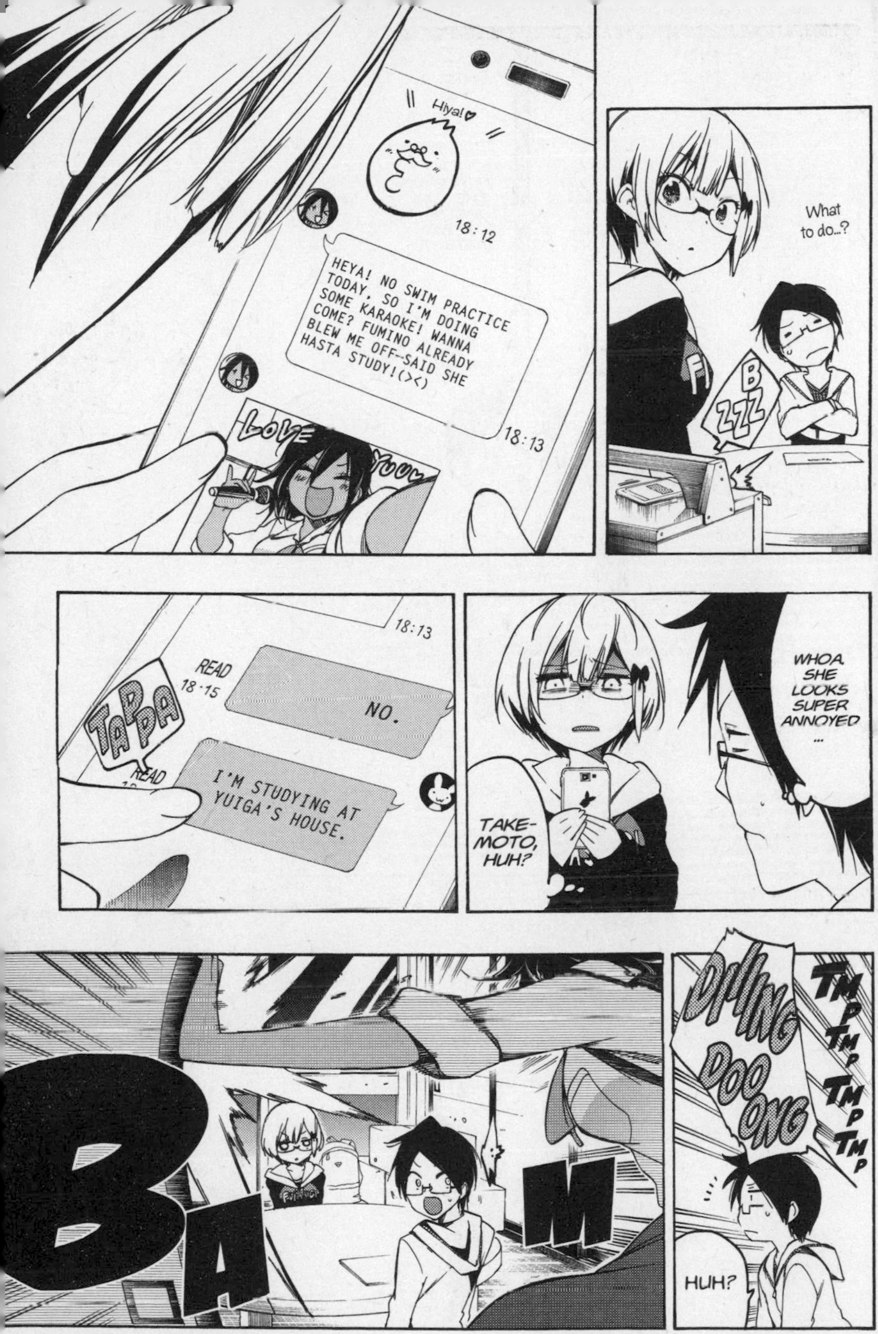
What to do...?
BZZZ
Hiya!♥
18:12
HEYA! NO SWIM PRACTICE TODAY, SO I'M DOING SOME KARAOKE! WANNA COME? FUMINO ALREADY BLEW ME OFF--SAID SHE HASTA STUDY!(><)
LOVE YOU
18:13
WHOA. SHE LOOKS SUPER ANNOYED...
TAKE-MOTO, HUH?
18:13
READ 18:15
NO.
TAPPA
READ
I'M STUDYING AT YUIGA'S HOUSE.
DIIING DOOONG
TMP TMP TMP TMP
HUH?
BAM

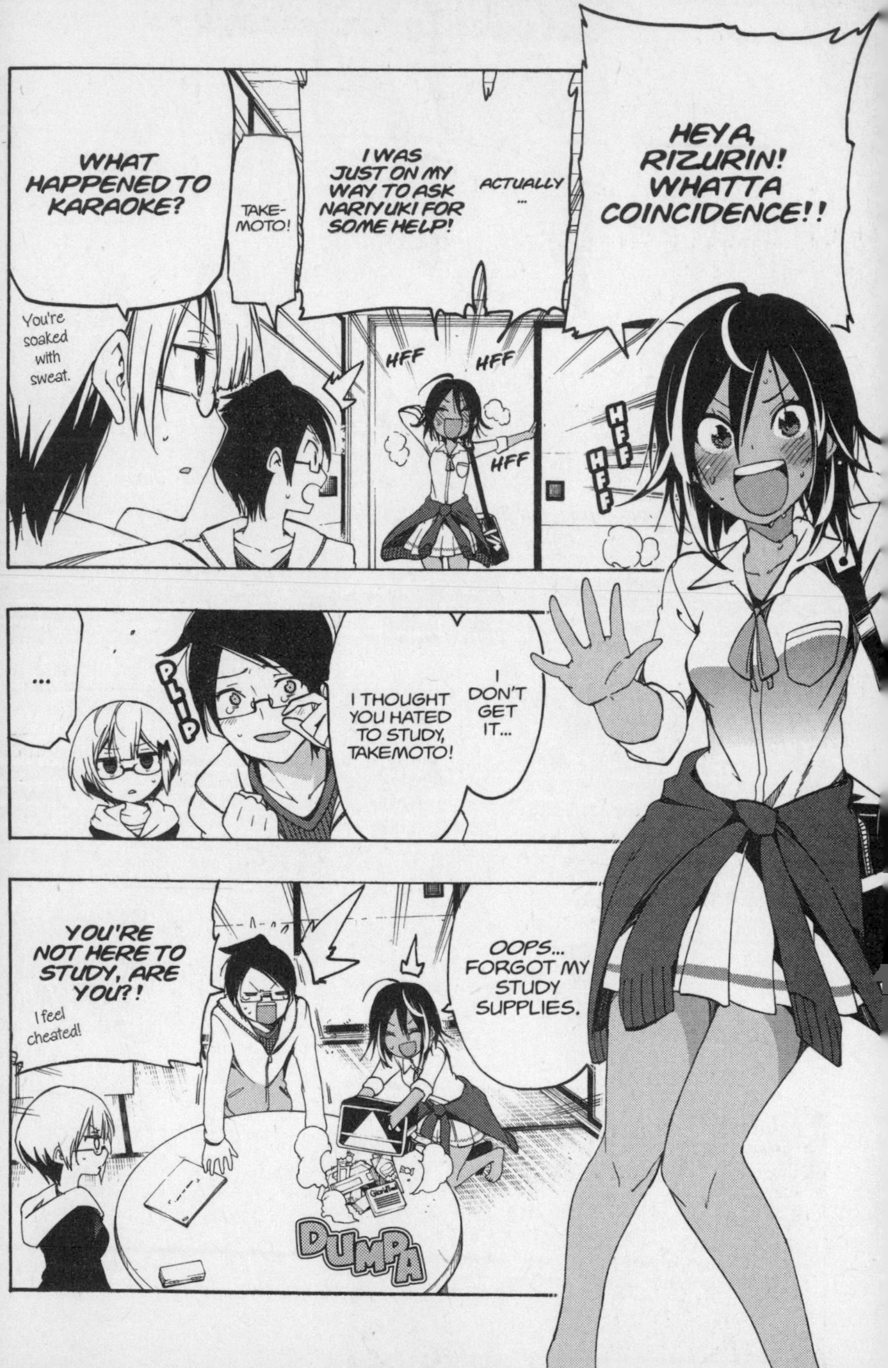
HEYA, RIZURIN! WHATTA COINCIDENCE!!
HFF HFF
ACTUALLY...
I WAS JUST ON MY WAY TO ASK NARIYUKI FOR SOME HELP!
HFF HFF HFF
TAKE-MOTO!
WHAT HAPPENED TO KARAOKE?
You're soaked with sweat.
I DON'T GET IT...
I THOUGHT YOU HATED TO STUDY, TAKEMOTO!
PLIP
...
OOPS... FORGOT MY STUDY SUPPLIES.
YOU'RE NOT HERE TO STUDY, ARE YOU?!
I feel cheated!
DUMPA

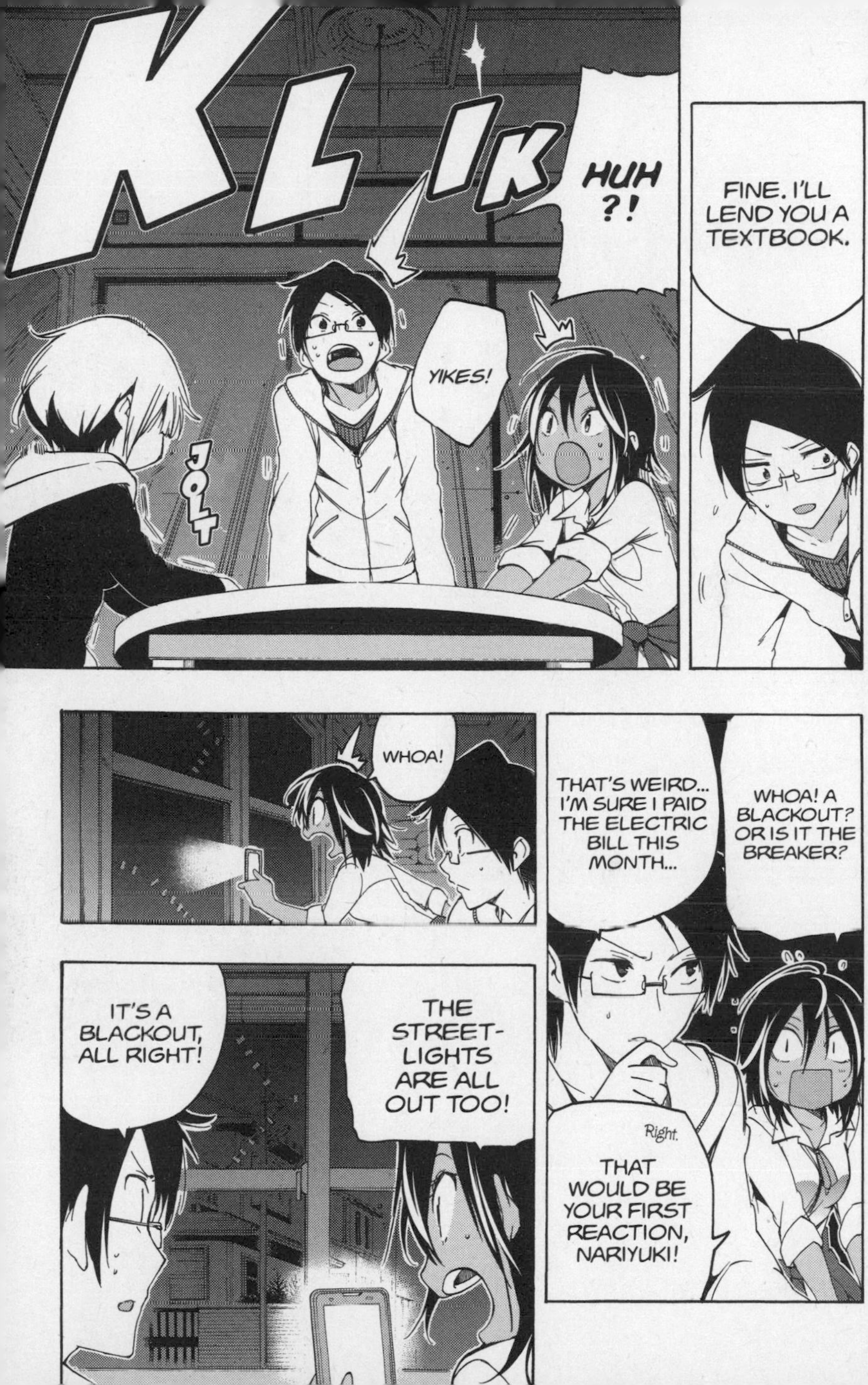
FINE. I'LL LEND YOU A TEXTBOOK.
HUH ?!
KLIK
YIKES!
JOLT
WHOA! A BLACKOUT? OR IS IT THE BREAKER?
THAT'S WEIRD... I'M SURE I PAID THE ELECTRIC BILL THIS MONTH...
Right.
THAT WOULD BE YOUR FIRST REACTION, NARIYUKI!
WHOA!
THE STREET-LIGHTS ARE ALL OUT TOO!
IT'S A BLACKOUT, ALL RIGHT!

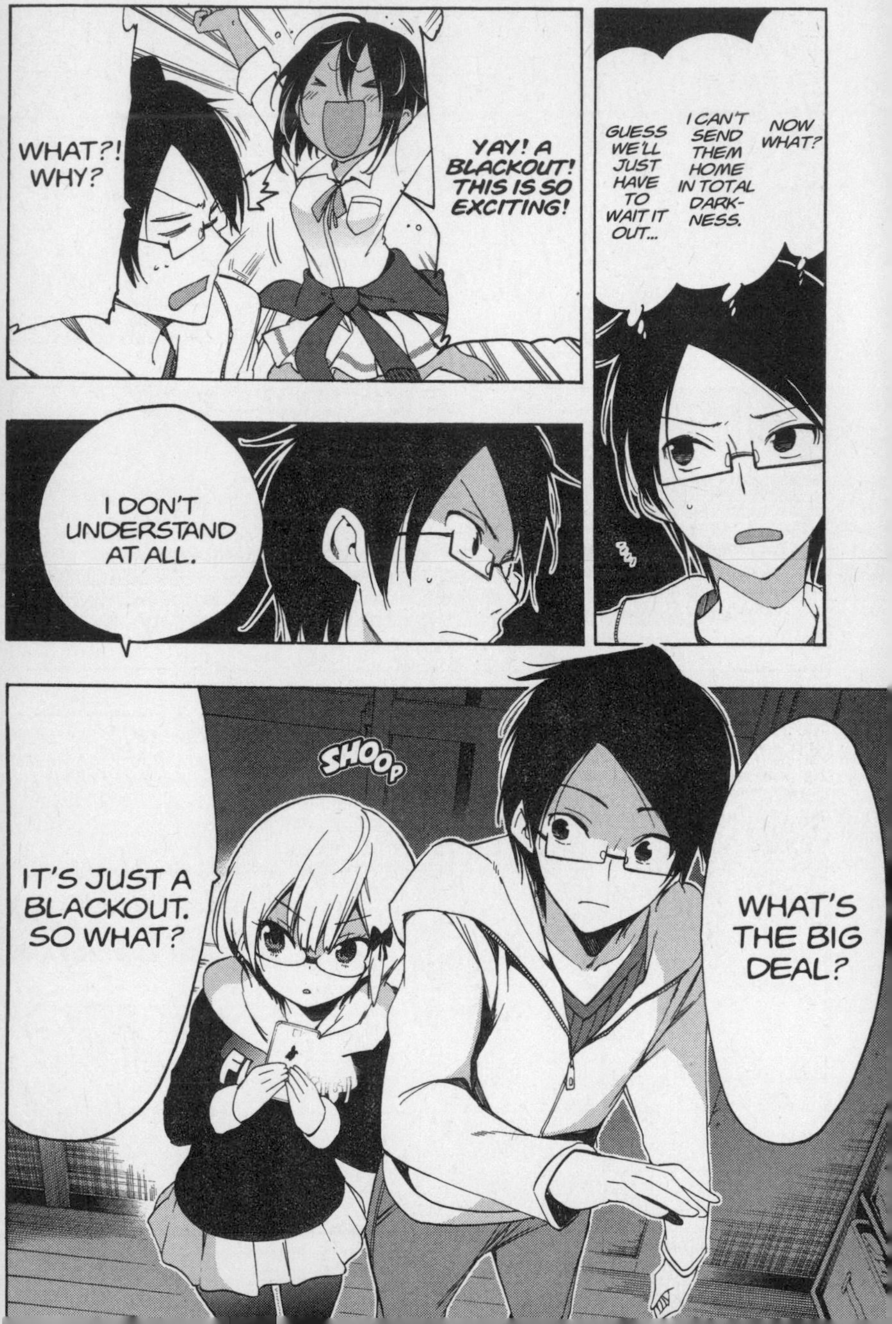
NOW WHAT?
I CAN'T SEND THEM HOME IN TOTAL DARKNESS.
GUESS WE'LL JUST HAVE TO WAIT IT OUT...
YAY! A BLACKOUT! THIS IS SO EXCITING!
WHAT?! WHY?
I DON'T UNDERSTAND AT ALL.
SHOOP
WHAT'S THE BIG DEAL?
IT'S JUST A BLACKOUT. SO WHAT?

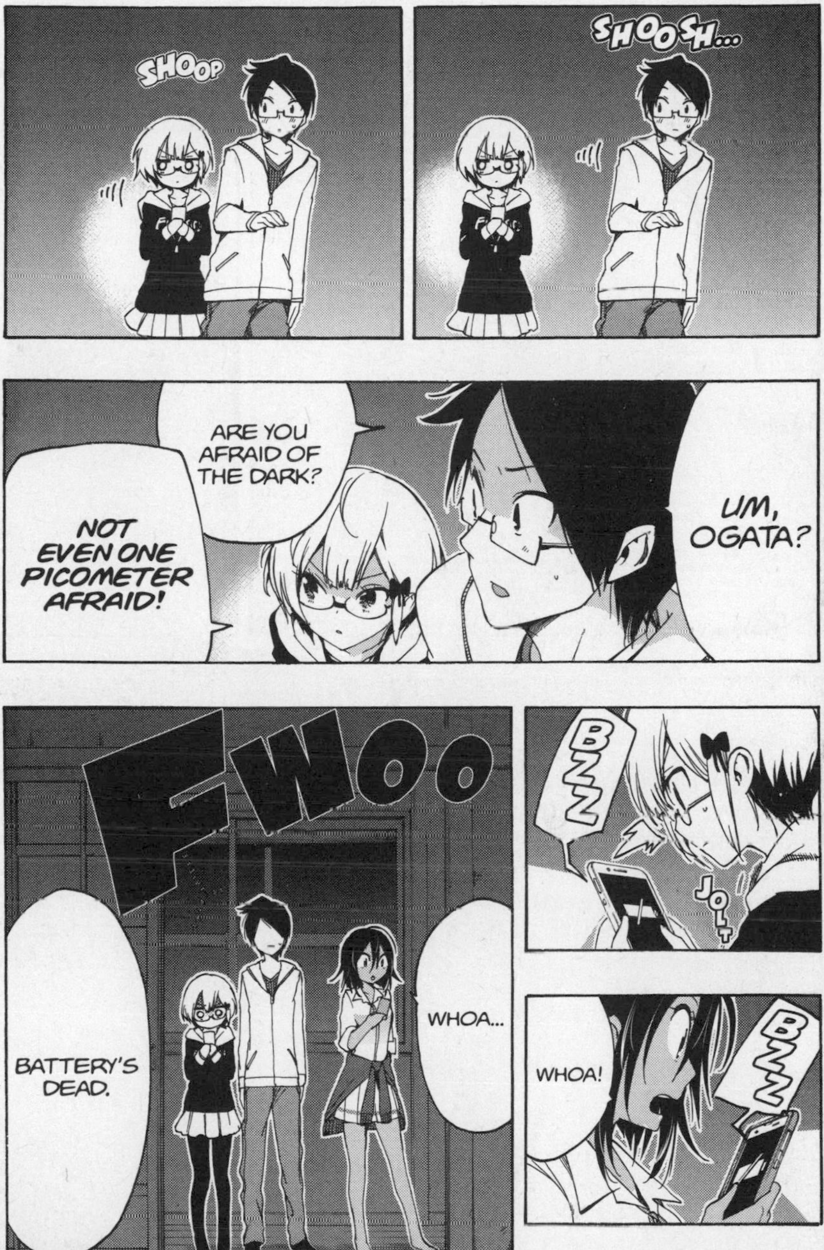
SHOOSH...
SHOOP
UM, OGATA?
ARE YOU AFRAID OF THE DARK?
NOT EVEN ONE PICOMETER AFRAID!
BZZ
JOLT
BZZ
WHOA!
FWOO
WHOA...
BATTERY'S DEAD.

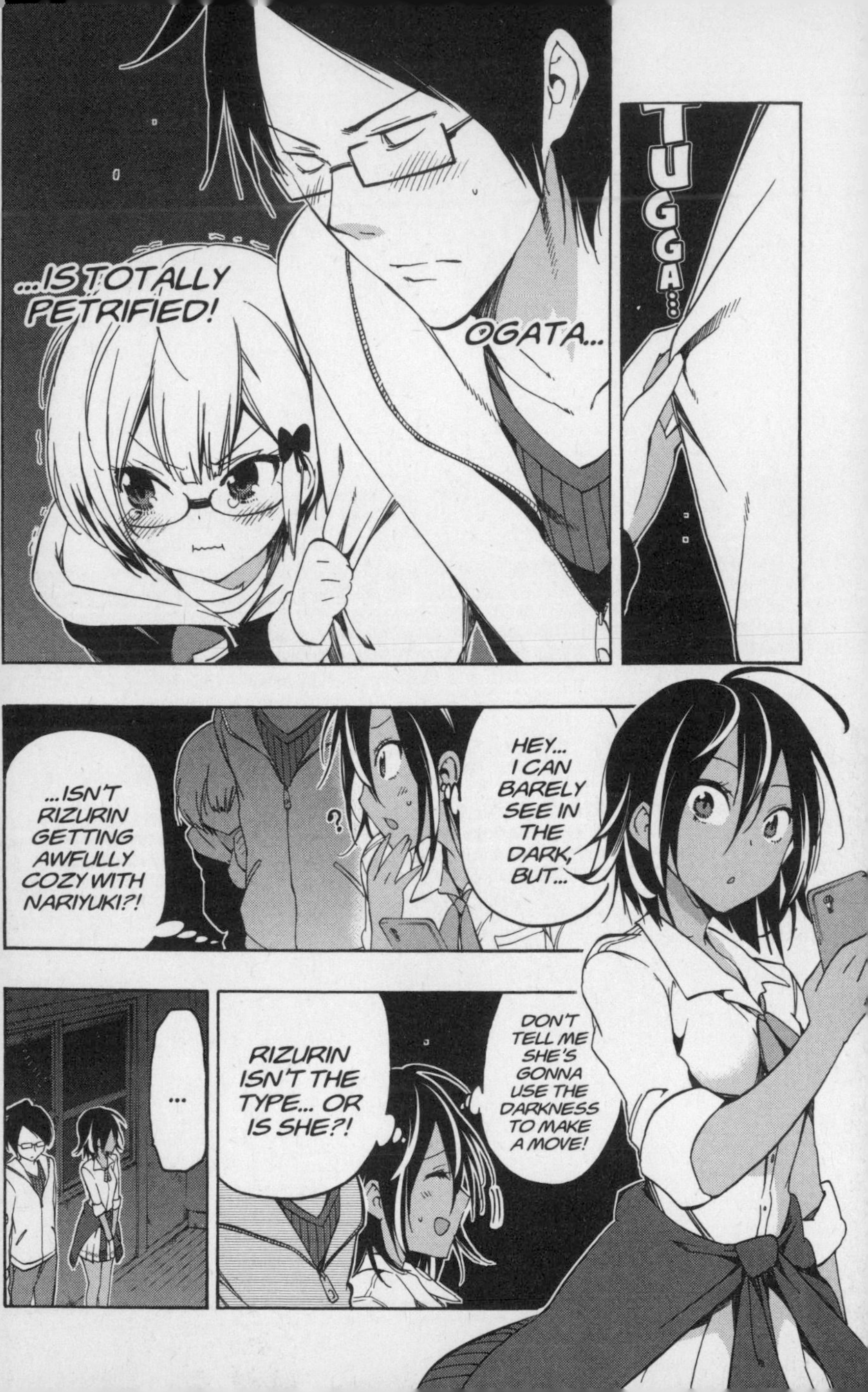
TUGGA...
OGATA...
...IS TOTALLY PETRIFIED!
HEY... I CAN BARELY SEE IN THE DARK, BUT...
...ISN'T RIZURIN GETTING AWFULLY COZY WITH NARIYUKI?!
DON'T TELL ME SHE'S GONNA USE THE DARKNESS TO MAKE A MOVE!
RIZURIN ISN'T THE TYPE... OR IS SHE?!
...

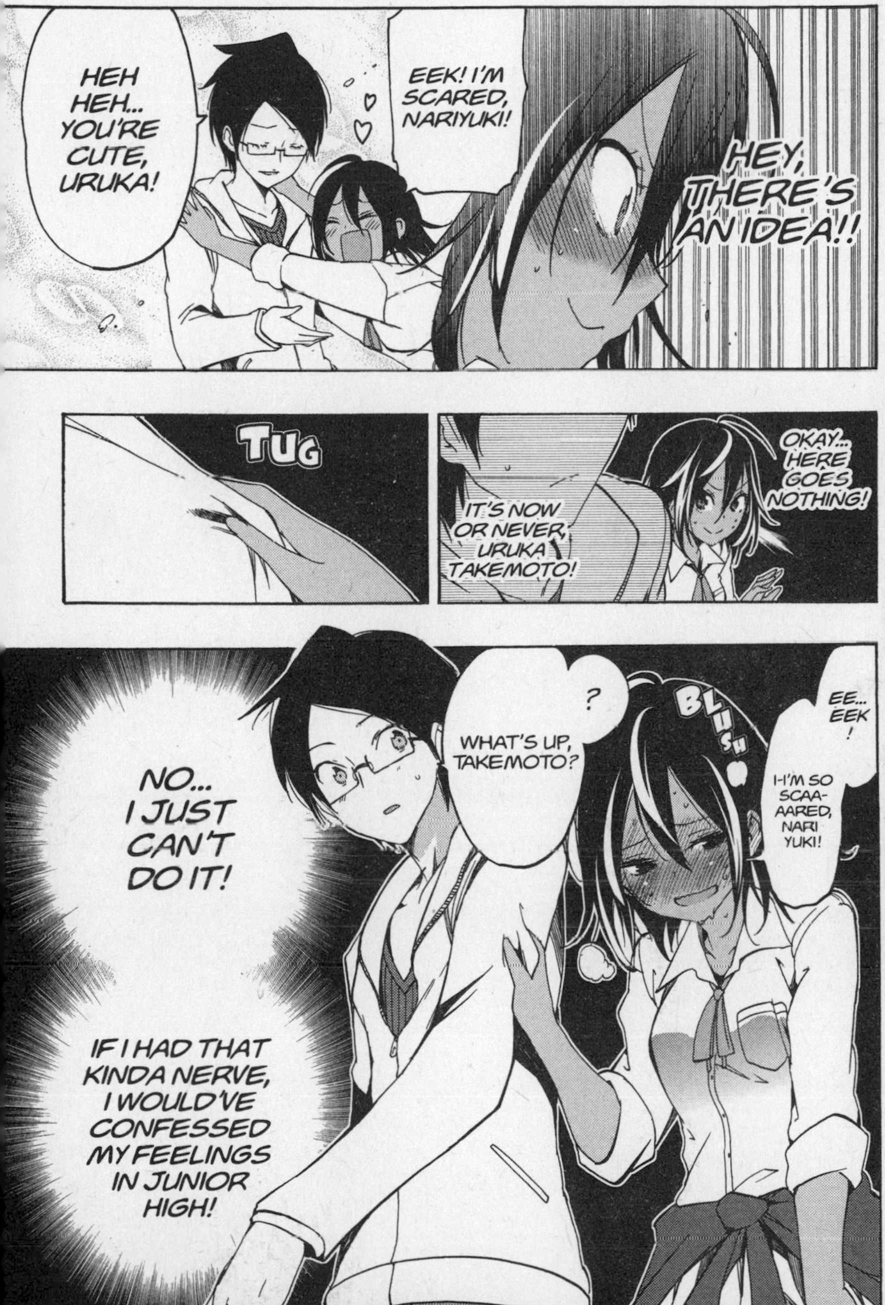
HEY, THERE'S AN IDEA!!
EEK! I'M SCARED, NARIYUKI!
HEH HEH... YOU'RE CUTE, URUKA!
OKAY... HERE GOES NOTHING!
IT'S NOW OR NEVER, URUKA TAKEMOTO!
TUG
EE... EEK!
I-I'M SO SCAAARED, NARI YUKI!
BLUSH
?
WHAT'S UP, TAKEMOTO?
NO... I JUST CAN'T DO IT!
IF I HAD THAT KINDA NERVE, I WOULD'VE CONFESSED MY FEELINGS IN JUNIOR HIGH!

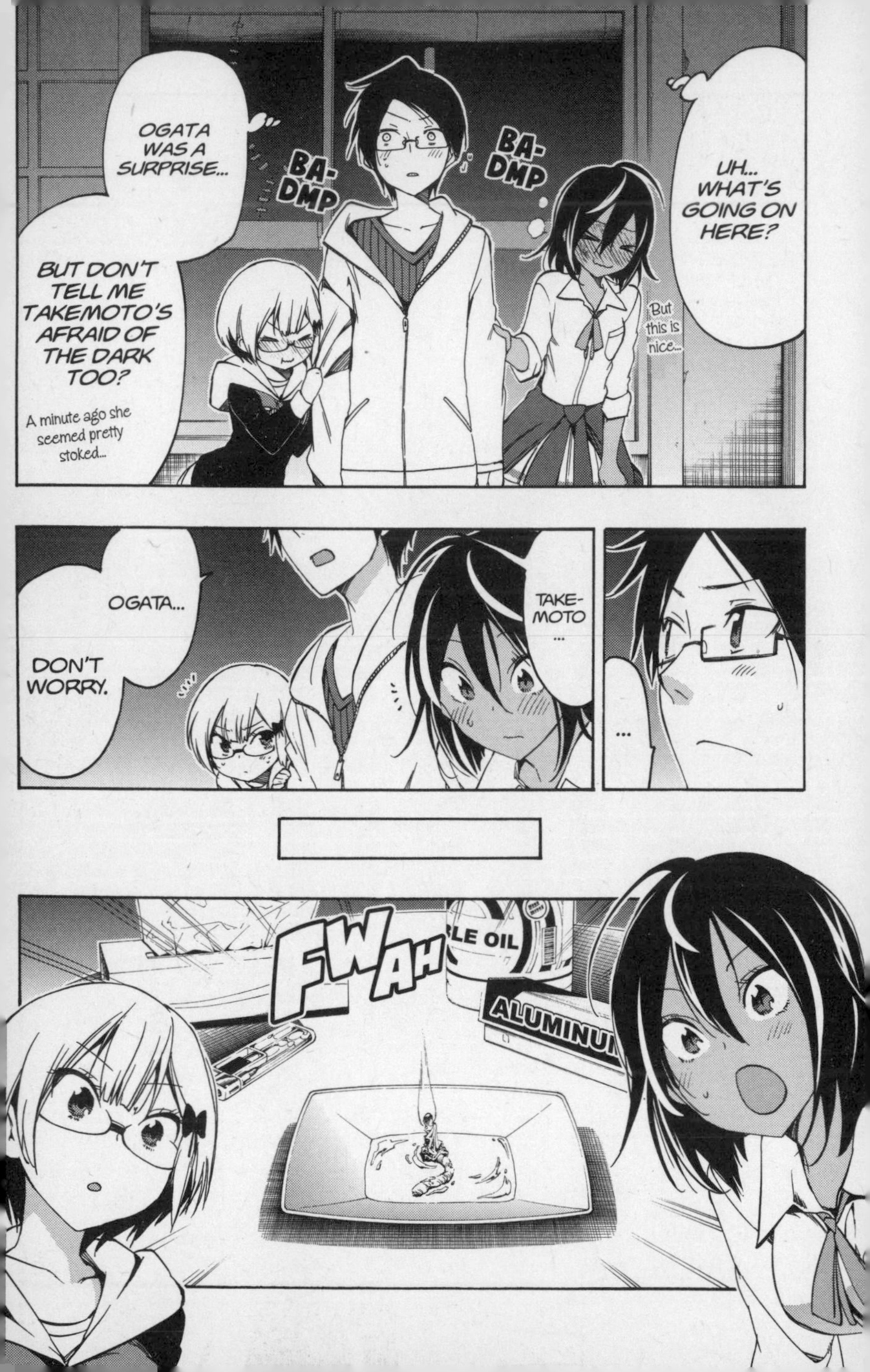
UH... WHAT'S GOING ON HERE?
But this is nice...
BA-DMP
BA-DMP
OGATA WAS A SURPRISE...
BUT DON'T TELL ME TAKEMOTO'S AFRAID OF THE DARK TOO?
A minute ago she seemed pretty stoked...
...
TAKEMOTO ...
OGATA...
DON'T WORRY.
FWAH
LE OIL
ALUMINU

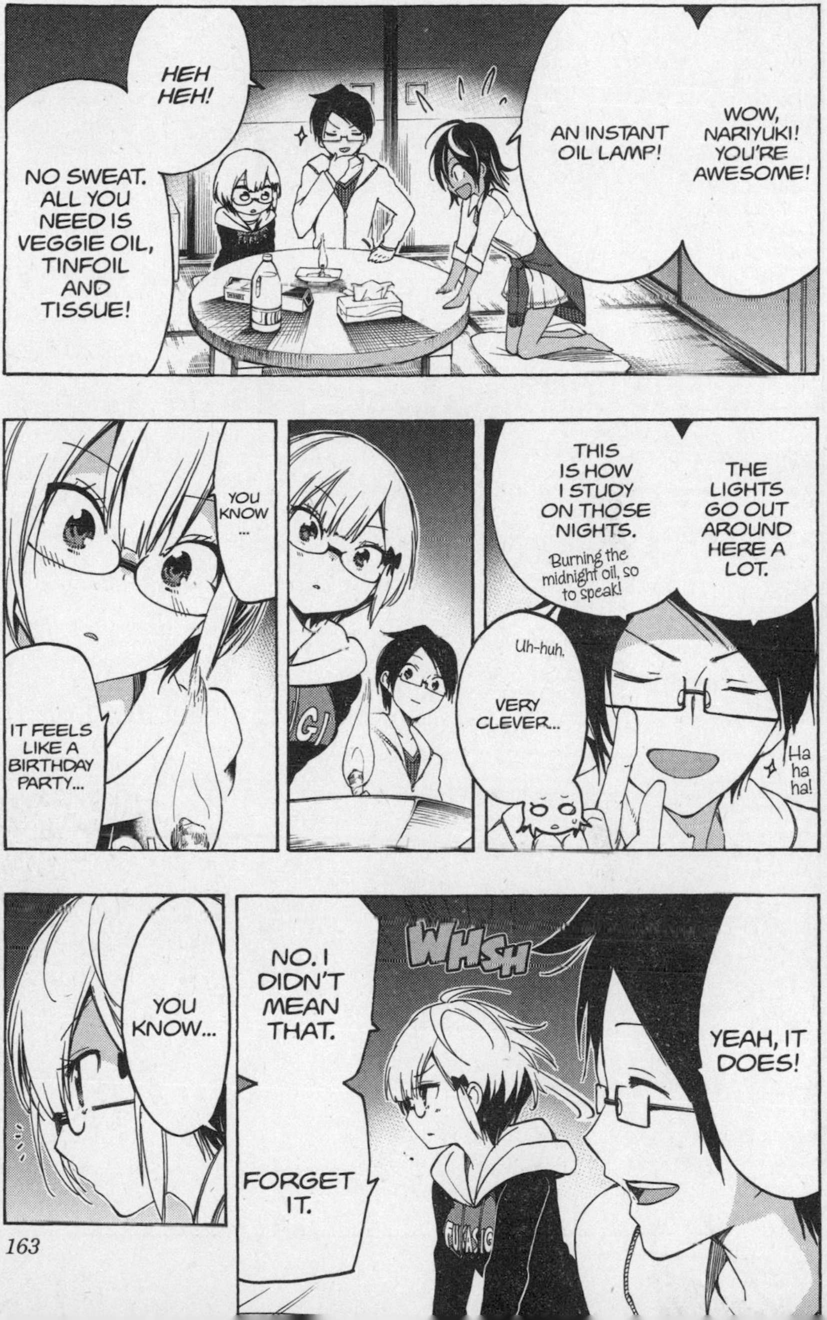
WOW, NARIYUKI! YOU'RE AWESOME!
AN INSTANT OIL LAMP!
HEH HEH!
NO SWEAT. ALL YOU NEED IS VEGGIE OIL, TINFOIL AND TISSUE!
THE LIGHTS GO OUT AROUND HERE A LOT.
THIS IS HOW I STUDY ON THOSE NIGHTS.
Burning the midnight oil, so to speak!
Ha ha ha!
Uh-huh.
VERY CLEVER...
YOU KNOW...
IT FEELS LIKE A BIRTHDAY PARTY...
YEAH, IT DOES!
WHSH
NO. I DIDN'T MEAN THAT.
FORGET IT.
YOU KNOW...

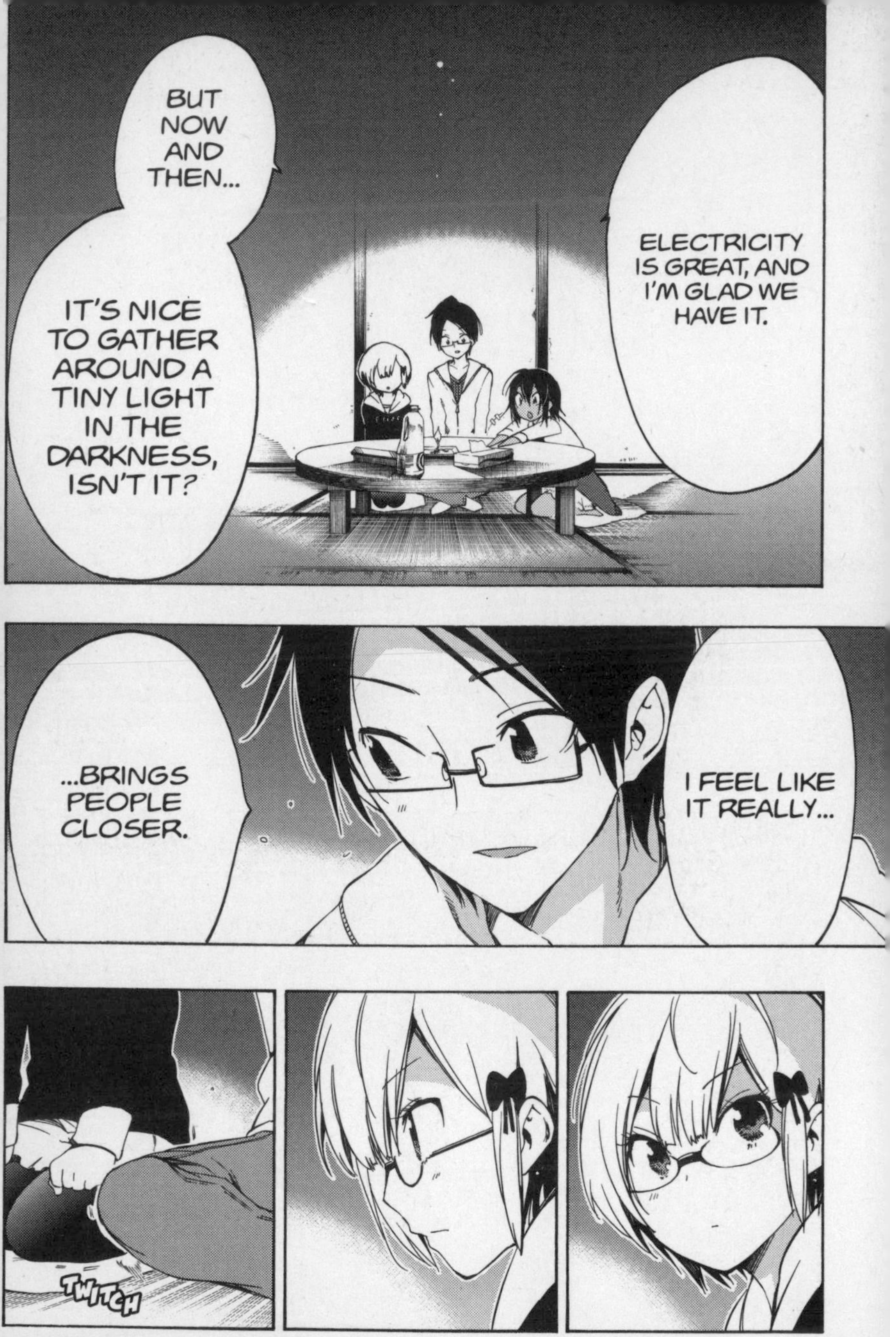
ELECTRICITY IS GREAT, AND I'M GLAD WE HAVE IT.
BUT NOW AND THEN...
IT'S NICE TO GATHER AROUND A TINY LIGHT IN THE DARKNESS, ISN'T IT?
I FEEL LIKE IT REALLY...
...BRINGS PEOPLE CLOSER.
TWITCH

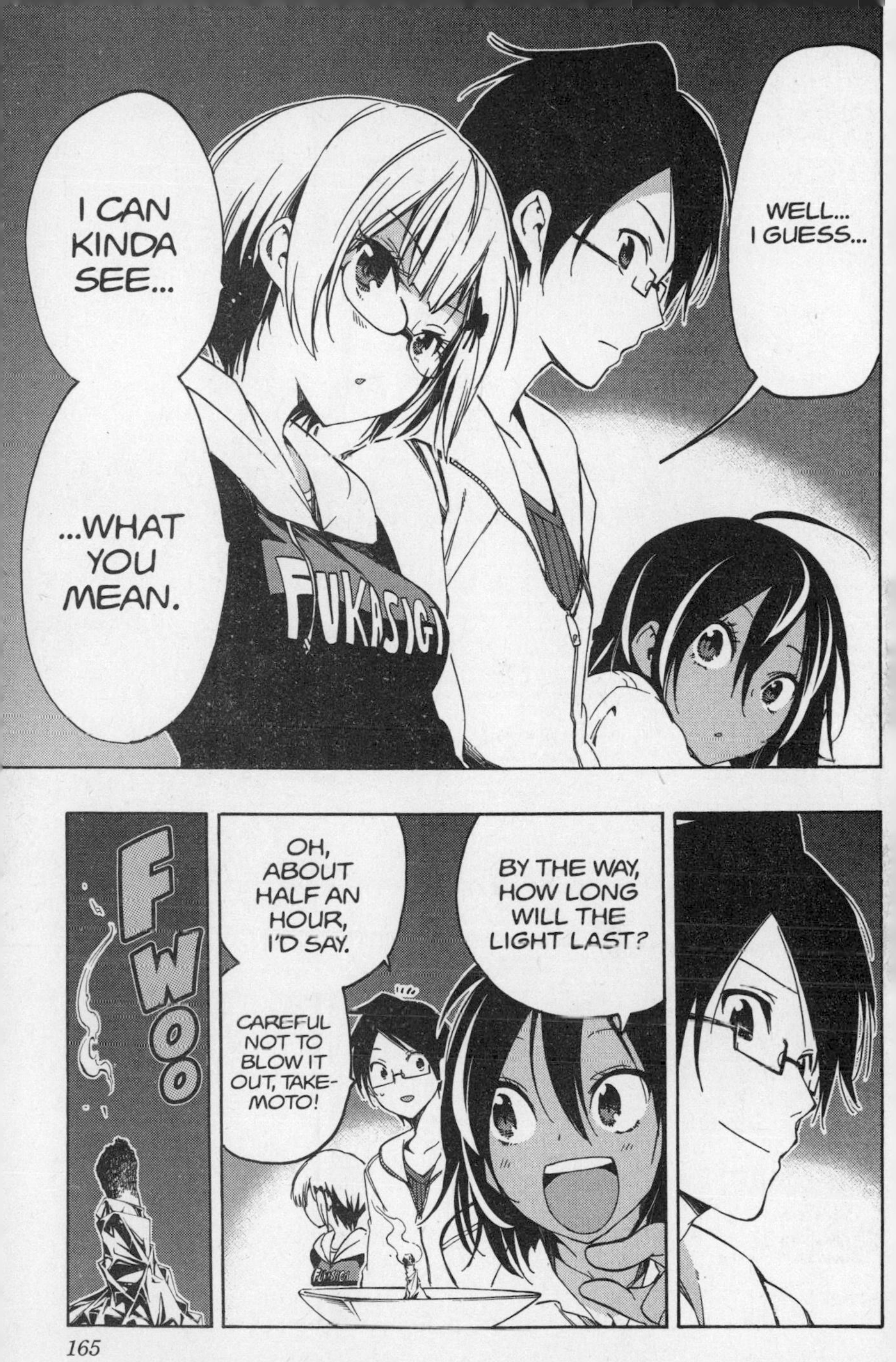
WELL... I GUESS...
I CAN KINDA SEE...
...WHAT YOU MEAN.
BY THE WAY, HOW LONG WILL THE LIGHT LAST?
OH, ABOUT HALF AN HOUR, I'D SAY.
CAREFUL NOT TO BLOW IT OUT, TAKE-MOTO!
FWOO

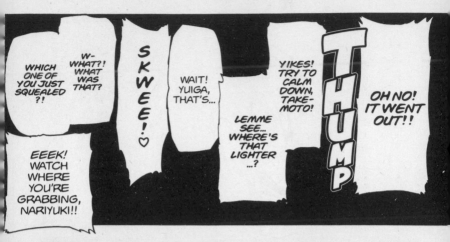

OH NO! IT WENT OUT!!
THUMP
YIKES! TRY TO CALM DOWN, TAKE-MOTO!
LEMME SEE... WHERE'S THAT LIGHTER ...?
WAIT! YUIGA, THAT'S...
SKWEE!♡
W-WHAT?! WHAT WAS THAT?
WHICH ONE OF YOU JUST SQUEALED ?!
EEEK! WATCH WHERE YOU'RE GRABBING, NARIYUKI!!
PAH
OH! THE LIGHTS ARE BACK!
THEY FIXED IT!
...
HUH ...?
WHAT'S WRONG, YOU TWO?

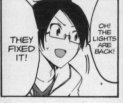

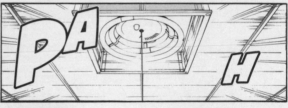

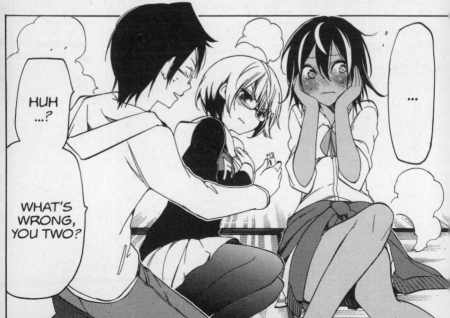

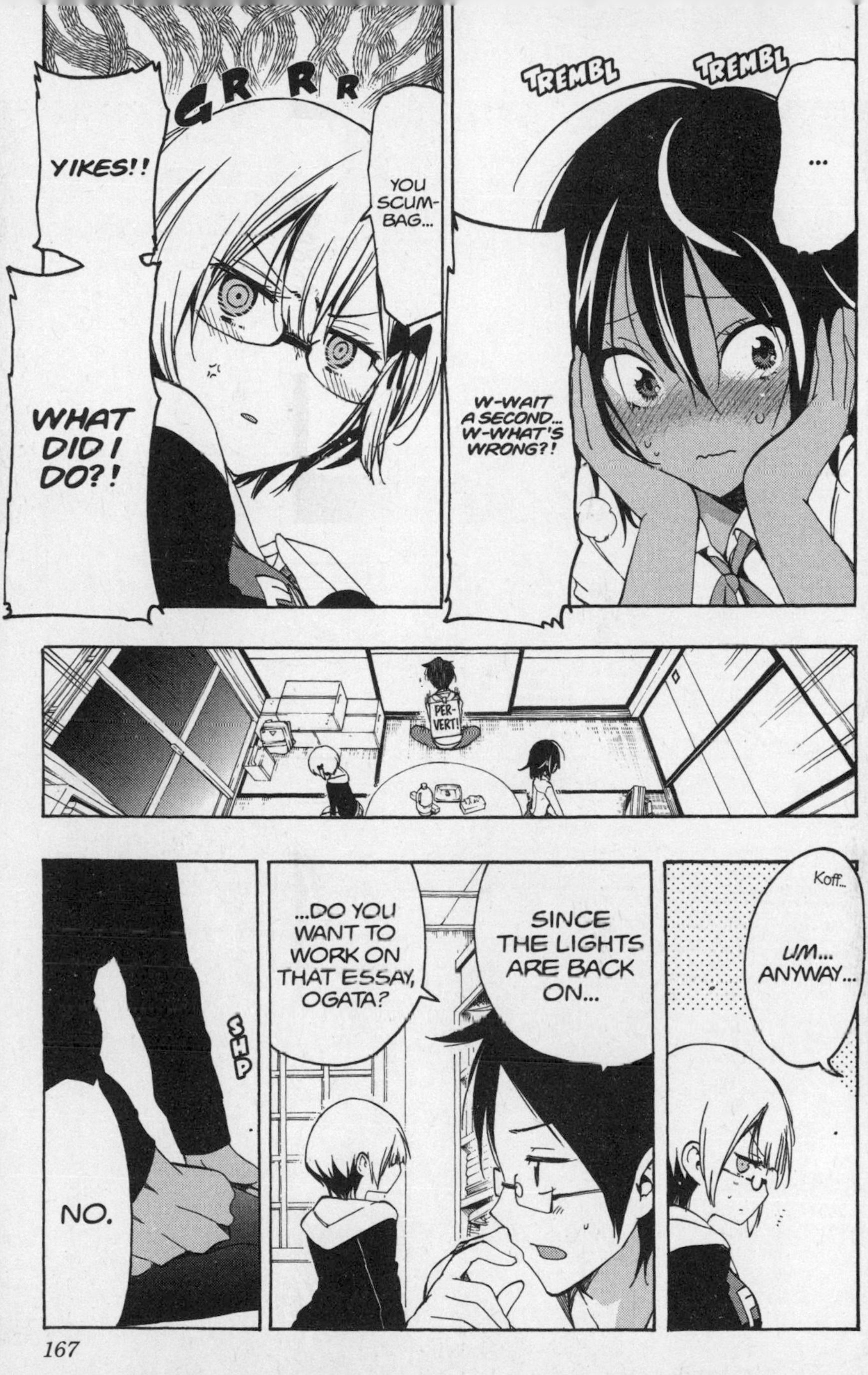
TREMBL
TREMBL
...
W-WAIT A SECOND... W-WHAT'S WRONG?!
GRRR
YOU SCUMBAG...
YIKES!!
WHAT DID I DO?!
PER-VERT!
Koff...
UM... ANYWAY...
SINCE THE LIGHTS ARE BACK ON...
...DO YOU WANT TO WORK ON THAT ESSAY, OGATA?
SHP
NO.

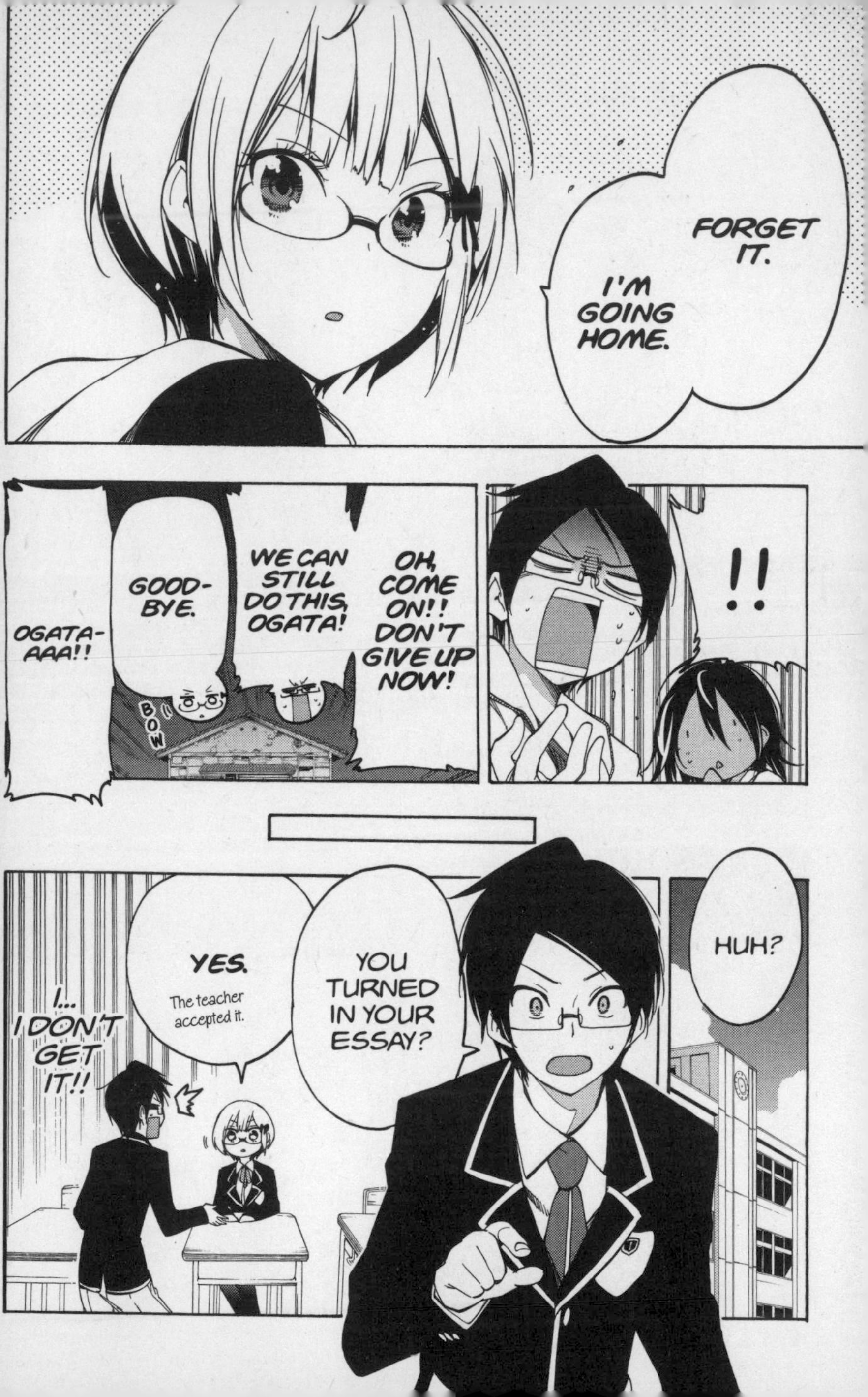
FORGET IT.
I'M GOING HOME.
!!
OH, COME ON!! DON'T GIVE UP NOW!
WE CAN STILL DO THIS, OGATA!
GOOD-BYE.
BOW
OGATA-AAA!!
HUH?
YOU TURNED IN YOUR ESSAY?
YES.
The teacher accepted it.
I... I DON'T GET IT!!

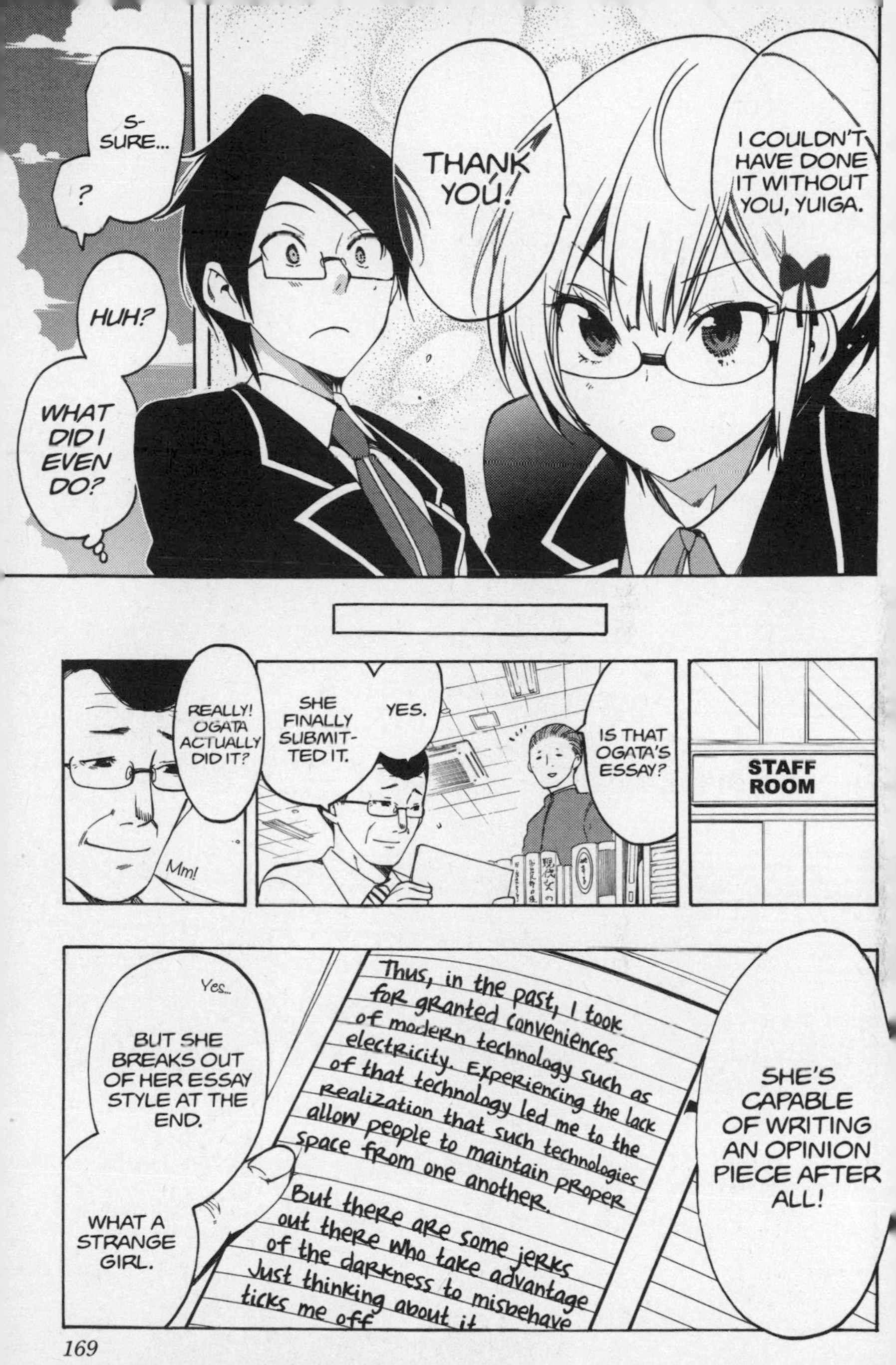
I COULDN'T HAVE DONE IT WITHOUT YOU, YUIGA.
THANK YOU!
S-SURE...
?
HUH?
WHAT DID I EVEN DO?
STAFF ROOM
IS THAT OGATA'S ESSAY?
YES.
SHE FINALLY SUBMITTED IT.
REALLY! OGATA ACTUALLY DID IT?
Mm!
SHE'S CAPABLE OF WRITING AN OPINION PIECE AFTER ALL!
Thus, in the past, I took for granted conveniences of modern technology such as electricity. Experiencing the lack of that technology led me to the realization that such technologies allow people to maintain proper space from one another.
But there are some jerks out there who take advantage of the darkness to misbehave Just thinking about it ticks me off
Yes...
BUT SHE BREAKS OUT OF HER ESSAY STYLE AT THE END.
WHAT A STRANGE GIRL.

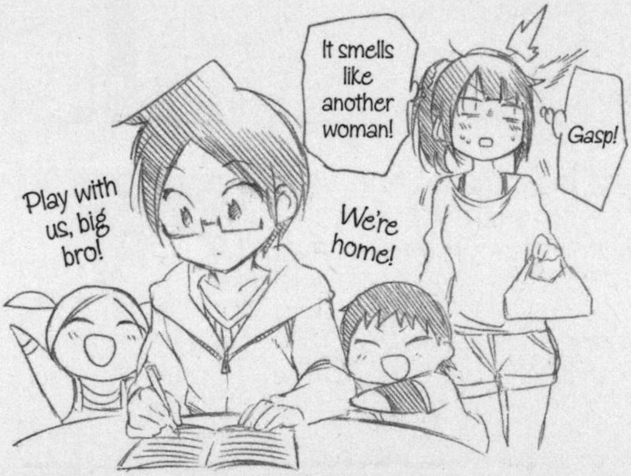
Gasp!
It smells like another woman!
We're home!
Play with us, big bro!

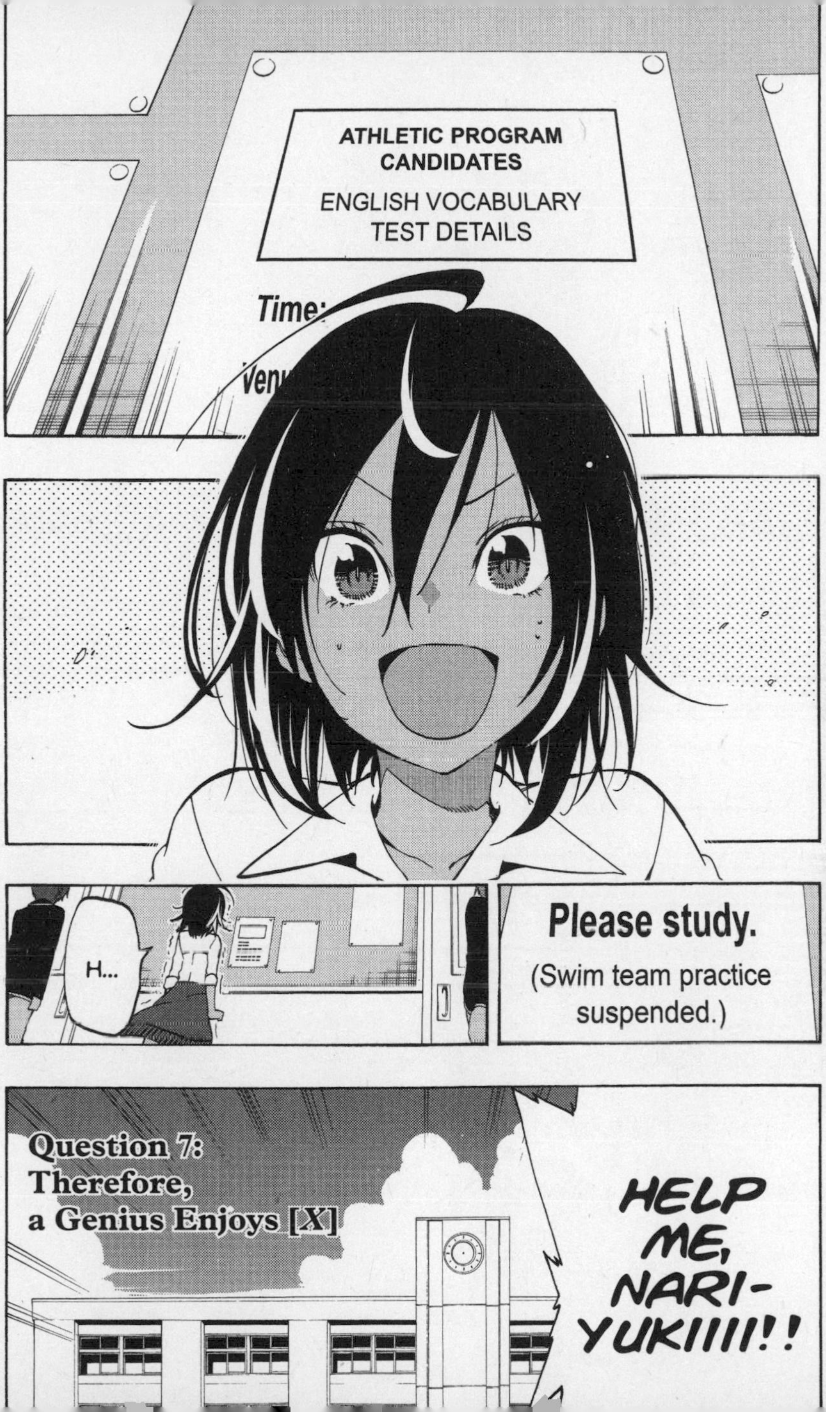
ATHLETIC PROGRAM CANDIDATES
ENGLISH VOCABULARY TEST DETAILS
Time:
Please study.
(Swim team practice suspended.)
H...
HELP ME, NARI-YUKIIIII!!
Question 7: Therefore, a Genius Enjoys [X]

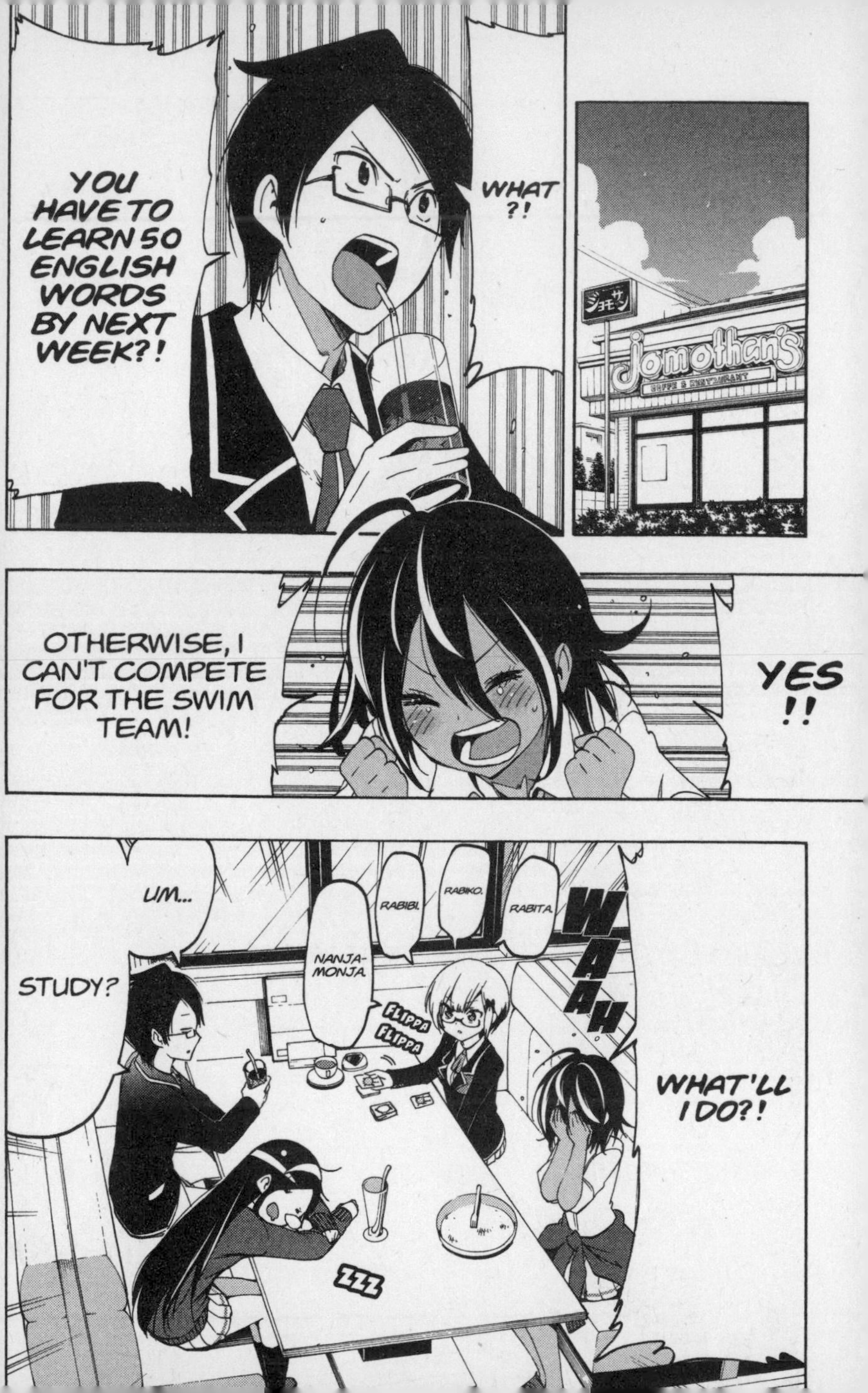
jomothan's
COFFEE & RESTAURANT
WHAT ?!
YOU HAVE TO LEARN 50 ENGLISH WORDS BY NEXT WEEK?!
YES !!
OTHERWISE, I CAN'T COMPETE FOR THE SWIM TEAM!
WHAAH
WHAT'LL I DO?!
RABITA.
RABIKO.
RABIBI.
NANJA-MONJA.
FLIPPA FLIPPA
UM...
STUDY?
ZZZ

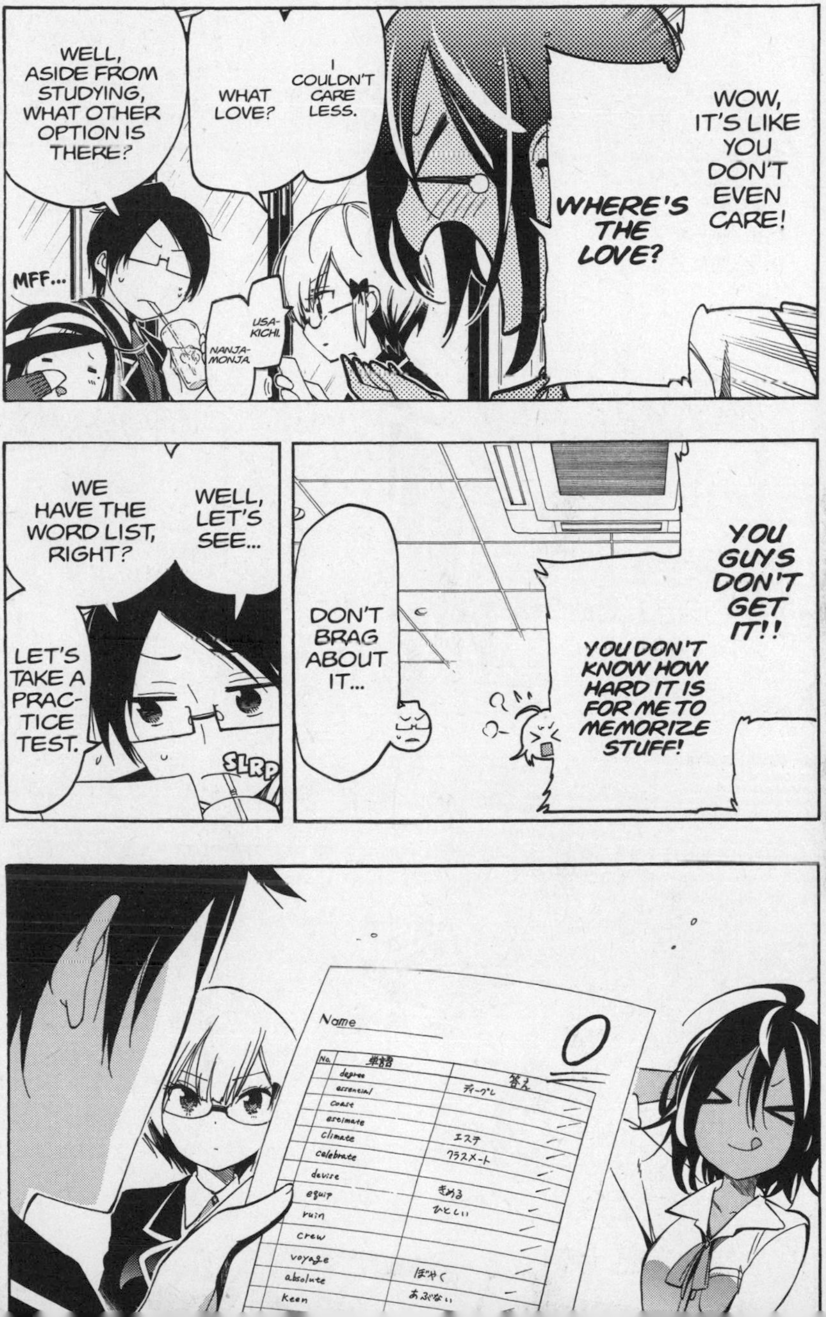
WOW, IT'S LIKE YOU DON'T EVEN CARE!
WHERE'S THE LOVE?
I COULDN'T CARE LESS.
WHAT LOVE?
WELL, ASIDE FROM STUDYING, WHAT OTHER OPTION IS THERE?
MFF...
USA-KICHI.
NANJA-MONJA
YOU GUYS DON'T GET IT!!
YOU DON'T KNOW HOW HARD IT IS FOR ME TO MEMORIZE STUFF!
DON'T BRAG ABOUT IT...
WELL, LET'S SEE...
WE HAVE THE WORD LIST, RIGHT?
LET'S TAKE A PRAC-TICE TEST.
SLRP
Name
No.
単語
答え
degree
essential
ディーグレ
coast
estimate
climate
エステ
celebrate
クラスメート
devise
equip
きめる
ruin
ひとしい
crew
voyage
absolute
ぼやく
keen
あぶない

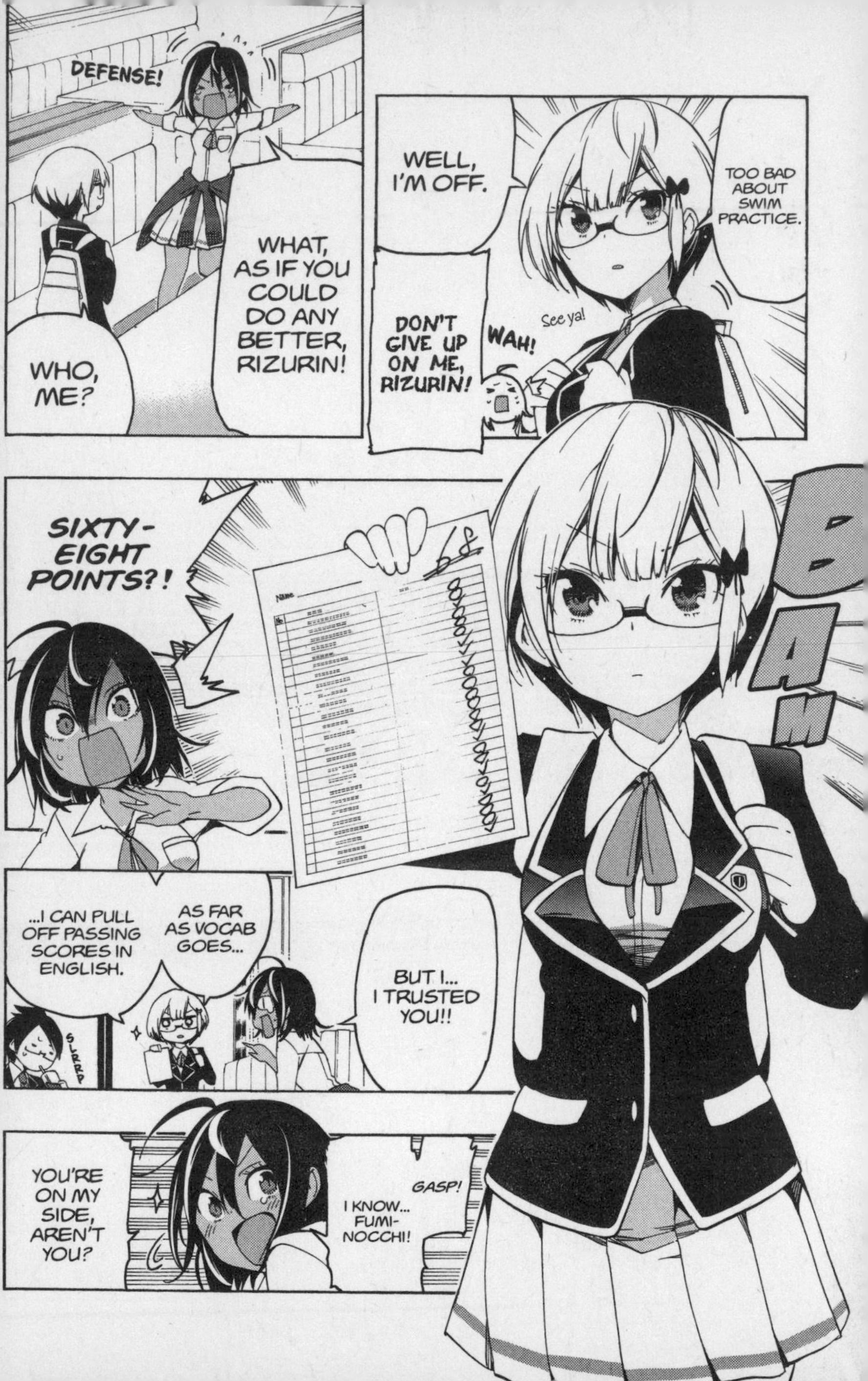
TOO BAD ABOUT SWIM PRACTICE.
WELL, I'M OFF.
See ya!
WAH!
DON'T GIVE UP ON ME, RIZURIN!
DEFENSE!
WHAT, AS IF YOU COULD DO ANY BETTER, RIZURIN!
WHO, ME?
BAM
SIXTY-EIGHT POINTS?!
68
BUT I... I TRUSTED YOU!!
AS FAR AS VOCAB GOES...
...I CAN PULL OFF PASSING SCORES IN ENGLISH.
SLRRP
GASP!
I KNOW... FUMI-NOCCHI!
YOU'RE ON MY SIDE, AREN'T YOU?

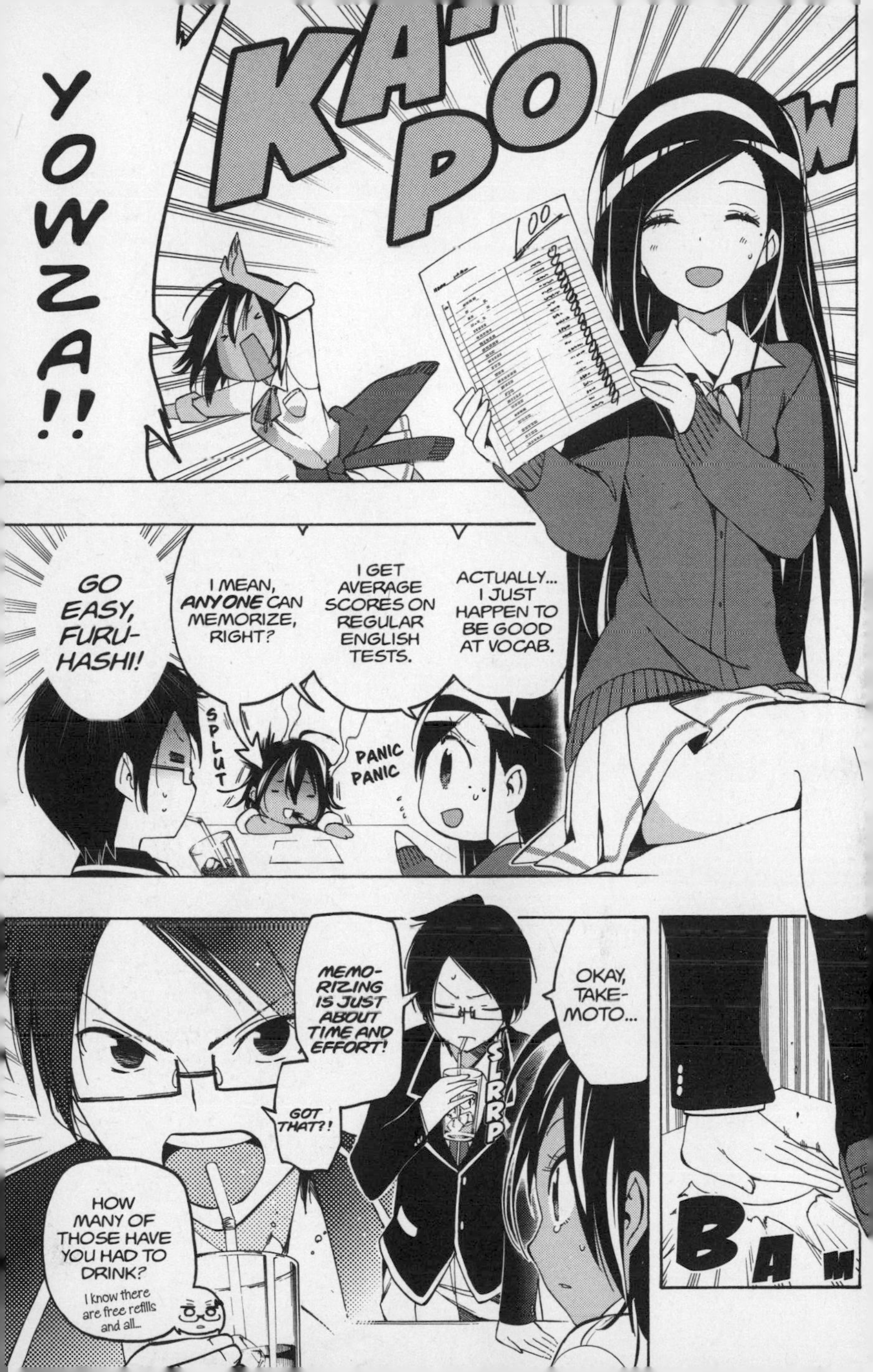
KA-POW
YOWZA!!
ACTUALLY... I JUST HAPPEN TO BE GOOD AT VOCAB.
I GET AVERAGE SCORES ON REGULAR ENGLISH TESTS.
I MEAN, ANYONE CAN MEMORIZE, RIGHT?
GO EASY, FURU-HASHI!
PANIC PANIC
SPLUT
BAM
OKAY, TAKE-MOTO...
MEMO-RIZING IS JUST ABOUT TIME AND EFFORT!
SLRRP
GOT THAT?!
HOW MANY OF THOSE HAVE YOU HAD TO DRINK?
I know there are free refills and all...

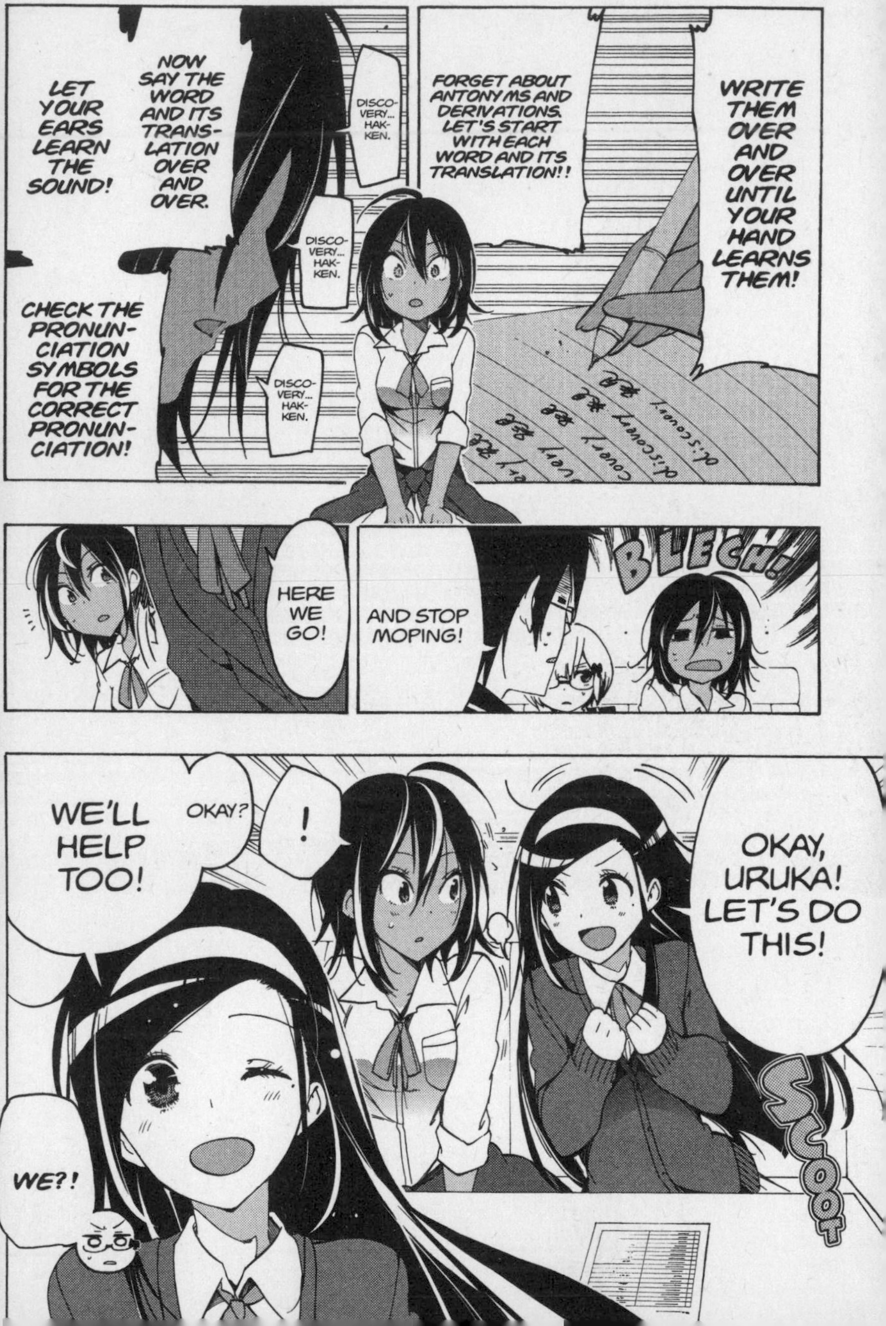
WRITE THEM OVER AND OVER UNTIL YOUR HAND LEARNS THEM!
FORGET ABOUT ANTONYMS AND DERIVATIONS. LET'S START WITH EACH WORD AND ITS TRANSLATION!!
DISCO-VERY... HAK-KEN.
NOW SAY THE WORD AND ITS TRANS-LATION OVER AND OVER.
LET YOUR EARS LEARN THE SOUND!
DISCO-VERY... HAK-KEN.
DISCO-VERY... HAK-KEN.
CHECK THE PRONUN-CIATION SYMBOLS FOR THE CORRECT PRONUN-CIATION!
BLECH!
AND STOP MOPING!
HERE WE GO!
OKAY, URUKA! LET'S DO THIS!
WOOT
!
OKAY?
WE'LL HELP TOO!
WE?!

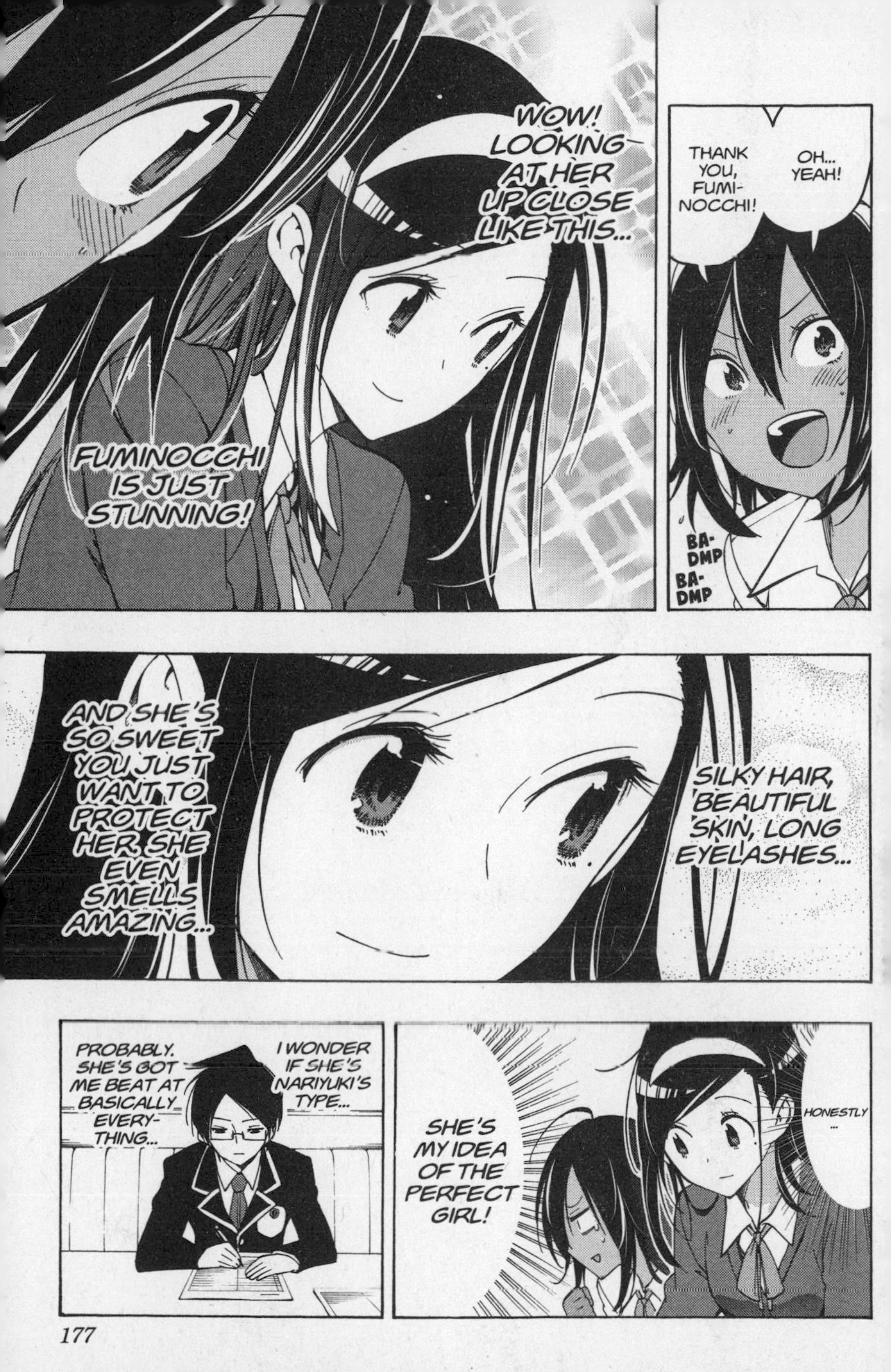
OH... YEAH!
THANK YOU, FUMI-NOCCHI!
BA-DMP BA-DMP
WOW! LOOKING AT HER UP CLOSE LIKE THIS...
FUMINOCCHI IS JUST STUNNING!
SILKY HAIR, BEAUTIFUL SKIN, LONG EYELASHES...
AND SHE'S SO SWEET YOU JUST WANT TO PROTECT HER. SHE EVEN SMELLS AMAZING...
HONESTLY...
SHE'S MY IDEA OF THE PERFECT GIRL!
I WONDER IF SHE'S NARIYUKI'S TYPE...
PROBABLY. SHE'S GOT ME BEAT AT BASICALLY EVERY-THING...

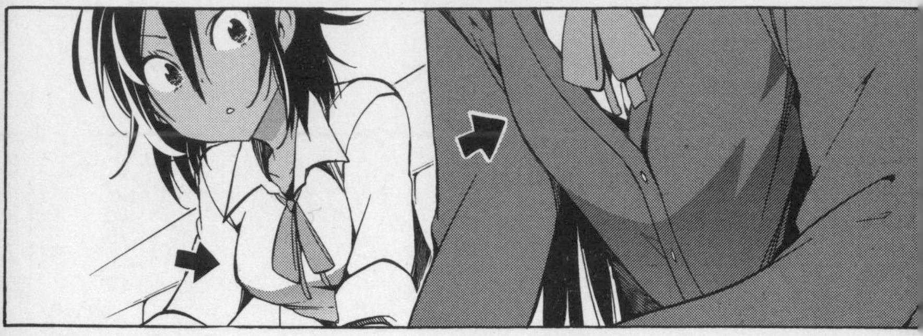

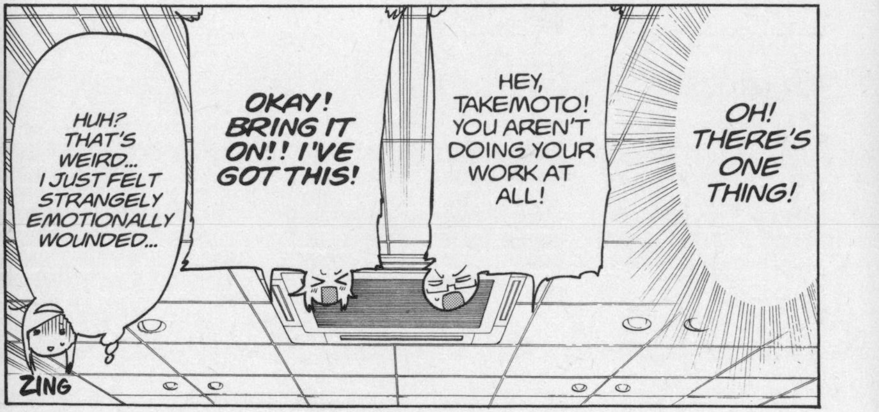
OH! THERE'S ONE THING!
HEY, TAKEMOTO! YOU AREN'T DOING YOUR WORK AT ALL!
OKAY! BRING IT ON!! I'VE GOT THIS!
HUH? THAT'S WEIRD... I JUST FELT STRANGELY EMOTIONALLY WOUNDED...
ZING

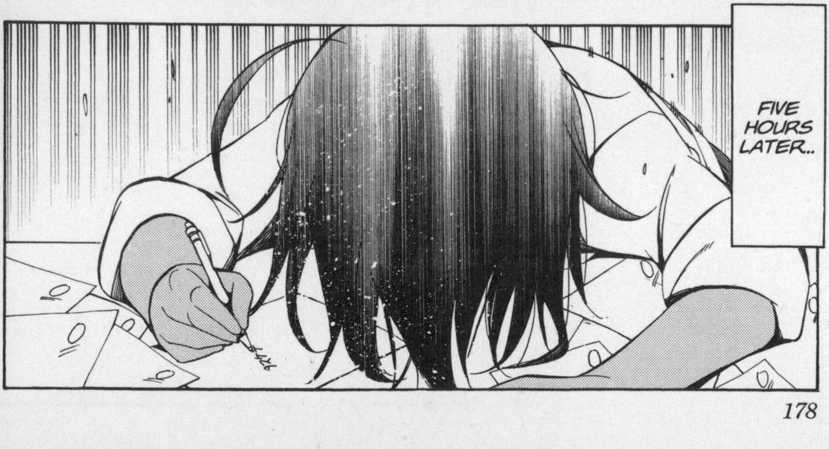
FIVE HOURS LATER...

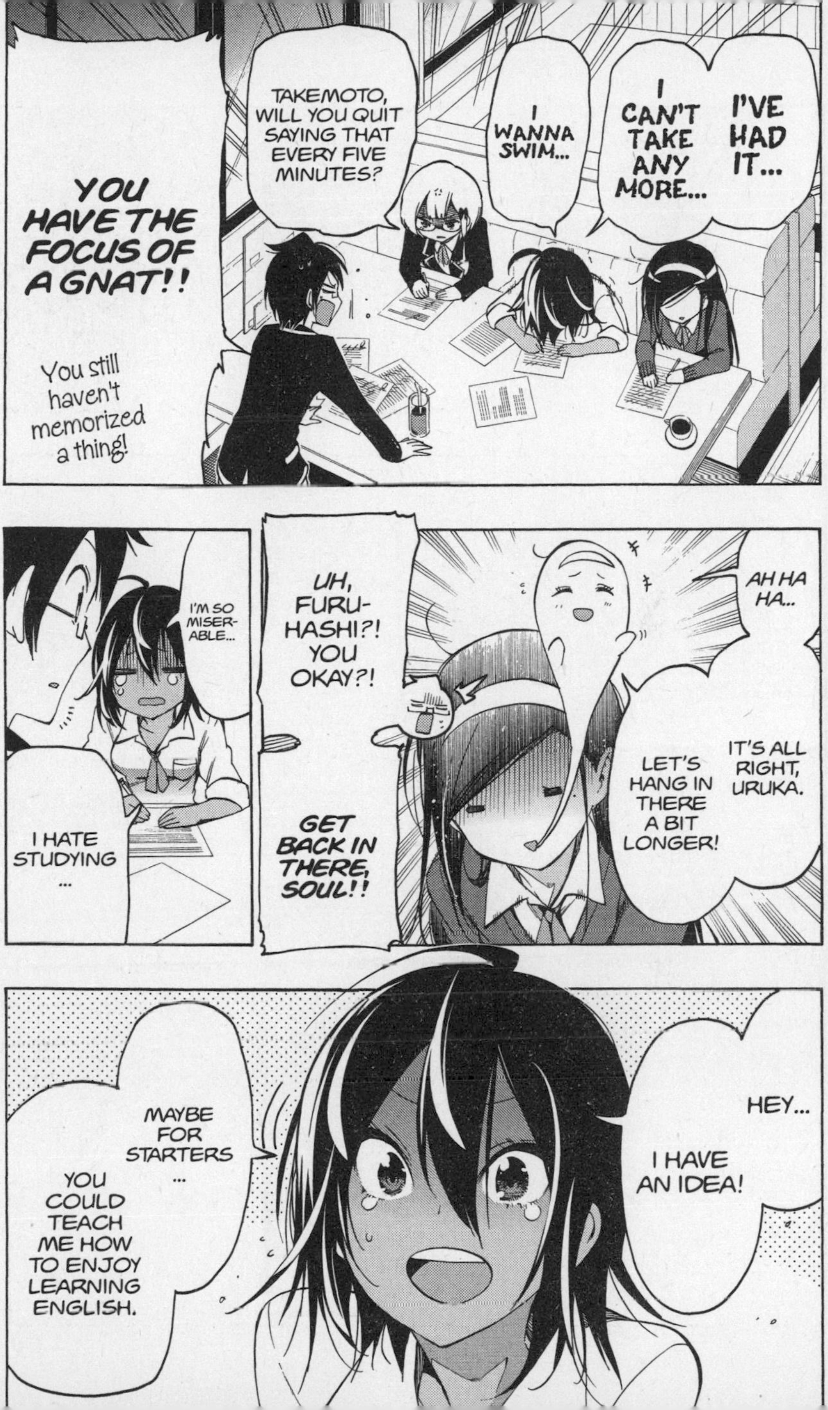
I'VE HAD IT...
I CAN'T TAKE ANY MORE...
I WANNA SWIM...
TAKEMOTO, WILL YOU QUIT SAYING THAT EVERY FIVE MINUTES?
YOU HAVE THE FOCUS OF A GNAT!!
You still haven't memorized a thing!
AH HA HA...
IT'S ALL RIGHT, URUKA.
LET'S HANG IN THERE A BIT LONGER!
UH, FURU-HASHI?! YOU OKAY?!
GET BACK IN THERE, SOUL!!
I'M SO MISER-ABLE...
I HATE STUDYING ...
HEY...
I HAVE AN IDEA!
MAYBE FOR STARTERS ...
YOU COULD TEACH ME HOW TO ENJOY LEARNING ENGLISH.

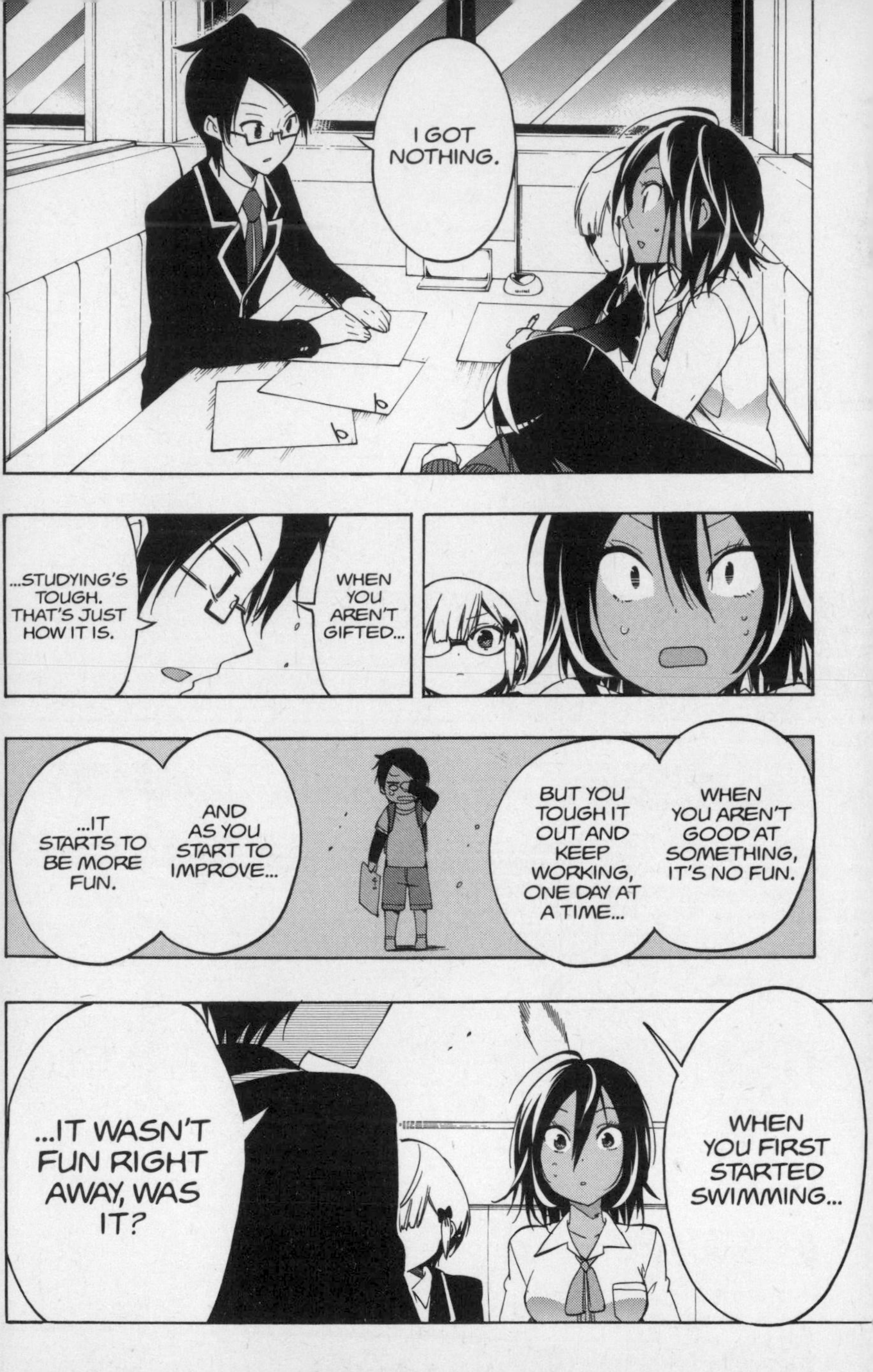
I GOT NOTHING.
WHEN YOU AREN'T GIFTED...
...STUDYING'S TOUGH. THAT'S JUST HOW IT IS.
WHEN YOU AREN'T GOOD AT SOMETHING, IT'S NO FUN.
BUT YOU TOUGH IT OUT AND KEEP WORKING, ONE DAY AT A TIME...
AND AS YOU START TO IMPROVE...
...IT STARTS TO BE MORE FUN.
WHEN YOU FIRST STARTED SWIMMING...
...IT WASN'T FUN RIGHT AWAY, WAS IT?

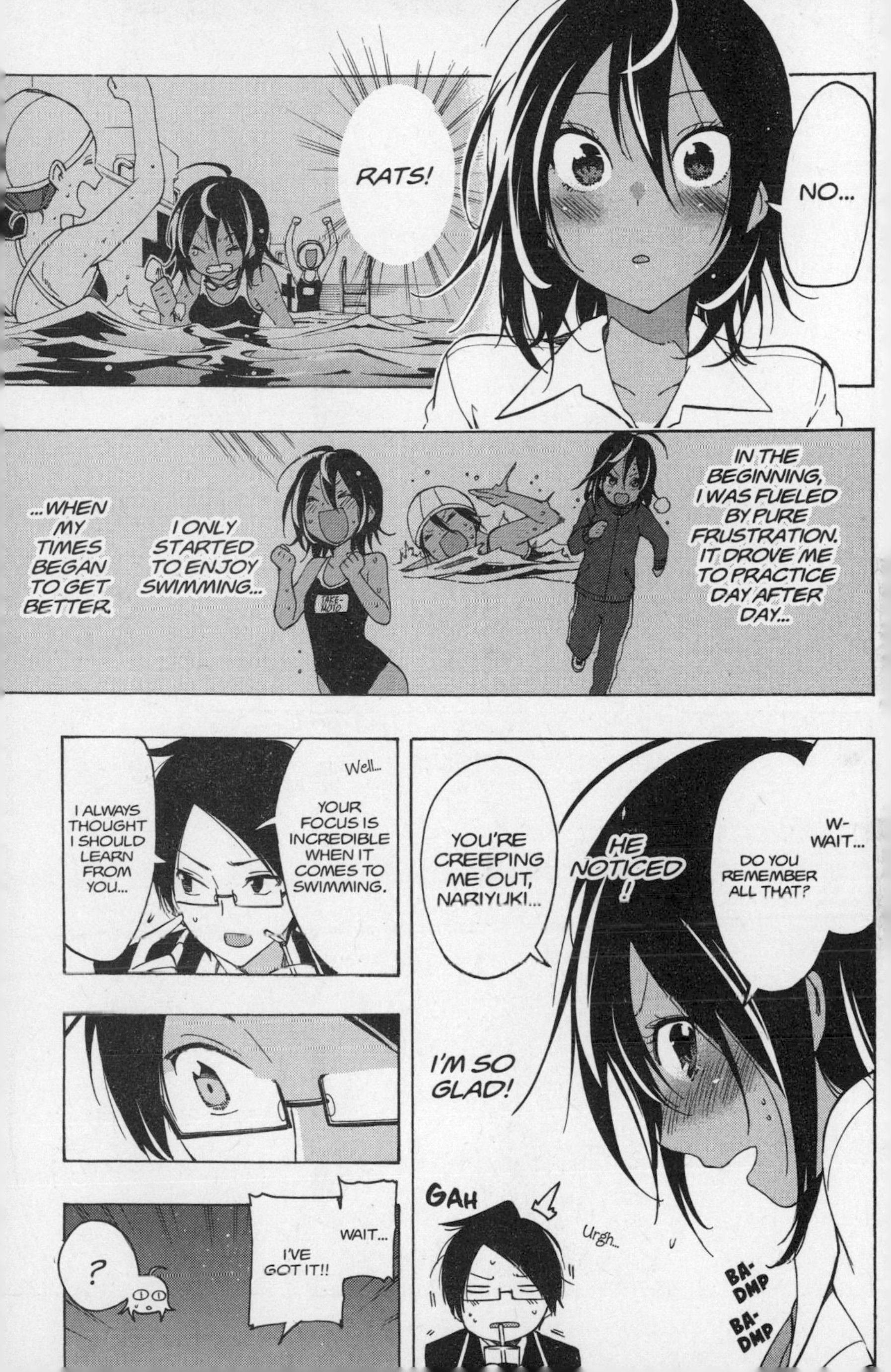
NO...
RATS!
IN THE BEGINNING, I WAS FUELED BY PURE FRUSTRATION. IT DROVE ME TO PRACTICE DAY AFTER DAY...
I ONLY STARTED TO ENJOY SWIMMING...
...WHEN MY TIMES BEGAN TO GET BETTER.
TAKE-MOTO
W- WAIT...
DO YOU REMEMBER ALL THAT?
HE NOTICED!
YOU'RE CREEPING ME OUT, NARIYUKI...
I'M SO GLAD!
GAH
Urgh...
BA-DMP
BA-DMP
Well...
YOUR FOCUS IS INCREDIBLE WHEN IT COMES TO SWIMMING.
I ALWAYS THOUGHT I SHOULD LEARN FROM YOU...
WAIT...
I'VE GOT IT!!
?

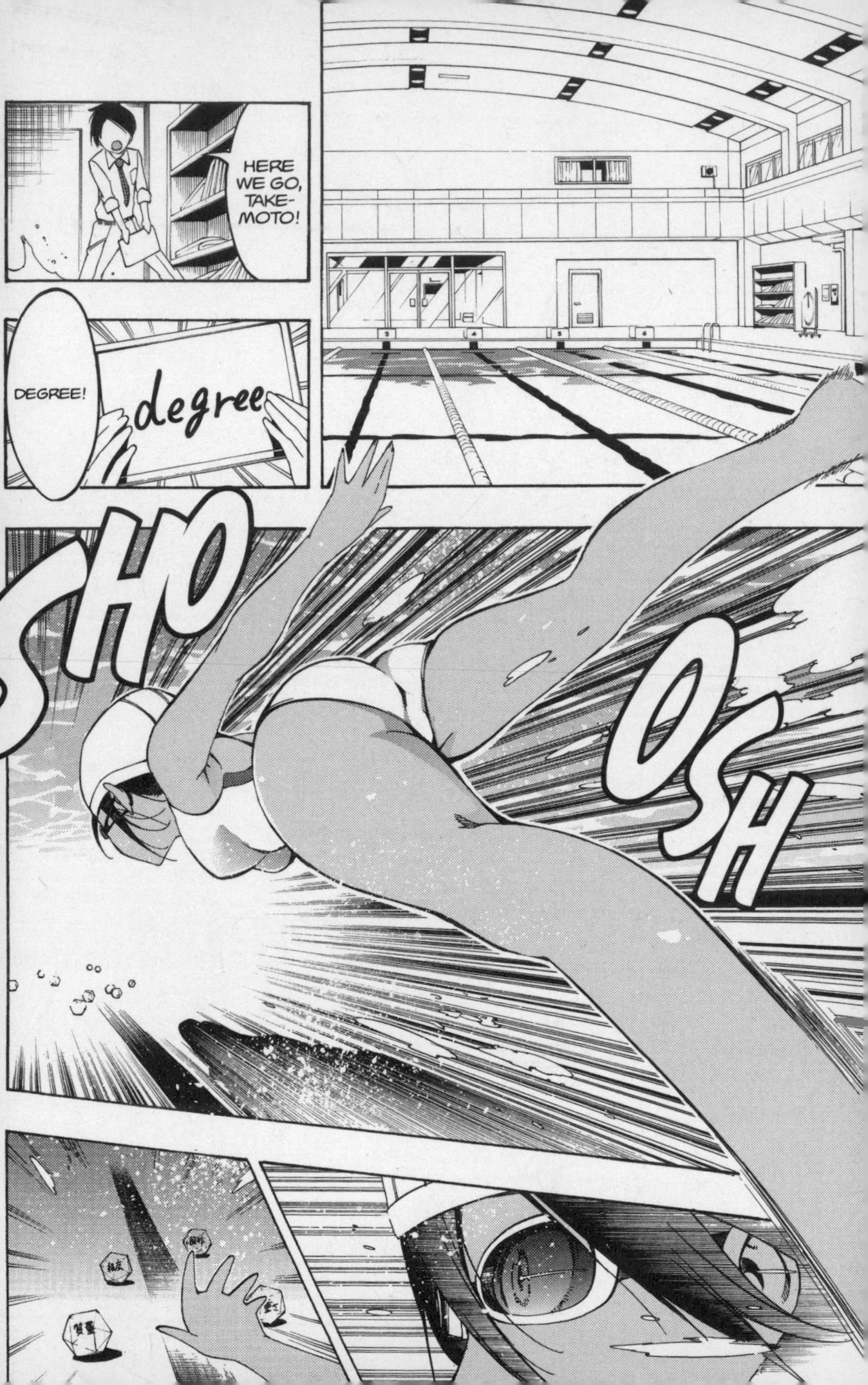
HERE WE GO, TAKE-MOTO!
DEGREE!
degree
SHOOSH

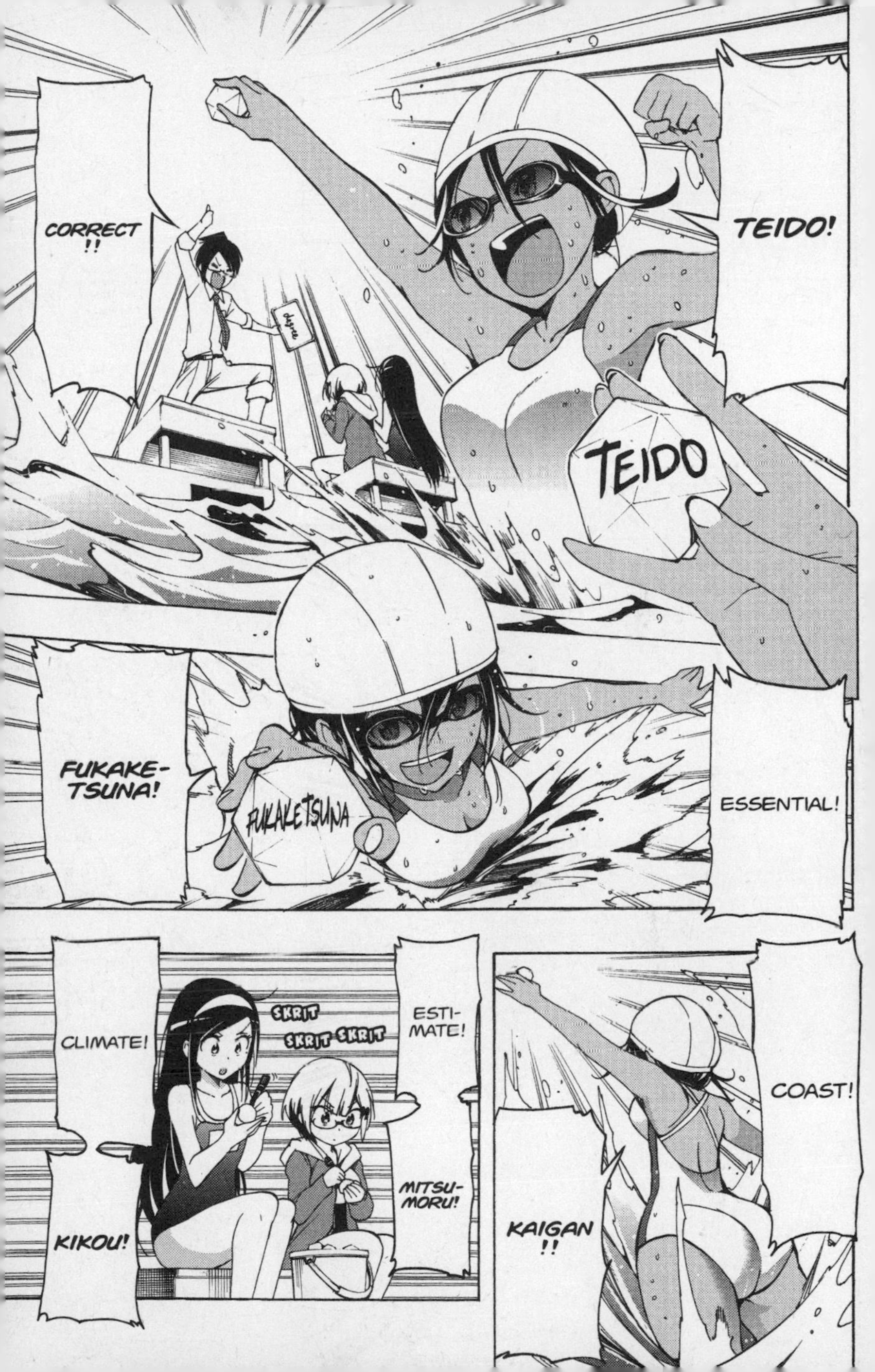
TEIDO!
TEIDO
CORRECT!!
ESSENTIAL!
FUKAKETSUNA
FUKAKE-TSUNA!
COAST!
KAIGAN!!
ESTI-MATE!
MITSU-MORU!
SKRIT
SKRIT SKRIT
CLIMATE!
KIKOU!

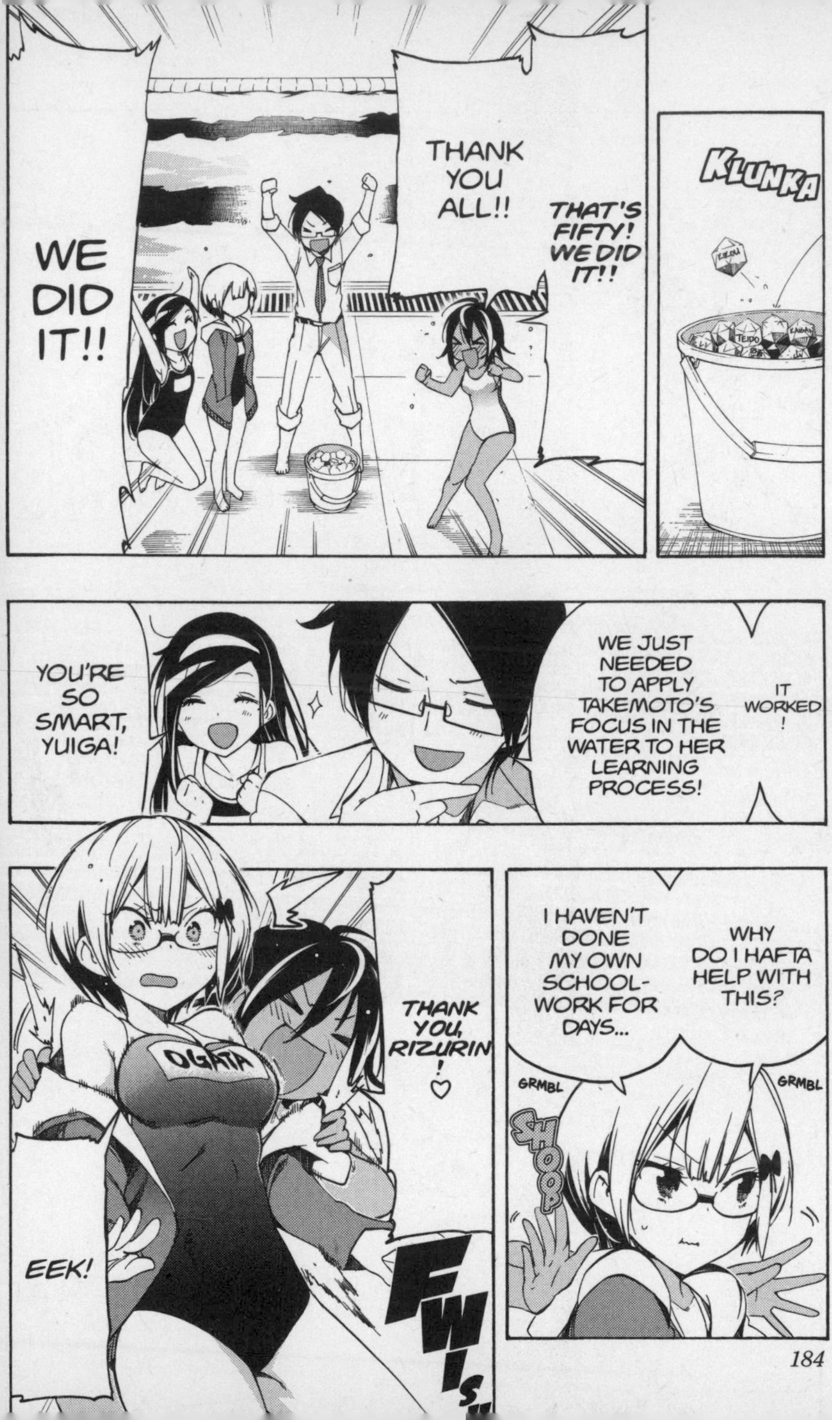
KLUNKA
THAT'S FIFTY! WE DID IT!!
THANK YOU ALL!!
WE DID IT!!
IT WORKED!
WE JUST NEEDED TO APPLY TAKEMOTO'S FOCUS IN THE WATER TO HER LEARNING PROCESS!
YOU'RE SO SMART, YUIGA!
WHY DO I HAFTA HELP WITH THIS?
I HAVEN'T DONE MY OWN SCHOOL-WORK FOR DAYS...
GRMBL
GRMBL
SHOOP
THANK YOU, RIZURIN! ♡
OGATA
EEK!
FWISH

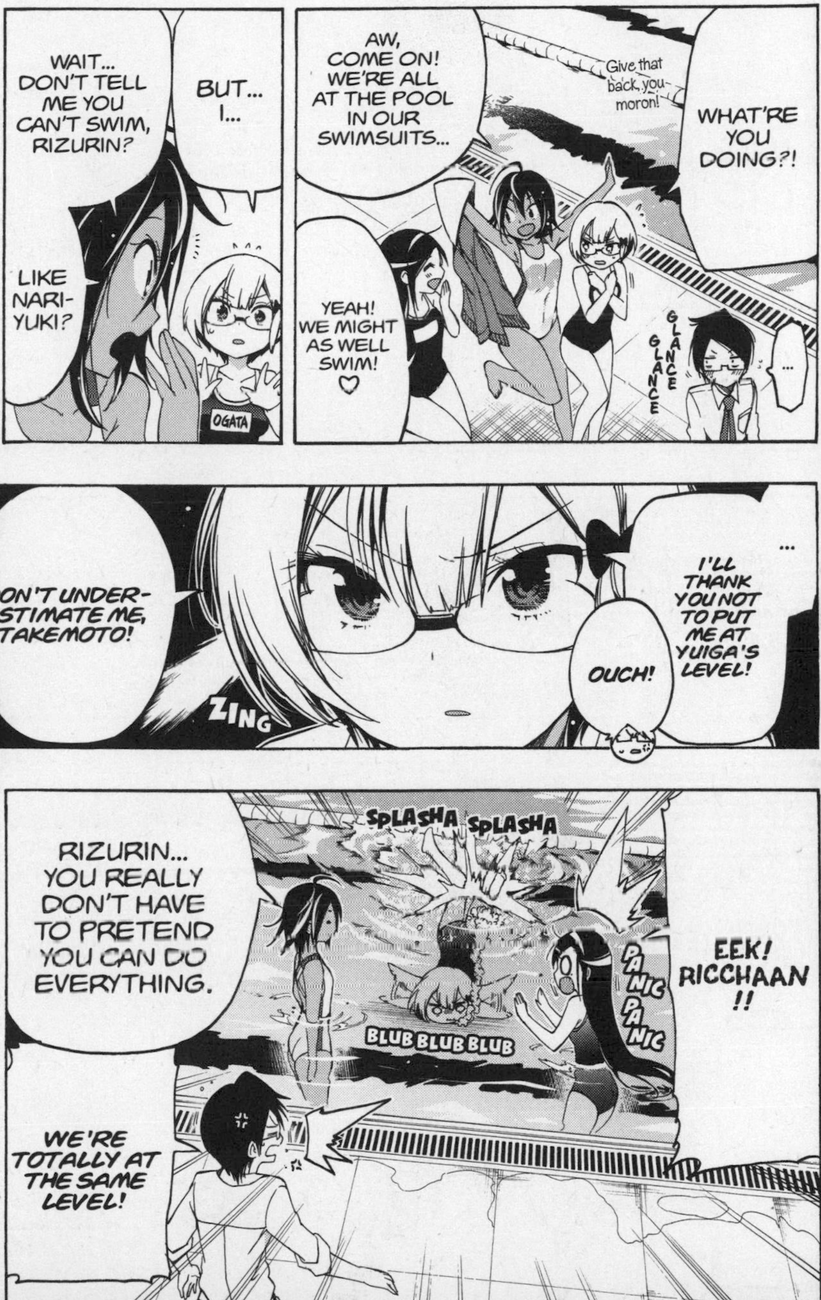
WHAT'RE YOU DOING?!
Give that back, you moron!
AW, COME ON! WE'RE ALL AT THE POOL IN OUR SWIMSUITS...
...
GLANCE GLANCE
YEAH! WE MIGHT AS WELL SWIM! ♡
BUT... I...
WAIT... DON'T TELL ME YOU CAN'T SWIM, RIZURIN?
LIKE NARI-YUKI?
OGATA
...
I'LL THANK YOU NOT TO PUT ME AT YUIGA'S LEVEL!
OUCH!
DON'T UNDER-ESTIMATE ME, TAKEMOTO!
ZING
EEK! RICCHAAN!!
SPLASHA SPLASHA
PANIC PANIC
RIZURIN... YOU REALLY DON'T HAVE TO PRETEND YOU CAN DO EVERYTHING.
BLUB BLUB BLUB
WE'RE TOTALLY AT THE SAME LEVEL!

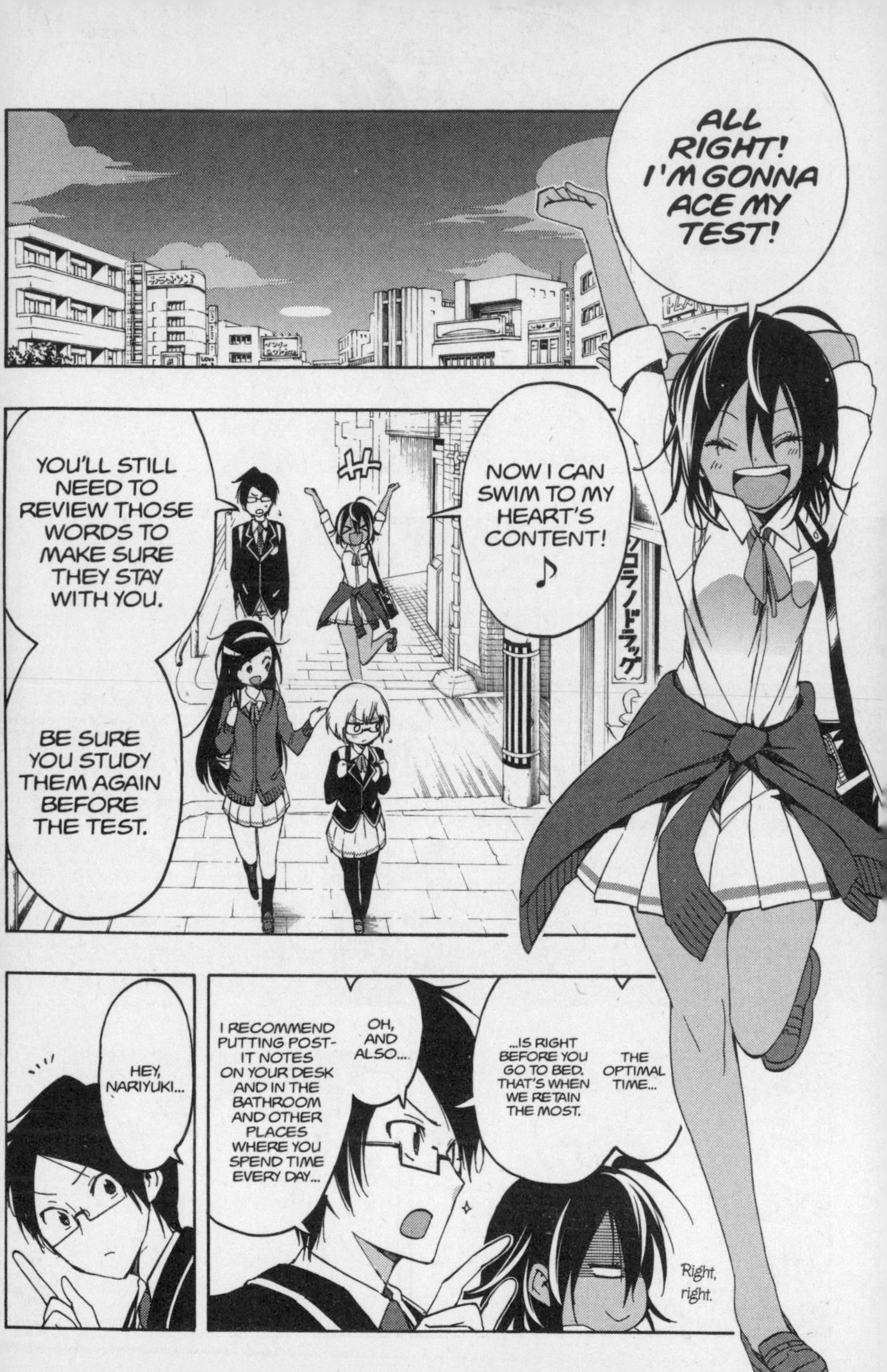
ALL RIGHT! I'M GONNA ACE MY TEST!
NOW I CAN SWIM TO MY HEART'S CONTENT! ♪
YOU'LL STILL NEED TO REVIEW THOSE WORDS TO MAKE SURE THEY STAY WITH YOU.
BE SURE YOU STUDY THEM AGAIN BEFORE THE TEST.
THE OPTIMAL TIME...
...IS RIGHT BEFORE YOU GO TO BED. THAT'S WHEN WE RETAIN THE MOST.
OH, AND ALSO...
I RECOMMEND PUTTING POST-IT NOTES ON YOUR DESK AND IN THE BATHROOM AND OTHER PLACES WHERE YOU SPEND TIME EVERY DAY...
Right, right.
HEY, NARIYUKI...

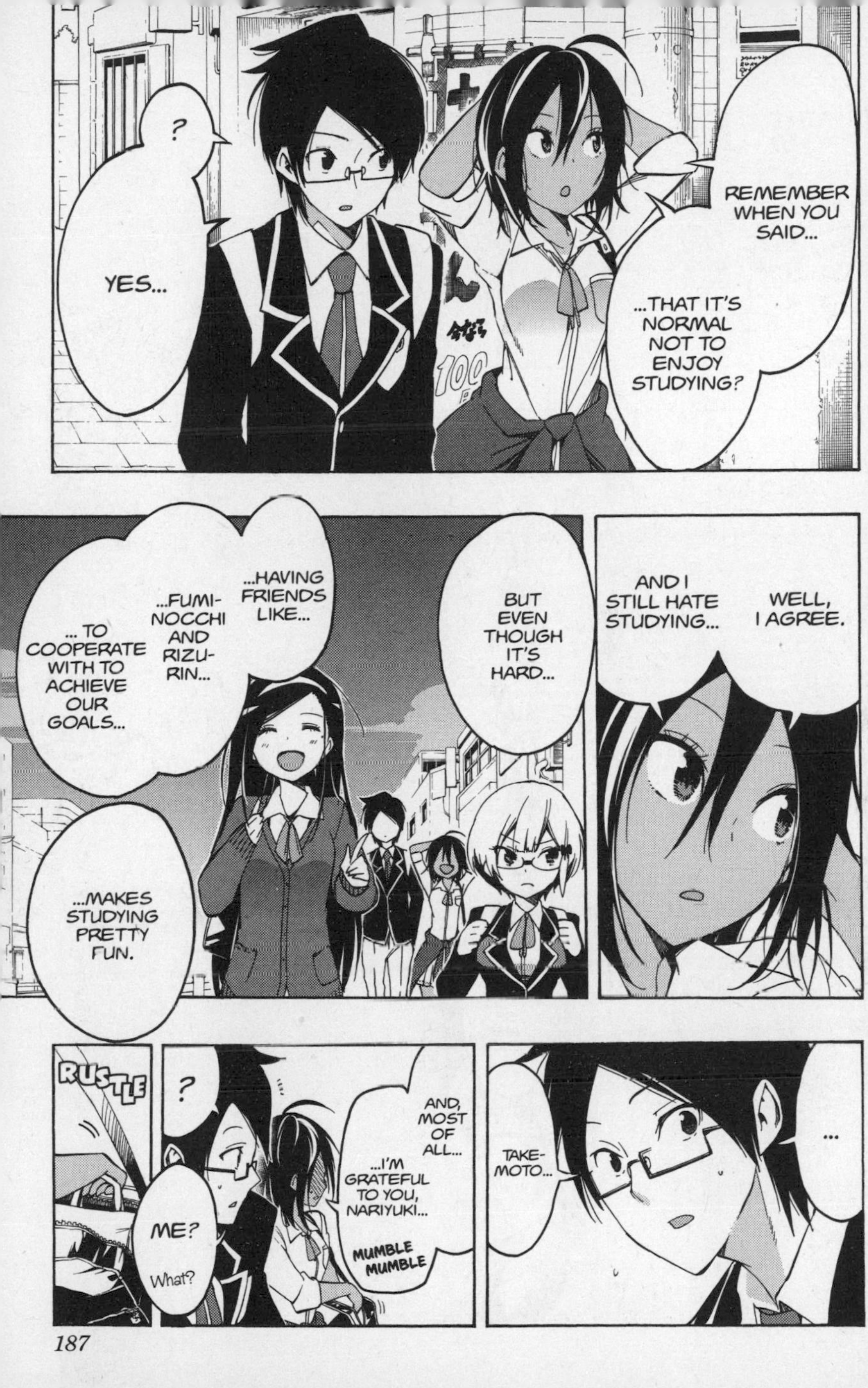
REMEMBER WHEN YOU SAID...
...THAT IT'S NORMAL NOT TO ENJOY STUDYING?
?
YES...
WELL, I AGREE.
AND I STILL HATE STUDYING...
BUT EVEN THOUGH IT'S HARD...
...HAVING FRIENDS LIKE...
...FUMI-NOCCHI AND RIZU-RIN...
... TO COOPERATE WITH TO ACHIEVE OUR GOALS...
...MAKES STUDYING PRETTY FUN.
...
TAKE-MOTO...
AND, MOST OF ALL...
...I'M GRATEFUL TO YOU, NARIYUKI...
MUMBLE MUMBLE
?
ME?
What?
RUSTLE

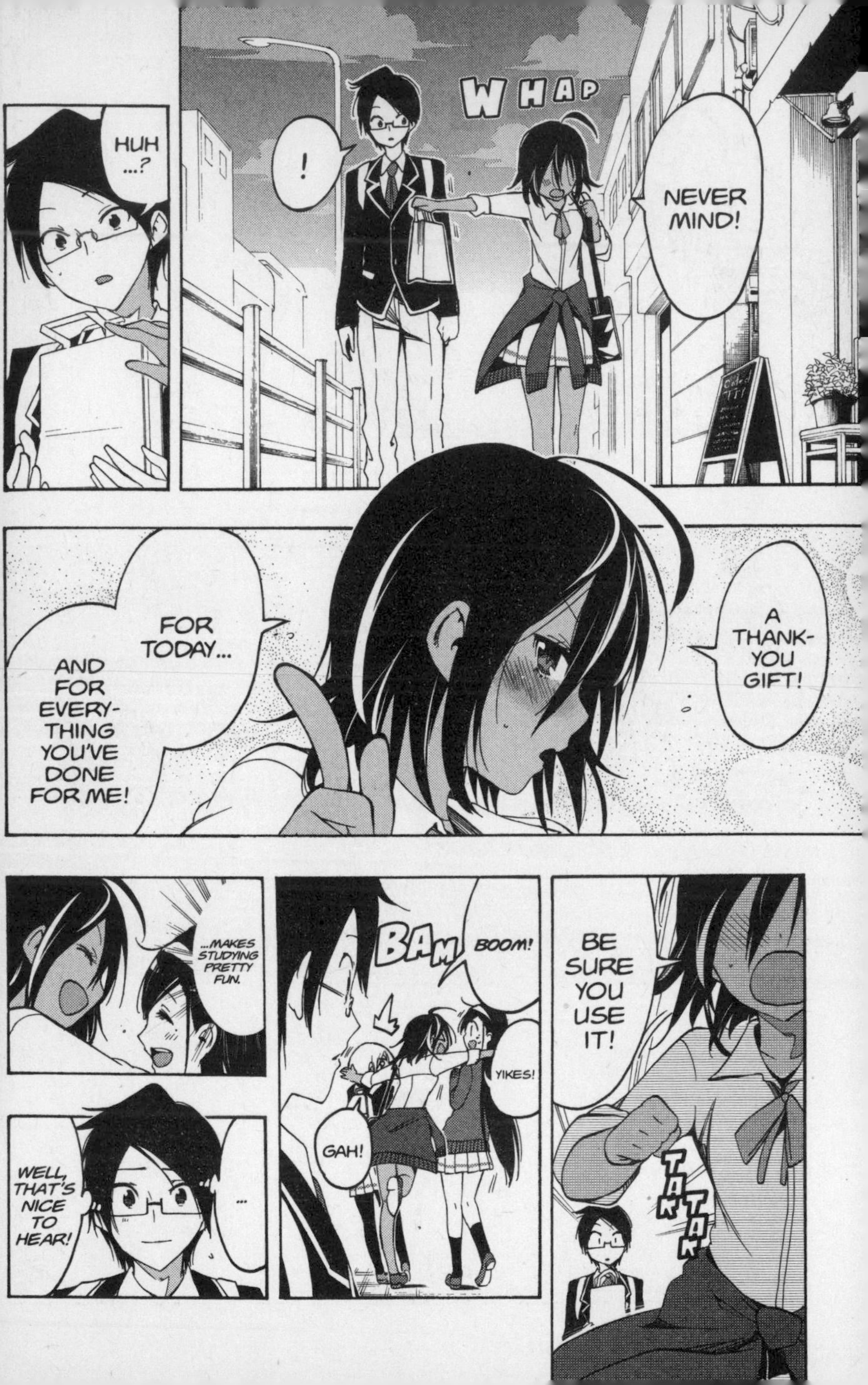
WHAP
NEVER MIND!
!
HUH ...?
A THANK-YOU GIFT!
FOR TODAY...
AND FOR EVERY-THING YOU'VE DONE FOR ME!
BE SURE YOU USE IT!
TAK TAK
BAM
BOOM!
YIKES!
GAH!
...MAKES STUDYING PRETTY FUN.
...
WELL, THAT'S NICE TO HEAR!

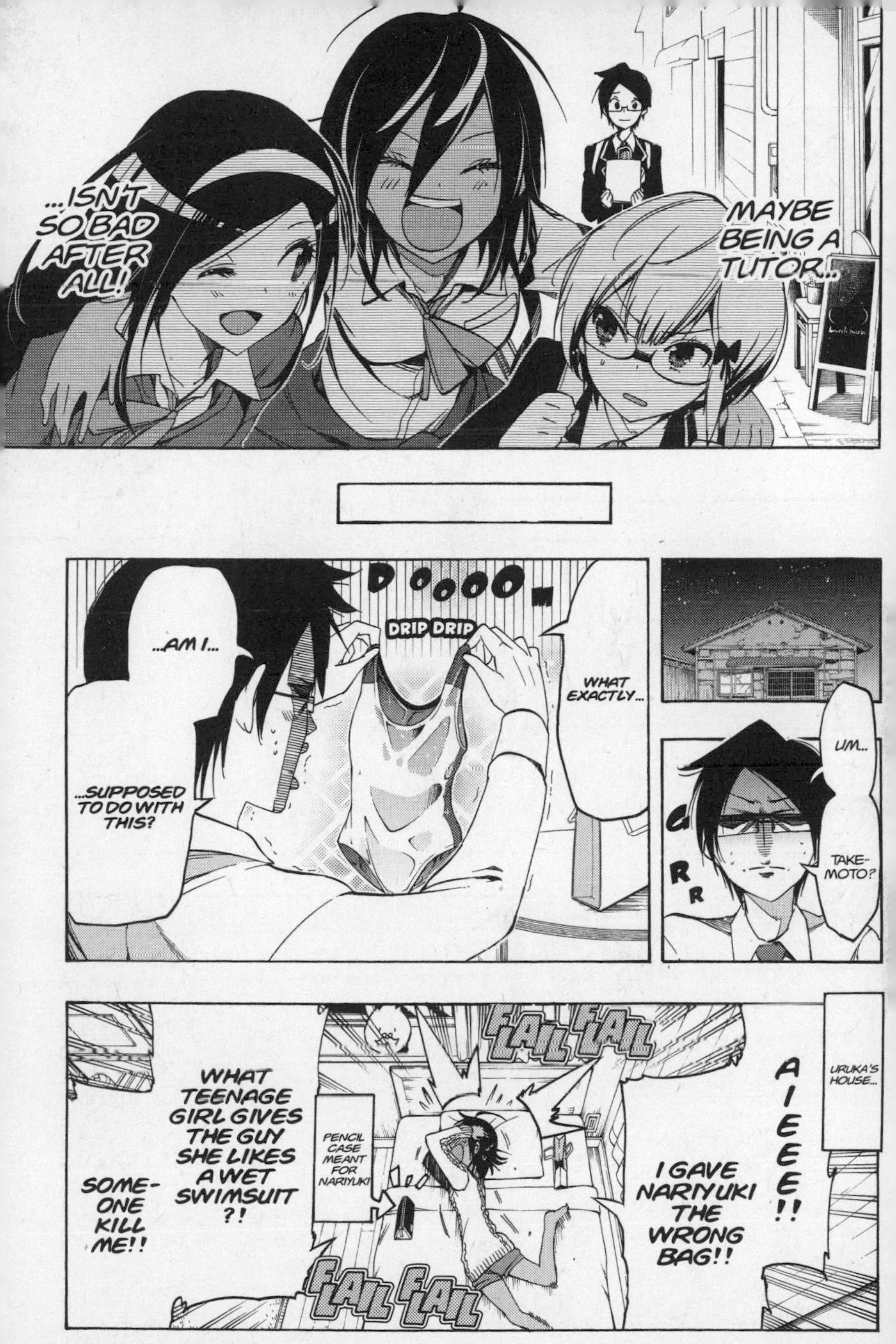
MAYBE BEING A TUTOR...
...ISN'T SO BAD AFTER ALL!
UM...
GRR
TAKE-MOTO?
WHAT EXACTLY...
DOOOOM
DRIP DRIP
...AM I...
...SUPPOSED TO DO WITH THIS?
URUKA'S HOUSE...
AIEEE!!
I GAVE NARIYUKI THE WRONG BAG!!
FLAIL FLAIL
PENCIL CASE MEANT FOR NARIYUKI
WHAT TEENAGE GIRL GIVES THE GUY SHE LIKES A WET SWIMSUIT?!
SOME-ONE KILL ME!!
FLAIL FLAIL

The next day...
She finally managed to give it to him!

Urk...

PSHOO

?

See you in
volume 2!

We Never Learn

1

STAFF

Taishi Tsutsui ....

....

Yu Kato ....

Shinobu Irooki ....

Yuji Iwasaki ....

Naoki Ochiai ....

HELP

Paripoi ....

Fuumin ....

Chisato Hatada ....

Kazuya Higuchi ....

Fuka Toma ....

Ookami Akaneharu ....

Chikomichi ....

S
T
A
F
F

L
I

S

T

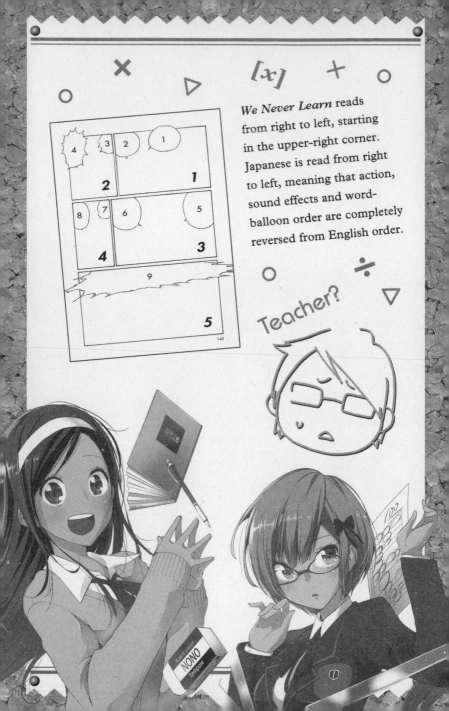

We Never Learn reads from right to left, starting in the upper-right corner. Japanese is read from right to left, meaning that action, sound effects and word-balloon order are completely reversed from English order.

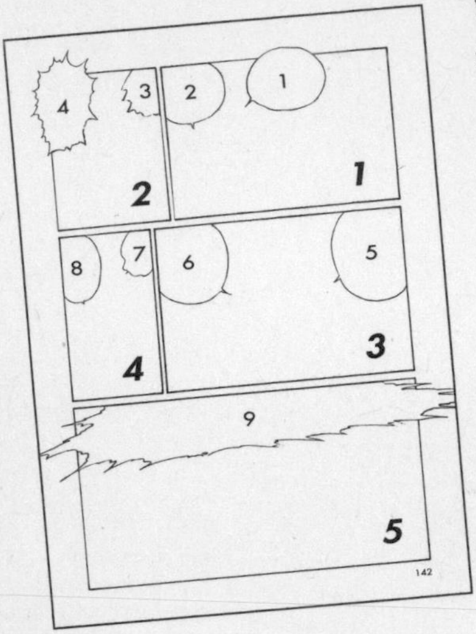
1
1
2
2
3
4
3
5
6
4
7
8
9
5
142

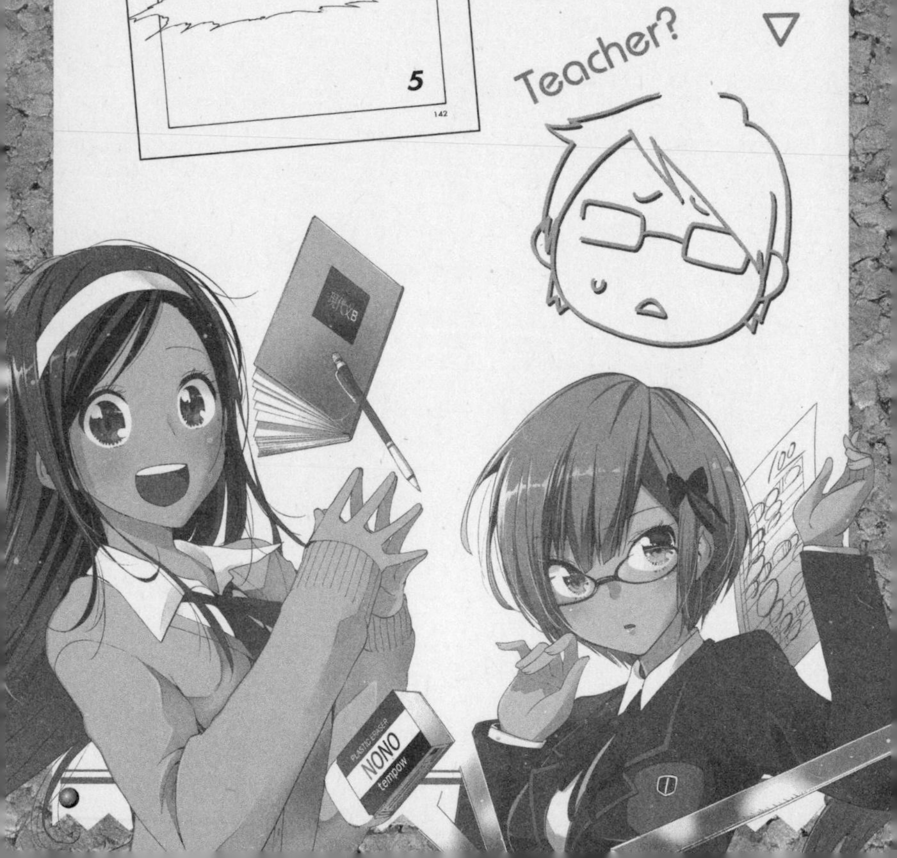
Teacher?
現代文B
100
PLASTIC ERASER
NONO
tempow